WELSH
GENEALOGY

WELSH
GENEALOGY

BRUCE DURIE

History is the dumping-ground of biology.
And genealogy is one way of keeping the score.

Bruce Durie, with thanks to Carlos Ruiz Zafón

The man who has only the excellence of his ancestry to boast of,
resembles that edible root, the potato, the best part being under ground.

Sir Thomas Overbury

A genealogist is someone who regards a step backwards as progress.

Unknown

Cover image: Caerphilly Castle, Wales. © Jeremy Voisey/iStockphoto

First published 2012

The History Press
The Mill, Brimscombe Port
Stroud, Gloucestershire, GL5 2QG
www.thehistorypress.co.uk

British Library Cataloguing in Publication Data.
A catalogue record for this book is available from the British Library.

ISBN 978 0 7527 6599 9

Typesetting and origination by The History Press
Printed in Great Britain

Contents

Preface

This book emerged from courses in genealogy, family history, heraldry, palaeography and related subjects at the universities of Strathclyde and Edinburgh, and from talks and lectures given elsewhere. It is not a list of sources, although a great many sources are mentioned. There are other places to get lists of books, archive holdings and websites. It is, rather, intended as a working manual for genealogists with an interest in Welsh records and family history, firmly based in the praxis of a genealogical researcher and educator, with worked examples, templates and methodologies. It is aimed at all those interested in pursuing proper research into Welsh records and archives for genealogical purposes. This includes:

– Anyone wishing to trace ancestors of a particular person of Welsh descent, including those in countries that accepted the Welsh diaspora – principally the USA, Canada, Australia, New Zealand, southern Africa and India;
– Archivists, librarians, registers and those who guide others in the use of records and archives;
– Those with a professional interest in Welsh genealogy – lawyers, records agents, researchers in archives and, of course, genealogists;
– Anyone needing a suitable textbook for a preparatory course on Welsh genealogy.

There are subjects here not routinely covered in most introductory genealogy books – for instance, the interpretation of mediaeval documents, Latin inscriptions and palaeography. Where possible and relevant, parallels and differences have been drawn between Welsh genealogy and that of Scotland, England, Ireland and other countries. As the basic family history sources – censuses, vital records and the various registers of property, electors and membership – become more readily available, genealogists will seek to push their research further back in time to the 1500s and earlier. There is much in this book that, with luck, will be of wider interest than the records of Wales, but as these are so rich and go back so far, there is a great deal every genealogist can learn from their study and careful application.

Finally, thanks are due to staff at The National Archives, Kew (TNA), the National Library of Wales, many local libraries, archives and societies, and to the numerous long-suffering university colleagues and family members who put up with the process of authorship.

To quote an old Welsh saying, particularly appropriate to the study of those long gone: *Yn araf deg mae dal iâr* (The way to catch a hen is slowly).

1

An Introduction to Genealogical Research

If you are new to family history, please read this chapter. If you are an experienced family history researcher, please read this chapter. Whether you agree or disagree with the techniques and tips in here, it may make you think about your existing practices. This is not a 'how to do it' menu so much as recipes born of years of experience in researching, teaching and writing about genealogy and local history. Nor is it the only way to approach research, but it is intended to help readers avoid some of the common pitfalls, and get the best out of their time and energies. Individual chapters may suggest a research strategy or source not previously considered, or a new approach to a long-standing problem.

Why are we doing this?

History is the great destroyer – it destroys reputations, illusions, myths and vanities; it reminds us that we are all mortal and passing; it teaches us that we have little control over our actions and their consequences, our destinies and even our motives. We have no hand in choosing our ancestors, and little over our descendants' choice of friends and spouses. Each of us is the product of our genes, our immediate family environment, our society and the influence of the wider world. Even our deepest-held beliefs, prejudices and bigotries dissolve when put under the microscope of history, and our seemingly complex human world is much like an ant colony when viewed from a sufficient distance. But where genealogy differs from history *per se* is that it moves the focus away from the grand sweep of civilisations and larger social groups to the lives and actions of individuals and immediate families. It is often as far from the 'Great Man' view of history the way it used to be taught (lists of kings and battles) as a cat is from a queen. Those interested in history itself often find it is best illuminated when seen through the life of one person, an ancestor with whom we have some commonality of feeling by virtue of no more than a shared surname or location, or a half-remembered family story.

However, the majority of such people led quiet, blameless lives and left very few traces, and almost all sources of biography come from collision with the authorities. This tends to be for purposes of registration (birth, marriage, death, census, taxes, poor relief etc.) or for legal reasons, whether criminal (arrests, trials, executions, witness statements) or civil (law suits, divorce, wills, property transfers). All of these generated records, which may still exist in some form, or at least as indexes or abstracts.

Being a small country, the set of records available in Wales is approximately one-twentieth of that of England, and is therefore of manageable proportions. Welsh genealogy is, to that extent, easier. However, there is far more to Welsh genealogy than merely searching for vital data in the old parish registers (OPRs – baptism, marriage and burial records from the 1500s to 1836), statutory records (births, marriages and deaths from 1837) and the decennial censuses from 1841).

The parish registers, by definition, only start with the birth of the Reformation in the 1500s, and only deal with the Established Church. Catholics, Episcopalians, the many Nonconformists in Wales and those who simply chose not to take part in parish registration (the nobility, often) are completely ignored until much later. Those registers that exist may not be easy to access. Equally, records of burials were not considered important until well after the Reformation, since it was only after that time that bodily resurrection at the last trump became an issue – before this, the location of physical remains hardly mattered except for royalty or anyone likely to achieve sainthood (and therefore be a source of relics and an object of veneration). Even then, the parish registers are incomplete.

So, before the 1500s, family history can become murky. However, names were often recorded in charters, especially when feudally held lands were passed on, or where grants of land, titles or other inheritances held of the sovereign had to be recorded. There were also records of pedigree and coats of arms in heraldic records, which are a rich source of name and place information.

Most genealogical research stalls somewhere in the seventeenth or eighteenth centuries. Between the 1500s and the 1830s to 1840s (the beginning of statutory registration, the censuses and much else, as the Victorians set about organising a secular society) not everyone will be recorded, especially Nonconformists and the poor, particularly in both the sparsely populated areas and the densely packed centres of very large towns and cities. Remember that it was mainly baptisms (not births) which were noted in the parish registers, and the same goes for the other sacraments – proclamation of marriage (banns) rather than the marriage itself, and burial or mort-cloth (shroud) rental rather than death.

Even after the 1840s, the records are incomplete. Not everyone was captured; there were considerable movements into, out of and within Wales; surname and place name variants and Welsh spellings were commonly recorded haphazardly – so they give a partial picture of an individual's life. At best, the researcher can get a person's given name at birth plus a date and place, and the names, address and (possibly) occupations of the parents and their date of marriage; the announcement of banns (pre-1837) or registration of a marriage may include the place, and the names and occupations of both spouses, and those of both sets of parents, plus names of witnesses; and at death, the place and time of death are given, and often the cause, with the names and occupations of the deceased's parents and of the registrant (witness). Such scraps can be filled in with census information from every decade between 1841 and 1911. For example, someone who was born in 1850, married in 1870 and died in 1920, will usually be able to be identified, along with their parents, spouse and spouse's parents, from BMD records; and all of these people can be further identified in the snapshots from the censuses of 1841 to 1901. This may take us back to the birth of that person's parents in the early 1800s and of *their* parents (if alive in 1841), that is, to 1780 or so.

But such scraps of information leave much to be told. Were they rich or poor? Owned land or rented it? Had children or otherwise? The accessible vital records give a very bare-bones account. Precisely because much of these data are digitised and available online, it is possible to imagine, as is often claimed, that 'all of genealogy is on the Internet'.

This is where most people stop looking. In truth, it may be enough for them to start building a family tree with a reassuringly complete and impressively precise set of dates and places. But there are many pitfalls: a child born a year or more after a dead sibling might be given the same name; there may be inconsistencies in ages across the various censuses, leading to inaccurate linkages of completely separate individuals; children of 'irregular' marriages may not be recorded; anyone could be away from home on census night; there is emigration and re-immigration; and we find seemingly identical individuals, stemming from the understandable but infuriating practice of naming children after parents, grandparents, uncles and aunts, leading to complete families with children of the same names, married to other people of the same names, probably their near relatives, and living in the same parish.

Fortunately, that's not all there is to it. There are other sources of information, which fill out the details of individual lives, and allow the grouping of individuals by family group, locality or occupation. These include: charters; wills; dissenting and Catholic church records; lair records (for churches or municipal cemeteries); local electoral and valuation rolls; court records; military lists; Poor Law records; registers of professions, trades and guilds; and many others. Then there are landed individuals They may be of the nobility (whether of the English, Scottish, Irish or British peerages), manorial or baronetage (which is a kind of hereditary knighthood), or be merely landowning persons. Often, these people will have had coats of arms, so heraldry is a useful adjunct to 'standard' genealogy.

Finally, there is DNA evidence, which may indicate surname links and deeper ethnic ancestry, but can also help in cases where documentary evidence is lacking. It can, furthermore, hold surprises – welcome or otherwise.

This book is intended to show researchers how to get beyond the standard BMD and census search, and dig deeper into genealogy and the social history surrounding an individual or family. Necessarily, there will be some discussion on other archives outside Wales: TNA in England; Scottish and Irish records; US and Canadian census data, ships' passenger lists and so on.

Is genealogy the same as family history?

Not really, but they have a lot in common, and each informs the other. Genealogy (as the term is used in this book) is the study and construction of familial relationships, mainly from vital records – birth, marriage, death, censuses etc. Family history concerns itself more with events and their social context. To that extent, genealogy is the Who and Where, while family history is the What and When. Sociology would doubtless claim to be concerned with the Why, although much sociological investigation centres on the collection of the sort of data used by family historians and genealogists, and then tends to turn it into statistical summaries. Perhaps it is better to think by analogy to the sciences – genealogy is more like mathematics while family history is chemistry, and sociology is nature study or population biology. Or, genealogy is the bones, and family history is the flesh on the bones, and each needs the other.

Frankly, such hair-splitting is rather fruitless. We all know a straightforward piece of genealogy when we see it (a pedigree, for instance) and a family history (such as a biography). It is rather pointless, or at least unilluminating, to collect only the dates of birth, marriage and death, and the locations of these, for a family tree or pedigree, without understanding something of why great-grandfather gave up the pastoral life to work in a coal mine, grandfather was a grocer in a different county, and father left for Australia but came back. Equally, it is difficult to understand a complex family history without a simple table of relationships and dates. A good example of this is the intermarriages of European royalty in the nineteenth and twentieth centuries, many of whom were related by descent from Queen Victoria and Prince Albert. But just having the rather useful charts at the back of such books tells us little about the politics or the social conditions of the time.

It is generally agreed that family history is more about who people were and how they lived, why they did this job or married that spouse in that place, the circumstances in which they were born, worked, loved, fought, died, and the wider social and economic milieu of the time. Like all narratives, family history is open to speculation and interpretation. Genealogy is, in a sense, more precise, as it deals largely with concrete parameters – dates and places, for example. Genealogy is about tracing (and proving) ancestry and descent, sometimes called 'pedigree' or 'lineage'.

The two interact, of course – the observation that one generation was Anglican (Church in Wales) and the next 'chapel' (Nonconformist) not only says something about changing social, family and even political conditions; it is also a clue as to which records to investigate.

Definitions

Properly, pedigree charts start with one individual and trace the ancestry backwards through time. These are sometimes called 'birth-briefs' and end up looking like an ice-cream cone (if laid out vertically) or a megaphone (if set down horizontally). Descendant charts or trees take the other approach – from one pair of ancestors at the top fanning out to a confusing tangle of distantly related nth cousins at the bottom. Each of these is a useful visual aid – but no more than that. The end point of any research project is information, not merely a diagram.

There are blank charts and other material to help with this listed on p. 277.

Be clear about your aims

One thing is certain about genealogy and family history – it can become an all-consuming passion. However, it can also swamp you with information, paper, file boxes and computerised data. Everything you discover will lead you onto more tantalising snippets, interesting ancestors, new connections and, ultimately, the whole sweep of human history. It is utterly absorbing, but can also be maddeningly complicated.

Every genealogist or family historian has discovered, or will at some point, that there is simply no sensible way to fit hundreds of interlinked individuals onto one chart the size of a roll of wallpaper, and no filing system that works without bursting at the seams. Even if you only search back five generations from yourself, and each generation has two siblings on each side of the family, that's over 250 people, without worrying about the children of your great-aunts and great-uncles and so on. Imagine the documentation associated with these, if you had the certificates for every birth, marriage and death, every census, military service and occupational record, and every will. You would need a library.

There is a solution, though, and it requires three things:

1. Know where you want to go and stick to it: if your aim is to track the male line back to a certain point, then do just that; if you want to find all descendants of one person, then make that your goal; if you decide to find every instance of a surname back to a particular year or in a particular place (a one-name study), then decide that's it – do not get sidetracked by interesting byways, but do note them and come back to them as a separate project.
2. The best way to swallow an elephant is one bite at a time: if it all seems too much (and it will) then concentrate on solving one aspect; if it defies solution, shelve it, move on and come back to it later.
3. Organisation is all: keep good records, have a decent but simple filing system, organise your computer files properly and buy a robust genealogy database programme (Chapter 16).

Do these things, following the recommendations in this book, and you just might save your life, sanity, marriage or whatever you value most – after your genealogy project, of course.

STEP ONE – Start with what you know

Almost every genealogy book, course and how-to guide starts with this advice. Generally, it's sensible – you and your family are already the experts on your family history. It is likely that you will be able to get reliable dates and places for births, marriages and deaths back to grandparents and even further. There may well be documents (certificates, wills, letters, inscriptions in family Bibles) as well as diaries, newspaper clippings and photographs. By talking to older relatives and family friends, and showing them photographs and records, you may trigger memories and elicit more information. Ask where deceased relatives are buried and visit the graves, to photograph or record the headstone information or lair records. But there are dangers, complications and pitfalls.

First, memory is a very good, if selective, editor. A family story, repeated by many relatives, may be wrong in detail, embroidered over time or just plain invented. What seems to be a crucial piece of information, repeated by a number of people you talk to, may turn out to be no more than hearsay, or even a carefully constructed lie. A family that has spent years trying to trace a great-uncle who had 'gone abroad to work' may be less than delighted to be told he had in fact died while serving time in prison.

Second, different family members may have very different views of an ancestor. The grandfather who seemed stern but upright to one may have been a brutal bully to another. A beloved aunt may have been an appalling mother or an ungrateful daughter.

Third, you may well discover a long-buried secret or an inconvenient piece of information that certain family members may prefer to forget or have spent years assiduously covering up, and they will not be pleased with you for bringing it into the light of day. An illegitimacy, a dead child, an earlier marriage, an abandoned family, disinherited offspring, debts, bankruptcies, collapsed business ventures, dishonourable war service, problems with drink, police records, illnesses, suspicious deaths, murders, suicides, the important job that turns out to be not what was claimed, violence, child abuse, disagreements over a will, stolen property – all of these may emerge, as well as other long-suppressed skeletons. You run the risk of alienating as many people as you delight. It is not uncommon for one side of the family to want to know something and for another side to be furious when it is out in the open. On the other hand, your researches may be the instrument for bringing together branches of a family who haven't spoken for years over some now-forgotten and irrelevant slight or misunderstanding.

Fourth, if you choose to start from some supposed distant ancestor ('we're all descended from Owain Glyndŵr, last native Prince of Wales' is not untypical) and work forwards to try to establish the link with living persons, it is more than likely you will hit a brick wall or end up researching some other family entirely. If the presumed great-great-great-grandfather had seven children, and so did each of them, which of these forty-nine branches do you track? Generally it is better to research backwards in time, one generation at a time. You can always explore collateral branches later, as a separate project.

Fifth, check it hasn't been done before. Another family member may have been an amateur or professional genealogist and collected a great deal of information. But do check every statement and assumption! Also, there may be a printed or manuscript family history out there in some local library or archive. Finding these may save time and effort. They may also be completely bogus.

Lists of family histories and pedigrees are held in various places and by numerous bodies – the Society of Genealogists (London), the Guild of One Name Studies, the College of Arms, local libraries and archives, the National Library of Wales, university libraries and others. Look at Chapter 4 and follow the links, but also check catalogues such as *The Genealogist's Guide*, available via the public library. And, of course, look on the Internet but do not accept anything undocumented, regardless of how many times you see it repeated (because all repeats will probably have a single source, which may be wrong).

STEP TWO – Get charting

As early as possible, start sketching out a family tree. You will probably need two versions – a 'drop-line' pedigree chart for yourself (or whoever is the starting point) working backwards and a descendant tree from a specific ancestor. These would show, where possible, full names (with maiden surnames for the females), dates and places of birth, marriage and death, address at census dates and occupations. Use a large piece of paper, use a pencil, leave room for additions and be prepared to redraw it often. Or, use a genealogy programme to organise the data and print charts.

Don't wait until the end of your research to produce a final, definitive family tree or family history narrative. Genealogical projects are never finished, and there is always more information to add.

Be prepared to copy or print ongoing versions of the work in progress and send it to relatives and others. This may, in itself, jog memories further.

STEP THREE – Arrange your material

Note everything you find, even the failed searches and blind alleys and false leads. This will save time and effort later when you find yourself heading off up the same garden path. Document every source as fully as possible and photocopy, photograph, scan, download or transcribe fully every document and record you find, writing the reference number on it.

Print, and keep all of these in a flexible, easy-to-access place. One good and flexible method is to take all the materials for one family and arrange it under the headings of Censuses, Births, Marriages, Deaths, Wills, Newspapers, Photographs and so on, chronologically in each section (i.e. not according to the person). A filing cabinet will probably be essential at some point. Until then, a system of folders, ring binders and file boxes should do. Use a bound (not loose-leaf) book for your notes, which you will type up or copy later into your filing system. (See Chapter 16.)

Don't forget the female line

for a variety of reasons – to do with land and property inheritance, the transfer of a name, the way documents are recorded and so on – family trees often concentrate on the male line. But there is no reason not to follow the female line too, if you wish. It is 50 per cent of everyone's genetic inheritance, after all.

Using the Internet

There is no question that the Internet has transformed genealogy and family history studies. Apart from more and more records and indexes to records appearing online, it is also possible to track down and keep in contact with a vast network of family and contacts around the world. With an email list of relatives and others interested, it is possible to share and contribute information. More and more surnames and areas have their own dedicated family history websites, online newsgroups and bulletin boards. To find the local family history society (FHS) for your area of interest, see the Chapter 4 and consult the website of the Federation of Family History Societies (www.ffhs.org.uk) as well as GENUKI (www.genuki.co.uk), the Guild of One-Name Studies (the 'GOONS' – www.one-name.org) and other places suggested.

Public records

Despite the scale of Internet genealogical material, it still represents only a fraction of the totality. Ultimately, if you want to pursue family history to the next level of detail and precision, you are going to have to look at original records. You may be able to see them online, on microfilm or microfiche, or you may have to seek out the real thing, such as original parish registers – wonderful historic documents, handwritten in copperplate script (if you're lucky!) and redolent of the past.

Britain has an extraordinary depth and breadth of public records. For family history, the most important are the censuses, then records of birth/baptism, marriage and death/burial (BMD). As noted above and elsewhere, the key date here is 1837, when statutory civil registration began in England and Wales. Before that, baptisms, marriages and burials were recorded in parish registers, some of which go back to the sixteenth century. (A similar system of civil registration was inaugurated in Scotland in 1855. In Ireland the records are patchier, because some censuses, wills and church archives were destroyed during the Civil War in 1922, but there is civil registration information from about 1854.) It can be hard to trace back family history beyond the generation born in the 1830s unless you belong to a well-documented line of landowners, nobility or royalty, or if the local church was especially punctilious about keeping – and maintaining – its records.

Such records will help you to fix the precise details (if not always 100 per cent accurately) about your ancestors: dates, occupations, where they lived – the bare bones of their histories, if not much else. You can consult the indexes to births, deaths and marriages, and order photocopies of the certificates; for English and Welsh records, you can do this through TNA, by going in person or via the Internet (www.nationalarchives.gov.uk). A large proportion of the indexes for England and Wales have been transcribed, and are accessible through www.freebmd.org.uk or commercial websites (see below). However, actual certificates have to be purchased for delivery by post (see Chapter 5).

You can get further details of your ancestors from the census returns. A national census has taken place in Britain every decade since 1801 (except 1941) and they are available up to 1911. These returns provide a fascinating snapshot of households, the names and ages of the residents, the relationships between them, their occupations and where they were born. The census returns are released to the public after a century has elapsed. You can see Welsh census returns for 1851 through to 1901 on microfilm at county records offices, or, for a modest fee, you can download them from official or licensed websites; some of these records have also been transcribed into print (see Chapter 5).

There are many other forms of records beyond this, any of which could help you to fill in vital gaps in your knowledge (military records, wills, tax records, company records, electoral rolls, overseas civil records etc.). Most of these cannot be seen on the Internet, but you can find out where they are located by using websites such as:

www.nationalarchives.gov.uk (Britain);
www.archon.nationalarchives.gov.uk/archon (UK government gateway to repositories of archives);
www.a2a.org.uk (the England and Wales strand of the UK archives network).

Are we there yet?

Remember that genealogy is the history of the future – and you are writing it. You are not just doing this for your own amusement. Your research is part of your family's legacy and future generations will either praise you or curse you depending on how good your work is and whether it can be accessed.

If you are intending to conduct professional genealogical research, you will naturally be expected to produce correct, well-indexed, properly assembled material with all 'facts' checked and documented and all records presented neatly and accessibly. But even if this is just a hobby, start with the same professional attitude, and your hard work will stand the test of time.

Bant â chi (Off you go, then!)

2

The Welsh – A Genealogist's Perspective

What is Wales and who are the Welsh?

Wales, the nation-state or geographical area, is intimately connected with the people called Welsh. Peoples are generally identified by geography, kinship (however loose) and language. In this case, the geographical definition of Wales is relatively simple – as a peninsula, it has an obvious boundary formed by drawing a more-or-less straight line from an inlet of the Irish Sea near Chester, south to the Bristol Channel. The actual eastern border with England is largely as defined by the Laws in Wales Acts 1535–42, based on the boundaries of medieval Lordships of the March. It follows the defensive line called Offa's Dyke, possibly established in the eighth century, but perhaps based on an earlier Roman structure built by Septimius Severus, Roman Emperor around 200. Offa's Dyke separated the ancient Welsh kingdom of Powys from the Anglian kingdom of Mercia, but about 40 miles from the north coast the modern border takes a diversion to the east from this. Strangely, the actual Welsh perimeter has never been formally confirmed by a Boundary Commission, although it is formed by the borders of the easternmost counties. There are some amusing anomalies – for example, Knighton is separated from its railway station, and in the village of Llanymynech the boundary runs straight through a pub.

Today, Wales is separated into twenty-two unitary areas but is thought of as having thirteen historic counties (see Chapter 4). It is part of the United Kingdom of Great Britain and Northern Ireland. However, it is not a separate country (as Scotland is), but is a principality of England. Its citizens are British citizens.

The other way to define Wales is where the Welsh (*Cymry*) lived and live. But who are they?

The Welsh

The term 'Welsh' defines the ethnic group native to Wales and associated with the Welsh language, but even that isn't straightforward. There was nothing that could reasonably be called a separate 'Welsh nation' until the Romans withdrew from Britain in the late fourth to mid-fifth centuries. They had met tribes in Wales that they called *Deceangli*, *Demetae*, *Ordovices* and *Silures*. However, these inhabitants were no different from anyone else in southern Britain – they were all Britons, speaking the common language, British. This is a Celtic tongue of the Brythonic group, which also includes Breton and Cornish. It is distinguished from the Goidelic group, comprising Irish Gaelic, Scots Gaelic and Manx. The Celtic tongue and the associated culture probably first arrived in Britain in the Late Bronze Age or Early Iron Age (around 1,200 BC), although DNA evidence suggests that this might be a cultural overlay of an Indo-European language and cultural shift onto pre-existing inhabitants.

These original inhabitants of Britain were mainly indigenous European Paleolithic (Old Stone Age) hunter gatherers, with a later and smaller Neolithic (New Stone Age) farming population. It seems, from various strands of evidence, that after the last ice age (8,000 BC) a small population survived in Iberia (present-day Spain and Portugal) and spread throughout

Europe during the Mesolithic period (up to 5,000 BC). Neolithic incomers were from further east in Europe. The Welsh themselves consider themselves Celts with a heritage traced back to the Iron Age tribes, superimposed to some extent by Romano-British culture and a language that has some Latin influence.

The prototype of the Welsh language was spoken farther afield – as far north as Strathclyde and the Lothians where it remained even after the encroachments from Ireland of the Gaelic *Scotii* and their Goedelic language into Argyll in the fifth and sixth centuries. It surprises many Scots that William Wallace's native language was one cognate with Welsh, and that 'Wallace itself' may mean 'Welsh', which is from the Germanic *walha* and indicates 'foreigner' or 'stranger' and is much the same word as 'Gaulish'. It also surprises many Welsh that their great early poem, *Y Gododdin*, was written in the Brythonic kingdom of Gododdin, which extended from the Tyne to the area around Stirling, with its capital at Din Eidyn (Edinburgh), and which rubbed up against the genetically and linguistically distinct Picts of Fife, Angus and the Mearns (Kincardineshire).

After the Romans left, Anglo-Saxons invaded Britain and gradually pushed west, possibly wiping out a large proportion of the indigenous population and forcing the remainder west. This makes the peoples of Wessex, Wales, Cumbria, Strathclyde and Lothian the original Britons; what became the 'English' were Germanic invaders who undertook a form of ethnic cleansing. So much for the claims of the British National Party to represent 'the original inhabitants'.

But if the Welsh are the Britons, why do they not call themselves that? There is evidence of the early use of the term *Brythoniaid* (Britons), but the first use of *Kymry* (which refers to the place, not the people) is in a poem from the 630s – around the time that the Brythonic language had changed to Welsh – and may have included the northern areas listed above. That explains the name of the region known as Cumbria, and the Brythonic language used there as Cumbric. Eventually *Cymru* came to indicate the land now called Wales, and *Cymry* the people. This makes sense – if 'Wales' derives from the a word meaning 'stranger' in the Romanised world, *Cymru* and *Cymry* come from the Brythonic word *combrogi*, meaning 'fellow-countrymen', a much more comfortable term than the English words Welsh and Wales, with their implications of 'foreign' and 'strange'. Modern Welsh has two words for the English: *Saeson* (singular *Sais*), originally meaning 'Saxon', and the less commonly used *Eingl*, meaning 'Angles'. The Welsh word for the English language is *Saesneg* and for England is *Lloegr*.

Of course, there have been later overlays too, both cultural and linguistic. Scandinavians invaded (as Vikings) and settled from the ninth century, as did the Normans (North-men, themselves descended from Vikings in northern France) after 1066; both of these had a much greater influence on language than the Romans. Any traces of Latin we now find in English are echoes of the language of Rome in Norman French, imports from the medieval church into law, and 'scholarly borrowings' after the Renaissance. It was the Normans who had the largest direct influence on the land and people of Wales, as Anglo-Normans were given lands in Wales and encouraged to settle there. There is a so-called 'Landsker Line' dividing the 'Englishry' and 'Welshry' of Pembrokeshire, and similar terms are used for parts of Gower.

Welsh identity in censuses and other surveys

The term 'Welsh' also applies to those from Wales and of Welsh ancestry who identify themselves or are identified as sharing a cultural, linguistic, geographical and ancestral heritage (as in 'Australian-Welsh'). Denied a chance to describe themselves as 'Welsh' in the 2001 census, about 14 per cent overall actually wrote on the form that they were ethnically Welsh (27 per cent in Gwynedd, 23 per cent in Carmarthenshire, 22 per cent in Ceredigion and 19 per cent in the Isle of Anglesey). The Welsh fought for the inclusion of added questions in 2011, and got: *What is your country of birth?* (with 'Wales' as an option), *How would you describe your national identity?* ('Welsh' and 'English' were among the options), *What is your ethnic group?* ('White Welsh/

English/Scottish/Northern Irish/British' was an option) and *Can you understand, speak, read or write Welsh?* At the time of writing (2012), there is no analysis available.

In 2001/02 the Labour Force Survey found that 87 per cent of Wales-born residents claimed to be ethnically Welsh. (The residential population includes 30 per cent born outside Wales.) Interestingly, a separate study by Oxford University identified that 18 per cent of respondents thought of themselves as 'Welsh and not British', 20 per cent 'more Welsh than British' and 39 per cent 'equally Welsh and British'. In general, younger people are more likely to identify themselves as 'Welsh' in some way. This Welsh/British distinction is at odds with history, but is indicative of the strong sense of identity that pervades what some refer to, rather dismissively, as 'Welsh Wales'.

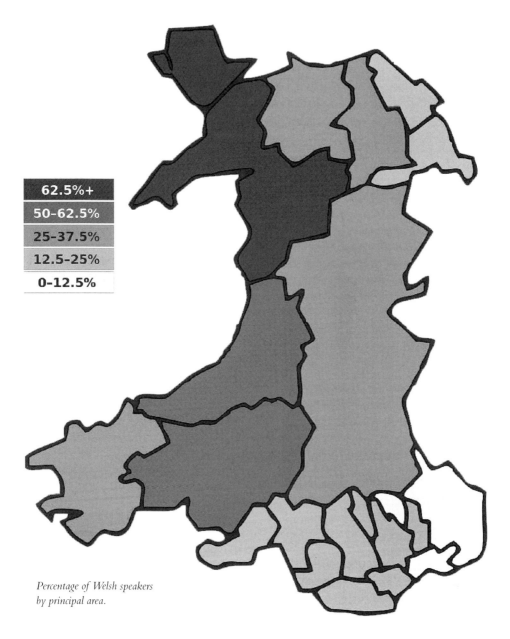

62.5%+

50-62.5%

25-37.5%

12.5-25%

0-12.5%

Percentage of Welsh speakers by principal area.

Language

Speaking Welsh is a central component of Welsh identity – more than speaking Gaelic or Scots is in Scotland. The Welsh themselves speak of *Cymry Cymraeg* (the Welsh-speaking Welsh), *Cymry di-Gymraeg* (the non-Welsh-speaking Welsh) and *Saeson* (English, not Welsh at all).

There is no question that the number of Welsh speakers in Wales is rising – there was a time when it was actively discouraged, especially in schools. The 2001 census (see above) may not have directly enumerated those considering themselves 'Welsh', but it did assess language, as did that of 2011. About 20 per cent of the population (so about 600,000 out of roughly 3 million) claimed to be fluent in Welsh, a further 28 per cent claimed to understand it. The increase over the last decade is most marked in large towns such as Cardiff (*Caerdydd*), and in the Rhondda. Welsh speakers in Gwynedd and Ceredigion have decreased, but these areas have had the greatest influx of new, non-Welsh residents. There is also evidence that non-Welsh-speaking residents moving to rural North Wales have diluted the language base – and also driven up property values so that Welsh-speaking 'locals' are displaced. About a quarter of Welsh residents are from outside Wales.

This means that Welsh is the first language in much of the rural north and west (the Isle of Anglesey, Gwynedd, central Denbighshire) followed by Powys, Ceredigion and Carmarthenshire, then North Pembrokeshire and western Glamorgan. Historically, this matches the places that did not have an influx of incomers for the slate-mining, coal-mining and other industries in the nineteenth and twentieth centuries. But there are first-language and fluent speakers all over Wales, including the urbanised south, especially now that Cardiff is home to many national organisations in the public and private sectors who need Welsh speakers.

There is hardly anyone who speaks only Welsh and almost everyone is truly bilingual in English and Welsh, but many Welsh speakers prefer to use Welsh rather than English. This also depends on the area – English is commoner in South Wales and large towns, and Welsh in North Wales and rural areas. Visitors often notice what linguistics specialists call 'code-switching', a shift from one language to the other depending on context, companions, presence or absence of other Welsh speakers and so on. Furthermore, because of the purposive promotion of the Welsh language, and the existence of the Welsh Assembly (with devolved but limited powers of self-government), learning and using the Welsh language is important in career and cultural openings.

The growth of interest in the language (and the use of it) since 1945 mirrors a rise in Welsh nationalism, the emergence of the political party *Plaid Cymru*, the increased activities of *Cymdeithas yr Iaith Gymraeg* (the Welsh Language Society), the existence of Welsh-only television and radio stations, road signs in Welsh and the teaching of Welsh in schools.

Surnames and population

Meat and drink to genealogists, surnames are an important aspect of identity. Strangely (according to a survey of Welsh surnames commissioned by the Welsh Assembly) only a third of the population of Wales have a family name of Welsh origin. The equivalent figure in the rest of the UK is about 5 per cent, and not much less in New Zealand, Australia and the USA. Over 16 million people worldwide are considered to be of Welsh ancestry – probably an underestimate.

Welsh surnames

Six out of the top ten commonest surnames in Britain are Welsh. The question is, though – why is the proportion of Welsh surnames in Wales not higher? (See Chapter 3.)

The population of Wales grew from less than 600,000 in 1801 to almost twice that in 1851, and twice that again by 1911. This trend was common during the Industrial Revolution in Britain – death rates (especially infant mortality) fell and birth rates were stable, but migration into Wales

WALES & the MARCH in the Time of Edward I.

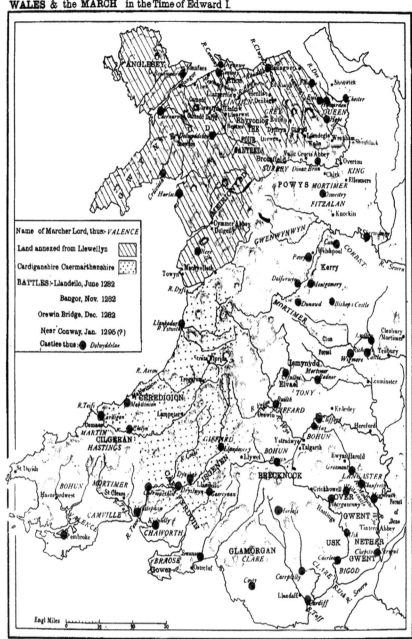

Wales in the time of Edward I.

was marked. Most immigrants were English, but Irish also figured, as did ethnic groups from elsewhere, notably Italians migrating to the South Wales coal mines.

In the twentieth century, as in the rest of Britain, there has been immigration from the British Commonwealth of African-Caribbean and Asian ethnic groups, and a more recent influx from new accession countries of the European Union such as Poland.

Partly this is to do with land inheritance. In Wales, and indeed for Catholics in Ireland, unlike in England (except Kent), a man's estate was divided equally among his sons – a custom known as 'gavelkind'. Someone's two sons who pass their share onto their two sons and so on could easily result in a number of unworkably small plots of land. So they left the land.

DNA

There is no particularly Welsh genetic pattern. The commonest marker is R1b (about 85 per cent) as with most Britons, who, after all, arrived from the Iberian Peninsula in the Mesolithic and the Neolithic times. Bryan Sykes in *Blood of the Isles* and Stephen Oppenheimer in *The Origins of the British*, summarise the genetic evidence. Oppenheimer claims that 96 per cent of lineages in Llangefni (North Wales) derive ultimately from Iberia. Y-chromosome markers amongst the Welsh, as with the Irish, show a common ancestry with the Basques of northern Spain and south-western France, perhaps with more Neolithic input than these. For more detail, start at http://en.wikipedia.org/wiki/Haplogroup_R1b_(Y-DNA).

Religion

The Anglican Church in Wales is the single largest denomination, but there is a long tradition of Nonconformists and Methodists, as well as other denominations such as the Presbyterian Church in Wales or Catholicism; about 70 per cent of the population consider themselves nominally Christian. There has been a Jewish community in Swansea from about 1730, but only Cardiff now has a sizeable Jewish population (some 2,000). The largest non-Christian faith in Wales today is Islam – there are about 25,000 members of some forty mosques (the first was in Cardiff in 1860). The 2001 census recorded about 7,000 practising 'other religions', including neo-Druidism, a form of the pre-Christian religion of Wales (this is not related to the bardic Druids of the *Gorsedd* at the National *Eisteddfod* of Wales).

As far as observance goes, the 2001 census showed that fewer than 10 per cent of the Welsh regularly attend church or chapel (lower than in England or Scotland). However, for the genealogist, that's not the point. Regardless of religious faith or none, people did tend to document their vital sacraments (baptism, marriage, burial) in the records of various churches. Knowing which is important – and, in Wales, this is complicated by the high proportion in Nonconformist denominations, not all of which kept good records, maintained them or have made them available (Chapter 6).

Welsh emigration

There has always been migration between Wales and the rest of Britain, in both directions. During the Industrial Revolution there were hundreds of thousands of Welsh who moved to work in the larger cities of England and Scotland or the coal mines in the north of England. There were also English, Scottish and Irish workers who migrated to Welsh cities such as Merthyr Tydfil or ports such as Pembroke, and to work in slate or coal mines. As a result, much of the British population today have ancestry from Wales. Therefore, Welsh surnames are fairly common in the rest of the UK, and many Welsh have surnames from Scotland, England and Ireland. The upshot is that it is rare, except in Welsh-speaking areas, to find anyone with exclusively Welsh ancestry, and there may be a need to consult records from other parts of the UK. It also means that genealogical investigations in Scotland, England or Ireland may lead back to Wales. (See also Chapter 9.)

Overseas emigration

Some Welsh moved to the European continent, but to rather specific places and for rather specific reasons. During the late nineteenth and early twentieth centuries there was a movement of contract miners from Wales to northern France, especially to the coal-mining towns of

Pas-de-Calais. There was not the same tradition of trade and migration with the Baltic and Scandinavian states as can be found with the Scots. However, Donetsk in the Ukraine was founded by John Hughes, an engineer and entrepreneur from Merthyr Tydfil, in 1869. Hughes built a steel plant and coal mines in the region and the town was named Yuzovska (or Yusovska) as 'Yuz' was as close as Russians or Ukrainians could get to Hughes).

Compared to the Irish, relatively few Welsh have emigrated to the USA; those that did moved predominantly to the coal-mining areas of Pennsylvania and Ohio. Jackson County, Ohio, has been called 'Little Wales' and Malad City, Idaho (originally a Welsh Mormon settlement), claims to have more people per head of Welsh ancestry than anywhere outside Wales – the high school football team is the Malad Dragons and flies the Welsh flag. About 1.75 million Americans claim they have Welsh ancestry – more than half the present population of Wales.

By the way, there is no evidence whatsoever for the legendary Prince Madog reaching North America in 1170 and founding the Mandan, a Native American tribe of the central USA.

As for Canada, Welsh settlers (and later Patagonian Welsh) arrived in Newfoundland in the early 1900s, and there are many Welsh-founded towns in Labrador. Almost 500,000 Canadians identified themselves as being of Welsh ancestry in the 2006 census.

The famous Welsh settlement, Y Wladfa in Patagonia, Argentina, is dealt with in Chapter 9. Rio Grande do Sul in Brazil was where Thomas Benbow Phillips of Tregaron established a Welsh community of about 100 in 1852. Individual Welsh may also have emigrated for particular reasons – as missionaries and evangelists, in the armed forces and so on, so records of these activities are valuable.

All of these aspects are considered in later chapters. But it should be clear that Welsh genealogy, as well being a study in its own right, touches many other genealogies worldwide. Ignore it at your genealogical peril! (See also Chapter 9.)

Further reading

John Davies, *A History of Wales* (Penguin, 1990).

Norman Davies, *The Isles* (Papermac, 1991).

Adrian Hastings, *The Construction of Nationhood: Ethnicity, Religion, and Nationalism* (Cambridge University Press, 1997).

Stephen Oppenheimer, *The Origins of the British: A Genetic Detective Story* (Robinson Publishing, 2007).

Bryan Sykes, *Blood of the Isles* (Corgi, 2007).

Gwyn A. Williams, *The Welsh in their History* (Croom Helm, 1982).

3

Welsh Surnames

When you are up to your neck in the undergrowth of a Welsh family history project, it can seem that everyone is surnamed Davies, Evans, Jones or Williams, all the men are David, Evan, John or William, all the women Anne, Gladys, Mary, Megan or Jane, and everyone in the same generation of cousins is named after the grandfather.

Well, that's the way it is. But it may help to understand how and when this came about.

Welsh surnames

Surnames as we recognise them today – passed down unchanged from father to children – are a relatively recent phenomenon. In Wales, they did not really exist until the Elizabethan times, before which people were known mainly by patronymics, place names and/or characteristics, like Rys du ap Llewelyn ap Kydwgan o Garog (a place in Cardiganshire) whose son was Rys Vychan Gentu (*vychan* or *fychan* later became Vaughan, which means 'the small' or 'the younger' in Welsh – and if you've ever heard of the Gentoo Penguin, reflect that *pen gwyn* is Welsh meaning, literally, 'head of white', which indeed the Gentoo has).

Not everyone Welsh is called Jones, and not every Jones is Welsh

There are relatively few Welsh surnames – fewer than forty names account for about 95 per cent of the Welsh, wherever they have ended up. That is not to say that everyone called 'Jones' (son of John) or 'Williams' (son of William) is of Welsh origin – they could be English, or simply have assumed the surname over time – but someone called Lloyd or Llewellyn and their variants most probably is. The most typically 'Welsh' surnames – Davies, Evans, Jones, Thomas and Williams – are also in the top ten found in England to this day, not as a result of Welsh out-migration, but because some of them also originated in England, long before they arose in Wales, in as early as the fourteenth century.

Now, in the twenty-first century, only a third of the Welsh population has a surname that would be considered of Welsh origin, but that is still six or seven times as many as in the rest of the UK. Many of them have spawned variants no longer thought of as being originally Welsh – the very old forename Madog has become Maddock, Maddox, Mattocks, Maddick and even Muddock (although considered to be from Suffolk, the earliest record is actually in Shropshire on the Welsh border).

Top 100 Welsh surnames

For the record, here are the top 100 surnames in Wales, in descending order of incidence, in the 1850s – about the time we can start to find census (Chapter 5) and statutory registration records (Chapter 6). The first ten account for more than half of all Welsh surnames, and the first thirty-five (the first column, below) for over 80 per cent.

Such lists are never perfect, vary according to locale (there are very few Joneses in the far south-west, for example) and may include or exclude certain variants. For instance, should Jones and Johns be considered separate, as they have a similar origin? As Preece and Price both arise from ap Rhys, should they be considered separately? Is everyone called Howell/Hywel necessarily related? However, armed with this list and knowing the origin of the name, it may be possible to track name changes back through the centuries.

Jones	Griffin	Bound
Williams	Bevan	Gwilt
Davies	Meredith	Beddoe
Thomas	Preece	Dacey
Evans	Prosser	Pendry
Robert(s)	Griffith	Reese
Hughes/Huw	Pierce	Doidrick
Lewis/Lewys	Reece	Brick
Morgan	Probert	Knill
Griffin/Griffith(s) –	Floyd	Evens
anglicised form of Gruffudd	Tudor	Gilliam
Owen/Owain	Breeze	Ace
Edward(s)	Pryce	Donne
Rees	Rosser	Bevans
James	Brice	Raikes
Jenkins	Gittins	Cleaves
Price	Beynon	Traylor
Morris/Morys	Mathias	Embrey
Richard(s)	Broderick	Leafe
Lloyd	Prowse	Connick
Phil(l)ip(s)	Gillam	Pumphrey
Parry	Morgans	Boore
David	Havard	Burris
Harris/Harries	Eynon	Games
John(s)	Beaven	Demery
Powel(l)	Coughlin	Glyn
Pritchard	Phoenix	Mabe
Howell(s)/Hywel	Press	Gwyn
Watkin(s)	Prichard	Scale
Rowlands	Gerrish	Yandle
Bowen	Prothero	Hargest
Humphreys	Speake	Beedles
Ellis	Breese	Boyde
Pugh	Cadogan	Skone
Llewelyn/Llywelyn		
Hopkins		

Origins of surnames

Surnames arise in a number of ways. In his classic *British Family Names* (1894) Henry Barber identified that 'most surnames will be found to come under one or other of the following headings':

1. Nicknames
2. Clan or tribal names
3. Place names
4. Official names
5. Trade names
6. Christian names
7. Foreign names
8. Foundling names

Modern practice tends to regroup these into six main origin groups (in no particular order):

- Patronymic (named after the father – Johnson = son of John).
- Fealtic (taken in order to show fealty to, or accepting the protection of, the local chief or landholder – as with many Scottish 'Mac' names, which may indicate nothing genetic, but simply that the person lived on the land of, accepted the protection of and swore loyalty to MacSomebody).
- Descriptive ('Small', 'White', 'Armstrong').
- Occupational ('Smith', Fletcher', Baker').
- Landed (indicating ownership or heritable possession – 'of Cardigan', 'de la Zouch').
- Locational (merely coming from – 'Glasgow', 'Bristol', Kent').

Consider the 'surnames' of Robin Hood and his Merry Men as they have come down to us in myth and literature:

- **Much the Miller's son** – Patronymic: family name combined with a trade name.
- **Little John (John Little)** – Descriptive: describing a physical characteristic.
- **Will Scarlet** – Descriptive or occupational: possibly referring to red hair, or he was a scarlet dyer (but could be a corruption of **Scathelock**, his actual surname).
- **Friar Tuck** – Occupational or status: in this case, clerical.
- **Alan a Dale** – Locational: 'Alan from the Dale'.
- **Robin Hood** – Descriptive: from 'Robin in the wood'. But he was also reputedly Sir Robert of Locksley, son of the Earl of Huntingdon, indicating landed territorial possession.

Let's take each of these in turn:

1. Patronymic

These are surnames derived from the name of a father or grandfather. Medieval England and English-speaking Wales had only some twenty popular male first names, the commonest being John. Richard, the son of John, might be known as Richard, John's son (Johnson), but by this scheme, Richard's son William would become William, Richard's son (Richardson) or even just William Richards. Over time, it became convenient and legally important to maintain the patronymic down the entire line.

There are also diminutives of the father's or grandfather's first name – Bartlett (Little Bartholomew), Hewitt or Hewlett (little Hugh), Perkin (Little Peter), Wilkin (Little William) and so on.

Sometimes there were changes in spelling – Anderson (Andrew's son), Harris (Harry's son), Henderson (Henry's son), Hughes (Hugh's son), Nixon (Nicholas's son), Simpson (Simon's son), Patterson (Patrick's son), Tennyson (Dennis's son) and Jones (the Welsh version of Johnson, which became the most common surname). Furthermore, the final '-son' was often elided to a single '-s' – Williamson becoming Williams, Evanson becoming Evans and so on.

After the Norman invasion of England in 1066 some surnames began with Fitz (from *fils*, French for 'son'), especially in Ireland – Fitzhugh, Fitzgerald – as is clear from the *Limerick Chronicle*, 22 May 1769: 'Last Tuesday James MOLONEY Fitzandrew …'. Later, Fitz was used for illegitimate but acknowledged offspring. For instance, King William IV (1765–1837, r. 1830) had no surviving legitimate children at his death (which is how Victoria came to be queen), although he was survived by eight of the ten illegitimate children he had by the popular actress, Dorothea

Bland, better known as Mrs Jordan, with whom he cohabited for twenty years. They were all surnamed FitzClarence as William had been Duke of Clarence.

In Scotland and Ireland, surnames often began with Mac (Gaelic for 'son of' or 'descendant of'), such as MacGregor (Gregor's descendant) or MacPherson (descendant of the parson). Incidentally, there is no distinction between Mac and its contractions Mc and M'. It is *not* the case that one is Scottish and the other Irish.

The Irish O' (O'Dwyer, O'Malley) indicated 'grandson of', or loosely 'descended from', in contrast to the prefix Mac or Mc, which would mean son of the ancestor specified. Scottish Gaelic has a similar word for grandson (*ogha*) but this has not made it into many surnames.) Gaelic names and customs were outlawed during the reign of Edward IV (from 1465) for Irishmen living within the 'Pale' (the area around Dublin); all had to take English names or forfeit their possessions. Many refused, and it took another 200 years of persecution and ridicule to make the Gaelic forms all but disappear – the anglicised version of Ua Dalaigh or O'Dalaigh became O'Daly and in Scottish Gaelic we find MacFhearghais (MacFergus) or Fearghasdan (Ferguson), MacFhionnlaigh (MacFinlay) and MacDomhnall (MacDonald or MacDonell).

The Welsh equivalent is *ap* or *ab* (before a vowel) as in ap John, which became Johns/Jones but also Upjohn; ap Rhys, which became Prees/Price; ab Owain, which turned into Bowen; and ab Ieuan, which became Bevan. The female equivalent is *ferch* (daughter of), such as Cerys ferch Dafydd ap Rydderch (Cerys, daughter of David, son of Roderick) and after marriage women would normally keep these maiden names – precisely because there was no 'surname' to adopt.

This patronymic system is still the pattern found in, say, Iceland, where Eric the son of Magnus becomes Eric Magnusson, and his son Thorvald, Thorvald Ericsson. Eric's wife might be Inge Baldursdottir. Eric and Inge's daughter, Bjork, would be Bjork Ericsdottir but it is also possible, although uncommon, to make a girl's last name from the name of the mother – Bjork Ingesdottir.

The same naming tradition existed in Sweden and Norway until the second part of the nineteenth century. In certain areas of western Sweden, it continued even longer.

In Russia and other Slavic countries, the full name includes a patronymic and the surname is altered to indicate gender – *ov* means 'son of' (Pavlov = son of Paul) and the female equivalent is *ova* (Pavlova = daughter of Paul). Igor, son of Mikhail Pisarev would be called Igor Mikhailovitch Pisarev and his daughter Svetlana would be Svetlana Mikhailovna Pisareva (note the feminine ending to the patronymic *and* surname).

In Italy *d'* or *di* indicates 'son of' – 'di Rollo', 'Dicaprio'.

Hungarians, for reasons best known to themselves, reverse the name order, so Gyula, the son of Bartok Bela, would be Bartok Gyula. A married woman, formally, takes a feminine form of her husband's Christian name, so Maria, wife of Rudnai Peter becomes Rudnai Peternye.

Remember also that in many Germanic countries, the wife adopts any professional titles of her husband, and all titles are given, so it is possible to meet Frau Professor Professor Doctor Doctor Schubert.

It is noticeable in the list of Welsh surnames on p. 24 that the commonest thirty-three (all in the first column) are all patronymic except Lloyd, which comes from *llwyd* (grey). The patronymics tend, in the main, to fall into three categories.

- Those derived from Christian names also common in England – like Jones, Thomas, Davies and Williams – or directly from Anglo-Norman names – as with Hughes, from Huw, the Welsh form copied from the notorious Hugh le Despenser (father and son both) who did such damage to Wales in the early 1300s; other examples of this are Robert and Richard.

- Surnames that originally contained the prefix *ap* (meaning 'son of' in the same way as the Scottish–Irish 'Mc' or 'Mac'). Examples of these are Pritchard (ap Richard) and Bowen (ap Owen with the 'p' hardened to a 'b').
- Surnames from English sources that became well known in parts of Wales, due to in-migration, or assimilation by native Welsh.

The patronymic system eventually ended and the father's name came to be treated as a surname to be passed on. For example, William ap John Thomas, standard bearer of King Henry VIII, became known as William Jones. Thomas ap Lewis, son of Lewis ap Sir David, was killed at the Battle of Banbury in 1469 and his son, Lord of the Manor of Raglan in Monmouthshire in 1487, was the first to adopt Lewis as a permanent surname.

At the same time as the patronymic system fell away – around the time of Henry VIII and into the beginning of the seventeenth century – traditional Welsh forenames (see p. 33) such as Ioan, Bleddyn, Huw, Geraint, Ieuan, Madog and Rhydderch were dying away, to almost disappear altogether or be replaced by English names and equivalents like John, Hugh, Evan, Richard, Thomas and William, which in turn became typically Welsh surnames (Jones, Hughes, Evans, Richards, Thomas, Williams, etc), and fixed in that form. This became the pattern among the gentry and the wealthy – especially in areas with a strong English presence or influence – and spread down the social scale.

The other implication of this is that two completely unrelated people in the same town or village – Owain ap William and Rhys ap William, say, both became Williams, confounding genealogists ever after.

That's not to say the old naming tradition isn't to be found in nineteenth-century and even later records, albeit largely in the Welsh-speaking areas. And there was another particularly Welsh issue – because there were suddenly so many people called Jones, Williams, Davies, Thomas and Evans, there had to be a system to distinguish them. The nineteenth century saw a trend for double surnames, made by prefixing the surname with the mother's first name or surname, as with Carys Williams, or with the name of the house, farm or parish, as in Betws Jones. Such names were sometimes hyphenated to make them double-barrelled, for example Evans-Williams or even Hughes-Hughes.

On the other hand, patronymic Welsh names are again becoming popular, in the light of the Welsh language and culture revival.

Furthermore, it may be that America derives its name from a Welsh patronymic – Richard ap Meric was a Bristol merchant who bankrolled the Venetian John Cabot's voyages to Nova Scotia and the north-eastern seaboard of North America around 1500, and Richard had anglicised his name to Amerike. Against this, the first use of America on a map drawn by German cartographer Martin Waldseemüller in 1507, and only applied to what is Brazil today, was based on measurements taken by Amerigo Vespucci of Florence, who was certainly there on his expeditions at exactly the same time as Cabot was further north, if his letters are to be believed. The debate goes on!

2. Fealtic

This doesn't really apply in Wales, and is more a feature of the clan system of the Highlands of Scotland, where a man and his family might take the name of the local clan chief, to indicate their fealty and service towards the chief, and the chief's protection of them. There need have been no blood relationship – many a Campbell family had its origin in someone who was under the protection of, or worked or fought for, the Dukes of Argyll, whose own surname was Campbell. The Gordons famously offered 'a bowl of meal' to anyone who came to live on their lands, swore fealty and took the name. Conversely, not all Mac- surnames indicate a relationship to a clan and there may be many a MacNab (son of the abbot) with no relationship to Clan MacNab at all, whose name arose independently.

3. Descriptive

The most obvious are common adjectives referring to:

- physical size (such as Vaughan from *vychan/fychan* meaning 'small', plus Little, Longfellow);
- hair colour or complexion (Lloyd for 'grey', Gwynn, for 'white' and therefore 'fair-haired'), plus Redhead, Black, Rufus);
- personal characteristics (Armstrong, Stern, Stout – meaning stout of heart, not stout of frame);
- social status (Knight, Bachelor, Laird).

Once the surname system was established there was no reason for a distant descendant to actually be a redhead or a long fellow. As for Vychan/Fychan becoming the surname Vaughan, the first major Vaughan family is found in Bredwardine, Hereford, on the border, which indicates the Anglicisation. The great Welsh surname scholars, T.J. Morgan and Prys Morgan (see *Further reading*) tell us that one Rhosier (= Roger), killed while protecting the body of Henry V at Agincourt in 1415, was himself the son of Rhosier, so the father had to be Rhosier Hen 'the Old' and the son Rhosier Fychan, that is, 'Young Roger'. Some, but not all, of Rhosier Hen's sons were called Fychan or Vaughan, so it became the surname of this Cardiganshire family – of which the first known member was Llywelyn Fychan, born *c.* 1250 – around that time.

Other examples of descriptive Welsh names and their derivatives:

- *bras* (gross, coarse) – Brace;
- *coch* (red), becoming *goch* – Gough, Goff, Gooch and Gouch;
- *du* (black, as is the Gaelic *dubh*) – Dee;
- *gwyn* (white) – Gwynn, Wynn.

4. Occupational

This especially made sense when sons followed fathers into their trades; these surnames are also mostly obvious – Smith, Farmer, Wright, Cooper and so on.

Occupational names are rare among Gaelic and Welsh surnames, which might be expected in predominantly agricultural communities where there were no specialised trades as such, except possibly the smith. Exceptions might be Crowther from *crythor* (a player of the *crwth*, a sort of lyre), Morgan from *morcant* (sea-chief), Priddy from *prydydd* (poet), Sears from *saer* (carpenter) and Wace from *gwas* (servant).

In Scotland, names beginning with Mael- signify a follower or devotee (Maeliesu, Mellish = follower of Jesus; Mael Colm, Malcolm = follower of Columba) and the equivalent in Ireland is Gil- or Kil-, from Giolla (Giolla Mhairtin or Gilmartin, follower of St Martin) or Mul-, from Maol (bald, of the monk's tonsure, and so Ó Maoilbhreanainn or Mulrennan, descendant of a follower of St Brendan).

Watch out for unusual or ancient occupational descriptions – Baxter (baker), Bailey (bailiff), Chandler (candle maker), Day (dairy worker), Fletcher (arrow maker), Frobisher (armour and sword polisher), Kellogg (hog-killer), Leach (doctor), Machin (stoneworker), Naylor (nailmaker), Proctor (steward), Redman (reed thatcher), Trinder (wheelwright), Ward (watchman), Webster (weaver).

Some surnames derived from an hereditary office, such as Stewart or Stuart (steward), Butler, Sheriff and Chamberlain.

Palmer describes a pilgrim who had returned from the Holy Land, bearing the traditional palm as a proof or souvenir (similar to the Islamic practice of adding *Haj* or *Haji* to the name after a pilgrimage to Mecca).

However, the most common form of occupational name in Wales is the nickname, used to identify people by their trade to this day. It's informal, but everyone in town knows that Jones the Brush is a house painter, Jones the Bread is a baker, Jones the Sheep is a farmer – and the undertaker may be known as Dai the Death!

5.   Landed surnames

A surname may be associated with land owned by the individual or his ancestors – either because they took their name from the land or vice versa. In 1260 or so a younger son of one of the Earls of Strathearn was given the land of Durie (possibly *dubh ri*, 'black stream' or *dobharach*, 'watery land') in Fife, becoming 'of Durie', from which time the surname was fixed. The Welsh surname Blayney is an English version of the Welsh town Blaenau. Dafydd ap Howel ap Ieuan ap Einion o Drelech ar Betws manages to combine the patronymics from three generations before adding the place in Carmarthenshire, which is now called Trelech-a'r-Betws.

However, although a surname equates to the name of some land, this does not indicate that an ancestor actually owned the land – it may simply be a locational description (below).

6.   Locational

When people started to move around more than they had previously, they may have called themselves, or been called, after their place of origin. John (from Gwent) who went to live in London might have been known as John (of) Gwent, to distinguish him from the hundreds of other Johns around. Inglis or Saes originally indicated English. In Scotland, Wallace meant Welsh (or, at least, from among the Britons of Strathclyde), which itself is from the Old English *waelis*, a foreigner, used to describe the Welsh themselves. A good half of all surnames in Britain derive from locational or geographic descriptions (Abernethy, Churchill etc.).

The suffix is often a clue, as in -lee (meadow), -bank, -don or -ton (town), -ham (village), -field, -house, -thorp (village). So is the prefix, as with Aber- (place where streams meet), Inver- (mouth of a river) and Mont- (a hill). Specifically Welsh is Glyn (a valley, similar to 'glen') – see pp. 249–54 for more Welsh place name meanings.

Charting surnames

Even with migration, until quite recently enough people of one particular surname did tend to stay in and around the same place to make it a good indicator of surname origin. Counties with the highest occurrence of a name are a good place to search for ancestors. With uncommon names, it may even be possible to identify one village or parish as the likely origin of the name, or birthplace of a common ancestor.

Plotting surnames for a certain timeframe (e.g. one census) onto a distribution map often illuminates a geographical bias, and 'hotspots'. There are a couple of good ways to find such information, although for the 'mapping' options below it tends to be rather large-scale and not very 'granular' (i.e. not down to parish level).

RootsMap (www.rootsmap.com) is a chargeable service where a searched surname is produced as a map, downloadable or mailed by post after payment. It uses a database of over 2,000 collected British surnames and plotted these on infill maps, covering England, Scotland and Wales, based on place of birth as given in the 1881 census and considering the dates of birth of the oldest people registered in the census, which allows for the mapping of birthplaces for individuals born as far back as the late 1700s.

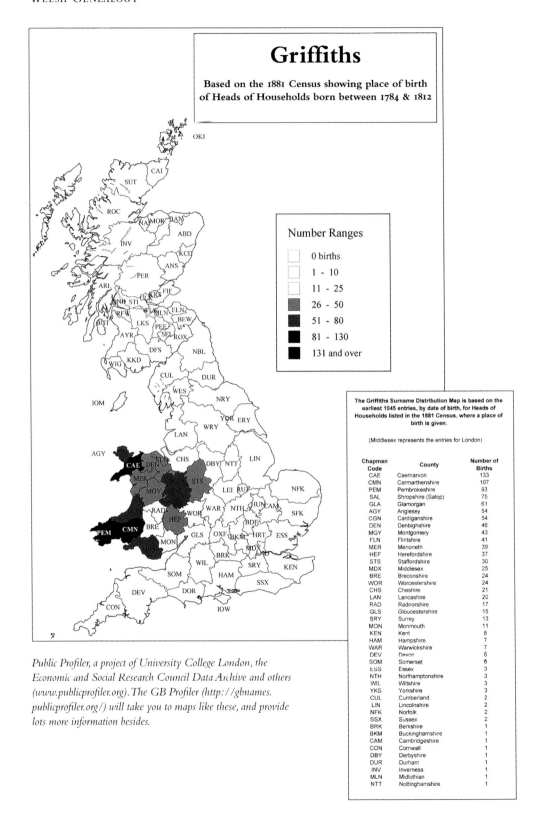

Griffiths

**Based on the 1881 Census showing place of birth
of Heads of Households born between 1784 & 1812**

Number Ranges

☐	0 births
☐	1 - 10
☐	11 - 25
▨	26 - 50
▨	51 - 80
■	81 - 130
■	131 and over

The Griffiths Surname Distribution Map is based on the earliest 1045 entries, by date of birth, for Heads of Households listed in the 1881 Census, where a place of birth is given.

(Middlesex represents the entries for London)

Chapman Code	County	Number of Births
CAE	Caernarvon	133
CMN	Carmarthenshire	107
PEM	Pembrokeshire	93
SAL	Shropshire (Salop)	75
GLA	Glamorgan	61
AGY	Anglesey	54
CGN	Cardiganshire	54
DEN	Denbighshire	46
MGY	Montgomery	43
FLN	Flintshire	41
MER	Merioneth	39
HEF	Herefordshire	37
STS	Staffordshire	30
MDX	Middlesex	25
BRE	Breconshire	24
WOR	Worcestershire	24
CHS	Cheshire	21
LAN	Lancashire	20
RAD	Radnorshire	17
GLS	Gloucestershire	15
SRY	Surrey	13
MON	Monmouth	11
KEN	Kent	8
HAM	Hampshire	7
WAR	Warwickshire	7
DEV	Devon	6
SOM	Somerset	6
ESS	Essex	3
NTH	Northamptonshire	3
WIL	Wiltshire	3
YKS	Yorkshire	3
CUL	Cumberland	2
LIN	Lincolnshire	2
NFK	Norfolk	2
SSX	Sussex	2
BRK	Berkshire	1
BKM	Buckinghamshire	1
CAM	Cambridgeshire	1
CON	Cornwall	1
DBY	Derbyshire	1
DUR	Durham	1
INV	Inverness	1
MLN	Midlothian	1
NTT	Nottinghamshire	1

*Public Profiler, a project of University College London, the
Economic and Social Research Council Data Archive and others
(www.publicprofiler.org). The GB Profiler (http://gbnames.
publicprofiler.org/) will take you to maps like these, and provide
lots more information besides.*

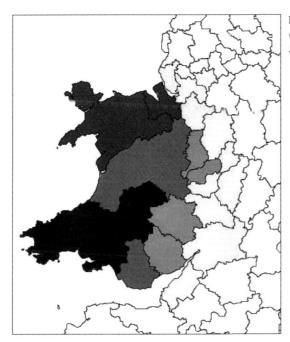

Left: *Surname map for Griffiths, 1881. Crown Copyright/database right 2008. An Ordnance Survey/EDINA-supplied service*

Below: *Surname map for Griffiths, 1998. Crown Copyright/database right 2008. An Ordnance Survey/EDINA-supplied service*

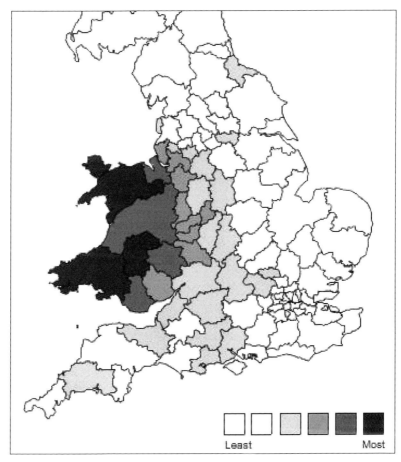

Least   Most

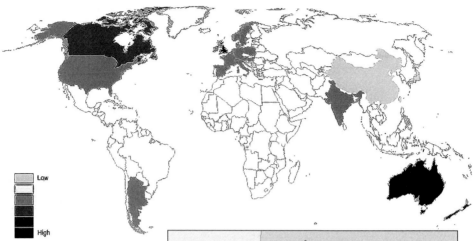

Above: *World surname map for Griffiths, 2012. Copyright 2010 Public Profiler*

Right: *Argentina surname map for Griffiths, 2012. Copyright 2010 Public Profiler*

The first map is taken from data gathered at the 1881 census, and the second from other sources in 1998. The surname entered was GRIFFITHS (without variants) – GRIFFITH shows a different distribution, more clustered in the north of Wales in 1881, so be careful.

You will notice that the 1881 maps from these sources are slightly different. The PublicProfiler one shows that the highest frequency of distribution is in Wales (unsurprisingly) with some spillover into the English counties the other side of the Marches and hardly anywhere else. The Rootsmap version shows some penetration into the rest of the UK (including Inverness-shire, which would bear investigation).

A similar exercise at the same site, using worldwide data, shows the highest density of GRIFFITH migrants as being in Australia and New Zealand – almost as great as in Britain as a whole – but note Argentina, especially Patagonia. This accords with what we know about Welsh emigration (Chapter 9).

It is possible to use these maps and the data behind them in other ways, such as in the sub-site www.censusprofiler.org, where you can derive maps of place of birth, religious affiliation and various socio-economic and demographic profiles, albeit based on very recent data.

The interesting result from this is good evidence that in the nineteenth century most people stayed fairly close to their birthplaces, and that many of the surnames in a particular place were highly represented there.

The third way is to search for the appearance of a surname as early as possible in parish records. This can be done free at www.familysearch.org by entering the surname and a date range. A search for GRIFFITHS in the whole of Wales and any 'Life Events' (birth, marriage, death, residence) from 1600 to 1700 produced twenty-seven results, mostly in Montgomeryshire and Denbighshire in the north-east, whereas the 1881 census maps show a concentration in the south-west: Cardigan, Pembroke and Carmarthen. This may reflect the different survival of church records more than anything else.

Welsh forenames of biblical origin

There is a list of 'native' Welsh forenames, with variants, at www.1911census.co.uk/content/default.aspx?r=144 but many of them became less popular as the Reformation took hold (1500s to 1600s) and were replaced by 'English' versions. What is noticeable after this time – and even more so when Nonconformism took hold – is the predominance of Old Testament first names (Abraham, Daniel, Elias, Emanuel, Gabriel, Isaac, Joseph and even Moses, not to mention David), which also became surnames by adding a terminal –s where possible. New Testament names were more popular with Anglicans and Roman Catholics – Matthew, Mark, Luke and John, of course, but also Andrew, Peter, Thomas and the rest.

Further reading

Books

T.J. Morgan and Prys Morgan, *Welsh Surnames* (University of Wales Press, 1985).

John and Sheila Rowlands, *The Surnames of Wales* (Federation of Family History Societies, 1966).

C.W. Bardsley, *A Dictionary of English and Welsh Surnames With Special American Instances* ([1901] Baltimore, Genealogical Publishing Company, 1967, 1980, 1988). Also available to download at *http://archive.org/details/adictionaryenglo1bardgoog.* ★

★ Not always reliable, but does give early referenced examples of surnames, and connects them with places where possible.

Online resources

GENUKI is the usual first port of call for researchers. The main site is www.genuki.org.uk but Welsh material starts at www.genuki.org.uk/big/wal/

The origins of Welsh Christian and surnames – http://www.amlwchhistory.co.uk/newdata/welshsurnames.htm

Welsh name meanings – www.behindthename.com/names/usage/welsh

How Common is Your Name? (Office for National Statistics). They used to release lists of first names and surnames, but now it's first names only. There are various versions available at www.ons.gov.uk/ons/rel/vsob1/baby-names--england-and-wales/index.html

Richard Webber, The Welsh Diaspora: Analysis of the Geography of Welsh Names, available at http://wales.gov.uk/firstminister/research/economic/completed/placenames/analysisgeographywelshnames.pdf?lang=en

The most common British surnames originally from Wales – www.britishsurnames.co.uk/lists/Welsh+Surnames

4

Administrative Areas and Local Records

Welsh 'County' Records

Wales is not as simple as '13 counties, 13 Local Records Centres'; although there are indeed thirteen local archives these serve twenty-two unitary authorities. For one thing, there are no counties any more in the formal sense, ever since the last-but-one reorganisation of regional government in 1974, which left eight regions. Then there was a further reorganisation in which regions disappeared. (Why do politicians think the answer to everything is to change the maps?) There are now, since 1996, twenty-two Welsh unitary authorities (UAs), with the added complication that the Welsh National Assembly has certain governmental powers. For simplicity's sake, genealogists continue to talk about 'county' archives, recognising that this is a convenient fiction.

For various historical reasons (discussed below) there is not a one-to-one mapping of UAs to archives. The functions of some of the smaller administrative units became subsumed within regions, which no longer exist. For example, the records of parts of the historic counties of Caernarfonshire and Denbighshire are now and forever bundled with Conwy Archives, but other areas of the historic County of Denbighshire (except Abergele, Colwyn Bay, Llandudno and surrounding areas) are at the Denbighshire Record Office. Others, though, retained some form of record independence: Flintshire became part of Clwyd but is once again Flintshire, a UA with its own archives, whereas Cardiganshire, Carmarthenshire and Pembrokeshire, united in Dyfed from 1974 to 1996, now each has its own archive (except that Cardiganshire is now called by its ancient name, Ceredigion). Also, some have delegated some records to a local library, or a dedicated local studies or family history centre. Some historical designations (e.g. Brecon) have had no real administrative validity for a long time, although they may have significance in that older censuses and BMD records will be tagged by county and then parish (see below). This all makes searching difficult and in some cases downright misleading.

The historic counties of Wales

Genealogists are used to seeing British census data, vital records, civil registrations and other information given in terms of county, and (in Scotland) burgh. But Britain has had no counties, nor Scotland any burghs, since 1975. It's important to know, therefore, how present-day administrative areas fit with the older system, and, more importantly, where the records are now held. In the process, we can have some fun with the history of how England and Wales were organised and managed. Americans will recognise concepts like 'County' and 'Sheriff', which they adopted from the British tradition.

The punchline is this – although counties no longer exist as administrative units of local government in the United Kingdom, the equivalent areas roughly correspond to the old historical counties, despite two major rearrangements in the 1970s and 1990s. These are sometimes known as the 'Ceremonial Counties' or 'Postal Counties'. But how did all this come about?

The monarchy

James VI, King of Scots, also became King James I of England and Wales in 1603. This amalgamation was further entrenched at the Union of Parliaments in 1707 under Queen Anne (the last Stuart monarch), when Great Britain, and later the United Kingdom of Great Britain and Ireland, were formed from two sovereign nations (Scotland is one, England and Wales the other) under one monarch. This was further complicated by union with Ireland in 1800–01, and the independence of the Irish Free State in 1922. What is left is the United Kingdom of Great Britain and Northern Ireland. At present, the sovereign is Queen Elizabeth II.

In 1707, Scotland retained control over its laws, courts, church, education, medical system, banks, censuses, civil registration and other activities. Since 1999 Scotland has had its own Parliament in Edinburgh, and largely runs its own affairs. Matters that affect the whole of the United Kingdom, or have an international dimension, like defence, international relations, economic policy, taxation and so on, are 'reserved powers', dealt with by the UK Parliament in Westminster. However, most of Scotland's administration was laid down before 1603 and much of it remained in place until well into the twentieth century.

Wales, however, was a 'principality' of England, directly governed from Westminster, but received a degree of autonomy with devolution and the opening of the National Assembly for Wales (*Cynulliad Cenedlaethol Cymru*) in 1998.

Counties and burghs/boroughs

First, some definitions: A county is the same as a shire, as in Glamorganshire (which is the county around the Vale of Glamorgan), but the two words have different origins. It's strange that Britain had counties at all, as it traditionally meant the realm of a count, as in many European countries, despite the fact that Britain has no counts. It does, however, have dukes, marquesses, earls, viscounts and barons (which aren't the same in Scotland). But an earl equals a count, and an earl's wife is a countess.

A shire was the area around a fortified castle, administered by a sheriff – an Anglo-Saxon official whose main job was to raise taxes. This defended place usually became the shire town. In Scotland, a burgh, sometimes called a 'schire' in old documents, is a town with special legal status. A city is a large town with a special charter (in England it also has to have a cathedral). Modern counties are therefore an amalgam of the medieval county (the land ruled by a noble) and the shire (an administrative unit), with the most prominent settlement becoming the county town, which may or may not be a burgh (Scotland) or borough (England). Be warned – it's about to get more complicated.

Genealogists often talk, somewhat loosely, of 'historic counties', as if they existed, unaltered, until 1974. But that's too simple. There are three types of 'county' – 'historic' or 'ceremonial' (not always the same thing), 'registration' and 'administrative' counties. A reference to 'county' in an historical document might be to any one of these three (depending on the date and the type of document). Before 1837 and the coming of civil registration (Chapter 6), 'county' meant 'historic county' (although there are some exceptions). So, the censuses of 1801–31 used historic counties. Registration districts (RD) were formed out of the Poor Law Unions, which often spread across historic county boundaries, so the later censuses use the concept of a 'registration county' – the county in which most of any particular RD sat, even if it crossed a historic county boundary. Meanwhile, the Local Government Act of 1888 created new 'administrative counties' and 'county boroughs', based upon the historic counties (not the registration counties), but not exactly the same. In 1974 it was all shuffled around again, as described below.

Finally, there are 'ceremonial counties' used for the purposes of shrievalty (the positions of High Sheriff, theoretically the queen's judicial representative in each county in England and Wales, but now purely ceremonial) and lieutenancy (Lord Lieutenants likewise, but the queen's personal representative) and based on the counties created in 1974. These were abolished in 1996, to be replaced by 'preserved counties', which largely correspond to the eight pre-1996 regions (Clwyd, Dyfed, South Glamorgan, Mid Glamorgan, West Glamorgan, Gwent, Gwynedd, Powys). The maps on p. 42 may help untangle this mess. The differences between historic counties, counties as designated under the 1972 Local Government Act, and those under the 1997 Lieutenancies Act are addressed at the website of the Association of British Counties (www.abcounties.co.uk/counties/countyconfusion).

How it all started

During Anglo-Saxon times, and when the Danes were in charge, England was run by four great jarls (earls) with taxes raised on the king's behalf by a sheriff, looking after a shire. Wales had a series of warrior-princes with their own principalities. Scotland had been a semi-unified country since the 850s, but in practice large swathes of the Highlands and Islands were still under the control of great *mormaers* (equivalent to earls or jarls) who more or less paid attention to the king in the Lowlands, but not much and not always. Ireland was still tribal, under a complex system of kings and a high king, whose position was largely ceremonial and federal – from the time of Brian Boru's rule (about AD 1000) up to the Norman takeover in 1171, the high king was anybody who could take the Hill of Tara and hold it until pushed off. American readers will recognise the echo of this situation in the children's game King of the Hill.

The Normans never conquered Scotland, as they did England in 1066, and Ireland from 1169 onwards, but there was considerable Norman influence over Scottish Lowland society, as the rulers of both countries intermarried and the nobles became exposed to each other's ways. The characteristic attribute of the Anglo-Norman structure was the feudal system of landholding. The political and military needs of medieval society were such that the monarch had to control the whole country – difficult at a distance – and also had to be sure of armed men when necessary. This became a social and economic system supported by law.

The main relationship in the feudal system was that between superior (lord) and vassal (tenant). The king ultimately owned all land but granted out parts of it 'in knight fief' – meaning that armed and mounted fighting men could be provided when needed, paid for out of the proceeds of the land. A fief could also be an office of the Crown, a right to hunt or fish, collect wood and so on. In turn, such a superior could give over part of his land or fief to a vassal, who then owed a duty of homage and fealty plus certain services. These could be military (the 'Knight's Fee', land in exchange for a stated amount of men and armed service), ceremonial (e.g. being a standard bearer), practical (such as supplying bread, flour, crops etc.) or monetary. In exchange, the superior guaranteed protection to the vassal. The provision of land was confirmed by a charter in writing. These charters are a great source for early genealogy, as they mention landholders and give the names of witnesses. Landholding by a vassal from a superior was a life interest only and not necessarily passed down. The superior needed to know that the land was held by loyal and capable men, and if the duty was military the Crown had the right to repossess the land if the heir in possession was a child or a female. However, an heir could negotiate to avoid this aspect of the tenure by redeeming the conditions by, say, paying money or goods instead. Nevertheless, the Crown retained an interest in the land. Later, when the development of longbow and artillery rather took away the point of mounted knights in armour, new forms of tenure emerged, particularly fee-based (payment of money or goods).

As well as being the ultimate landholder, the king was also the fount of justice. Just as the land was parcelled out, so was local administration and the justiciary courts, so the feudal system also became a decentralised government.

Shires and sheriffs

Whereas a county is properly the land controlled by a count (or earl), a shire is the land controlled from a castle. Such an area needs administering and, building on another Anglo-Saxon model, King David I also established the office of sheriff (originally shire-reeve, from the Old English *scīrgerefa*) in Scotland. The function of the sheriff was to administer the local area, to represent royal judicial power, and to carry out other military and financial functions, with civil and criminal jurisdictions. In time, the office became hereditary. Scotland still has sheriffs (essentially local judges) and it is easy to see how this evolved into the American concept of the local lawman for a county. The position of Highe Sheriff (the monarch's judicial representative) and Lord Lieutenant (personal representative) still exist, associated with the historic counties, but are purely ceremonial. Confusingly, the Latin for a county or sherrifdom is *vicecomitatis*, not a reference to a viscount.

The modern age

As the power and responsibilities of large landowners and nobles fell away, they were replaced with civil administration. By the twentieth century, most of the UK's local government had become organised in two broad tiers, each with its own responsibilities – the county councils and, below them, an admixture of city, burgh or borough, metropolitan district, urban district and rural district councils. However, some of the larger cities and towns had a single layer of local government and were designated a 'county borough' or a 'county of itself', or, in Scotland, a 'county of a city'. Scotland also had royal burghs as administrative units until 1975.

Most county council boundaries were the same as those of the geographical counties, but those with larger land areas or populations were subdivided – in England, Yorkshire had three 'ridings' (meaning a 'thirding'), North, East and West; there was East and West Sussex; and Lincolnshire and Suffolk were similarly divided. London was also different, as it consisted of two cities (the City of London, the square mile around the Bank of England and the financial district, and the City of Westminster, where Parliament is) plus a number of boroughs, all of which were properly in counties. For example, Richmond was in Surrey, Islington in Middlesex and Ilford in Essex. In 1899 the County of London was forged from the city plus parts of the surrounding counties of Middlesex, Kent and Surrey, and their boroughs.

In 1965 the long-used but informal concept of Greater London became official, with the formation of the Greater London Council, taking in London, Westminster and the area covered by the former counties of London and Middlesex, together with parts of Essex, Kent, Surrey and Hertfordshire, including three former county boroughs (Croydon, West Ham and East Ham). The tier below this, which had consisted of eighty-two borough, metropolitan and urban district councils, was reorganised into thirty-two London boroughs and the City of London.

All change in the 1970s

There was a similar situation in Northern Ireland, but on 1 October 1973 the seventy-three councils (the six counties of Antrim, Armagh, County Down, Fermanagh, County Londonderry or Derry and Tyrone, two single-tier county boroughs, plus ten boroughs, twenty-four urban districts and thirty-one rural districts), became twenty-six single-tier district councils. For administrative purposes at least, the six historic counties were gone. Be aware that everything to do with Northern Ireland is loaded with political meaning, including what it gets called. Unionists and Loyalists in the North itself often refer to it by the inaccurate term 'Ulster' or 'The Province', both a reference to the centuries-old Four Provinces, of which Ulster was one, but which included the six counties plus another three now in the Republic. Nationalists, Republicans and even some official bodies in the Republic avoid using 'Northern Ireland' on the grounds that this implies acceptance of the political divide of 1921, and instead call it 'the

Six Counties' or 'the Occupied Six Counties', and refer to the Republic as 'the Twenty-Six Counties', or else refer to it as 'the North of Ireland' or 'the North', ignoring the fact that the most northerly part of Ireland, in County Donegal, is in the Republic.

Six months later, on 1 April 1974, England and Wales were reorganised. Apart from Greater London, the two-tier system was extended with the abolition of county boroughs; the county councils were reduced from fifty-eight to fifty-three (six of which, around the larger cities, became metropolitan county councils); and the 1,250 local councils were replaced by 369 district councils. Several historic counties disappeared, such as Rutland, and most had major boundary changes, to the fury of local inhabitants. One month later, it was Scotland's turn. Over 400 councils, including thirty-four historic counties, were replaced by nine regions, fifty-three district councils and three single-tier authorities covering some of the islands. Also lost were the royal burghs, many of which had stretched back 600 years or more.

On 31 March 1986 the government, jealous and suspicious of the power, popularity and political colour of the Greater London Council and the six metropolitan county councils, abolished these. The London boroughs and the metropolitan district councils gained a status similar to the pre-1974 county boroughs, but the counties as administrative units were gone.

All change again in the 1990s

Frankly, none of this worked. People had a long-standing loyalty to their historic areas, which any family historian will recognise as pride of place, and resented being told that their county no longer existed, or that suddenly they lived in a different county because of a boundary change. In Scotland, almost everyone hated the regions – Strathclyde was too big, nobody felt any warmth towards a region called 'Central' and there was a yearning for the old names. Only Fife was relatively unscathed. Properly known as the Kingdom of Fife (although it has not had a king since Pictish times) it has remained more or less the same size and shape throughout recorded history. It may be the longest-standing recognisable geopolitical entity in Europe, apart from some islands.

There have been subsequent changes to all of Wales and Scotland and most of England, some of which simply reversed the reorganisations of 1974–75. In Wales the eight counties and thirty-seven district councils were abolished in 1996, to be replaced by twenty-two new unitary authorities called either counties or county boroughs. At the same time in Scotland the nine unpopular regions, the three island authorities and the fifty-three second-tier districts, were replaced by thirty-two unitary authorities, known by the unlovely term 'council areas'.

Counties and burghs/boroughs have gone forever. In England there were various changes, with some areas being unaffected but others moving over in a phased manner, between 1995 and 1998. Four of the 1974 county councils were abolished and the rest turned into a number of unitary authorities or given the two-tier county and district structure. This move reinvented a number of the old county and county borough names, but the boundaries are different in almost all cases. Frankly, it's a mess. More recently, the reality of Greater London was again recognised and it now has a unified government under a mayor.

Genealogist's Guide

That was all a bit complicated. Some counties have disappeared forever, particularly in Scotland and in South Wales; the old Glamorgan is now ten or so units. The real question is, to find information on someone who lived in 1881 in, say, Montgomeryshire (Wales) or Huntingdonshire (England) or Roxburghshire (Scotland) or County Fermanagh (Northern Ireland), where would you now look? These tables and maps are intended to help track down the likely current repositories of information. But be careful – check the neighbouring places too! To tie down a particular place, try the parish locator covering the whole of the UK (but not the Republic of Ireland) at GENUKI (www.genuki.org.uk/big/churchdb). For a brief description of the administrative changes in the United Kingdom see 'Local Government Changes in the United Kingdom' (www.genuki.org.uk/big/Regions/UKchanges.html).

Some of the old abbreviations for counties may cause confusion. Oxford is Oxon, from the Latin name Oxonia; Shropshire is Salop, from the earlier name Saloppsberrie; Hampshire is still known as Hants, from the old name Hantshaving, and the same goes for Northants (Northamptonshire). In Scotland, Forfarshire is the old name for Angus (which is an older name still), and there is considerable confusion between Nairnshire, Elginshire, Morayshire plus parts of Inverness-shire. Buchan and others have just disappeared, and there are at least four places (including a county) called Kincardine. You will need to get a map or a parish list for the historic period of interest, and consult www.genuki.org.uk but also see the list below. The first table shows the historic counties and their administrative subdivisions before the first round of changes and lists the successor counties for each, that is, the post-change counties, which contain some or all of the original county area. The second table shows the counties after the first round of changes and lists their successor unitary authorities. In all cases only the top-tier authority is shown – either the top tier in a two-tier arrangement or a single-tier authority (shown italicised).

The following abbreviations are used in these tables:

(CB) = County Borough
(UA) = Unitary Authority

Single-tier local authorities are shown italicised. Additional information is provided where appropriate and available – for example, the common abbreviation for the area and the Chapman County Code (CCC), a unique three-letter code for counties and regions.

Wales – Counties and Unitary Authorities			Successor Unitary Authorities
pre-1974 (13)	CCC	1974–96 (8)	post-1996 (22)
Anglesey	AGY	Gwynedd	Anglesey
Brecon★	BRE	Powys, Gwent, Mid Glamorgan	Powys
Caernarvonshire	CAE	Gwynedd	Aberconwy and Colwyn
			Gwynedd
			Conwy
Cardiganshire	CGN	Dyfed	Ceredigion
Carmarthenshire	CMN	Dyfed	Carmarthenshire
Denbighshire	DEN	Clwyd, Gwynedd	Denbighshire
(parts of Denbigh and Flint became)			Wrexham
Flintshire	FLN	Clwyd	Flintshire

★Also known as Brecknockshire

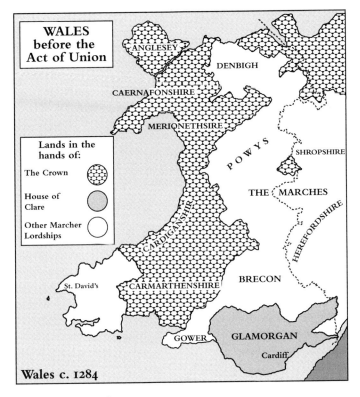

Wales before the Act of Union.

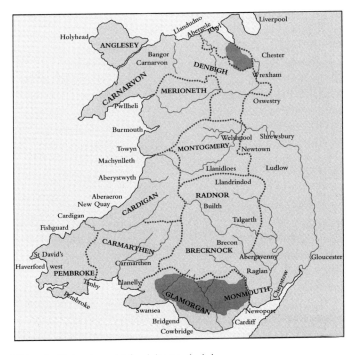

Wales after Tudor times: chief coal districts shaded.

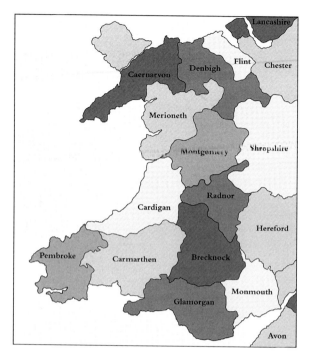

Counties of Wales (with English border counties), pre-1974.

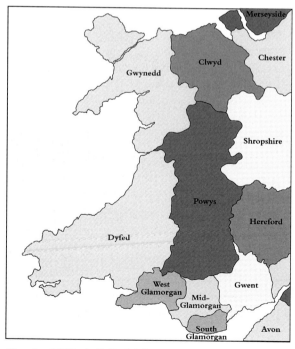

Counties of Wales (with English border counties), 1974–96.

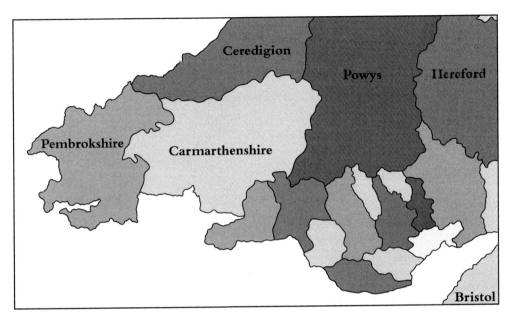

Ceremonial 'Counties' and larger Unitary Authorities of Wales (with Hereford and Bristol border counties), post-1998.

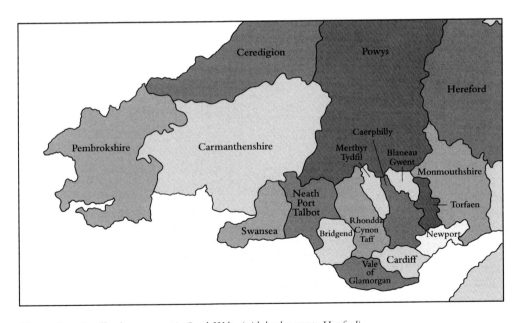

The smaller units of local government in South Wales (with border county Hereford).

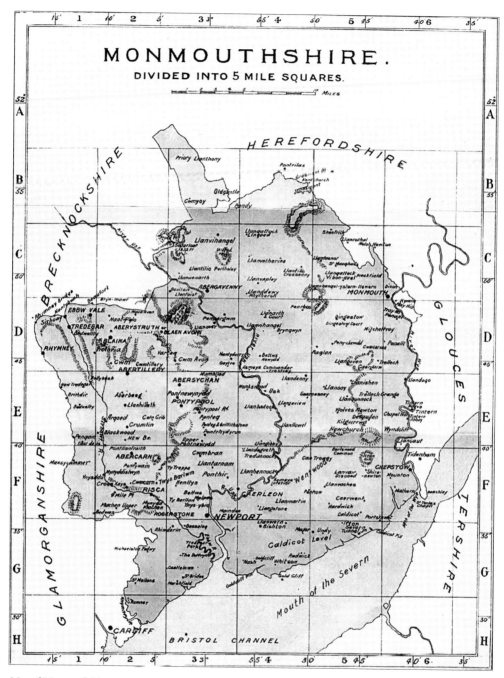

Map of Monmouthshire c. 1907.

Glamorgan *Cardiff (CB)* *Merthyr Tydfil (CB)* *Swansea (CB)*	GLA	Mid Glamorgan	Merthyr Tydfil
			Bridgend
			Rhondda Cynon Taff
		South Glamorgan	Vale of Glamorgan
			Cardiff
		West Glamorgan	Swansea
			Neath Port Talbot
Merionethshire	MER	Gwynedd, Clwyd	Gwynedd
Monmouthshire			
Newport (CB)	MON	Gwent, Mid Glamorgan, South Glamorgan	Monmouthshire
			Caerphilly
			Blacnau Gwent
			Newport
			Torfaen
Montgomeryshire	MGY	Powys	Powys
Pembrokeshire	PEM	Dyfed	Pembrokeshire
Radnor	RAD	Powys	Powys

Administration 1974–96	CCC	Successor Unitary Authorities
Clwyd *Denbighshire (UA)* *Flintshire (UA)* *Powys (UA)* *Wrexham (UA)*	CWD	*Conwy (UA)* *Denbighshire (UA)* *Flintshire (UA)* *Powys (UA)* *Wrexham (UA)*
Dyfed	DFD	*Cardiganshire (UA)* *Carmarthenshire (UA)* *Pembrokeshire (UA)*
Gwent	GNT	*Blaenau Gwent (UA)* *Caerphilly (UA)* *Monmouthshire (UA)* *Newport (UA)* *Torfaen (UA)*
Gwynedd *Anglesey (UA)* *Gwynedd (UA)*	GWN	*Aberconwy and Colwyn (UA)* *Anglesey (UA)* *Gwynedd (UA)*

Mid Glamorgan	MGM	*Bridgend (UA)*
		Caerphilly (UA)
		Cardiff (UA)
		Merthyr Tydfil (UA)
		Rhondda Cynon Taff (UA)
		Vale of Glamorgan (UA)
Powys	POW	*Powys (UA)*
South Glamorgan	SGM	*Cardiff (UA)*
		Vale of Glamorgan (UA)
West Glamorgan	WGM	*Neath and Port Talbot (UA)*
		Swansea (UA)

Example – administrative changes to Bedwellty

Bedwellty is in Monmouthshire. The original parish included most of the upper Ebbw and Sirhowy valleys and covered a large area. As the many coal-mining communities grew in the nineteenth century, these became large enough to justify separate local government units, so in 1874 local boards of health and local government districts were formed – Ebbw Vale, Rhymney and Tredegar – and what was left became a local government district in 1891, although Bedwellty remained the overall civil parish. The local boards became urban districts in 1894, and Bedwellty, Ebbw Vale, Rhymney and Tredegar urban districts each became its own civil parish, with Bedwellty including Argoed, Bargoed, Blackwood, New Tredegar, Pengam and Rock. In 1926, the neighbouring urban districts of Bedwellty and Mynyddislwyn came together as West Monmouthshire Omnibus Board (to control the bus services), but the boundaries between them were changed in 1935. Urban districts were abolished in 1974 – Aberbargoed, Cwmsyfiog, New Tredegar and Phillipstown joined the Rhymney Valley district of Mid Glamorgan, while everything else became part of the Islwyn borough of Gwent. That lasted a mere twenty-two years until the reorganisation of 1996 put the former urban district of Bedwellty into the county borough of Caerphilly (which includes Argoed, Bargoed, Blackwood, Cefn Forest, New Tredegar, and part of Darran Valley).

However, that is all different from the parliamentary constituency of Bedwellty. Created in 1918, it was replaced in 1983 by the constituency of Islwyn in the County of Gwent.

Then there is the registration district (RD) of Bedwellty, for purposes such as census (Chapter 5) and BMD registration (Chapter 6). This was created in 1861 out of Abergavenny RD, with the sub-districts of Abertillery, Aberystruth, Ebbw Vale, Rhymney Valley, Rock Bedwelty and Tredegar. In 1939 it gained that part of the Parish of Bedwellty which had been part of the Parish of Mynyddislwyn in Caerleon RD until 1935.

Where are the parish registers and other documents now kept? 'Monmouthshire County Record Office' would be the obvious answer, but there is no such beast – Gwent Archives (co-managed by the local authorities of Blaenau Gwent, Caerphilly, Monmouthshire, Newport and Torfaen) have the records, and the register office is at Bedwellty House in Tredegar, which belongs to the RD of Blaenau Gwent.

To make sense of this, visit www.genuki.org.uk/big/wal/MON/Bedwellty/index.html and see the list of county record offices on pp. 50–52.

Local Resources

It may seem strange to start a discussion of local resources with two national archives, but it's often forgotten that the National Library of Wales has a lot of genealogy-related collections, and that TNA, though in London, is the British national archive, and has records from Wales (as well as Scotland and Ireland), despite whatever is held locally. A good example is military records from the British armed services, which are held there regardless of where the regiment is based.

The National Archives (TNA)	Tel: (020) 8876 3444
Kew, Richmond, Surrey	Web: www.nationalarchives.gov.uk
TW9 4DU	Email: enquiry@nationalarchives.gov.uk

This is one of the world's largest and best largest archival collections (100 miles of shelving, they say) and has records right back to the time of the Norman Conquest in 1066, plus government and court papers (including over 1 million 'PCC' wills proved at the Prerogative Court of Canterbury between 1384 and 1858), taxation records (death duties, hearth taxes, land taxes, lay subsidies), criminal and prison records, military records and Nonconformist BMDs.

Not all material is online, but see the online catalogue (www.nationalarchives.gov.uk/catalogue/default.asp), which is free to search, and links to the catalogues of many other archives.

Research guides – www.nationalarchives.gov.uk/catalogue/researchguidesindex.asp.

A reader's ticket is required if consulting original documents.

There is a paid search service if you are unable to visit.

National Library of Wales	Tel: (0) 1970 632800
Aberystwyth	Fax: (0) 1970 615709
Ceredigion	Web: www.llgc.org.uk
Wales	Email: enquiry@llgc.org.uk
SY23 3BU	

This is the best place to start when researching Welsh genealogy as it holds a wide collection of original documents (pre-1858 Welsh wills, many Welsh parish registers, microfilm/microfiche copies of records held elsewhere, such as GRO BMD indexes post-1837, Nonconformist records etc.).

There are also church records (baptism, marriages and burials, bishops' transcripts, marriage bonds and diocesan records), wills and probate records, maps, images (pictures, photographs, sound and movies), legal records (great sessions, quarter sessions, manorial records), Poor Law and parochial records, education registers, estate and personal papers, pedigree books and much more besides.

A reader's ticket is required for the reading rooms and online access to Ancestry and so on.

There is no paid research service provided.

Online Catalogue of Archival Databases is www.llgc.org.uk/index.php?id=searcharchivaldatabases.

National Library of Wales Digital Mirror (images of some archived documents) – www.llgc.org.uk/index.php?id=127.

Archives Network Wales (*Archifau Cymru*) – www.archivesnetworkwales.info/
Online catalogue of more than 7,000 collections of historical records held at twenty-one archives in Wales, under a single search. Get individual archive contact details at Archon – www.nationalarchives.gov.uk/archon/

Access to Archives (A2A) – www.nationalarchives.gov.uk/a2a

TNA coordinates an online catalogue of archive collections held in record offices and other repositories – some 400 holding 10 million entries, with keyword searches including surnames and places. The individual places in Wales covered in A2A, Archives Network Wales and the Archon (contacts) directory include the following:

Aberdare Library
Aberystwyth University
Andrew Logan Museum of Sculpture
Anglesey Antiquarian Society and Field Club
Archifau Ynys Mon / Anglesey Archives
Bangor University, Archives and Special Collections
Brecknock Museum & Art Gallery
Brecon Branch Library, Local Studies Department
Bridgend Reference and Information Centre and Local Studies Library
Cadw, Welsh Historic Monuments
Cardiff Central Library
Cardiff Roman Catholic Archdiocesan Archives
Cardiff University
Cardiff University: Sir David Owen Population Centre
Carmarthenshire Archive Service
Carmarthenshire County Museum
The Castle and Regimental Museum, Monmouth
The Cathedral School, Llandaff
Central Register of Air Photography for Wales
Centre for Performance Research
Ceredigion Archives
Chapel of Art
Chepstow Museum
Coleg Harlech
Conwy Archive Service
Cyfarthfa Castle Art Gallery and Museum
Denbighshire Record Office
Estyn (Inspectorate for Education and Training in Wales)
Flintshire Record Office
Glamorgan Archives (previously Glamorgan Record Office)
Gwent Archives
Gwent Wildlife Trust
Gwynedd Archives, Caernarfon Record Office
Gwynedd Archives, Meirionnydd Record Office
Haverfordwest Library
Jerome Gatchouse Collection
Llandudno Museum
Llanelli Public Library
Lloyd George Museum
Menevia Roman Catholic Diocesan Archives
Merthyr Tydfil Libraries
National Library of Wales: Department of Collection Services
National Monuments Record of Wales

National Museum Cardiff (formerly St Fagans National History Museum)
National Museum of Wales
National Screen and Sound Archive of Wales
Neath Antiquarian Society
Neath Reference Library
Nelson Museum and Local History Centre
Newport Central Library
Newport Museum and Art Gallery
Oriel Ynys Mon
Pembrokeshire Museum Service
Pembrokeshire Record Office
Pontypridd Library
Port Talbot Library
Powys County Archives Office
Queens Dragoon Guards Regimental Museum
Rhayader and District Museum
Robert Owen Memorial Museum
Royal Institution of South Wales
Royal Mint
Royal Welch Fusiliers Regimental Museum
Royal Welsh Regiment Museum
South Wales Borderers Museum
St Deiniol's Library
St Michael's College
Swansea Central Library Local Studies Department
Swansea Metropolitan University
Swansea Museum
Swansea University Archives
Tata Steel UK Ltd
Tenby Museum and Art Gallery
Treorchy Library
University of Wales, Aberystwyth Ceramic Collection and Archive
University of Wales, Lampeter Archives
Welsh Baptist Union Library
Welsh Industrial and Maritime Museum
West Glamorgan Archive Service
West Wales Chamber of Commerce
Wrexham Archives and Local Studies Service

County Archives Research Network readers' ticket scheme (CARN)

Some local authority record offices will supply a single reader's ticket for admission to any archive in the scheme, which is most of them. Apply in person with two proofs of identity bearing your name, permanent address and signature, plus two passport-size photographs.

Local Archives

These are the places to get parish registers, chapel records, newspapers, local directories and more. Visit their websites for holdings, access hours and so on. Addresses and contact details are correct as of 2012. Website links also change, so if any one doesn't work, use the top-level address (e.g. www.anglesey.gov.uk) and search for 'Archives'. In each case, check if there is also an associated or nearby local studies centre. Details may change from time to time.

Anglesey County Archives Service

Anglesey Archives, Industrial Estate Road, Bryn Cefni Industrial Estate, Llangefni, Anglesey LL77 7JA

Tel: +44 (0)1248 751930
Email: archives@anglesey.gov.uk
Web: www.anglesey.gov.uk/leisure/records-and-archives/

Caernarfon Record Office

Gwynedd County Council covers the former counties of Caernarfonshire and Merionethshire. See Meirionnydd Record Office (below) for Merionethshire archives
Victoria Dock, Caernarfon
Address for postal communication: Caernarfon Record Office, Swyddfa'r Cyngor, Caernarfon, Gwynedd, LL55 1SH

Tel: +44 (0)1286 679095
Email: archives.caernarfon@gwynedd.gov.uk
Web: www.gwynedd.gov.uk/gwy_doc.asp?cat=3693&doc=12971&Language=1

Carmarthenshire Archives Service

Parc Myrddin, Richmond Terrace, Carmarthen, Carmarthenshire, SA31 1HQ

Tel: +44 (0)1267 228232
Email: archives@carmarthenshire.gov.uk
Web: www.carmarthenshire.gov.uk/English/education/archives/Pages/Home.aspx

Ceredigion Archives

Tel: +44 (0)1970 633697
Email: archives@ceredigion.gov.uk
Web: http://archifdy-ceredigion.org.uk/

Conwy Archives

Covers parts of the historic counties of Caernarfonshire and Denbighshire. Records for Abergele, Colwyn Bay, Llandudno and surrounding areas are at the Conwy Archives. Records for other areas of the historic County of Denbighshire are at the Denbighshire Record Office (see below)
The Old Board School, Lloyd Street, Llandudno, Conway, LL30 2YG

Tel: +44 (0)1492 577550
Email: archifau.archives@conwy.gov.uk
Web: www.conwy.gov.uk/section.asp?cat=772

Denbighshire Record Office

Records for Abergele, Colwyn Bay, Llandudno and surrounding areas are at the Conwy Archives
Ruthin Gaol, 46 Clwyd Street, Ruthin, Denbighshire, LL15 1HP

Tel: +44 (0)1824 708250
Email: archives@denbighshire.gov.uk
Web: www.denbighshire.gov.uk/en-gb/DNAP-6ZQKTQ

Flintshire Record Office

The Old Rectory, Rectory Lane, Hawarden, Flintshire, CH5 3NR

Tel: +44 (0)1244 532364
Email: archives@flintshire.gov.uk
Web: www.flintshire.gov.uk and search for 'Archives'

Glamorgan Archives

This is managed jointly by the local authorities of Bridgend, Cardiff, Caerphilly, Merthyr Tydfil, Rhondda Cynon Taff and the Vale of Glamorgan. Records for Mid Glamorgan and South Glamorgan (Cardiff, Bridgend, Caerphilly, Merthyr Tydfil, Rhondra, the Vale of Glamorgan) are at the Glamorgan Archives – see below for contact details.

Records for West Glamorgan (Swansea, Neath, Port Talbot) are at the West Glamorgan Archive Service – see below for contact details

Glamorgan Archives

Clos Parc Morgannwg, Leckwith, Cardiff, CF11 8AW
  Tel: +44 (0)29 2087 2200
  Email: glamro@cardiff.gov.uk
  Web: www.glamro.gov.uk/

West Glamorgan Archive Service

City and County of Swansea and the County Borough of Neath Port Talbot
Civic Centre, Oystermouth Road, Swansea, SA1 3SN
  Tel: +44 (0)1792 636589
  Email: westglam.archives@swansea.gov.uk
  Web: www.swansea.gov.uk/westglamorganarchives/

Gwent Archives

Managed by the local authorities of Blaenau Gwent, Caerphilly, Monmouthshire, Newport and Torfaen
Steelworks Road, Ebbw Vale, Blaenau Gwent, NP23 6DN
  Tel: +44 (0)1495 353363
  Email: enquiries@gwentarchives.gov.uk
  Web: www.gwentarchives.gov.uk/

Meironnydd Record Office

Gwynedd County Council, incorporating the former counties of Merionethshire and Caernarfonshire, which manages both the Meirionnydd Record Office, which holds the Merionethshire archives, and the Caernarfon Record Office, see above

Meirionnydd Archives, Ffordd y Bala (Bala Road), Dolgellau, Gwynedd, LL40 2YF
  Tel: +44 (0)1341 424682
  Email: archives.dolgellau@gwynedd.gov.uk
  Web: www.gwynedd.gov.uk/gwy_doc.asp?cat=3693&doc=12971&Language=1
            &p=1&c=1 *scroll down*

Pembrokeshire Record Office

The Castle, Haverfordwest, SA61 2EF
  Tel: +44 (0)1437 763707
  Email: record.office@pembrokeshire.gov.uk
  Web: www.pembrokeshire.gov.uk/content.asp?nav=&id=8057&Positioning_Article_
            ID=&Language=&d1=0

Powys County Archives Office
Official repository for the records of the current County of Powys from 1974 and the three former counties of Breconshire, Montgomeryshire and Radnorshire
County Hall, Llandrindod Wells, Powys, LD1 5LG

    Tel: +44 (0)1597 826088
    Email: archives@powys.gov.uk
    Web: www.powys.gov.uk/index.php?id=647&L=0&

Radnorshire
See Powys (above).

Family History Societies
Family history societies (FFHs) have links to many other local resources.

Federation of Family History Societies (FFHS) – http://ffhs.org.uk/. An educational charity that represents family history societies and other genealogical organisations worldwide. Online shop. Most Welsh FHSs are members.

Association of Family History Societies of Wales – www.fhswales.info. Coordinating body for Welsh family history societies. Website has a useful translation of 1911 census schedules in Welsh.

Gwynedd Family History Society (also covers Anglesey, Caernarfonshire and Merionethshire)
    Contact: J. Bryan Jones, 7 Victoria Rd, Old Colwyn, Colwyn Bay, LL29 9SN
    Email: bryan.jones8@btinternet.com
    Web: www.gwyneddfhs.org

Powys Family History Society (covers Breconshire, Montgomeryshire and Radnorshire)
    Contact: Mrs Angela Jones, Briar Patch, The Ridgeway, Penally, Tenby. Pembrokeshire, SA70 7RJ
    Email: angieprobertjones@hotmail.com
    Web: www.rootsweb.ancestry.com/~wlspfhs

Ystradgynlais Family History Society (covers Breconshire)
    Contact: Ystradgynlais Family History Society, c/o Ystradgynlais Library, Temperance Lane, Ystradgynlais
    Email: caryljones@talktalk.net
    Web: www.ystradgynlaisfhs.co.uk

Cardiganshire Family History Society
    Contact: Menna Evans, Hon. Sec. Cardiganshire FHS, c/o Adran Casgliadau, National Library of Wales, Aberystwyth, Ceredigion, SY23 3BU
    Email: ymholiadau@cgnfhs.org.uk
    Web: www.cgnfhs.org.uk

Dyfed Family History Society (covers Cardiganshire, Carmarthenshire and Pembrokeshire)
    Contact: Joan Beckingsale, Llethr Bach, Ffostrasol, Llandysul, Ceredigion, SA44 5JT
    Email: membership@dyfedfhs.org.uk
    Web: www.dyfedfhs.org.uk

Clwyd Family History Society (covers Denbighshire and Flintshire)

Contact: Clwyd Family History Society Resource Centre, Community Enterprise Centre,
           Well Street, Cefn Mawr, Wrexham, LL14 3AL
Tel: Phone: 01978 814924 (open Tue, Thu, Sat)
Email: membership@clwydfhs.org.uk
Web: www.clwydfhs.org.uk

Glamorgan Family History Society

Contact: Mrs R. Williams, 93 Pwllygath Street, Bridgend CF36 6ET
Email: secretary@glamfhs.org
Web: www.glamfhs.org

Gwent Family History Society (covers Monmouthshire)

Contact: Nicola Thomas, 11 Rosser Street, Waunfelin, Pontypool, Gwent NP4 6EA
Email: secretary@gwentfhs.info
Web: www.gwentfhs.info

Montgomeryshire Genealogical Society

Contact: Mrs M. Woosnam, 24 Dysart Terrace, Canal Road, Newtown, Powys SY16 2JL
Web: home.freeuk.net/montgensoc

Church of the Latter-day Saints (LDS) Family History Centers (FHCs) in Wales

In all cases, check opening hours, make an appointment before visiting, and remember that, unlike family history societies and local libraries, they have no staff or volunteers. Individual church members may be willing to help you, but that is not why they are there.

Each FHC can get anything that exists in the main library at Salt Lake City, Utah, USA, given time. More and more information is online rather than as microfilm, which may need to be posted to the FHC. However, some resources are available at most family history centres in Wales including:

- Computer access to the 1881 Census Index.
- Computer access to the British Isles Vital Records Index.
- Computer access to the International Genealogical Index (IGI).
- Microfiche copies of the General Register Office master indexes of births, marriages and deaths in England and Wales since 1837.
- Microfiche copies of the National Probate indexes from 1858 to 1957.
- Microfiche copy of the complete Family History Library catalogue.
- Microfilm copies of the death duty registers from 1796 to 1857.
- Microfilm copies of the source documents (e.g. parish registers etc.) on which the IGI is based – the relevant microfilm is ordered from Utah for viewing at the local FHC for a small fee.
- Microfilm/fiche copies of all census records from 1841 to 1901 – following an online catalogue search for its reference number, the relevant microfilm reel can be ordered and subsequently viewed at the local FHC for a small fee.

Cardiff Wales Family History Center

Heol-Y-Deri, Riwbina, Cardiff, CF14 6UH
  Tel: +44 (0)292-062 5342

Cwmbran Wales Family History Center
The Highway, Croesceilog, Cwmbran, NP44 2NH
Tel: +44 (0)163-348 3856

Gaerwen Wales Family History Center
Holyhead Road, Gaerwen, LL60 0RW
Tel: +44 (0)124-842 1894

Merthyr Tydfil Wales Family History Center
Nantygwenith Street, Merthyr Tydfil, CF48 1BS
Tel: +44 (0)168-572 2455

Newcastle Emlyn Wales Family History Center
Cardigan Road, Newcastle Emlyn, SA38 9RD
Tel: +44 (0)123-971 1472

Rhyl Wales Family History Center
171 Vale Road, Rhyl, LL18 2PH
Tel: +44 (0)174-533 1172

Swansea Wales Family History Center
Cockett Road, Swansea, SA2 0FD
Tel: +44 (0)179-258 5792

Wrexham Wales Family History Center
Herbert Jennings Avenue, Wrexham, LL12 7YD
Tel: +44 (0)1978-358997

5

The Welsh Censuses of 1841 to 1911

The best place to start with any genealogical research is by knowing where people were at a particular time, and their relationships. From there it is possible to work backwards to births and marriages, forward to marriages and deaths, and laterally to other information such as occupations and land ownership.

For any new family history research project, start if possible with the oldest living family members. If you can get a name, age, address and other details (spouse, children, place of birth etc.) for someone alive in 1911, then the censuses are a great starting point.

Do not forget the two most basic rules of family history:

1. ALWAYS talk to the oldest living relatives.
2. NEVER (necessarily) believe anything they tell you.

That said, if you can track down grandparents, older uncles and aunts and so on, and use their reminiscences (or documents) to build a picture of at least one nuclear family group, then you are well on your way.

A census return will (usually) give names of everyone living at a particular address on the census night (see below), their occupations, ages, relationships and places of birth. The ages will be approximate – a year either side – but will be a clue as to year of birth, so you can find birth or baptism records. The date of a marriage can be inferred from the age of the oldest child, although this isn't always reliable – there may be older children living away from home, or elder children may be from a previous marriage of one of the spouses, for example – but with luck and perseverance you might get to a marriage record, which will provide the maiden name of the wife and the addresses of the happy couple at the time the marriage was registered or solemnised. Someone who disappears between two censuses may have died (or emigrated, Chapter 9), but this clue may lead you to a death record, which might give you the cause of death as well as age and address at the time of death.

The reasons for the 'might', 'may' and 'usually' in the paragraph above is, as we will see, due to the fact that:

- not all records are accurate;
- not all records are transcribed or indexed accurately;
- not all censuses contain all the information;
- earlier censuses will lead you back to church BMD records pre-1837, which are often lacking in detail, if they exist at all.

Statutory (post-1837) records are dealt with in Chapter 6 and parish (pre-1837) records in Chapter 7, but for now just accept that cross-referencing from the starting point of census details is a good way to begin.

Censuses in Welsh, 1841–1901

Householder's Schedules were printed with instructions and column headings in both Welsh and English for each of the censuses from 1841–1901, for issue to Welsh-speaking households, who would complete them in Welsh. The enumerator copied the details into his book, but in English, which are the images we see on websites. If the enumerator was not Welsh-speaking, this could lead to inaccurate entries, especially with regard to place names.

The 1911 Census in Welsh

The 1911 census was the first in which there were no Enumerators' Books; these were replaced by Enumerators' Summaries of Households (in English). The original Householder's Schedules in Welsh can be viewed, but this may present a problem. See the Association of Family History Societies of Wales for more details of transcriptions available (www.fhswales.org.uk/censuses/Schedules.htm).

Case study – Frederick Ebenezer Griffiths

The background to the 1841–1911 censuses will be covered later. For now, if we look at an example of a census return, we can see how much information can be gleaned. The only information we have to go on is that Frederick Ebenezer Griffiths was from Wales, and that his middle name was after his grandfather. There is no 1911 census record for Frederick (we'll see why later) so we are going to track an individual called Ebenezer Griffiths, and some of his children and grandchildren, back in time from 1911.

Census 1911

First we should look at the structure of the census form for 1911. (There is a full-page version of the blank form for each of the censuses in Chapter 16, which can be copied and used for recording information.) It is worth looking at the exact descriptions of information to be collected in each of the columns, but, in abbreviated form, they are:

Number of Schedule: The box at the top right gives the order in which the census was taken, but be aware that adjacent houses may not be adjacent in the records – the enumerator may have taken a 'postman's walk' up one side of a street, around the corner, back along a different road, and finally down the other side of the first street. The British predilection for having even numbers on one side of the street and odd numbers the other means that No. 1 High Street might be many pages away from No. 2.

Name and Surname: NOTE: this is a record of people actually on the premises on census night (Sunday, 2 April in this particular year, but always around that time) *not* those who 'normally'

The Welsh census of 1911 – column headings.

live there, such as students, family members away from home for some reason, those in hospital, prison, the armed services and so on. Any family member elsewhere – in a hotel, on a ship, away at school, on holiday and so on – will be recorded in those places. Anyone just visiting this address on that night will be enumerated there. This can lead to confusion over 'missing' family members, unrelated 'visitors' and the like, so take care. On the other hand, a visitor may be a relative – often a vital clue to the rest of the extended family.

Relationship: This will normally include head, wife, sons, daughters, but also relatives (son-in-law, cousin etc.) as well as servants, lodgers and visitors.

Age of Males, Age of Females: Notice these are in different columns, for ease of tallying later, and giving the gender. As the date or enumeration is early April, take care when working out birth years – a boy born on 1 April 1901 would have passed his 10th birthday, whereas a boy born on 3 April 1901 would not, but both might be down as 10. Older people would think of themselves as 'in my 82nd year', for example, meaning after the 81st but before the 82nd birthday, so the birth year for someone claiming to be 82 in 1911 could be 1828, 1829 or 1830, depending on the actual birth date. Also, older people would often exaggerate their ages (especially if near 100), while unmarried women nearing an important birthday (40 or 50) had a tendency to shave a few years off. In censuses earlier than 1911 there was a tendency to make children aged 12–14 either older (so they could work rather than attending school) or younger (so as to avoid military service), although this was harder to get away with as registration and other records improved. Anyway, always allow a window of one or two years either side.

Particulars as to Marriage: This meant single, married, widower or widow for everyone over 15, and can be a clue as to the date of a spouse's death.

The 'Fertility Census': For reasons explained later, the 1911 census recorded, for women, the length of the present marriage, number of children born alive within that marriage, the number still alive and the number dead. This is where to pick up hints about infant deaths, earlier marriages, children born before the marriage and the like. The questions were not asked for the benefit of genealogists a century later, but have turned out to be immensely valuable.

Profession or Occupation: This gives the precise occupation, the industry or service involved, whether employer, worker or 'Working on Own Account' (self-employed) and 'Whether Working at Home' – this can be a valuable nugget of social history.

Birthplace: For someone born in the UK, the county and town are given, but the details are less helpful for anyone born elsewhere. Often (to the continuing fury of genealogists), anyone born in Ireland may just be down as 'Ireland', but in 1911 details were required as to whether the person was 'Resident' (in England and Wales) or a 'Visitor'.

Nationality: This is not the same as residence, of course – the child of the Italian Ambassador might be born in the UK and resident there, but have Italian citizenship, and the whole business of whether someone was a British subject (by virtue of being born somewhere in the British Empire to British parents) or naturalised (after arriving) is complicated. When Jews were being hounded out of Poland and Lithuania in the 1880s, many went to South Africa, especially those in the jewellery business, as gold and diamonds had just been discovered there. Some became British subjects (South Africa was British then) and later moved to Britain. So, you might find a father, who was naturalised British, but born in Poland, with children born in the UK and therefore British.

Infirmity: We may be uncomfortable with terms like 'Deaf and Dumb', 'Lunatic', 'Imbecile' and 'Feeble-minded' in today's enlightened times, but these had actual legal definitions in 1911. This section is blanked out in all 1911 census images, because the information might still be sensitive even 100 years later.

Language Spoken: This is the only difference between the censuses in Wales and England (the Scottish census asked about Gaelic).

Address: Another way in which the 1911 census differed from previous years was in having one page per household, so the address details are at the foot, rather than in a column. The address is the 'Postal Address', not the registration district (RD), sub-registration district, enumeration district (ED), civil or ecclesiastical parish and so on, which earlier censuses recorded; these will have to be inferred from the form's index number. Finally, we get the actual signature of whoever completed the form – usually the householder.

We can now look at an actual example. In the image below, information from two adjacent pages has been assembled into one, for purposes of contrast. We find that:

- The address is Greenhill, Pentrecagal, Newcastle Emlyn, which is in Carmarthenshire (now Dyfed). Ebenezer Griffiths, the head of the household, is male and aged 82 (therefore b. *c.* 1829), widowed (so no marriage particulars), is a retired butter merchant, is living on private means (scored out, because that wasn't asked for, as he is retired), is not working (obviously), was born, he says, in Llanfairtrefeligen, Cardiganshire (probably Llanfairtrefhelygen, also called Llanfair Trelygen, a parish associated with registration district 594, Newcastle-in-Emlyn, see the map on p. 67), is of British nationality (by default) and can speak both English and Welsh. The other numbers, clearly written on later, are for coding by the census officials (e.g. 350 for 'Retired').
- Ebenezer is living with Martha Rees, aged 22, a servant (general domestic) from Cenarth, Carmarthen, and therefore a local girl.
- The Howells family added below (in reality, on the previous page) provide more information. John is 32 and Maria 30, they have been married for nine years, and their oldest child living, Hannah, is aged 7. Four sons and a daughter are listed (Hannah, 7;

1911 Census. Crown Copyright (courtesy of The National Archives)

Mary, 6; Rachel Anne, 3; Benjamin Daniel, 1; and Miriam, 11 months, sometimes recorded as 11/12) but Maria has had seven children, two of whom have died. Was there an older child? Did the other two die as infants, or later, and of what? These are questions to be answered from death records (Chapter 6).

- That's the bare bones of the information in the census, but what else could we divine from it? Well, first, Ebenezer is probably comfortably off in his old age – own house (probably) and a live-in servant (quite common amongst the middle classes of the time) – and his wife died before 2 April 1911. He has no family members living with him, so perhaps he is of independent mind and still fairly healthy, or a complete curmudgeon nobody else can stand! Alternatively, all his children may be living elsewhere. Ebenezer has moved from his birthplace in Llanfairtrefhelygen, Cardiganshire.

Scottish censuses from 1861 had a useful column headed 'Number of rooms with windows', which is an indication of the size and structure of the dwelling, but this information was not collected in England and Wales. Looking up the address on Google Maps Street View (http://maps.google.co.uk) is an alternative if the building has survived, but leads to a disappointing result in this case – it is not clear whether Greenhill Cottage refers to one of a number of newbuild houses, or an older building across the road.

Census 1901

This census has an Ebenezer Griffiths, aged 72 (confirming birth *c.* 1829) living with his wife, Rachel (71), in Green Hill, Penboyr, Newcastle in Emlyn, Carmarthenshire (the same parish and registration district as in 1911), with a female servant called Rachel Jones (19). In this census Ebenezer claims to have been born in Llandyfriog, Cardiganshire (now Ceredigion, the original Welsh form of 'Cardigan'). This is just across the old Cardigan/Carmarthen county border from Newcastle Emlyn, so Ebenezer didn't move far at all. It is the same person – how many retired butter merchants could there be of the exact right age? – but more proof would be welcome.

However, there is also a 1901 census for Frederick E. Griffiths, so let's concentrate on that, assuming for the moment it's the correct family. In this case, the actual page from the census book has been compacted to show only one family, although there are five households on the page. Other edits have been made in order to pull the relevant information together.

Administrative County etc.: This is Monmouthshire, Civil Parish of Tredegar, Ecclesiastical Parish of St George – although the census taker has written 'Ecclesiastical Parish of St. James' as an amendment in the right margin – Tredegar Urban District, Georgetown Ward, West

Crown Copyright (courtesy of The National Archives)

Monmouthshire Parliamentary Division and Town of Tredegar (see Chapter 4 for definitions of these administrative units). Inferred from the index data, the RD is Bedwellty; sub-registration district is Tredegar: ED 11.

Address: 11 James Street (Tredegar), an inhabited dwelling with five or more rooms occupied.

Head of Household: Godfrey J. Griffiths (45, b. *c.* 1856). Others are Elizabeth A. Griffiths (wife, 33), Frederick E. Griffiths (son, 21, b. *c.* 1880), Edgar F. Griffiths (son, 10), Gertrude E. Griffiths (daughter, 7), Edith M. Griffiths (daughter, 4) and Elizabeth G. Bamford (m[other]-in-law, 61).

Occupation: Godfrey is a colliery timekeeper (and therefore middle management) while Frederick is a blacksmith's striker – this is a skilled occupation: the blacksmith's assistant or apprentice would swing the large, heavy hammer while the smith held the hot iron with tongs on the anvil and indicated the striking-point by tapping the iron with a smaller hammer.

Where Born: Godfrey J. (Glamorganshire, Dowlais); Elizabeth A., Frederick and Edgar (Monmouthshire, Tredegar); Gertrude, Edith (Monmouthshire, Sirhowy); Elizabeth (Glamorganshire, Neath).

Language: they all speak only English, except mother-in-law Elizabeth, who is from the previous generation.

Notice a few other things.

- The double stroke after the household indicates it is separate from the next building – households in a tenement or a row of cottages would have a single stroke between them.
- Some of the information seems to have been crossed out – this is not an indication of mistakes, but 'tally-marks' made by the registrar when counting his totals.
- There is some later writing over the top of the entries, but the '(above)' under Godfrey's occupation may indicate his above-ground work (as opposed to 'below', underground).

What else can we discern?

- Godfrey was born in Dowlais and his children in Tredegar and Sirhowy, which are all within a few miles of each other, between Merthyr Tydfyl and Ebbw Vale. The Dowlais Iron & Steelworks was founded in the eighteenth century and at one time – when Godfrey was working – was the largest steel producer in Britain. However, in 1901 Godfrey worked in a colliery in Tredegar at the head of the Sirhowy Valley, considered the centre of the Industrial Revolution in South Wales, albeit with everyone, children included, working in near-slavery conditions in the 1830s, and the place being the site of major anti-Irish riots in 1882 and similar anti-Jewish unrest in 1911. It wasn't all sweetness and light in South Wales, which goes a long way to explaining emigration.
- Elizabeth's maiden name is probably Bamford, unless Godfrey has two mothers-in-law, which he might if Elizabeth is his second wife. She is 12 years younger than Godfrey, and Frederick simply cannot be her son (she is 33, he is 21) but Edgar (10) could be.
- If she is Elizabeth A. Bamford, it is possible her parents moved to Tredegar from Neath, a coastal industrial town some 30 miles to the south-west, where she met Godfrey.

Do we have the right family? We have no idea what anyone's middle initials stood for. The answer may be in the previous census, when Godfrey would be 35, Frederick 11 and Edgar just born.

Census 1891

This one was hard to find because it is indexed as 'Griffeiths' – not a surname variant, nor yet a census taker's error, but a transcriptional mistake by whoever compiled the index. Living at

1891 Census. Crown Copyright (courtesy of The National Archives)

1881 Census. Crown Copyright (courtesy of The National Archives)

33 Alexandra Place, Tredegar, is Godfrey, right age, same occupation, same place of birth, married to Elizabeth A. aged 23 and with son, Edgar F. 2 months old. So where is Frederick?

The clue may be in Edgar's age – if Elizabeth has just had a child, the 11-year-old Frederick may have been packed off to relatives while his mother recovered. There is no sign of him at this point.

And look who was living next door – postmistress Elizabeth G. Bamford, a 51-year-old widow born in Neath. Now we know how Godfrey and Elizabeth met! (Strangely, Godfrey's house seems to be 'Uninhabited', so perhaps they have all moved in with mother-in-law for the duration of the 'confinement', as childbirth was known.) Notice that the two addresses are separated by a single tick and share a front-door number (33) – it's possible Godfrey and Elizabeth were living 'above the shop' courtesy of her mother, not an unusual situation for newly-weds.

Census 1881

Frederick should be aged just 1, and here he is, living at 63 Fourth Row South Side (the street address is on the previous page) with father Godfrey J. (but indexed as Godfrey G. Griffiths) and mother Sarah E., aged 26 and born in Tredegar. Another mystery solved – Godfrey has indeed been married before, and his first wife presumably died before 1890 (because in early 1891 he had a 2-month-old son by Elizabeth). We can check this from the relevant birth, marriage and death records (Chapter 6). Again, the houses are 'double-stroked', so separate. Fourth Row, in an area known as Georgetown, was renamed York Terrace *c.* 1904, and is still there (although the reference to 'South Side' is confusing, as the street itself runs north–south).

Notice that the language question was not asked in 1881 or in earlier censuses.

1871 Census. Crown Copyright (courtesy of The National Archives)

Census 1871

In 1871, Godfrey would be 15 or so, and presumably living with his parents, so perhaps finally we can tie down whether the 'middle-name-Ebenezer' story is correct.

At last! Godfrey (15) is at 7 Park Place, Tredegar (literally around the corner from Fourth Row), with parents Ebenezer (43, b. *c.* 1828) and Mary (39, born in Lanehead, Staffordshire, England) plus sister Melissa Ann (8) and four gloriously named brothers – Alphonso F. (17), Orpheus Stentor (5), Faustus Mentor (3) and Cuthburt Ernest (7 months). Orpheus was a Greek minstrel and Stentor was the Greek herald with the loud voice in the *Iliad*, so perhaps this young chap had a healthy set of lungs. Alphonso was a contemporary of Dr Faust. Mentor was the Greek tutor and counsellor Odysseus picked to educate his son. Cuthburt is not a mistake for 'Cuthbert' – *The Confessions of Cuthburt: A Ballad* by Sydney Melmoth (1827) was a well-known poem at this time although rather ignored today. It does seem that Ebenezer liked to show off his knowledge of literature.

Other research (p. 60) shows that Ebenezer obviously got Godfrey into the time keeper business after he started as a striker, but Alphonso was in an even more skilled occupation, patternmaker (see pp. 76–77 for a list of occupations and abbreviations), and ended up in Pennsylvania like so many Welsh, as we shall see. Baby Cuthbut was dead within three or four months; Orpheus Stentor died in 1875; Faustus was not to survive the winter of 1886; but Melissa Ann remained unmarried, looking after her aged mother in Floral Cottage, Dukestown, Tredegar, according to the 1911 census.

No wonder that Godfrey's son, Frederick, should become the apple of his grandfather's eye, and be given his name.

Census 1861

The top line is a different house. The address is simply given as Charlestown, Bedwellty.

The inhabitants are:

– Head, Mary Turner (60), Widow, Dependent on her children, b. Staffordshire, Willenhall (a town on the River Tame in Black Country area of the English West Midlands, between Wolverhampton and Walsall);
– Levinia Turner, Daughter (25), unmarried, Dressmaker, b. Monmouth[shire], Mynyddislwyn (halfway between Cardiff and Tredegar, and 8½ miles north-west of Newport);
– Selina Turner, Daughter (21), unmarried, Milliner (hat maker), also b. Monmouth, Mynyddislwyn;

1861 Census. Crown Copyright (courtesy of The National Archives)

– Mary Griffiths, Daughter (29), married (no occupation given but presumably the wife of Ebenezer), b. Staffordshire, Lanehead;

– Ebenezer Griffiths (33), married, Son-in-law (confirming that he was married to Mary Turner), Proprietor of houses (suggesting he earned money by renting them out, and that he had accumulated capital at some time), b. Monmouth, Tredegar;

– Alphonso Turner Griffiths (7), unmarried (obviously!), Grandson (of Mary Turner and therefore son of Ebenezer and Mary), Scholar (meaning 'at school'), b. Glamorgan[shire], Dowlais (indexed, confusingly, as Dowland, Gloucestershire, England, which shows the flaw in depending on place name lists when transcribing. We can see that the middle name Turner came from his mother's maiden surname, which is often a vital clue for family researchers);

– Godfrey James Griffiths (5), Grandson, Scholar, b. Glamorgan, Dowlais (finally we have his middle name, James); William Hadley (5), Nephew (which suggests that Levinia, Selina or perhaps another Turner daughter not in the household, either married a man called Hadley or had a child by him out of wedlock).

Notice that Mary Turner is 'Head of Household' rather than Ebenezer and, again, the Welsh language question was not asked.

Census 1851

This may be a leap of faith, as there is no real evidence in this census that we have the same Ebenezer, except that there is no other of that name, age and place of birth in 1851. However, it should be confirmed from a record of the marriage of Ebenezer Griffiths and Mary Turner between 1851 and 1853 (as Alphonso was 7 in 1861).

If so, Ebenezer, a butcher by trade, is living in his older brother's house at Polar Place, 26 Church Street. His brother is Thomas Ja[me]s (41), 'Builder and Tallow Chandler Employing 6 men', married to Elizabeth R (44). There is no hint here of Ebenezer's parents.

Notice that in this census, households were separated by a long underline, rather than the single or double strokes of later censuses.

Census 1841

The structure of the 1841 census records is different. There is less information, and it is collected on one side of a double page.

1851 Census. Crown Copyright (courtesy of The National Archives)

1841 Census. Crown Copyright (courtesy of The National Archives)

There are two 13-year-olds (or near that age) called Ebenezer Griffiths in the 1841 census for Wales, one in Llandyfriog, Cardiganshire (see below), and one in Garth Cottage, Hamlet of Graig, Bassaleg, Monmouthshire, shown above. Bassaleg is on the west of Newport, 20 miles to the south of Tredegar. This may not be the correct family, but this can be checked by following these names forward into later censuses, and by using birth, marriage and death records (Chapter 6).

PLACE	HOUSES		NAMES of each Person who abode therein the preceding Night.	AGE and SEX		PROFESSION, TRADE, EMPLOYMENT, or of INDEPENDENT MEANS.	Where Born	
	Uninhabited or Building	Inhabited		Males	Females		Whether Born in same County	Whether Born in Scotland, Ireland or Foreign Parts
Pensarne		1	Anna Griffiths	55		Publican	Y	
			Margaret do		20	do	Y	
			Anne do		15		Y	
			Ebenezer do	13			Y	

1841 Census. Crown Copyright (courtesy of The National Archives)

Notice what is missing from the 1841 census – no relationships (head, wife, son, daughter etc.), state of marriage or widowhood, and the 'Place of Birth' columns only have 'Y[es]' if born in the census county (Monmouthshire in this case) or 'S[cotland]', 'I[reland]' or 'FP' (foreign parts). It's not very revealing – the bottom two entries for Charles and Sarah Vincent only say they were not born in Monmouthshire, but as there is no S, I or FP, they could be from any county in England or Wales.

We might assume that Thomas Griffiths (65), a builder, is widowed and living with daughters Ann (20), Jemima (16) and Mary (8) plus son Ebenezer (13), and that Thomas's wife died some time in the previous eight years, but equally these could all be the grandchildren of Thomas, and their parents could be dead or elsewhere.

There is one other peculiarity of the 1841 census (and only 1841) – the ages of those over 15 were rounded down to the nearest 5, although some enumerators ignored this and collected the actual ages. That's why almost all adults have ages ending in 0 or 5. So, in the example above, Thomas Griffiths might be anywhere from 65–69 (or possibly 64 if he meant 'in my 65th year') and Ann is 20–4, but Ebenezer really is 13 (assuming his age was correctly given).

The Cardiganshire Ebenezer Griffiths family is shown above, and the same caveats apply about Anna being 54–59 and so on.

Pensarne, Llandyfriog (today called Pensarn), is very near Newcastle Emlyn. At this point we can loop back to the 1911 censuses. Remember Ebenezer Griffiths, retired butter merchant living at Greenhill, Pentrecagal, Newcastle Emlyn, Carmarthenshire? It is more likely that this is the Ebenezer at Pensarne in 1841 and the butcher of Bedwellty in 1851. (It isn't a far stretch from butcher to butter merchant.)

To check this, all entries for Ebenezer Griffiths of the right age from the 1841–1911 censuses were collated, as shown in the table overleaf.

Census Year	Forename	Surname	Age	Occupation	County	Estimated Birth Year	Place of Birth
1841	Ebenezer	Griffiths	13	(None given)	Monmouthshire	1828	Monmouthshire
1841	Ebenezer	Griffiths	13	(None given)	Cardiganshire	1828	Cardiganshire
1851	Ebenezer	Griffiths	23	Butcher	Monmouthshire	1828	Tredegar, Monmouthshire
1851	Ebenezer	Griffiths	22	Carpenter	Cardiganshire	1829	Llanfertichligion, Cardiganshire
1861	Ebenezer	Griffiths	33	Proprietor Of Houses	Monmouthshire	1828	Tredegar, Monmouthshire
1861	Ebenezer	Griffiths	32	Carpenter	Cardiganshire	1829	Llandyfriog, Cardiganshire
1871	Ebenezer	Griffiths	45	Time Keeper	Monmouthshire	1826	Tredegar, Monmouthshire
1871	Ebenezer	Griffiths	42	Butter & General Merchant	Cardiganshire	1829	Llanfairtrefhelygen, Cardiganshire
1871	Ebenezer	Griffiths	47	Slate Quarry Labourer	Carnarvonshire	1824	Lancashire, Liverpool
1881	Ebenezer	Griffiths	53	Inn Keeper & Druggist	Brecknockshire	1828	Bedwellty, Monmouthshire
1881	Ebenezer	Griffiths	52	Butter Provision Merchant & Farmer	Cardiganshire	1829	Llanfair Trefhelygain, Cardiganshire
1891	Ibenezer	Griffiths	62	Butter Merchant	Cardiganshire	1829	Llandyfriog, Cardiganshire
1901	Ebenezer	Griffiths	72	Butler [sic] Merchant	Cardiganshire	1829	Llandyfriog, Cardiganshire
1911	Ebenezer	Griffiths	82	Retired Butter Merchant	Cardiganshire	1829	Llanfairtrefeligen, Cardigan

It is quite clear there are two Ebenezers. We can discount the in-migrant 'Slate Quarry Labourer' from Liverpool in 1871, and possibly the 1881 'Inn Keeper & Druggist' although Brecknockshire or Brecon borders both Cardigan and Monmouth counties, as the maps below show, and boundary changes might well have put his residence in Brecon (Chapter 4). There is the Cardiganshire 'Carpenter/Butter Merchant', present in all eight censuses, and there is the Monmouthshire 'Butcher/Proprietor Of Houses/Time Keeper', who seems to go missing before 1881. There are three possibilities – he died, he migrated or he really was an innkeeper and druggist in 1881 and died before the 1891 census. Other records would tell us.

There is another clue in the 1911 census (see p. 68). The Ebenezer from Tredegar, Monmouthshire had a sister called Melis(s)a Anne. She turns up, aged 47 and single, living with her widowed mother Mary Griffiths (79) at Floral Cottage, Dukestown, Tredegar. What is interesting about this entry is that, although Mary is a widow, her marriage particulars have been recorded – 60 years married (presumably meaning the wedding was in 1851, when she was 19) and she had seven children, four of whom have died (we know about Orpheus Stentor, Faustus Mentor and Cuthburt Ernest) and three alive (possibly Godfrey and Alphonso, if they hadn't died by then, plus Melissa Ann) but that makes six, so there is a child missing. That would bear further investigation.

Summary

We were looking for Frederick Ebenezer Griffiths, and initially started down the wrong track – a different Ebenezer Griffiths to Frederick's grandfather, in the 1911 census. But in the process, we got back on the rails and showed that:

- Frederick Ebenezer was born *c.* 1880 in Tredegar, Monmouthshire, son of Godfrey J. Griffiths (45, b. *c.* 1856) and Sarah (maiden name as yet unknown) b. *c.* 1855, who died before 1891.

Map showing Newcastle-in-Emlyn and northern Cardiganshire.

1911 Census. Crown Copyright (courtesy of The National Archives)

- Godfrey's father and Frederick's grandfather was Ebenezer Griffiths, b. *c.* 1828 in Tredegar, who worked as a butcher, proprietor of houses and a time keeper at an ironworks or colliery.
- Frederick trained as a blacksmith's striker, but either died or disappeared after the 1901 census.

We will find out which when we pick up his trail again in later chapters, specifically those on statutory BMD records (Chapter 6) and emigration (Chapter 9).

Finding Census Records

See pp. 49–54 for places and websites where censuses can be seen. In some cases the actual record images can be viewed, and some have transcriptions.

Here, for example, is an extract of all Griffiths in the 1891 census for Penboyr, compiled by Alan Jones (who has also done 1841 and 1851) and available at www.genuki.org.uk/big/wal/CMN/Pen-Boyr/1891surnameindex.txt – GENUKI has such a number of such transcripts for individual parishes. These have been re-sorted into households for display here.

Where	Forename	Surname	Relation	Status	Age	Occupation	County Born	Parish Born
Gilwen Terrace	John	Griffiths	Head	Married	26	Tailor	Carmarthen	Newcastle Emlyn
Gilwen Terrace	Mary	Griffiths	Wife	Married	25		Carmarthen	Brechfa
Gilwen Terrace	William	Griffiths	Brother	Single	23	Tailor	Carmarthen	Llangeler
Gilwen Terrace	Lizie A.	Griffiths	Daughter		3		Pembroke	Manordeifi
Gilwen Terrace	Mary J.	Griffiths	Daughter		2		Carmarthen	Cilrhedyn
Green Hill	Ebenezer	Griffiths	Head	Married	62	Cheese & butter merchant	Cardigan	Llandyfriog
Green Hill	Rachel	Griffiths	Wife	Married	61		Carmarthen	Llangeler
Green Hill	Mary	Griffiths	Daughter	Single	30		Carmarthen	Penboyr
Green Hill	John H.	Griffiths	Son	Single	25	Cheese & butter merchant	Carmarthen	Penboyr
Pantyffynon	John	Griffiths	Step-son	Single	26	Farmer's stepson	Carmarthen	Penboyr

Penlangribin	Griffith	Griffiths	Head	Widower	58	Farmer	Carmarthen	Penboyr
Penlangribin	Ruth	Griffiths	Daughter	Single	24	Farmer's daughter	Carmarthen	Penboyr
Penlangribin	Sarah	Griffiths	Daughter	Single	26	Farmer's daughter	Carmarthen	Penboyr
Penlangribin	David	Griffiths	Son	Single	20	Farmer's son	Carmarthen	Penboyr
Penlangribin	John	Griffiths	Son	Single	29	Farmer's son	Carmarthen	Penboyr
Shop	Sarah	Griffiths	Head	Widow	90	Shop keeper (Grocer)	Carmarthen	Cenarth
Pentre	Jane	Griffiths	Sister	Single	47	Living on her own means	Cardigan	Trefilan
Pentrecagal shop	Elizabeth	Griffiths	Servant	Single	15	General servant (domestic)	Cardigan	Llandissuliogogo [Llandysiliogogo]
Rhuddgoedfawr	Ann	Griffiths	Daughter	Married	29	Farmer's daughter	Carmarthen	Cilrhedyn
Rhuddgoedfawr	Elizabeth	Griffiths	Grand-daughter		5		Carmarthen	Penboyr
Rhuddgoedfawr	Evan	Griffiths	Grandson		3		Carmarthen	Penboyr
Ty-isaf	Mary	Griffiths	Head	Widow	35	Woollen weaver	Cardigan	Llandyfriog
Ty-isaf	Anne	Griffiths	Daughter		11	Scholar	Carmarthen	Penboyr
Waunfawr	John	Griffiths	Head	Widower	34	Farmer	Carmarthen	Penboyr
Waunfawr	David	Griffiths	Brother	Single	22	Farmer's brother	Carmarthen	Penboyr
Waunfawr	Dinah	Griffiths	Sister	Single	23	Farmer's sister	Carmarthen	Penboyr

How the census came about

The first census of England had been carried out under William I (William the Conqueror) and the results collated as the Domesday Book in 1086. ('Domesday' refers to 'domertie' not 'doom'.) There were later census-like exercises, for example, in the sixteenth century when bishops enumerated the number of families in their dioceses, and there was an 1851 religious census in Wales. Landowners also conducted periodic censuses of their workers and tenants, although usually only heads of households.

The first national census in Britain took place in 1801, and there has been a further census every ten years since, except for 1941 when the Second World War took priority – although there was a similar but simpler exercise on Friday, 29 September 1939, for the purposes of issuing National Identity Cards, which became the basis of the National Health Service Central Register in 1948.

However, the earliest four censuses (1801, 1811, 1821, 1831) were rather different in aim and character from the later ones, and it was only from 1841 that censuses are of much use to genealogists, as names were recorded.

Census dates 1801–1911

These were generally, but not always, a Sunday night at the end of March or the beginning of April.

1801 – 10 March	1811 – 27 May	1821 – 28 May	1831 – 30 May
1841 – 7 June	1851 – 30 March	1861 – 7 April	1871 – 2 April
1881 – 3 April	1891 – 5 April	1901 – 31 March	1911 – 2 April

The 1801 census

The first modern census, in 1801, was considered necessary because of growing unease about the demand for food in Britain, especially in the aftermath of the publication of Thomas Robert Malthus's *Essay on the Principle of Population* in 1798. The upshot was the Census Act or Population Act 1800 ('An Act for taking an Account of the Population of Great Britain, and the Increase or Diminution thereof' 41 Geo. III c.15), which legislated for a census of Scotland, England and Wales, the Channel Islands and the Isle of Man. Ireland was not included until 1821. The process was remarkably swift, which underlines the importance attached to it – the Census Bill was presented to Parliament on 20 November 1800, was passed on 3 December, and received Royal Assent from King George III on 31 December. The first census was held just fourteen weeks later, on Monday, 10 March 1801. This was possible because a House of Commons clerk called John Rickman was passionate about the idea and was prepared to take on the analysis of the results and the preparation of abstracts and reports, which he did for the 1801 census and the next three.

The 1801 census collected two sorts of information: the first was the numbers of families and houses, the numbers of individuals and their occupations; the second was the numbers of marriages, christenings (not births) and burials, which allowed those who followed the new science of population statistics to estimate the rate at which the population was growing or declining, what proportion was of working age and so forth.

In an earlier century, it might have fallen to the church to collect such data. Even at this time, it was parish registers collated by the local ministers that recorded individual baptisms, banns and burials, also recorded as bishops' transcripts (see Chapter 8).

This exercise would have taken a greater army of recorders than the church could muster, and in any case it was seen as a secular exercise and the province of government. Luckily, there was already an administrative infrastructure in place. In England and Wales, the local census enumerators were usually the Overseers of the Poor. (In Scotland, it tended to be the local schoolmaster, often known 'the Dominie', along with other literate, educated and trustworthy individuals – doctors, clergymen, lawyers, merchants – who acted as the army of paid volunteers.) These enumerators would visit each household, institution or ship within their allocated district just before the census date and deliver a form (called a schedule) to the 'Head', or the person in charge of the house, who was required to complete it for collection on the day after the night of the census. The enumerator would check the completed forms – or complete them if they were not, by questioning whoever was in – copy the information into pre-printed books of blank forms, and take them to the local registrar, who checked the data again and forwarded it onto the central office in London, where it was checked again, collated and published in summary as a parliamentary paper. The individual details of households and people, which would have been of great value to later generations of historians, sociologists and genealogists, were destroyed in the vast majority of cases. The summaries include the totals of:

Houses: Inhabited, By how many families occupied, Uninhabited.
Persons: Males, Females.

Occupations: Persons chiefly employed in agriculture, Persons chiefly employed in Trade, Manufactures, or Handicraft, All other Persons not comprised in the two preceding Classes.
Total of persons: England, Wales, Scotland, Army, Navy, Seamen and Convicts.

As well as the overall national summaries there were county tables organised by Hundred, Parish, Township or Extra parochial place, and separate tables for the Cities of London and Westminster. The diligent Mr Rickman managed to complete his work and publish the *Enumeration of England and Wales* by 21 December 1801, with Scotland following on 9 June 1802.

The 1801 census estimated the population of England at 8.3 million; Wales at 541,000; Scotland at 1.6 million; the number of those in the army, navy and merchant marine about 370,000; and 1,410 'convicts on hulks' (see box on p. 72). This made almost 11 million souls, plus a further 4 million in Ireland (estimated from hearth tax returns) and 80,000 on the Channel Islands, the Scilly Isles and the Isle of Man.

Local censuses

Approximately fifty places in eighteen counties have census fragments from 1801–31. Consult the booklet *Local Census Listings 1522–1930* by Jeremy Gibson and Mervyn Medlycott, published by the Federation of Family History Societies and available via the Federation's online bookshop, www.familyhistorybooks.co.uk, for more information. Some local libraries and family history societies have census information from 1801 for certain parishes. They can be obtained from the FHS in question, or the Society of Genealogists in London.

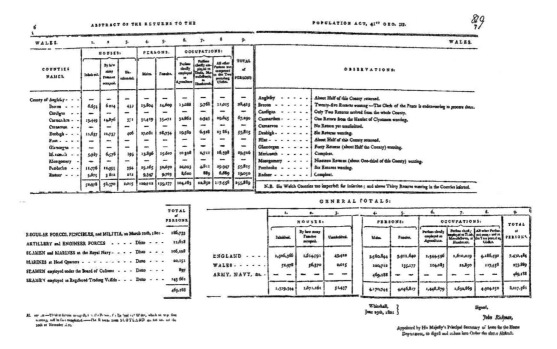

A redacted copy of the population abstract for Wales, 1801.

The 1811, 1821 and 1831 censuses

The next three censuses used the same model as that of 1801. Again, there is little individual information given and no names. More information and images of statistical summaries are available at the website of the Great Britain and Ireland Historical GIS Project, based at the Centre for Data Digitisation and Analysis, The Queen's University of Belfast (www.qub.ac.uk/cdda), and at Histpop – The Online Historical Population Reports Website (www.histpop.org/ohpr/servlet/). There is also some limited statistical information at county and, in some cases, parish level at A Vision of Britain (www.visionofbritain.org.uk/gbhdb/index.jsp). It may be useful to know how a particular area's population changed in these years, in terms of total number, age distribution or occupations. Scottish parishes tend to have better population statistics and other data available than burghs, where the amount of information (and whether it was collected at all) depended to some extent on size.

PRISON HULKS

These were decommissioned warships, and were originally used to relieve overcrowding in English and Welsh prisons in the 1700s. The Industrial Revolution at the end of the eighteenth century led to mass movements of people into the cities, with a consequent increase in petty crime. There were more and more debtors and, towards the end of the century, French prisoners of war. The problem the authorities had was that there were no 'national' prisons, only local gaols.

Misdemeanours could be dealt with locally and the miscreants imprisoned there, but for more severe crimes (felonies) prisoners had to be transported to London. This was carried out by private contractors, who also had the idea of keeping the prisoners on derelict ships or 'hulks' in the Thames, in the Medway, off south coast ports and elsewhere. There were also hulks in Bermuda. The conditions on these floating prisons were appalling, but there was no desire to go back to the old days of execution for minor crimes, so a more humane idea developed – transport them to the North American colonies. Some 50,000 transportees were settled there, but after the War of Independence in 1776 America decided it didn't want any more, thank you. Fortunately, Australia was discovered about then and so provided an alternative. The first fleet (775 prisoners) went in 1786, followed by another three large transports between 1787 and 1791. They weren't all thieves and brigands.

There is a persistent story that transportees temporarily housed at Millbank prison wore jackets with POM (Prisoner of Millbank) stencilled on the back, which explains why, to this day, Britons in Australia are called 'Poms'. Well, perhaps.

There were no prison hulks in Scotland, although the overseer of the Thames hulks was one Duncan Campbell, son of the Principal of Glasgow University, a major tobacco shipper, prisoner-transporter and slave-runner, and the man who put Captain Bligh in charge of the *Bounty* for that notorious voyage to bring breadfruit from Tahiti as cheaper food for slaves.

Prison ships have been used since, notably for the internment of Republicans during the Irish 'troubles' of 1922 and for internees during the Second World War. In 1997 the first prison ship for 200 years off mainland UK was opened off Portland, Dorset, but within ten years was due to be closed as 'unsuitable, expensive' and 'in the wrong place'. However, severe prison overcrowding meant that the idea was revived in 2006 and again in 2010. Interestingly, detaining prisoners of war on hulks was outlawed by the 1949 Geneva Convention.

For example, Tredegar was founded in 1799 when the landowner, Lt. Col. Sir Charles Gould Morgan, leased land on the east bank of the Sirhowy River to Samuel Homfray and his partners in the Tredegar Ironworks Company, in order for them to build the works and a town to accommodate the workers. It's no coincidence that Homfray married Sir Charles's daughter Jane in 1800, and anyway the west bank of the Sirhowy was owned by someone else – Lord Tredegar. Why there? A travel book published in 1801 (*An Historical Tour in Monmouthshire* by William Coxe) paints an idyllic picture:

> The features of this vale are more wild and romantic than those of the Ebwy; it is narrower and
> deeper; and the shelving declivities, laid out in meadows, stretch to the edges of the torrent, which
> roars in a profound abyss, obscured by overhanging trees.

There were few people in the area at the time, and they were mostly Welsh-speaking, living in small cottages and from subsistence agriculture, or working on the surrounding large estates. But what they did have plenty of were ironstone, coal, wood, limestone and water – all necessary for ironworks. There had been small-scale furnaces as far back as 1600.

Once in charge, Homfray made some infrastructure improvements – including a horse-wagon track along the 25 miles to Newport in 1805, and the acquisition of one of Mr Stephenson's newfangled steam locomotives in 1829.

It is no surprise, then, that the parish population swelled from 1,132 in 1801 to 34,685 in 1881.

Homfray, however, turned out to be every bit the Dickensian factory owner: anyone who wanted to set up a business in his 'company town' had to buy a franchise at a percentage; the workers were paid in private coin (no banks were allowed to operate in the town), which they could only spend in local, company-controlled 'Truck Shops' ('truck' meaning 'exchange') or 'Tommy Shops', which stocked inferior quality goods at inflated prices (the origin of 'Tommy-rot'). Homfray was known as a martinet to work for. The result was poverty, consequent malnutrition and disease. The poor housing and sewerage conditions led to a cholera outbreak in 1832–33 and an even worse one in August and September 1849, which required a devoted cholera burial ground at Cefn Golau, now a scheduled ancient monument, although largely abandoned to sheep. Incidentally, 'trucking' was largely outlawed by the 1831 Truck Act, due in no small part to a heartfelt speech in the House of Commons by Sir Charles Morgan, after which employees, albeit those in certain trades only until 1887, had the right to be paid in normal money. (For more historical detail, see www.tredegar.co.uk.)

The parish population rose steadily, but it is noticeable how many people lived in the small, cramped dwellings, and that the infant mortality rate in the 1890s was one in five:

Year	Population	Households	People/House
1801	1,132		
1811	3,958		
1821	5,404		
1831	8,567		
1841	19,929	3,658	5.45
1851	24,544	4,460	5.50
1861	28,598		
1871	33,697		
1881	34,685	6,356	5.46

1891	35,628	6,623	5.38
1901	40,831	7,761	5.26
1911	57,008	10,967	5.20
2011	15,000		

Notice that the population of Tredegar in 1911 is fifty times that of 1801

For comparison, here is the total population of Wales over a similar time period. The increase from 1801 to 1911 is only five-fold, showing how much growth there was in the industrial south.

Year	Wales, Total Population
1801	533,235
1811	600,612
1821	708,105
1831	805,749
1841	921,792
1851	1,027,023
1861	1,208,304
1871	1,389,588
1881	1,570,873
1891	1,770,633
1901	2,053,111
1911	2,442,041
1921	2,656,474
2001	2,903,085

The 1841 census

The passing of the Population Act 1840 (Act 3° & 4° Victoria, Cap. 99, intituled 'An Act for taking an Account of the Population of Great Britain'), inspired a new form of census. For the first time individual names were recorded and there were stiff penalties for giving misleading information (see p. 76). The census enumerators delivered forms to each household, which they would later collect, check and enter into their printed book of forms. The census information we have today is from the enumerators' transcript books, as few of the original schedules have survived. The enumerator entered marks to show where each household and/or building ended (see p. 76–77), and indicated whether the house was uninhabited (U) or being built (B).

Census returns were collected according to enumeration districts (ED – roughly equivalent to the pre-existing parishes) and brought together according to registration district (RD, the same area as was used to record births, marriages and deaths, BMD). Larger EDs were divided into sub-districts. This was to ensure that an enumerator could reach every household on the same day, so reducing the chance of a duplicate or missed entry if someone happened to be in another house.

In 1837, when civil registration of BMD began, each RD was given a number, applied retrospectively to the pre-1837 parishes. The numbers run roughly north to south and east to west by county, and within a county are numbered by alphabetical parish or RD name. Therefore, a complete reference for a census record includes the parish/RD number, ED number, piece, folio and schedule numbers.

The year codes for England and Wales are:

1841	HO107
1851	HO107
1861	RG9
1871	RG10
1881	RG11
1891	RG12
1901	RG13
1911	RG14

HO = Home Office; RG = Registrar General.

As an example, the full reference for the 1891 census for 33 Alexandra Place, Bedwellty, shown on p. 61 above, would be: RG12/4357, 20, 96, 59

RG12 tells us it's 1891; RD 4357 = piece number (Bedwellty); Sub-RD – Tredegar; ED = 20; 96 = folio; 59 = schedule no.

This can be confusing at first sight. Because each enumerator's pre-printed book had about twenty to forty double-sided sheets, when collected these were later bound into a larger book called a 'census piece', with fifty to 200 leaves. Each sheet in a piece would be given a folio number (which is the front and back of the sheet, in other words, two pages, but not on a double-page spread), which was stamped on the upper right corner of the 'recto' (the front of the sheet), not the 'verso' (the back) Therefore, the original page number is largely irrelevant. The schedule number is the order in which the household was visited (see p. 56).

There is a list of RDs in the census years 1841–1901 in Chapter 5 along with instructions on how to search for piece numbers and so on.

Bear in mind that a household may appear across two pages, so if the relevant entries are near the top or bottom of a page, check the page before or after.

Problems with the 1841 census

The major problem with 1841 is the rounding-down of adult ages. Ages of anyone over 15 were rounded down to the nearest five. If someone aged 30 made a mistake, or lied, and said 29, this would be recorded as 25, giving later researchers a headache when trying to establish a birth date. Someone aged 34 would go down as 30. Sometimes the householders or enumerators ignored this and inserted the actual ages, for which we thank them!

EXTRACT from the Act 3° & 4° Victoria, Cap. 99, intituled

'An Act for taking an Account of the Population of Great Britain'
Penalty for refusing Information, or giving false Answers
XX. And the better to enable the said Commissioners, Enumerators, Schoolmasters and other Persons employed in the Execution of this Act to make the said Inquiries and Returns, be it enacted. That the said Commissioners, Enumerators, Schoolmasters and other Persons shall be authorized to ask all such Questions as shall be directed in the Instructions to be issued by the said Commissioners, with the Approval of One of Her Majesty's Principal Secretaries of State, which shall be necessary for making the preliminary Inquiries and for obtaining the Returns required by this Act; and every Person refusing to answer, or wilfully giving a false Answer to such Questions, or any of them, shall for every such Refusal or wilfully False Answer, forfeit a Sum not more than Five Pounds, nor less than Forty Shillings, at the Discretion of any Justice of the Peace or Magistrate before whom Complaint thereof shall be made.

The above may be shown by the Enumerator to any person refusing to answer, showing his authority to require an Answer, or giving an Answer which he suspects is false.

There were stiff penalties for evading or misleading the census takers.

The 1851–1901 Censuses

From 1851 on, the head of the household was asked to provide more information, which is a boon to family historians. In particular, each household was given a schedule number, the relationship of each individual to the head of the family was collected, correct ages were taken instead of adults, being rounded down, and there was more birthplace detail – including the place and parish of birth. In the 1891 and 1901 census taken in Wales, there was also a question on language spoken, read or understood (English, Welsh or both).

Occupation was recorded according to a standard set of abbreviations. The table below is taken from the instructions to enumerators at the time of the 1841 census: 'Alphabetical List of Abbreviations which may be used and no others, unless a large class occurs in any Enumerator's District, when, if he uses another abbreviation, it must be carefully noticed in the page left for observations of Enumerators.' These instructions were not always followed!

Agricultural Labourer.	Ag. Lab.	To signify all Agricultural Labourers, whether in the fields, or as Shepherd, Ploughman, Carter, Waggoner, or Farm Servant generally.
Apprentice.	Ap.	The letters Ap., which must be accompanied by the name of the trade, will signify Apprentice.
Army.	Army.	All persons of whatever rank in the Military Land Service of Her Majesty, whether Cavalry, Infantry, Artillery, Engineers, &c. must be inserted Army – add for Half-pay, H.P.; for Pensioners, P.
Calico Printer.	Cal. Prin.	Insert Cal. Prin. as the sign for all persons engaged in that trade.
Clerk.	Cl.	All persons employed as Clerk or Book-keepers, &c. may be inserted 'Cl.'
Factory.		(See Manufacturer)

Hand Loom Weavers.	H.L.W.	Always add H.L.W. to each person engaged in Hand-Loom Weaving, after the words Silk, Cotton, &c. as the case may be.
Journeyman.	J.	The letter J. following the name of the trade or handicraft, will signify Journeyman.
Male Servant.	M.S.	All Male Servants may be entered M.S. This class to include, without further distinction, all Bailiffs, Game-keepers and Domestic Servants; Butlers, Coachmen, Footmen, Grooms, Helpers, Boys, &c.
Maid Servant.	F.S. (Female Servant.)	This class is to include all females employed in houses as House Keeper, Ladies Maids, Nurses, &c.
Maker.	m.	The letter J. (Jorneyman) following the trade of any person designated as a maker.
Manufacturer.	Manf.	Master Manufacturers to have 'Manf.' following the name of the staple commodity in which they are engaged.
Merchant Seaman.	Mer. S.	Add Mer. S as the designation of all persons engaged in Merchant Service, whether in the Coasting or Foreign Trade.
Miners.	M.	Always add the name of the Mineral in which each person is employed to the occupation in which he is engaged. If only general work add M., as 'Coal M.', 'Copper M.', 'Iron M.'
Navy.	Navy.	All persons, of whatever rank, engaged in the Sea Service of Her Majesty, whether in the Navy or Marines; must be inserted as Navy – adding H.P. for Half-pay; and P. for Pensioner.
Operatives.		Insert the staple commodity in which workmen are employed, as Cotton, Flax or Hemp, Silk, Woollen, Worsted, Linen, &c. &c., along with the particular designation of the branch of the trade in which the person is engaged, as 'Silk Throwster', 'Cotton Weaver', 'Wool Carder', &c. &c.
Power Loom Weavers.	P.L.W.	Always add P.L.W. to the name of each person engaged in Power Loom Weaving, after the words Silk, Cotton, &c. as the case may be.
Shopman.	Sho.	All persons employed by retail Traders in their Shops, must have the name of the trade prefixed to this abbreviation.
Spirit Dealers.	Sp. Deal.	Add Sp. Deal. to the trade of all persons who are also engaged in vending Spirits.

Censuses after 1851

There are no further surprises in the structure of censuses from 1861 to 1901 – all ask for more or less the same information and use the same layout to record the answers. (In 1911 new 'fertility census' questions were included – see p. 57.) However, in Scotland after 1861 the administrative arrangements were different. The new Registrar General for Scotland had been appointed as a result of the 1854 Registration of Births, Deaths and Marriages (Scotland) Act, and the responsibility for the censuses, as with statutory registration, fell to him. Thus, the 1861 census was the first carried out by the office of the Registrar General and the new network of local registrars.

Generally, the census information gets more and more detailed over the years. In 1871 there is information on those with what would now be called disabilities (deaf, dumb, blind etc.), mental

DIRECTIONS

Respecting the manner in which Entries should be made in this Book.

The process of entering the Householder's Schedules, in this book should be as follows:–

The Enumerator should first insert, in the spaces at the top of the page, the name of the Parish, Quoad Sacra Parish, City or Burgh, Town or Village, to which the contents of that page will apply, drawing his pen through all the headings which are inappropriate.

He should then, in the first column write the No. of the Schedule he is about to copy, and in the second column the name of the Street, Square, &c. where the house is situate, and the No. of the house, if it has a No., or, if the house be situate in the country, any distinctive Name by which it my be known.

He should then copy from the Schedule into the other columns, all the other particulars concerning the members of the family (making use if he please of any contractions authorised by his Instructions); and proceed to deal in the same manner with the next Schedule.

Under the last name in any house he should draw a line across the page as far as the fifth column. Where there is more than one Occupier in the same house, he should draw a similar line under the last name of the family of each Occupier; making the line, however in this case, commence a little on the left hand side of the third column, as in the example on page vi. By the term 'House', must be understood 'a distinct building separated from other buildings by party-walls'. Flats, therefore, must not be entered as houses.

Where he has to insert an uninhabited house or a house building, this may be done, as in the example, by writing in the second column on the line under the last name of the last house inhabited, 'One house uninhabited', 'Three houses building', as the case may be, drawing a line underneath as in the example.

At the bottom of each page for that purpose, he must enter the total number of HOUSES in that page, separating those inhabited from those uninhabited or building.

If the statement regarding any one inhabited house is continued from one page to another, that house must then be reckoned in the total of the page on which the first name is entered. He must also enter on the same line the total number of males and of females included in that page.

When he has completely entered all of the Schedules belonging to any one Parish or Quoad Sacra Parish, he should make no more entries on the LEAF on which the last name is written, but should write across the page, 'End of the Parish [or Quoad Sacra Parish] of ——'; beginning the entry of the next Schedule on the subsequent LEAF of his book. The same course must be adopted with respect to any isolated or detached portion of a distant Parish; which portion, for the sake of convenience, may have been included in his district. When he has entered all the Schedules belonging to any Burgh, Village, &c., he should make no more entries on that PAGE, but write underneath the line after the very last name, 'End of Burgh [or Village &c.] of ——'; making his next entry on the first line of the following PAGE.

In this way he will proceed until all his Householders' Schedules are correctly copied into his Book; and he must then make up the statement of totals, at page ii of this book, in the form there specified. He must also, on page iii, make up the summaries mentioned, in the form according to the instructions there given.

Directions for enumerators from the 1851 census.

health problems or learning difficulties. From 1891 we can learn employment status (employee, self-employed, employer, of independent means) and whether the individual was a Welsh or English speaker.

General Difficulties with Census Records

Genealogists are always advised to consult original records where possible. However, even original sources can be incomplete or just wrong, and census records are no different. Add to this the inevitable errors that will creep in during indexing and transcribing, and it is clear why nothing can be taken at face value. Knowing what the likely problems are and how they occur should help in recognising them when they arise.

Limitations on the census

Because of the need to protect the privacy of living individuals, census records are released only 100 years after they were recorded. The 1911 census became available in April 2011.

PERSONS NOT IN HOUSES, AND COMPLETION OF THE ENUMERATION BOOK.

After having completed the entry of all the Enumeration Schedules according to the above directions, commence a fresh page, and writing across the top 'List of Persons not in Houses', proceed to copy from your 'Memorandum Book' the particulars contained in the list of Persons who slept in Barns, Sheds, &c. When marking up the totals at the foot of that page, the column headed 'Houses' must be left blank, as Barns, Sheds &c. are not to be reckoned as houses. Then, having satisfied yourself of the correctness of your book, fill up the tables on pages iv and v, and sign the Declaration on page vi.

CONTRACTIONS TO BE USED BY THE ENUMERATOR

ROAD, STREET, &c. – Write 'Rd.' for Road; 'St.' for Street; 'Pl.' for Place; 'Sq.' for Square; 'Ter.' for Terrace.

NAMES – Write the First Christian Name in full; Initials or first letters of the other Christian names of a person who has more than one may be inserted.

When the same surnames occur several times in succession, write 'do.' for all such surnames except the first, which should be written out in full.

When the name or any particular is not known, 'n. k.' should be entered in its place.

In the column 'RELATION TO HEAD OF FAMILY', write 'Head' for head of family; 'Daur.' for daughter; 'Serv.' for servant.

In the column 'CONDITION', write 'Mar.' for married; 'Un.' for unmarried; 'W.' for widow; 'Widr.' for widower.

In the column for AGE, write the number of years carefully and distinctly in the proper column for 'Males' or 'Females' as the case may be; in the case of Children under One Year of age, as the age is expressed in months write 'Mo.' distinctly after the figure.

In the column for 'RANK, PROFESSION, or OCCUPATION', the following contractions may be used: 'Ag. Lab.' for agricultural labourer; 'Ap.' for apprentice; 'Cl.' for clerk; 'Serv.' for servant.

Further instructions to the enumerator, taken from the 1861 census.

Making sense of the census

Bear in mind the following when you hit the inevitable 'brick wall':

– the census records for the parish of your interest may just be missing (some are, especially about half of those for Fife, Scotland, in 1841).

– married women were usually, but not always, recorded by the married surname – however, if the maiden surname is given, it is not necessarily the case that the couple was unmarried; also, widows sometimes reverted to their maiden names and children often took the name of the stepfather if the mother remarried; check married and maiden surnames if at all possible.

– if the birthplace of a child (especially the eldest) is different from that of the parents or the census place, it may be that the mother had gone back to her family for the first birth; this can be a clue as to the address of her parents.

– it is often said that people did not move around much in the nineteenth century, but it only took the opening or closing of a mine or a mill, or better work to become available in a nearby parish, for someone to disappear from one district and turn up in another; check the neighbouring county, especially if the district is near a county boundary, and always check adjoining parishes.

– it is also worth checking nearby workhouses, hospitals, asylums, prisons, barracks and prison hulks, and any ships or other vessels.

Not collected or lost

Various censuses have been lost for a variety of reasons. See the list on p. 92. There is no point looking for something that just isn't there. For some reason Denbighshire seems to be especially badly hit, particularly in 1861. One theory has it that the Registrar General had a disagreement with the Public Records Office about handing over the original census books to go into archive until the 100-year mark was passed, and in the meantime they were kept in less than ideal conditions. The 1861 books were not given up until 1962, and it is said that at one point they were discovered stored, if that's the word, under the roof at the Houses of Parliament, where they were exposed to damp, mould, dirt and all the other depredations over which archivists have sleepless nights.

Information partial

The 1841 census contains less information than later exercises – little or nothing on birthplace, for example, and adults' ages rounded down to the nearest five years (p. 75). Every census has individuals for whom some information is simply not recorded.

Information not given or wrongly given

Despite the severe warnings and penalties for giving wrong or no details, it still happened. Unmarried women claimed to be married and took the surname of the 'husband'; ages were given wrongly, especially when there were implications of eligibility for military service, factory work or marriage (at a time when parental consent was required if not 'of full age' – 21, or 25 in some circumstances). Some people were simply unclear about where or when they were born, or chose to change it. Enumerators, officials at institutions, ships' captains and proprietors of boarding houses made mistakes when recording information, but they may have been given wrong data in the first place and transmitted it in good faith. Someone living in a hotel with a good reason not to provide a true name, age and occupation could easily provide alternatives. In prisons, asylums and hospitals, and in the armed services, there must have been many who either did not know, or had changed or simply invented details about themselves.

In the nineteenth century, the numerous prostitutes would hardly have put that on the form, so 'Dressmaker' and 'Of independent means' were common euphemisms for ladies of negotiable affection. Children listed as 'scholars' (i.e. at school) may have in fact been sent out to work; if underage, their parents were breaking the law.

Information wrongly recorded or transferred

Illiteracy was common, especially in the earlier nineteenth century, and many individuals asked friends, neighbours or enumerators to help them complete the forms. Any spelling or numerical errors may not have been spotted. Where the official in charge of a ship, hospital, school, prison and so on took notes and transferred the information onto the census form, there was the possibility for errors at both stages. Typical mistakes were in spelling names, recording ages or writing down occupations. Occasionally, enumerators misheard or failed to catch the Welsh spelling and recorded the English instead (Hugh instead of Huw, for instance). See 'Censuses in Welsh' (p. 56).

Information wrongly transcribed or keyed

There is many a slip between record and transcription. Genealogists are eternally grateful to all the volunteers and commercial organisations who have indexed and transcribed the various censuses plus other records, but despite checks, error-trapping and validation routines, glitches do still get through. There are examples of 'John Smith Senior' being indexed as if 'Senior' were the surname. The examples of 'Griffeiths' and 'Ibenezer' were seen earlier in this chapter.

Onomastics

This is to do with naming, which is the very stuff of genealogy (from the Greek, *onomastikos* 'of or belonging to naming'). First, there is the spelling issue. This was standardised – especially for names – only comparatively recently. Even when almost everyone could read and write, many simply spelled what they heard. The Mc/Mac controversy rolls on, with some writers even suggesting that one is Scottish and one Irish. This is nonsense. All Scottish surnames of this type are Mac (meaning son of) but were often abbreviated to Mc or even M', so that MacKay could be written as McKay, M'Kay or Mackay and so on. The same goes for Owain (thought to be Welsh) and Owen (English), which have an identical origin.

Spelling was largely a toss of the coin until names got recorded somewhere official, such as in a birth record after statutory registration, or in an earlier record of land purchase, sale, mortgage, rental etc.; and so the same could be said for Johns/Jones or Thomson/Thomsson/Thompson. Always check all likely (and unlikely) variants.

Marriage and remarriage are obvious reasons for a name change. But there are also professional, personal and political reasons for this. A bigamist, convicted felon or fraudster would have good reason to find a brand new surname. The celebrated Victorian novelist and detective story author James Edward Muddock (the name probably originally derived from Madoc), changed his first names to Joyce Emmerson Preston (Muddock), which has led to him being included in several databases of female authors. For similar professional reasons Diana Fluck became Diana Dors, and Marion Michael Morrison became John Wayne.

Some changed their names from Welsh to a more anglicised form, either to suit the political climate or for convenience – Evan Preece is easier to spell than Ifan ap Rhys, and may have been more acceptable when trying to make good in an English-dominated milieu.

Given names

The British have always used interchangeable first names and diminutives, such as Meg, Maggie and Peggy for Margaret (although Meg could also be Megan); Eliza, Lizzie, Liza, Lisbet, Lillibet, Beth or Betty for Elizabeth; Isa, Bel, Isabelle or Issie for Isobel; and Janet, Jean, Jane or Jessie for each other. Jackie may have been christened John; Andy was almost certainly baptised Andrew;

Tom and Tommy are really Thomas; Ted could be Edward or Frederick. Adding to that confusion, enumerators (or the individuals themselves) would abbreviate names – Thos for Thomas, Jas or Jac (Latin – Jacobus) for James, Rbt for Robert, Alexr for Alexander, Wm for William.

In the decade between two censuses a lot may have happened to a person or a family – a marriage or even two, resulting in a wholesale name change, not just for the wife but all the children; or a radical change in fortune (up or down), necessitating a change in surname. Prime Minister David Lloyd George (1863–1945) was plain David George when born – in Chorlton-on-Medlock, Manchester, England, incidentally. When his father died in 1864, his mother took the young David to her brother, Richard Lloyd, in Tŷ Newydd, who was a great influence on the boy's education and politics. David added Lloyd to his surname and nailed it firmly in place with a hyphen when created 1st Earl Lloyd-George three months before his death.

Welsh naming patterns

As a follow-on from the patronymic naming system prevalent before the seventeenth century (pp. 25–27), an eldest son would often be named for the paternal grandfather, an eldest daughter for the maternal grandmother, the next son for the maternal grandfather, the next daughter for the paternal grandmother, the third son after the father, third daughter after the mother, and other children after aunts and uncles and so on. This is confusing where a number of families live in close proximity – especially if they share an ancestor – but can sometimes provide a valuable clue as to family relationships. It is quite possible for a whole set of first cousins, and their uncles, to have the same first name. However, an unusual first name might repeat itself every other generation down a single line.

It isn't always even that simple! Major Francis Jones, in his classic *An Approach to Welsh Genealogy* (trans. Hon. Soc. of Cymmrodorion, 1948, p. 448) cites the story told by William Jones of Llangollen in the nineteenth century:

> As an example of the old-fashioned habits of Beddgelert in my early days, I may mention the way in which wives and children used to be named. The custom was that the wife never took her husband's family name, but retained the one she had as a spinster. Thus, my grandmother on my mother's side was called Ellen HUGHES, daughter of Hugh Hughes of Gwastad Annas. The name of her husband, my grandfather was William PRICHARD, son of Richard WILLIAM, of the Efail Newydd. The name of their eldest son, my uncle (brother to my mother) was Hugh HUGHES and the second son's name was Richard WILLIAMS. The mother had the privilege of naming her first born after her own family, in case it was a boy; but if it happened to be a girl, she took her name from the father's family, for which reason my mother's maiden name was Catherine WILLIAMS. This remained her name to the day of her death, and the old people of Beddgelert persisted in calling me, so long as I was at home, William PRICHARD, after my grandfather, as I was my mother's eldest child.

Moving around

People did move around to a degree. There was seasonal work, and times when mills, mines or new factories opened up or closed. Miners and weavers in particular moved around the country. There was a great deal of migration in the nineteenth century – from the pastoral north of Wales to the industrial south, and to the cities of England, as well as transportation and, after that, mass emigration to the USA, Canada, South America, Australia, southern Africa (then Rhodesia, Transvaal, Orange Free State etc.), New Zealand and elsewhere. Many went to work in India, or joined the armed services and moved abroad.

The Irish moved into Wales to find work (and often hostility, see p. 82) in the southern counties. For this reason, if no other, a genealogist might have to delve into English or Irish records, or even into the murky waters of ships' passenger lists, immigration records, and overseas census and death records (Chapter 9).

Young, unmarried women were often in domestic service and living with their employers rather than their families, while young, unmarried agricultural labourers would frequently live in a communal dormitory or bunkhouse and be counted as part of the farm household on census night. It was not uncommon for assistants in large department stores to live on the premises, or together in accommodation provided by their employer.

A sailor may have been at sea on the census night – both the Royal Navy and Merchant Service lists will appear under 'shipping' rather than a county – or in dock elsewhere in a Welsh, Scottish or English port, in which case he would be recorded at the ship's address.

Medical staff working in hospitals, prison wardens, policemen, factory night-shift workers and others would be recorded at those institutions instead of their home addresses. The same is true of schoolchildren, if at boarding school, and university students.

People who were not where they 'should' be on a particular census night – working away from home, visiting friends, staying at an hotel – were collectively known as 'Census Strays'. There are websites and other resources dedicated to identifying these, such as the 1901 Carmarthenshire Census Strays Index, available from http://carmarthenshire-online.info/carmarthenshirefhs/.

Just for fun (and interest), there is a list of Wigtownshire (Scotland) strays in the 1861 Welsh census at: http://archiver.rootsweb.ancestry.com/th/read/SCT-WIGTOW NSHIRE/2005-07/1122751348. A list like this can readily be generated by manipulating the 'Birth' and 'Residence' search criteria in any of the finding aids, such as Ancestry, FamilySearch or especially Origins.net, which makes a virtue of this particular aspect of census searching (for example, www.origins.net/help/helpio-census1871.aspx).

Finding Census Records
The census is available in various forms – on the web, as microfilm, on CD-ROM and in print.

Online
The most convenient source of census information is via the web. Officially, TNA, Kew, London, is where all census forms are held, so visit there first, especially as there are useful guides to help you understand the censuses (www.nationalarchives.gov.uk/records/census-records.htm). However, the censuses are not available online there, as TNA partnered with Ancestry (www.ancestry.co.uk or www.ancestry.com) for the 1841–91 records; with www.1901censusonline.com for 1901; and with another arm of the same organisation, FindMyPast, for 1911 (www.1911census.co.uk and www.findmypast.com). However, certain of these sites do have all census years 1841–1911, so anyone with a subscription to one or other will find this most convenient. Bear in mind that for 1911 only the summary books (as shown in Chapter 5) exist. The most convenient website is Ancestry, where complete books can be browsed, as well as searched. These sites have a variety of subscription and pay-as-you-go options, plus deals, which change at times, so do check.

FreeCEN
FreeCen (freecen.rootsweb.com) is part of the larger FreeUKGEN project, which aims, in time, to have all registration data and other primary (or near-primary) records of genealogical relevance available free online. There are equivalent FreeBMD (civil registrations of births, marriages and deaths) and FreeREG (church records) projects, all transcribed by a network of over 2,000 volunteers worldwide.

Their work is incomplete, as the table below (correct in 2012) shows, so check at www.freecen. org.uk/statistics.html for the latest status.

County	Status	County	Status
Anglesey	1861, 1871, 1891	Flintshire	1861, 1871, 1891
Caernarvonshire	1861, 1871, 1891	Glamorganshire	1871, 1891
Cardiganshire	1891	Merionethshire	1871, 1891
Carmarthenshire	1871	Monmouthshire	1871, 1891
Denbighshire	1861, 1871, 1891	Montgomeryshire	(Parts only) 1861, 1891

FamilySearch.org

The reason the year 1881 is conspicuous by its absence from FreeCEN (above) is that this has been fully transcribed by the LDS Church (Mormons) for the website FamilySearch (www. familysearch.org), and is also available as a CD. The website, which is free to use, now has all censuses, with a full transcript and, in some cases, with images or links to where these can be found (FindMyPast, for example, where the information will then have to be paid for). Sadly, for reasons best known to FamilySearch itself, and against the wishes of almost every genealogist asked, the old 'classic' search system has been abandoned in favour of a new one considered to be 'user-friendly', which has destroyed much of the functionality.

However, it is possible to search for, say, Ebenezer Griffiths, residence Wales, dates 1841–1911, birth, from 1828–30 ('Exact result only'), which produces fifty-seven results. These can then be filtered by 'Collections (Census & Lists)'. A search for 'Residence 1911–1911' (i.e. one census year) produced seventeen Ebenezer Griffiths results.

It is also possible to see the images by appointment at a family history centre (see p. 53).

Microform

Census images are available as microfilm or microfiche at various places, chiefly local libraries, family history society premises and LDS family history centres. Bear in mind that local facilities may only have census data for that parish, area or county, and perhaps those adjoining. These films and fiches cannot be searched by name, only by place, so the best first step is to identify the individuals in question through an Internet search or other index (see below), then use the GRO data (folio and piece no.) to identify the correct reel for that parish, enumeration district and page.

Using the 1881 Census Index on microfiche

There are four parts to the fiche version.

People Index – individuals listed in alphabetical order by surname, given name and age, plus other details including relationship to 'Head of Household'.

Birthplace Index – people in alphabetical order by surname and birthplace, for example, everyone called Jones born in Llangefni, Anglesey, will be grouped together, regardless of whether they are related. This index does not contain all the other census information.

Census Place Index – individuals in alphabetical order by surname and census place, for example, all Edwards recorded in Beguildy, Radnorshire, will be grouped together, regardless of relationship. Again not all enumerators' information is in this index.

Enumerators List – places and individuals in the order in which they appear on the census. Use the reference numbers from the other indexes to find the page. This shows complete households, not just family members.

Printed and CD versions

Local family history societies often have census indexes and street indexes available for purchase as printed booklets, parish by parish, and sometimes as whole counties on CD-ROM. Again, the FFHS, AFHSW or a local Family History Society may have these for sale. They are usually available at the many family history fairs up and down the country, and for sale online. LDS family history centres and local libraries may have these booklets or CDs available for consultation free of charge. There are also commercial companies who produce census records on CD, and as good a place as any to start is S&N Genealogy Supplies at www.genealogysupplies.com, although the local FHS may also have these.

Census headers

At the beginning of each census book is a description of the district concerned. This can be helpful in deciphering the names of streets or finding the position of addresses that have disappeared in the years since. On microfilm, check the creation of each district. On Ancestry, when in an image, click on 'District' in the top bar then 'View description of enumeration district' to produce a description of the district, list of streets covered and so on.

Other 'Censuses'

Marriage Tax

In 1695 the Marriage Duties Act or 'Marriage Tax' was introduced on births, marriages, burials, bachelors over 25 and childless widows in England and Wales. It only lasted ten years but it meant that parishes or townships had to make lists of inhabitants liable to pay tax. A small number of these lists have survived in county, borough, parish and some private archives.

See Chapter 7 for more on parish records and Chapter 10 for hearth tax and poll tax lists.

Ecclesiastical censuses

See Chapter 7, Parish Registers Pre-1837.

Scottish censuses

These are naturally very similar to other UK censuses. They are available as full images (pay-per-view) at the official website ScotlandsPeople (www.scotlandspeople.gov.uk), as partial transcripts and

Header page for the enumeration district. Crown Copyright (courtesy of The National Archives)

images at www.ancestry.co.uk or www.ancestry.com for 1841 to 1891, and elsewhere as transcripts only. FreeCen (http://freecen.rootsweb.com) has transcribed some of the censuses.

Most local and large municipal libraries in Scotland have microfilm or microfiche copies of the census returns for their areas, as do the LDS family history centres. In addition, IGI and FamilySearch have the 1881 census.

Irish censuses

Remember that until 1922 Ireland was one country, and part of the United Kingdom. Therefore, do not necessarily expect records relating to the (present-day) Northern Ireland to be in Belfast or Republic records to be in Dublin.

The census started in Ireland in 1821. That sounds like good news, but almost all nineteenth-century census returns were either pulped for paper during the First World War (1861, 1871, 1881 and 1891) or destroyed during the 1922 Civil War (1821, 1831, 1841 and 1851). However, a few census fragments and surname indexes exist for some areas, chiefly Co. Fermanagh for 1821, Co. Londonderry for 1831 and Co. Antrim for 1851. The 1901 and 1911 censuses can be seen at the National Archives of Ireland in Dublin and online at www.census.nationalarchives.ie. The normal 100-year rule for census availability has been relaxed, because only 1901 and 1911 are intact, and these have been made available online. The 1926 census may be released soon – check at http://www.cigo.ie/campaigns_1926.html for updates.

Ireland is unusual in that the original household manuscript returns – the forms filled in by the head of the household – still survive, as well as the enumerators' books. The records are organised by county, district electoral division, and townland or street. Irish censuses are particularly detailed. As well as the usual name, address, occupation, age and other details familiar to anyone looking at Scottish or English censuses, the Irish also recorded religion, the number of years women had been married, the number of their children born alive and the number still living (www.proni.gov.uk).

Old age pension records, which have some of the information from the 1841 and 1851 censuses, are at the Public Record Office, Dublin, and the Public Record Office of Northern Ireland (PRONI) in Belfast.

Welsh registration districts (RDs) for the census years 1841–91

The sub-RDs do not appear in all years, as in 1841 each county was an RD in its own right.

However, it is possible to determine piece numbers and so on at the National Archives online catalogue (www.nationalarchives.gov.uk/catalogue/search.asp).

EITHER: Enter the series code and the piece number. For example, if looking for Penboyr, Carmarthenshire, in the 1881 census, type *Penboyr* in the 'Word or phrase' search box and *RG 11* in 'Department or Series code'. This will return the information shown, and clicking on 'Civil Parish, Township or Place: Penboyr (Carm)' will produce the result below. This tells us that Penboyr is in RD 602 Newcastle-in-Emlyn, and can be found as piece no. 5430.

Likewise, typing RG 11/5430 in the upper-left search box will produce a list of all the places in that piece.

The year codes for England and Wales censuses are: 1841 – HO107; 1851 – HO107; 1861 – RG9; 1871 – RG10; 1881 – RG11; 1891 – RG12; 1901 – RG13; 1911 – RG14 (HO = Home Office; RG = Registrar General).

Thus (from the table below), somewhere in Bryngwran, Anglesey, in the 1901 census would be in series RG12/5295, RG12/5296 or RG12/5297; this can be refined as above.

Crown Copyright (courtesy of The National Archives)

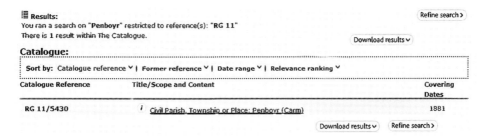

Crown Copyright (courtesy of The National Archives)

Item reference RG 11/5430

Civil Parish, Township or Place: Penboyr (Carm)

Jump to : Summary | Access   ‹ Back to search results   Browse from here ›

Ordering and viewing options ›

Context

RG Records of the General Register Office, Government Social Survey Department, and Office of Population Censuses and Surveys
▸ **RG 11** General Register Office: 1881 Census Returns
  ▸ CARDIGANSHIRE
    ▸ Registration District 602.NEWCASTLE IN EMYLN
      ▸ **RG 11/5430** Description available at other catalogue level

^ Top of page

Record Summary

Scope and content	Civil Parish, Township or Place: Penboyr (Carm)
Covering dates	1881
Held by	The National Archives, Kew
Legal status	Public Record(s)

Crown Copyright (courtesy of The National Archives)

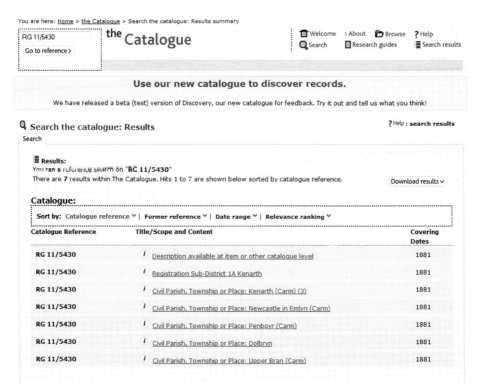

Crown Copyright (courtesy of The National Archives)

Registration districts and sub-RDs

	1841	1851	1861	1871	1881	1891	1901
ANGLESEY	1358–1364	2520–2522	4361–4373	5741–5754	5585–5595	4675–4677	5291–5294
HOLYHEAD (Bryngwran, Holyhead, Llanddeusant)	–	–	–	–	–	4678–4681	5295–5297
BRECONSHIRE or BRECKNOCK	1365–1371	–	–	–	–	–	
BRECKNOCK (Brecknock, Dyfynnock, Llangorse, Pencelly)	–	2489	4208–4214	5576–5582	5456–5461	4568–4572	5167–5170
BUILTH (Abergwessin, Builth, Colwyn, Llanwrtyd)	–	2488	4205–4207	5572–5575	5453–5455	4565–4567	5161–5165
CRICKHOWELL (Beaufort, Crickhowell, Cwmdu, Llanelly)	–	2490	4215–4222	5583–5590	5462–5467	4573–4577	5171–5175
HAY							5177–5178

CAERNARVONSHIRE	1388–1398	–	–	–	–	–	
BANGOR (Bangor, Beaumaris, Llanfairfechan, Llanllechid)	–	2517–2518	4346–4356	5724–5735	5572–5580	4663–4669	5276–5285
CARNARVON (Carnarvon, Llandwrog, Llanidan, Llanrug)	–	2515–2516	4336–4345	5711–5723	5562–5571	4655–4662	5268–5275
CONWAY (Conway, Creuddyn)	–	2519	4357–4360	5736–5740	5581–5584	4670–4674	5286–5290
PWLLHELI (Aberdaron, Criccieth, Nevin, Pwllheli)	–	2513–2514	4328–4335	5702–5710	5555–5561	4650–4654	5262–5290
CARDIGANSHIRE	1372–1378	–	–	–	–	–	
ABERAYRON (Llandsantffraid, Llandysilio)	–	2484	4190–4193	5553–5558	5440–5443	4555–4556	5148–5151
ABERYSTWTH (Aberystwth, Geneurglynn, Llanrhystyd, Rheidol)	–	2485–2486	4194–4200	5559–5567	5444–5449	4557–4561	5152–5156
CARDIGAN (Cardigan, Llandygwydd, Newport)	–	2481	4173–4178	5538–5542	5425–5429	4542–4545	5134–5137
LAMPETER (Lampeter, Llanwenog, Llanybyther, Pencarreg)	–	2483	4186–4189	5549–5552	5436–5439	4551–4554	5143–5147
NEWCASTLE IN EMLYN (Cenarth, Llandyssil, Penbryn)	–	2482	4179–4185	5543–5548	5430–5435	4546–4550	5138–5140
TREGARON (Gwnnws, Llangeitho, Tregaron)	–	2487	4201–4204	5568–5571	5450–5452	4562–4564	5157–5159
CARMARTHENSHIRE	1379–1387	–	–	–	–	–	
CARMARTHEN (Carmarthen, Conwil, Llangendeirne, St Clears)	–	2472–2474	4134–4145	5490–5504	5393–5401	4514–4520	5112–5116
LLANDILOFAWR (Llandebie, Llandilo, Llanfynydd, Llangathen, Talley)	–	2471	4127–4133	5482–5489	5387–5392	4508–4513	5102–5108
LLANDOVERY (Cilycwm, Conwil Caio, Llanddausant, Llandingat, Llanfairarybryn, Llangadock, Llansadwrn)	–	2470	4118–4126	5473–5481	5379–5386	4500–4507	5094–5101

LLANELLY (Llanelly, Llanon, Loughor, Pembrey)	–	2468–2469	4110–4117	5464–5472	5370–5378	4491–4499	5086–5093
DENBIGHSHIRE	1399–1406	–	–	–	–	–	
LLANRWST (Bettws y Coed, Llanrwst, Yspytty)	–	2508	4304–4307	5676–5679	5534–5537	4631–4634	5241–5245
RUTHIN (Gyffylliog, Llanarmon, Llandyrnog, Llanelidan, Llanrhaiadr, Ruthin)	–	2504–2505	4289–4294	5659–5666	5521–5526	4620–4625	5227–5233
ST ASAPH (Abergele, Denbigh, St Asaph)	–	2506–2507	4295–4302	5667–5675	5527–5533	4626–4630	5237–5240
WREXHAM (Holt, Ruabon, Wrexham)	–	2502–2503	4277–4288	5651–5658	5510–5520	4611–4619	5215–5225
FLINTSHIRE	1407–1413	–	–	–	–	–	
HOLYWELL (Flint, Holywell, Mold, Whitford)	–	2500–2501	4266–4276	5636–5650	5500–5509	4603–4610	5207–5214
GLAMORGAN	1414–1426	–	–	–	–	–	
BRIDGEND (Bridgend, Cowbridge, Maesteg, Ogmore)	–	2461	4072–4079	5412–5422	5326–5333	4449–4456	5040–5051
CAIFF (Central Cardiff, East Cardiff, Llandaff, Penarth, St Nicholas, West Cardiff)	–	2454–2456	4028–4044	5354–5373	5275–5292	4384–4408	4984–4996
GOWER (Gower Eastern, Gower Western)	–	–	4108–4109	5460–5463	5367–5369	4488–4490	5083–5085
MERTHYR TYDFIL (Aberdare, Gelligaer, Lower Merthyr Tydfil, Upper Merthyr Tydfil)	–	2457–2460	4045–4071	5387–5411	5307–5325	4431–4448	5021–5032
NEATH (Cadoxton, Margam, Neath, Ystradvellte)	–	2462–2464	4080–4094	5423–5441	5334–5345	4457–4466	5052–5062
PONTAAWE	–	–	–	–	5346–5349	4467–4469	5063–5066
PONTYPRIDD (Eglwysilan, Llantrisant, Llanwonno, Ystradyfodwg)	–	–	–	5374–5386	5293–5306	4409–4430	4997–5020
SWANSEA (Llandilo Talybont, Llangafelach, Llansamlet, Swansea)	–	2465–2467	4095–4107	5442–5459	5350–5366	4470–4487	5067–5082

MERIONETHSHIRE	1427–1432	–	–	–	–	–	
BALA	–	2510	4314–4316	5685–5687	5542–5543	4639–4640	5250–5251
CORWEN (Corwen, Llangollen)	–	2509	4308–4313	5680–5684	5538–5541	4635–4638	5246–5249
DOLGELLY (Barmouth, Talyllyn)	–	2511	4317–4321	5688–5693	5544–5547	4641–4643	5252–5253
FESTINIOG (Deudraeth, Festiniog, Tremadoc)	–	2512	4322–4327	5694–5701	5548–5554	4644–4649	5257–5261
MONMOUTHSHIRE	742–752	–	–	–	–	–	
ABERGAVENNY (Blaenavon, Llanarth, Llanvihangel)	–	2446–2448	3991–3996	5307–5314	5232–5238	4345–4350	4927–4932
BEDWELLTY (Aberystruth, Rock Bedwellty, Tredegar)	–	–	3997–4006	5315–5330	5239–5249	4351–4360	4933–4943
CHEPSTOW (Chepstow, Lydney)	–	2443	3974–3979	5292–5297	5217–5222	4335–4337	4915–4919
MONMOUTH (Coleford, Monmouth, Trelleck)	–	2444–2445	3980–3990	5298–5306	5223–5231	4338–4344	4920–4926
NEWPORT (Caerleon, Llantarnam, Mynyddislwyn, Newport, Rogerstone)	–	2451–2453	4013–4027	5339–5353	5258–5274	4367–4383	4953–4969
PONTYPOOL (Llangibby, Pontypool, Usk)	–	2449–2450	4007–4012	5331–5338	5250–5257	4361–4366	4944–4952
MONTGOMERYSHIRE	1433–1442	–	–	–	–	–	
FORDEN (Chirbury, Montgomery, Welshpool)	–	–	–	5619–5625	5489–5494	4595–4598	5198–5202
LLANFYLLIN (Llanfair, Llanrhaiadr, Llansantffraid)	–	2499	4259–4265	5626–5635	5495–5499	4599–4602	5203–5206
MACHYNLLETH (Darowen, Machynlleth, Towyn)	–	2495	4239–4242	5601–5605	5477–5479	4586–4588	5187–5191
MONTGOMERY (See Forden, above)	–	2498	4253–4258	–	–	–	
NEWTON (Kerry, Llanidloes, Llanwnog, Newtown, Tregynon)	–	2496–2497	4243–4252	5606–5618	5480–5488	4589–4594	5192–5197

PEMBROKESHIRE	1443–1452	–	–	–	–	–	
HAVERFOWEST (Fishguard, Haverfordwest, Milford, St David's)	–	2477–2480	4160–4172	5522–5537	5415–5424	4533–4541	5127–5133
NARBERTH (Begelly, Llanboidy, Narberth)	–	2475	4146–4151	5505–5511	5402–5407	4521–4526	5117–5119
PEMBROKE (Pembroke, Roose, Tenby)	–	2476	4152–4159	5512–5521	5408–5414	4527–4532	5120–5126

	1841	1851	1861	1871	1881	1891	1901
RADNORSHIRE	1453–1459	–	–	–	–	–	
KNIGHTON (Knighton, Llanbister, Presteigne)	–	2493	4233–4236	5595–5598	5471–5474	4581–4583	5181–5183
Presteigne	–	2492	4227–4232	5594	–	–	5179–5180
RHAYADER (Nantmel, Rhayader)	–	2494	4237–4238	5599–5600	5475–5476	4584–4585	5184–5184

Missing census books

Based partly on Ted Hackett, 'The Incomplete Census', *Dyfed Family History Journal*, vol. 10, pp. 33–36 (see p. 80).

1841

County	Parish	Place/Township
Breconshire	Vaynor (Y Faenor)	Cefn Coed y Cymmer, Dyffrin, Gelli, Vaynor (Y Faenor)
Denbighshire	Bangor is y Coed	Eyton, Pickhill, Royton, Sesswick
	Clocaenog	Clocaenog, Clocaenog Isa, Clocaenog Ucha
	Derwen	Derwen, Derwen Dyfanedd, Derwen Ysgeifiog
	Erbistock	Erbistock
	Gresford	Allington, Borras Riffri, Burton, Erddig, Erlas, Gresford, Gwersyllt, Llay (Llai)
	Holt	Caca Dutton, Dutton Diffeth, Dutton y Bran, Holt, Isycoed, Ridley, Sutton
	Llanarmon yn Iâl	Alltgymbyd, Banhadlen, Bodidris, Bodigre'r Abbot, Bodigre'r Iarl, Chwileiriog, Creigiog is Glan, Creigiog uwch Glan, Cyfnant, Eryrys, Gelligynan, Gwaunyffynnon, Llanarmon yn Iâl
	Llanelidan	Bodlywydd, Bryncyme, Garthneuoedd, Nantclwyd
	Llanfair Dyffryn Clwyd	Derwen Llanerch, Euarth, Faynol, Garthgynan
	Marchwiel	Marchwiel, Sontley

	Nantglyn	Blaenau, Cwmllwm, Gwmllwm, Hendre, Hendre, Waun, Nantglyn, Plas
	Ruabon	Belan, Bodylltyn, Coed Cristionydd, Cristionydd Cynrig/Kenrick, Dinhinlle Isaf, Dinhinlle Uchaf, Hafod, Morton Above, Morton Anglicorum, Morton Below, Rhos y Medic, Rhyddallt, Ruabon
	Wrexham	Abenbury Fawr, Acton, Bersham, Bieston, Borras Hwfa, Broughton, Brymbo, Esclusham Above, Esclusham Below, Gorton, Minera, Stansty, Wrexham★, Wrexham Abbot★, Wrexham Regis★ ★Available on CD from the Clwyd Family History Society (www.clwydfhs.org.uk).
Flintshire	Bangor is y Coed	Bangor is y Coed
	Erbistock	Erbistock
	Gresford	Marford and Hoseley
	Hope	Caergwrle, Cymau, Estyn, Rhanberfedd, Shordley, Uwch y Mynydd Isaf, Uwch y Mynydd Uchaf
	Mold	Tryddyn (Treuddyn)
	Threapwood	Threapwood
	Worthenbury	Worthenbury
	Wrexham	Abenbury Fechan
Glamorgan	Cowbridge	Cowbridge
	Llanblethian	Aberthin, Treinghill
	Merthyr Tydfil	Dowlais or Merthyr Tydfil (Upper)
Montgomeryshire	Castle Caereinion	Trehelig

1851
None [missing]

1861

County	Parish	Place/Township
Caernarvonshire	Denio	Denio, Pwllheli
Cardiganshire	Aberporth	Aberporth Llanannerch, Aberporth Rectorial, Rectorial
	Caron ys Clawdd	Berwyn
	Cellan	Blaen Caron, Caron ys Clawdd, Croes and Berwyn, Cellan
	Llanbadarn Fawr	Broncastellan, Clarch, Uchaf yn Dre, Upper Vaynor
Carmarthenshire	Pencarreg	Coedmore, Pencarreg
	St Clears	St Clears

Denbighshire	Abergele	Brynffanigl, Garthgogo, Nant
	Betws Abergele/ Bettws Yn Rhos	Tai, Betws Abergele, Beniarth, Bodlyman, Cilcen, Maesegwig, Peniarth, Tre'r Llan, Trofarth
	Bryneglwys	Bodynwyddog, Bryneglwys, Bryntangor, Gwythina, Talybidwal
	Denbigh	Denbigh
	Derwen	Derwen, Derwen Dyfanedd, Derwen Ysgeifiog
	Efenechtyd	Efenechtyd
	Llangwm	Disgarth
	Llanarmon Dyffryn Ceiriog	Lloran, Llowarch
	Llanarmon Mynydd Mawr	Llanarmon Mynydd Mawr
	Llanddulas	Llanddulas
	Llanefydd	Berain, Carwedfynydd, Talybryn
	Llanelian yn Rhos	Twynnan (or Dolwen)
	Llanelidan	Bryncume, Garthneuoedd, Llanelidan, Nantclwyd, Trewyn Bodlowydd
	Llanfair Dyffryn Clwyd	Derwen Llannerch, Euarth, Faynol
	Llanfair Talhaearn	Barog, Cynnant, Prysllygoed, Talhaearn
	Llanfihangel Glyn Myfyr	Cysilog, Llanfihangel Glyn Myfyr, Llys Dinmael, Llysan, Maes yr Odyn
	Llangollen	Crogen Wladus, Cysylltau, Llangollen Abad, Llangollen Fawr, Llangollen Fechan, Nantygwryd, Pengwern, Rhisgog, Vivod (Feifod)
	Llangwm	Cefn Cymer, Penyfed
	Llannefydd	Bodysgaw, Brisgill, Bryneaubychain, Dinas Cadfel, Llannefydd, Myfoniog, Pen y Gribin Bach, Penfron Chill, Penporchell, Pentre Isaf, Sychnant, Ty Newydd
	Llanrwst	Garthgyfannedd, Tybrith Uchaf
	Llansanffraid Glyn Ceiriog	Glyn Fechan
	Llantysilio	Cymo, Llandynnan
	St George	Dinorben, Meifod, St George
Flintshire	Cilcain/Cilcen	Cefn, Cilcain, Tre Llan, Trellyniau
	Dyserth	Dyserth
Glamorgan	Llandyfodog	Blackmill, Pant y Rid
	Machen	Rhydgwern
	Welsh St Donats	Welsh St Donats
Merionethshire	Beddgelert	Nantmor
	Llanfihangel Glyn Myfyr	Cefnpost

Monmouthshire	Bettws	Bettws
	Magor	Redwick
	Tredynog	Tredynog (Tredunnock)
	Whitson	Whitson
Pembrokeshire	Yerbeston	Yerbeston

1871

County	Parish	Place/Township
Glamorgan	Nicholaston	Manselfield (Mansel), Nicholaston
	Port Eynon	Overton
	Oxwich	Oxwich
	Penmaen	Paviland, Penmaen
	Penrice	Penrice, Pilton Green
	Port Eynon	Port Eynon
	Reynoldston	Reynoldston

1881

None [missing]

1891

County	Parish	Place/Township
Glamorgan	Dowlais	Merthyr Tydfil – part of Dowlais

1901

None [missing]

Further reading

Books

Peter Christian and David Annal, *Census: The Expert Guide* (TNA, 2008).

Jeremy Gibson and Elizabeth Hampson, *Marriage and Census Indexes for Family Historians*, 8th edn (Bury: Federation of Family History Societies, 2000).

——, *Census Returns 1841–1881 in Microform: A Directory to Local Holdings in Great Britain; Channel Islands; Isle of Man*, 6th edn (Bury: Federation of Family History Societies, 2001).

Jeremy Gibson and Mervyn Medlycott, *Local Census Listings, 1522–1930: Holdings in the British Isles*, 3rd edn (Bury: Federation of Family History Societies, 2001).

Edward Higgs, *A Clearer Sense of the Census, the Victorian Censuses and Historical Research*, Public Record Office Handbooks, No. 28 (London: HMSO, 1996).

Dennis Mills and Kevin Schurer (eds), *Local Communities in the Victorian Census Enumerators' Books* (Oxford: Leopard's Head Press, 1996).

Geoff Riggs, *Distribution of Surnames in the 1881 British Census* (London: Guild of One-Name Studies, 2001).

Using Census Returns (Richmond: Public Record Office, 2000).

Tom Wood, *An Introduction to British Civil Registration*, 2nd edn (Bury: Federation of Family History Societies, 2000).

Online resources

Always start with GENUKI for hints, tips and places to find more information – www.genuki. org.uk/big/wal/

Also consult www.genuki.org.uk/big/Census.html

1901 Census Online – www.1901censusonline.com

Ancestry – www.ancestry.com or www.ancestry.co.uk

Census finder – www.censusfinder.com/wales.htm

Census info – www.histpop.org

FamilySearch – www.familysearch.org

FindMyPast – www.1911census.co.uk and www.findmypast.com

FreeCen – http://freecen.rootsweb.com and www.freecen.org.uk

Origins.net – www.origins.net

S&N Genealogy Supplies – www.genealogysupplies.com

The National Archives (TNA, Kew, London) – www.nationalarchives.gov.uk/records/ census-records.htm

UK Census Online – www.ukcensusonline.com

UKBMD – www.ukbmd.org.uk

Vision of Britain – www.visionofbritain.org.uk

6

Statutory Registers of Birth, Marriage and Death Post-1855 1837!

In 1837 the formal civil registration of births, marriages and deaths (BMD) began in England and Wales. Scotland followed some eighteen years later, with the Registration of Births, Deaths and Marriages (Scotland) Act 1854. This took over from the voluntary registration system operated by the church, which was interested in baptisms (not usually births), proclamations of marriage (and sometimes marriages themselves) and records of burials or mort-cloth records (occasionally deaths). These were recorded in parish registers, also known as the old parish registers (OPR) – see Chapter 7.

Statutory registration (SR) was the province of the newly formed General Register Office (GRO) and a network of local registrars, under a Registrar General. In Scotland, the equivalent body (GROS) also took in the OPRs up to 1819, while those from 1820 to 1854 were given over to the local registrars, but sent to GROS thirty years later. Thus, GROS has control of all BMD records back to the beginning of the Church of Scotland in 1563 or thereabouts. The earliest parish record available is for Errol, Perthshire, in 1553, but this is exceptional.

In England, OPRs – and derivative records called bishops' transcripts – have largely have remained with local and county archives (Chapter 4). These records are by no means perfect, so it can be difficult to trace family history back beyond this unless the family concerned already had a well-documented pedigree, was connected to the church, nobility or royalty, or owned land.

A similar system of civil registration was started in Ireland in 1845 for non-Roman Catholic marriages, and for all births, marriages and deaths since 1864. This was an outgrowth of the Irish public health system, which was in turn based on the poor relief for the destitute, using the areas covered by the Poor Law Unions. For that reason, the responsibility for registration in the Republic of Ireland is still with the Department of Health. Local health boards have the original registers and the General Register Office of Ireland (GROI, 8–11 Lombard St, Dublin) has the master indexes to all thirty-two counties up to 1921, and to the twenty-six counties of the Republic from then on. For Northern Ireland, the indexes and registers from 1921 and after are at Oxford House, Chichester St, Belfast. Originally, local registrars forwarded records to Dublin for copying, after which they were returned. GROI has microfilms of the copy registers as well as the master indexes. The registers can be consulted at the offices of the local registrars (at their discretion). Some of the local heritage centres have transcripts on databases. The Latter-Day Saints have copies of almost all GROI indexes and registers, accessible at LDS family history centres, and the indexes of some of these (primarily birth registrations from 1864 to 1875 inclusive) are in the IGI – searchable online at www.familysearch.org – and on the LDS British Isles Vital Records CDs. The often-repeated story that most of the records were lost when the Four Courts in Dublin were destroyed during the events of 1922 is simply untrue – it was mainly censuses, wills and some church records. Statutory BMD records were not involved.

BMD Registration After 1837

The introduction of the register of births, marriages and deaths was effected by the 1837 Births, Marriages and Deaths Act (passed a month after Victoria took the throne, so signing this into law was almost her first action as queen). This law provided that after 1 July that year all such records had to be kept centrally, regardless of whether the ceremony took place in a church, chapel or registry office. These were compiled into quarterly indexes from Q3 (Jul-Aug-Sep) 1837, and annually after 1984. The quarters are often referred to by the last month of each, such as Q3 (September).

These can be consulted in print, on microfiche and (in the main) online. However, much to the annoyance of English and Welsh researchers, there is no access to images of the actual registers, as there is in Scotland. The only route is to take a stab at the likely B, M or D event and order up a certified copy of a particular entry, which comes by post as a certificate, and at considerable cost. This process is explored later in the chapter.

There was an attempt to digitise the registers a few years ago (a project called DOVE – Digitisation Of Vital Events – started in 2003) but, among a great deal of recrimination, backsliding and shifts of position within GRO and the other government bodies involved, it was unsuccessful. A more recent effort by petition to the prime minister's office to get this decision reversed, and to have the records from 1837 to 1908 digitised and online in some form, produced the following reply in 2009:

> The Government understands that many family researchers want to have full and open access to the information in historic birth, death and marriage registers and accepts that the current legislation is overly restrictive with these records.
>
> Under current legislation – the Births and Deaths Registration Act 1953 and the Marriage Act 1949 – access to the information in birth, death and marriage registers is only possible by means of a certified copy (certificate) of a particular entry, when that entry has been identified from the index and the statutory fee paid. There are other pieces of legislation which allow for the release of information in birth, death and marriage registers for specific purposes, e.g. statistical data, but there is no power to provide full and open public access.
>
> The Government proposed in 2003 a wide-ranging set of reforms to the civil registration service in England and Wales. These proposals included an intention to digitise all the records with historic records being accessible to view on a database, possibly with a small charge, but without the need to purchase a certificate. It did not prove possible to introduce the necessary legislation by a Regulatory Reform Order as we had intended and there has not been a suitable opportunity to legislate since then. Nevertheless, we remain committed to modernising the way in which these records can be accessed and the Registrar General keeps this under active review.

In other words, it's unlikely this will happen any time soon.

Registration Districts (RDs)

There is a list of Welsh RDs in Chapter 4 and it would be worth re-reading the information on censuses (Chapter 5) to see how this worked. The same RDs are used for BMD. However, do not assume, if working forwards in time, that an RD and a parish have the same name. As most research will be pre-1911 (the latest censuses that can be seen) or pre-1920 (availability of most BMD indexes), later administrative changes to local government in Wales (Chapter 4) won't matter much.

At times, RDs were merged or given new names. This can make life difficult for historians, as it may look like whole families moved about through the years, while in fact they may have stayed put as the RD boundaries changed around them. There is a useful parish locator programme, ParLoc, available as downloadable freeware (www.dmbceb.me.uk).

Using BMD indexes from 1837

The best way to understand the complexities of this is to follow a real example. This follows on from the search for Frederick Ebenezer Griffiths, which started with the census (Chapter 5). From census information, Frederick Ebenezer Griffiths was born in or near Bedwellty around 1879.

Births

A search at Ancestry (www.ancestry.co.uk) produced this result:

England & Wales, FreeBMD Birth Index, 1837-1915 about **Frederick Ebenezer Griffiths**

Name:	**Frederick** Ebenezer **Griffiths**
Date of Registration:	Jul-Aug-Sep 1879
Registration district:	Bedwellty
Inferred County:	Monmouthshire
Volume:	11a
Page:	104

(Bedwellty is about 6 miles due south of Tredegar and both are now in Blaenau Gwent, but were in Monmouthshire at this time.)

The relevant index page (part of) is:

(The relevant entry is highlighted here, not in the original.)

This doesn't actually give us any more information than the transcript above it – his birth was registered in the RD of Bedwellty in Q3 (Jul-Aug-Sep) 1879, vol 11a, p. 104. There is no actual birth date, no parents' names, no address. So this is not much help, except for the fact that he is the only Frederick Ebenezer (or Frederick E.) Griffiths who fits the information we have.

This search was in the FreeBMD Birth Index, 1837–1915. For the sake of completeness the search should have been extended to include England and Wales, birth, marriage and death indexes, 1916–2005. In this case, there were no other births for that name and date. There were, however, sixty-four other births during the period 1878–80 where the name contained 'Frederick Griffiths' (such as George Frederick Griffiths); eleven of these were in Wales and one of these was in Monmouthshire (Newport, in this case, and Q4 1880). It is only because we are confident about the birth in Bedwellty that we can exclude the other individual at this point – but remember that if the birth date/place turns out to be a red herring, we may have to revisit the other possible Frederick Griffiths.

Ancestry is a subscription/pay-as-you-go service, and there are others (see *Further reading*), but they will all lead to the same index page image as above, and provide no extra information. The Ancestry database is actually taken from FreeBMD (www.freebmd.org.uk) for dates up to 1983. A search there provides exactly the same result, but at no cost whatsoever. In this case, searching for Frederick E.★ Griffiths (notice the 'wild card' ★), between Mar (that is, Q1) 1878 and Dec (Q4) 1880, a two-year span, and in all counties of England and Wales, gives the following results:

Birth	Surname	First name(s)	District	Vol	Page
Sep 1878	Griffiths	Frederick Edgar	Stourbridge	6c	206
Jun 1879	Griffiths	Frederick Ernest	Chorlton	8c	749
Sep 1879	Griffiths	Frederick Ebenezer	Bedwelty	11a	104

Only one is in Wales – but notice the spelling of Bedwel(l)ty. There is a link on the web page that shows the index page image in each case, downloadable in a variety of formats (gif, jpeg, tiff, pdf), but these are identical to the example shown above.

Marriages
A similar search showed no marriages (or deaths) for Frederick Ebenezer Griffiths b. *c.* 1879 in Wales, which means either:

- he never married (possible) and he died after 2005 (so he would be about 126!);
- he went elsewhere between the 1901 and 1911 censuses (including Scotland and Ireland, but also overseas);
- he didn't get married under that name (it could been just Frederick, depending on how punctilious the registrar or minister was, and what his actual birth certificate said).

We could possibly exclude 1, 2, 9, 17 and 19 in the table below on the grounds of middle name(s), but transcriptional errors are not unknown. For the same reason, it would be sensible to check for variants such a Fred/Frederik, Ebenezer/Ebeneezer/Inenezer, Griffith/Grifiths/Griffeiths and so on.

However, here is what came back from this fairly straightforward search:

	Marriage	Surname	First name(s)		District	Vol	Page	
1	Dec 1902	Griffiths	Frederick Ernest		Chorlton	8c	1195	
2	Mar 1903	Griffiths	Frederick Edgar		King's N.	6c	529	
3	Dec 1910	Griffiths	Frederick E		Shoreditch	1c	242	
4	Dec 1919	Griffiths	Frederick E	Hughes	Llanelly	11a	2874	(Wales)
5	Sep 1922	Griffiths	Frederick E	Frake	Yeovil	5c	810	
6	Jun 1926	Griffiths	Frederick E	Radford	Axbridge	5c	1064	
7	Sep 1927	Griffiths	Frederick E	Haggett	Cardiff	11a	1065	(Wales)
8	Sep 1928	Griffiths	Frederick E	Dethloff	Wrexham	11b	417	(Wales)
9	Dec 1929	Griffiths	Frederick E C	James	Wandsworth	1d	901	
10	Jun 1930	Griffiths	Frederick E	Willard	Wandsworth	1d	1276	
11	Sep 1932	Griffiths	Frederick E	Harrison	Birmingham N.	6d	1372	
12	Jun 1936	Griffiths	Frederick E	Sylvester	Barnsley	9c	639	
13	Jun 1938	Griffiths	Frederick E	McDermott	Birmingham	6d	968	
14	Sep 1938	Griffiths	Frederick E	Alnwick	Gateshead	10a	2105	
15	Mar 1940	Griffiths	Frederick E	Cave	Mt. Harbro'	7a	79	
16	Sep 1941	Griffiths	Frederick E	Barrell	Colchester	4a	2820	
17	Mar 1943	Griffiths	Frederick E D	Lee	Liverpool S.	8b	95	
18	Sep 1943	Griffiths	Frederick E	Lewis	Holywell	11b	278	(Wales)
19	Jun 1959	Griffiths	Frederick E F	WILLIS	Edmonton	5e	680	

There are nineteen results for marriages of Frederick and Frederick E.★ Griffiths (from 1919, with the spouse's surname) to as late as 1959. None has age, place of birth, names of parents or any other information – such information could only be checked by:

1. cross-referencing these individuals with census, birth and death records (a laborious but sometimes necessary task);
2. ordering the actual certificates from GRO (expensive but often necessary).

In the event, as we'll see, there is no need to in this case, but we are not to know that at this stage.

Only four of the marriages found are in Wales, but there is no reason to assume that's where Frederick would have married. One of these results might be him.

Deaths

A similar search was made for deaths post-Q1 1901 and pre-Q4 1983. We know he was in the 1901 census and not in the 1911, so why search after 1911? Because he could have been temporarily away and not counted, but have returned later. However, these gave a similar result – nothing terribly convincing. Because age at death was recorded, it was possible to exclude any not b. c. 1879; however, this search would have been easier using Ancestry, as it includes the year of birth as one of the search criteria. Using FreeBMD, the results had to be inspected for anyone aged, say, around 60 in 1939 and the years of birth added manually. Also, middle names are never expanded in the death indexes, so there was no point searching for 'Frederick Ebenezer', as this would necessarily have given a null result.

Death Year	Surname	First name(s)	Age	District	Vol	Page	Birth Year
1902	Griffiths	Frederick	23	Lambeth	1d	211	1879
1910	Griffiths	Frederick W	31	Reading	2a	176	1879
1918	Griffiths	Frederick	39	Stoke T.	6b	209	1879
1934	Griffiths	Frederick P	55	W. Derby	8b	392	1879
1936	Griffiths	Frederick C	57	Medway	2a	1019	1879
1942	Griffiths	Frederick E	63	Chesterfield	7b	924	1879
1943	Griffiths	Frederick H	64	Liverpool S.	8b	98	1879
1944	Griffiths	Frederick	65	Brentford	3a	331	1879
1948	Griffiths	Frederick R	69	Rowley R.	9b	217	1879
1949	Griffiths	Frederick	70	Bury	10b	968	1879
1949	Griffiths	Frederick J	70	Gloucester C.	7b	407	1879
1950	Griffiths	Frederick E	71	Birmingham	9c	236	1879
1958	Griffiths	Frederick	79	Prescot	10f	325	1879
1942	Griffiths	Frederick	62	Prescot	8b	504	1880
1949	Griffiths	Frederick	69	Shrewsbury	9a	273	1880
1951	Griffiths	Frederick L	71	Cheltenham	7b	321	1880
1957	Griffiths	Frederick	77	Shrewsbury	9a	222	1880
1959	Griffiths	Frederick	79	W. Cheshire	10a	912	1880

We could probably discount Frederick W. and so on if another initial is given. None of these is in Wales, but Frederick E. (or any of the other Fredericks with no middle initial) could be 'our' Frederick Ebenezer, now living, or at least dying, in Liverpool, Birmingham, Shrewsbury, Cheltenham or Cheshire (all near Wales), or even further afield in Lambeth or Bury. No reason why not – more investigation is needed, and we haven't even considered Ireland, Scotland or overseas.

Case study – Godfrey J[ames] Griffiths

It's disappointing (although often informative) to have negative results – but it's encouraging to get a proper answer! We were, originally, looking for the ancestry of Frederick Ebenezer Griffiths, and we do know his father was Godfrey J(ames) Griffiths b. *c.* 1856. We may have more luck with him. Using FreeBMD only, and restricting the searches to Godfrey J.,* and to births 1855–57, marriages 1870–80 and deaths 1896–1956 (from the year before the birth of his youngest child to his year of death if 100), but not assuming county, the following emerged.

Birth Mar 1856	GRIFFITHS	Godfrey James		Merthyr Tydfyl	11a	321
Marriage Sep 1876	GRIFFITHS	Godfrey James		Bedwelty	11a	134
Marriage Sep 1889	GRIFFITHS	Godfrey James		Bedwelty	11a	123
Death Jun 1951	GRIFFITHS	Godfrey J	95	Bath	7c	55

This looks very much like 'our' Godfrey – and we were right not to make any assumptions about the county (he died in Bath, Somerset, England) or likely age at death (he was, indeed, almost 100). Note also the two marriages.

Here are the relevant index pages, which are less than informative. To completely confirm this is the correct Godfrey, it would be essential to order the GRO certificates (see below).

Handwritten entries in the 1856 births register.

By 1876 these were typeset.

Notice the later manual addition for an entry missed by the original typist or typesetter in 1889.

GRI

DEATHS REGISTERED IN APRIL, MAY AND JUNE, 1951.

	Age.	District.	Vol.	Page.		Age.	District.	Vol.	Page.
— Sarah									
GRIFFITHS, Abel	73	Maidenhead	6 a	32	— George	94	Hawarden	8 a	502
— Abraham G.	80	Holywell	8 a	529	— George A.	0	Wrexham	8 a	456
— Abraham L.	64	Cardiff	8 b	183	— George W.	49	Marylebone	5 d	314
— Ada	73	Chard	7 c	128	— Gertrude D.	61	Romford	5 a	378
— Ada	56	Bradford	2 b	219	— Glyndur L.	50	Whitehaven	1 a	165
— Ada L.	73	Christchurch	6 b	211	— Godfrey J.	95	Bath	7 c	55
— Adah	75	Runcorn	10 a	452	— Gomer	82	Pontypridd	8 b	455
— Agnes E.	55	Lewisham	5 d	17	— Griffith	55	Leigh	10 d	7
— John	66	Caernarvon	8 a	133	— Francis	72			

Crown Copyright (courtesy of The National Archives)

Is this really the death of 'our' Godfrey James Griffiths? He is the correct age, and we haven't come across any other births or marriages for that name of the right age, but what is he doing in Bath, Somerset? In the 1901 census he was still in Tredegar, Monmouthshire, Wales. We will pick up this particular mystery in later chapters.

There is one more thing we can do from the marriage information. By clicking on the page (in this case 134), we get a list of everyone on that page – although this refers to the page of the original marriage register, not the index, and there are typically only four names – two marriages – on each page.

Marriages Sep 1876				
Surname	**First name(s)**	**District**	**Vol**	**Page**
GRIFFITHS	Godfrey James	Bedwelty	11a	134
HOGAN	Catharine	Bedwelty	11a	134
PUGH	Sarah Emily	Bedwelty	11a	134
WYPER	Peter	Bedwelty	11a	134

Godfrey's wife was thus either Catharine Hogan or Sarah Emily Pugh. We know from the 1881 census that his wife was Sarah, so now we have her full name – Sarah Emily Pugh (a very Welsh surname, and a variant of 'ap Hugh').

Marriages Sep 1889				
Surname	**First name(s)**	**District**	**Vol**	**Page**
BAMFORD	Elizabeth Annie	Bedwelty	11a	123
GRIFFITHS	Godfrey James	Bedwelty	11a	123
PRICE	Jane	Bedwelty	11a	123
WATKINS	William	Bedwelty	11a	123

By also looking at 1889, we have confirmed our surmise from the censuses that his second wife was Elizabeth Annie Bamford. Incidentally, there are a number of deaths recorded for Elizabeth Griffiths b. *c.* 1865 (note – search by married name), and a few around the Merthyr/Bedwellty area, but none in Bath.

Search Tips

In general, it is best to do a 'wide' search first – put in as little information as possible – as anything too restrictive may exclude some possibilities, such as recording or transcriptional errors, variations in name, dates and places.

There are some advantages to using FreeBMD over other BMD search sites:

1. It is free.

2. The records are mostly double-transcribed, and so have a greater likelihood of being correct (poor original handwriting or mistyping by the indexers notwithstanding).

3. The transcribers can be contacted by a link against each entry and there is a separate 'Corrections' link – so we might query the spelling of 'Bedwelty' for example, although that's how it is spelt in the original indexes. The correct Welsh spelling was Bedwellte ('abode of Mellteu').

4. It is possible to use a number of search filters for information that is already known.

5. After Q3 1911, birth indexes come with mother's maiden name included, for example:

52

GRI

BIRTHS REGISTERED IN JANUARY, FEBRUARY AND MARCH, 1944.

	Mother's Maiden Surname.	District.	Vol.	Page.		Mother's Maiden Surname.	District.	Vol.	Page.
Griffiths, Ann L.	Bates	Birmingham	6 d	76	Griffiths, David W.	Cass	I.Wight	2 b	925
— Ann O.	Ewald	Blaby	7 a	46	— David W.	Green	Northwich	8 a	497
— Anne	Holland	Ince	8 c	124	— David W.	Davies	Walsall	6 b	1068
— Annie	Jones	Holywell	11 b	192	— Dean T.	Amesbury	Bridgend	11 a	1022
— Annie E.	Parry	Woobley	6 a	965	— Denis D.C.	Town	Hammersmith	1 a	323
— Anthony	Cox	Pontypridd	11 a	883	— Derek G.	Longstaff	W.Glamorgan	11 a	1481
— Anthony F.	Tranter	Ploughley	3 a	2831	— Diana H.	Yates	Wellington	6 a	1253
— Anthony H.	Griffiths	Hammersmith	1 a	247	— Dilys J.	Evans	Carmarthen	11 a	1619

Do remember a few other things here:

The indexes are national (i.e. they relate to the whole of England and Wales, and are not specific to county or RD).

They are compiled into quarters – Q1 = Jan, Feb, Mar; Q2 = Apr, May, Jun; Q3 = Jul, Aug, Sep; Q4 = Oct, Nov, Dec., and are sometimes called March, June, etc.

What is recorded is the date of registration, not the event itself – a birth or death in late March (which is in Q1), might not be registered until early or mid-April (in Q2), and a death in late December (Q4) one year might be registered in Q1 the year after. Marriages are registered when they happen.

A marriage is always registered where it took place, but a birth or death could be registered anywhere. An English or Welsh birth must be registered within forty-two days (twenty-one in Scotland), and a death that takes place in England and Wales must be registered within five days. These events should be registered at a register office, but although the district where the event took place must be given, the events can be registered at any office. This can lead to complications and a lot of chasing around, especially if the birth or death subject normally lived in one place, was born or died in another (in the nearest large hospital, say), was buried in a third (the family plot, for instance) and got registered by a relative living somewhere else completely. It would be wonderful if all such records were online and searchable in the same place.

There is an 'Official Districts' list at FreeBMD (www.freebmd.org.uk/DistrictInfo.html) as well as pages for alternate and misspelt districts. These are linked to GENUKI, where there will be more information on the district in question.

GRO certificate ordering

It is possible to obtain these in person at any local register office in England and Wales – not necessarily the one where the event was registered. However, it may be more convenient to do it online. Many of the BMD search sites offer a certificate ordering service. There is no need to use these as it is very straightforward and much cheaper to do it yourself.

1. Bear in mind this relates to England and Wales only – Scotland and Ireland have their own separate operations.

2. Go to www.gro.gov.uk/gro/content/certificates/.

3. Log in (if registered) or register first – name, full address and an email address are required.

4. Use the Name(s), Year, Quarter, Volume and Page information from the indexes to order your certificates. You can make multiple orders at the same time. Certificates available are:

   Birth Certificate
   Adoption Certificate (the birth certificate will be in the post-adoption name – only the adoptee can get any other information)
   Marriage Certificate
   Civil Partnership Certificate
   Commemorative Marriage Certificate (Silver, Ruby, Gold and Diamond Wedding Anniversaries)
   Death Certificate (age at death must be given for deaths registered in the last fifty years)
   Overseas versions of the above

5. Pay by credit card.

6. The document(s) will be mailed to arrive within four working days if you supplied the full GRO reference information, fifteen days if not. Mailing takes longer if overseas. There is a more expensive 'next-day' service (£23.40).

Burials

Death is one thing – burial is another, and gravestones can be hard to find. The best way is the National Burial Index (NBI), available online at various search sites (for a fee) or as a set of CD-ROMS from the FFHS or various commercial suppliers. This is dealt with in more detail in Chapter 7 (Old Parish Records pre-1837).

After 1860, it will usually be necessary to contact the local authority (council) to request burial information. This is sometimes the responsibility of 'Cems and Crems' or 'Bereavement Services' but in some authorities the registrar can look up the information for you.

Local authority and private burials

A death certificate will not give the burial place, although the place of death or usual residence should help narrow down the search for a record of interment. All burials before 1853 were in churchyards, church crypts and so on, but always 'consecrated ground'. However, Britain was

CERTIFIED COPY OF AN ENTRY OF BIRTH
COPI DILYS O GOFNOD GENEDIGAETH

GIVEN AT THE **GENERAL REGISTER OFFICE**
FE'I RHODDWYD YN Y **GENERAL REGISTER OFFICE**

Application Number
Rhif y Cais | 4109759-1

REGISTRATION DISTRICT		MERTHYR TYDFIL	
DDOSBARTH COFRESTRU			
1856	BIRTH in the Sub-district of GENEDIGAETH yn Is-ddosbarth	Merthyr Tydfil Upper	in the Counties of Glamorgan and Brecon yn

Columns: Colofnau No. Rhif	1 When and where born Pryd a lle y ganwyd	2 Name, if any Enw os oes un	3 Sex Rhyw	4 Name and surname of father Enw a chyfenw'r tad	5 Name, surname, and maiden surname of mother Enw, cyfenw a chyfenw morwynol y fam	6 Occupation of father Gwaith y tad	7 Signature, description and residence of informant Llofnod, disgrifiad a chyfeiriad yr hysbysydd	8 When registered Pryd y cofrestrwyd	9 Signature of registrar Llofnod y cofrestrydd	10 Name entered after registration Enw a gofnodwyd wedi'r cofrestru
4	Twenty fifth January 1856 Church Row Dowlais	Godfrey James	Boy	Ebenezer Griffiths	Mary Griffiths formerly Turner	Roll Turner	Ebenezer Griffiths Father Church Row Dowlais	Nineteenth February 1856	J. L. White Registrar	

CERTIFIED to be a true copy of an entry in the certified copy of a Register of Births in the District above mentioned.
TYSTIOLAETHWYD ei fod yn gopi cywir o gofnod mewn copi y tystiwyd iddo o Gofrestr Genedigaethau yn y Dosbarth a enwyd uchod.

Given at the GENERAL REGISTER OFFICE, under the Seal of the said Office
Fe'i rhoddwyd yn y GENERAL REGISTER OFFICE, o dan Sêl y Swyddfa a enwyd.

the 7th day of June 2012
y dydd o fis

CAUTION: THERE ARE OFFENCES RELATING TO FALSIFYING OR ALTERING A CERTIFICATE AND USING OR POSSESSING A FALSE CERTIFICATE. © CROWN COPYRIGHT
GOFAL: MAE YNA DROSEDDAU YN YMWNEUD Â FFUGIO NEU ADDASU TYSTYSGRIF NEU DDEFNYDDIO TYSTYSGRIF FFUG NEU WRTH FOD AG UN YN EICH MEDDIANT. © HAWLFRAINT Y GORON

WBXZ 419561

WARNING: A CERTIFICATE IS NOT EVIDENCE OF IDENTITY.
RHYBUDD: NID YW TYSTYSGRIF YN PROFI PWY YDYCH CHI.

IPS 046687 39899 03/11 3M5PSL 028904

KEG

Above and below, see caption overleaf.

CERTIFIED COPY OF AN ENTRY OF MARRIAGE
COPI DILYS O GOFNOD PRIODAS

GIVEN AT THE **GENERAL REGISTER OFFICE**
RHODDWYD YN Y **GENERAL REGISTER OFFICE**

Application Number
Rhif y Cais | 4109759/2

1876.	Marriage solemnized at Holy Trinity Church in the District of Nantyglo					in the County of Monmouth	
No.	When Married	Name and Surname	Age	Condition	Rank or Profession	Residence at the time of Marriage	Father's Name and Surname	Rank or Profession of Father
165	Sept 14th 1876	Godfrey James Griffiths	21	Bachelor	Time keeper	Nantyglo	Ebenezer Griffiths	Agent
		Sarah Emily Pugh	22	Spinster	-	Nantyglo	John Pugh	Mason

Married in the District Church according to the Rites and Ceremonies of the Established Church, by ____ or after Banns by me, S. Morgan

This Marriage was solemnized between us, Godfrey James Griffiths / Sarah Emily Pugh in the Presence of us, Robert Edey x by mark / Elizabeth Bevan x by mark

CERTIFIED to be a true copy of an entry in the certified copy of a Register of Marriages in the Registration District of Bedwellty
TYSTIOLAETHWYD ei fod yn gopi cywir o gofnod mewn copi y tystiwyd iddo o Gofrestr Priodasau yn Nosbarth

Given at the GENERAL REGISTER OFFICE, under the Seal of the said Office
Fe'i rhoddwyd yn y GENERAL REGISTER OFFICE, o dan sêl y Swyddfa a enwyd y

11th day of June 2012
dydd o fis

CAUTION: THERE ARE OFFENCES RELATING TO FALSIFYING OR ALTERING A CERTIFICATE AND USING OR POSSESSING A FALSE CERTIFICATE. © CROWN COPYRIGHT
GOFAL: MAE YNA DROSEDDAU YN YMWNEUD Â FFUGIO NEU ADDASU TYSTYSGRIF NEU DDEFNYDDIO TYSTYSGRIF FFUG NEU WRTH FOD AG UN YN EICH MEDDIANT. © HAWLFRAINT Y GORON

WMXZ 302392

WARNING: A CERTIFICATE IS NOT EVIDENCE OF IDENTITY.
RHYBUDD: NID YW TYSTYSGRIF YN PROFI PWY YDYCH CHI.

IPS 046687 39915 03/11 3M5PSL 028916

JMK

CERTIFIED COPY OF AN ENTRY OF MARRIAGE
COPI DILYS O GOFNOD PRIODAS

GIVEN AT THE **GENERAL REGISTER OFFICE**
RHODDWYD YN Y **GENERAL REGISTER OFFICE**

Application Number 4109759-3
Rhif y Cais

1889. Marriage solemnized at the Parish Church in the Parish of Bedwellty in the County of Monmouth

No.	When married.	Name and Surname.	Age.	Condition.	Rank or Profession.	Residence at the time of Marriage.	Father's Name and Surname.	Rank or Profession of Father.
210	Sep. 5th 1889	Godfrey James Griffiths	33	Widower	Time Keeper	7 Chapel Street Tredegar	Ebenezer Griffiths	Clerk
		Elizabeth Annie Bamford	22	Spinster	—	13 Alexandra Place Tredegar	Francis Bamford	Hosier

Married in the Parish Church according to the Rites and Ceremonies of the Established Church, by — or after Banns by me,

This Marriage was solemnized between us, Godfrey James Griffiths / Elizabeth Annie Bamford in the Presence of us, Francis Newham Bamford / Melissa Anne Griffiths — Samuel John, Vicar

CERTIFIED to be a true copy of an entry in the certified copy of a Register of Marriages in the Registration District of } Bedwellty
TYSTIOLAETHWYD ei fod yn gopi cywir o gofnod mewn copi y tystrwyd iddo o Gofrestr Priodasau yn Nosbarth

Given at the GENERAL REGISTER OFFICE, under the Seal of the said Office the } 11th day of } June 2012
Fe'i rhoddwyd yn y GENERAL REGISTER OFFICE, o dan sêl y Swyddfa a enwyd y } dydd o fis }

WMXZ 302418

CAUTION: THERE ARE OFFENCES RELATING TO FALSIFYING OR ALTERING A CERTIFICATE AND USING OR POSSESSING A FALSE CERTIFICATE. © CROWN COPYRIGHT
GOFAL: MAE YNA DROSEDDAU YN YMWNEUD Â FFUGIO NEU ADDASU TYSTYSGRIF NEU DDEFNYDDIO TYSTYSGRIF FFUG NEU WRTH FOD AG UN YN EICH MEDDIANT. © HAWLFRAINT Y GORON

WARNING: A CERTIFICATE IS NOT EVIDENCE OF IDENTITY.
RHYBUDD: NID YW TYSTYSGRIF YN PROFI PWY YDYCH CHI.

Above and below and previous page: Birth certificate – For births pre-1969, this has the name and sex of the child, date and place of birth, father's name and surname, father's occupation, mother's name, surname and maiden name (after Q3 1911). The certificate also gives the district, sub-district and county of registration, the date registered, the name and signature (or mark) of the informant and relationship to the child, plus the name of the registrar. Birth certificates issued after 1969 are in a different format ('portrait' rather than 'landscape') and also give the place of birth of both parents (with mother's occupation after 1984). Both parents will appear on the certificate if they were married to each other; if not, the only way that the father's details will appear on the birth certificate is if both attended the register office at the time, or if he completed a statutory declaration, which was taken to the register office by the mother.

CERTIFIED COPY OF AN ENTRY OF DEATH

GIVEN AT THE **GENERAL REGISTER OFFICE**

Application Number 4109759-4

REGISTRATION DISTRICT BATH

1951 DEATH in the Sub-district of Bath in the County Borough of Bath

Columns:-	1	2	3	4	5	6	7	8	9
	No.	When and where died	Name and surname	Sex	Age	Occupation	Cause of death	Signature, description and residence of informant	When registered	Signature of registrar
	473	Twelfth June 1951 St. Martins Hospital U.D.	Godfrey James GRIFFITHS	Male	95 years	of 9 First Avenue, Bath U.D. Colliery Timekeeper (Retired)	1(a) Pyelonephritis (b) Chronic Cystitis (c) Hypertrophied Prostate Certified by E. Mountjoy Powrie M.R.C.S.	Godfrey J. Cole Grandson 9 First Avenue, Bath.	Twelfth June 1951	G. Field Registrar

CERTIFIED to be a true copy of an entry in the certified copy of a Register of Deaths in the District above mentioned.

Given at the GENERAL REGISTER OFFICE, under the Seal of the said Office, the 8th day of June 2012

DYD 291538

See note overleaf

CAUTION: THERE ARE OFFENCES RELATING TO FALSIFYING OR ALTERING A CERTIFICATE AND USING OR POSSESSING A FALSE CERTIFICATE © CROWN COPYRIGHT
WARNING: A CERTIFICATE IS NOT EVIDENCE OF IDENTITY.

running out of church interment space by 1853, so an Act of Parliament was passed enabling local authorities to buy and use land for burials. Civic and private cemeteries sprung up, and some private ones were later taken over ('adopted' is the term) by local government. One consequence is that it becomes increasingly difficult to track down burial records, especially in large towns.

If the burial was on private land, and not registered anywhere, there was always the risk of the accidental disturbance of remains by later owners or land developers. To prevent this, details of the burial may be with the title deeds to the property, or with the family's solicitor.

Local or national archives may have the business records of undertakers, which could contain burial information.

DeceasedOnline

A new commercial service is becoming available – www.deceasedonline.com – to help track down local authority and other burial places. This is a partnership between the company that provides one of the popular cemetery records computer systems the councils use, and the councils themselves. It is based on the very simple idea that if all records are going into a database, they might as well go online as well. The great advantage is that a person's name can be searched for with or without locality information. Searches and a simple index return are free, with a low one-off cost for more details.

So far, there are a number of English and Scottish boroughs and councils involved, but none in Wales. This changes quickly, so check the website for the up-to-date coverage. It will, in time, include register records, maps and photographs (headstones, for instance) in digital form, mainly from the 1850s onwards. The councils and DeceasedOnline are also working to image and index manual registers ('lair records') and memorial inscriptions as far back as possible. This may well include pre-1855 records, and those of private cemeteries later adopted by councils.

Newspapers

Newspaper obituaries (and birth, engagement and marriage announcements) are a great source of information for family historians. There are many online search directories (unfortunately, most not free) of newspaper obituary archives:

1. The British Library newspaper collection index should be the first port of call (www.bl.uk/reshelp/findhelprestype/news/blnewscoll/).

2. A great and often neglected source for genealogy is the *London Gazette*, the official government newspaper – which is free to search, and has military records, notices of wills, bankruptcies, changes of names and more (www.gazettes-online.co.uk).

Gravestones

Many local FHSs have CDs or online sites of gravestones, collected by 'Recording Angels' – volunteers who spend their spare time haunting graveyards with camera, notebook and rubbing paper. However, be aware that details on headstones and memorials are not always correct, so check names, dates and places with the documentary records.

Further reading

John Rowlands (ed), *Welsh Family History: A Guide to Research* (Association of Family History Societies of Wales in conjunction with the Federation of Family History Societies, 2nd edition from Genealogical Publishing Co Inc., 2009).

John and Sheila Rowlands (eds), *Second Stages in Researching Welsh Ancestry* (Federation of Family History Societies in conjunction with the Department of Continuing Education, University of Wales, Aberystwyth).

Copies of the GRO indexes are not available to buy on microfiche, print or CD-ROM, but complete sets are available to view at these places, among others:

Wales

Bridgend Reference and Information Library, Wales

National Library of Wales – subscribes to Ancestry and Findmypast within the library reading rooms

England

British Library, London (requires a reader's card)

City of Westminster Archives Centre, London

Birmingham Central Library

Manchester City Library

Newcastle City Library

Plymouth Central Library

Scotland

The Mitchell Library, Glasgow

The indexes held include:

Births, Deaths and Marriages 1837 to 2009

Provisional indexes for births and deaths from January 2010 to June 2011

Overseas Index: Births, Deaths and Marriages 1761 to 2009

Civil Partnerships 2005 to 2010

Adoptions 1927 to 2010

Online websites with BMD for England and Wales from 1837

FreeBMD – www.freebmd.org.uk (now 268+ million records of BMD, and free to use, with index images).

Ancestry – www.ancestry.co.uk and www.ancestry.com use FreeBMD data up to 1984 and GRO data 1985–2005. Currently about 200 BMD databases are available for England and thirty specifically for Wales.

FamilySearch – www.familysearch.org.

The Church of Jesus Christ of Latter-day Saints website is also free, and includes:

* Wales Births and Baptisms, 1541–1907
* Wales Deaths and Burials, 1586–1885
* Wales Marriages, 1541–1900

Be careful – some entries have been uploaded by church members, have no source attribution and are frequently just plain wrong.

A useful add-on to FamilySearch and the International Genealogical Index (IGI) is http:// freepages.genealogy.rootsweb.ancestry.com/~hughwallis/

Hugh Wallis is to be congratulated for providing additional search options such as a search within a specific county, then parish (Britain and North America) by using IGI batch numbers – births/christenings and marriages only. It is a useful way to find all the children of a particular marriage.

Findmypast – www.findmypast.com/
>   Apart from BMD indexes for England and Wales 1837–1983 and a database search available for 1984–2005, there are indexes to the British overseas 1761–2002, BMD at sea from 1854, death duty registers and the National Burial Index (1538–2005).

The Genealogist – www.thegenealogist.co.uk/
>   The same DMD indexes 1837–2005 and GRO database 1984–2005 as everyone else, plus over 1,100 parish register transcripts.

UK BMD – www.ukbmd.org.uk
>   Links to over 2,000 websites offering transcriptions of births, marriages, deaths and censuses.

Dustydocs – http://dustydocs.com.au/
>   An Australian links site for BMD 1538 to 1900. Some information is user-uploaded, but is validated.

Specifically Wales

Genealogy Links (Wales) – www.genealogylinks.net/uk/wales/
>   County-based links site to cemeteries, censuses, marriages, military info., passenger lists, societies and more.

Multi-Region BMD Search – www.ukbmdsearch.org.uk/
>   Combined searching, including the North Wales BMD (www.northwalesbmd.org.uk/) from 1837 – an ongoing project.

Wrexham Council Marriage Index – www.wrexham.gov.uk/english/community/genealogy/ MarriageIndexSearchForm.cfm
>   Another ongoing project, in collaboration with the Clwyd Family History Society, to provide online indexes to Wrexham births and deaths in the 1837–1950 period.

7

Parish Registers Pre-1837

Statutory civil registration started in 1837 in England and Wales, and the earliest census with any genealogically useful information is that of 1841. After consulting these, it is possible to home in on likely dates of births, marriages and deaths in the previous century. Someone aged 5 in the 1841 census may have a birth date in 1835–36. If the parents are given as age 25 (remember the 1841 census rounded ages down to the nearest five years) they could be 24–29 and thus b. c. 1812–17 and married c. 1835–36. Someone recorded aged 70 in 1841 was b. c. 1767–72, and if widowed there may be a corresponding burial record of the spouse sometime before 1837 or 1841.

The next obvious step in this trip back through time is to consult the parish registers. Each of the 500 or so Church in Wales (Anglican) parishes kept – or were supposed to have kept – registers of baptisms and/or births, of marriages and/or the proclamations of banns, and of deaths and/or burials. This was a rather haphazard system for a number of reasons.

1. This only applied to Church in Wales members, and, after 1538 or so, while this was the predominant denomination of the population, there were still Catholics, Episcopalians and those of other faiths such as Judaism. However, these were very much in the minority (and some did choose to be registered by the Church in Wales). Nonconformism (Chapter 8) was not widely popular until well into the nineteenth century; also, many Nonconformist chapels, especially in rural areas, were not licensed for marriages, and may not have had a burial ground.

2. There is no absolute starting date for these records, although not many date much further back than the early 1600s, some are even later, and some parishes have no records at all.

3. Despite attempts to enforce a standard format this was not always adhered to by individual ministers or parish clerks, while many parishes have no death or burial registers at all.

4. Not everyone chose to register a birth, marriage or death, or to have the event itself celebrated in church, as it generally cost money; in particular, the imposition from 1783 to 1794 of a 'stamp duty' of threepence on each registration was a serious inhibition.

5. As the population grew, and people moved from villages and hamlets to the larger towns towards the end of the eighteenth century, their ties with their local church loosened and registration was less likely.

6. Some registers have just been lost, or are damaged beyond recovery.

7. Individual parishes have appeared, merged and/or disappeared over time – as a starting point consult the Church in Wales website (www.churchinwales.org.uk) for details of all current churches and parishes.

It is always worth checking the parish registers, not least because the births and marriages are often accessible and searchable (as transcripts and occasionally as images), or on microfilm at National Library of Wales or at the appropriate county record office (see Chapter 4), online through FreeReg.org, FamilySearch.org and the LDS family history centres, on other websites (see below) or on CDs from a family history society. Some caveats to remember, though:

1. The amount of information in a parish register is often less than ideal; baptisms will usually give the name of the child and the date, but the parents' names, place of residence and occupations are not always documented; the mother's name may be unrecorded, or the baptised child's sex not given.

2. Remember that a date of baptism is not a date of birth; one of the pitfalls of IGI and FamilySearch.org is that many well-meaning people uploading information have assumed that one is the same as the other, but a birth could precede a baptism by some weeks or months; do not accept any date given as either 'born' or 'baptised/christened' without checking the original document.

3. Do not assume that the baptism date was close to the birth date – a child may have been baptised almost immediately (if it was thought not likely to survive long), or months later (to see if it survived), when the father returned from work away or from being at sea, when moving to a new parish (often all the children in the family at once), twice in different parishes (father's and mother's) or not at all.

4. Baptisms (and indeed marriages) were usually held on Sundays, but if a child was not likely to live it might be baptised at any time, and by anyone, because canon law held that in such circumstances anyone in good standing with the church could perform the rite to save the soul, even after the child had actually died – this might be registered as 'P.B.' (private baptism) and entered into the parish register later.

5. You might also see 'C.B.' (conditional baptism) in a record of confirmation when the child was older, usually 12 or 13 – if it was unclear whether there had been a previous baptism (a prerequisite for confirmation) then another would be performed just in case, but on the condition that if it had happened already, this one didn't count. Most churches regard baptism as a once-and-for-all-time event, except Baptists, who don't accept infant baptism, as the child could not have made a decision about religion. Even today, some ministers will perform a C.B. before a religious marriage if there is no proof of baptism. Confirmation is where the candidate affirms his or her Christian belief and displays an appropriate understanding of the faith and the Bible.

6. You may find two people married in a certain parish, but be unable to find their births there, or in any other parish; sometimes a will or other testamentary document throws up names of children even though their births – and the parents' marriage itself – seems not to be registered.

7. Sometimes there appear to be double entries, the same child apparently 'born' on two different dates; this is usually because one is a birth date and the other the date of baptism, but could be due to the proud parents being from different parishes and wishing to having the baby baptised at both.

8. Likewise, marriage entries (which are usually a record of the proclamation of banns) might be made in two parishes, those of both the bride and groom, and one register entry may give more details than the other; however, typically what appears are the names of the parties to be wed, their places of residence and the date of the proclamation. Sometimes there is also a statement that the marriage took place (although this was not required).

9. Burial records often have no more details than the name of the deceased and the date of interment, but if the deceased was a child, their age is often given.

10. If the actual burial took place elsewhere – in a municipal cemetery, for example, or if the body were cremated – there will be no parish record unless a memorial service had been held. Cremation became legal, and then popular, after 1884, when Welsh physician, socialist, vegetarian and neo-Druid Dr William Price was unsuccessfully prosecuted for cremating his 5-month-old son, named named Iesu Grist, the Welsh for Jesus Christ.

Every so often a particular vicar – whether because he thought it was his religious duty, or just because he had a tidy mind – would choose to give other information, such as a mother's maiden name in a baptismal entry, or those of godparents (at a baptism) or witnesses (at a marriage), or a cause of death. You may even be told whether a child was legitimate or illegitimate, and the relationships of witnesses or godparents to the married couple or child. These could be relatives, useful information for the family historian. Ages are rarely recorded, except in the case of child burials, but a surviving spouse might be mentioned.

The single major hazard of consulting parish registers is overenthusiastic identification. A small town or isolated parish may have a number of individuals with the same name and of a similar age – cousins, for instance, all christened with the grandfather's first name – who married others with common or locally predominant names.

Incidentally, baptism and christening are not the same thing – baptism 'washes away sins', whereas christening is the welcoming into the church and the giving of a 'Christian' name. They usually happen together, but do not need to.

How the Parish Registers Came About

In 1530, Henry VIII had split from Rome, largely because if he ran his own church, he could decree his divorce from Catherine of Aragon, which he managed in 1533. By that time he had, however, married Anne Boleyn regardless, and Catherine died three years later anyway. On 5 September 1538, Henry's Vicar General, Thomas Cromwell, was busy tidying up the new Church of England (and the Anglican Church in Wales and Ireland) and so decreed that clergy in England and Wales should maintain weekly records of baptisms, marriages and burials, to be kept in a 'sure coffer' with two locks (one for the vicar, one for the churchwardens). It was not a great success, for a number of reasons.

First, if records were kept at all, they were usually written on paper, sometimes as loose sheets, and were liable to deterioration, damage and loss. Second, there was a fine of 3s 4d for failure to comply, and as many parishes thought this was the thin end of a taxation wedge they just ignored it. To allay their fears on this score, the order was issued again in 1547, making it clear that the fine, if any, should to go to the poor relief fund.

Interestingly, this all came about at more or less the same time as the first printed book in Welsh, *Yny lhyvyr hwnn* (literally, 'In this book') of 1546, the author of which, Sir John Price of Brecon, had an earnest wish for 'reform in religion, to ensure that ordinary people learnt the basic tenets of the Christian faith'. (The book is viewable at the National Library of Wales

'Treasures', http://digidol.llgc.org.uk/METS/YLH00001/frames.) The first Welsh translation of the complete Bible was in 1558 (see www.llgc.org.uk/index.php?id=digitalmirror).

The Roman Catholic Church finally issued a general order to keep baptismal and marriage records in 1563.

In 1598, Henry's rather more organised daughter, Elizabeth I, made a further attempt at getting parish registers kept. Clergy were instructed to use parchment (more likely to last than paper) onto which they were to copy the old records, although by that time many were unreadable or lost. A reasonable number of the new parchment registers contained records from 1538, but many more began in 1558, the first year of Elizabeth's reign. The 1598 order also required that transcripts of the registers should be sent annually to the diocesan registry – known as bishops' transcripts (p. 97). The books were to be kept in a chest – with three locks this time – and the entries for the week were to be read out in church after evening service every Sunday. How would this be paid for? Well, the long-dreaded tax finally arrived to support what were called 'great decent books of parchment'; each parish could meet this by charging a fee per entry, with a percentage to the minister for his trouble. This met with predictable opposition and was not really enforced until 1603 when James VI of Scotland also became James I of England and Wales and took a properly Scottish view of his income.

During the turbulent Commonwealth or Cromwellian period, after Charles I lost his crown and head, registration became a matter for the state rather than the church. From 1653, the new post of parish register (rather than 'registrar') was created. This holder of this job, who was elected by the ratepayers of the parish, kept the registers of births and baptisms and deaths and burials. In 1654 the concept of civil (i.e. not controlled by the church) marriage, solemnised by a Justice of the Peace, was introduced. During this period, the date of birth as well as baptism is usually recorded. This system only lasted until the Restoration of King Charles II in 1660, at which point the registers were handed back to the parishes who got on with it (or didn't) as before.

In 1678, Charles was worried about the wool trade so he devised, or someone devised for him, a scheme to promote this – it was made compulsory for all corpses to be buried in a woollen shroud, with a sworn statement made to that effect and recorded in the parish register. At this time, coffins were only for the rich, although the body was usually taken to the graveside in a rented parish coffin, then removed for burial in the shroud alone.

In 1694, James II increased the cost of parish registration spectacularly – from 4d to 2s (six-fold) for a baptism entry, 1s to 2s 6d (two-and-a-half times) for a marriage and 4d to 4s (twelve times) for a burial, plus (in 1696) a tax of 6d for any birth not reported within five days, and a fine imposed on the vicar of £2 for failing to record it. As a vicar might be living on £30–£100 per annum, that represented at least a week's income. This was not from any aspiration to support a decent registration system, but was actually so that James could raise cash for war against France. The whole idea was dropped in 1706, as it was feared, justifiably, that it would be the financial ruin of many clergymen.

There was a new attempt to regulate the keeping of registers in 1711, during the last days of Queen Anne's reign and with a new Tory Parliament in power, when it was decided that the registers' pages should be ruled and numbered (few were). Then, in 1733, the Hanoverians issued yet more changes as George II declared that all entries should at last be in English rather than Latin (and certainly not in Welsh!).

Why register your marriage in an Anglican church anyway? Before 1754, ecclesiastical law required that marriage be performed after banns or by licence, but common law meant that a couple could have an informal or 'irregular' marriage, valid and recognised by the civil authorities, even though the church hated the very idea. The legal age for marriage was 14 for a boy and 12 for a girl, although parental consent was required for both up to 21. Many lied about their ages, and there wasn't always proof of age, except by reference to a baptism entry back in the home parish – not a possibility if the individual had moved away.

The 1753 Hardwicke Act

Hardwicke's Marriage Act of 1753 changed all this. It was made compulsory for all marriages, except Jewish and Quaker, to be performed and registered by the Church of England. To add financial insult to religious injury, from 1783 to 1794 there was a stamp duty of 3*d* on entries (to help pay for the ill-fated war to keep America British with an exemption for the poor. This proved to be a great boost to the marriage trade in Gretna Green and other Scottish border towns (see below), and was so unpopular that it was finally repealed in 1794. It was also stipulated that marriage registers should be in a standard format, and volumes of printed forms were at last produced to make this happen. Up to then, the information recorded was usually fairly basic – baptisms, for example, give the name of the child, the date of baptism, the name of the father and sometimes, but not always, the name of the mother (the mother's maiden name is hardly ever stated).

As for burial, that was the hardest one to avoid as there was no choice really but to be interred by the church.

Dade registers

At this point, two well-meaning men of the cloth – Dade and Barrington – decided to sort things out.

The Rev. William Dade was a Yorkshire clergyman who saw the value of recording as much information as possible in parish register entries. He even referred to 'the researches of posterity'. In 1777 Dade persuaded Archbishop William Markham to introduce this format in his Archdiocese of York. The baptism entries, known as 'Dade registers', include the child's name, date of birth and baptism, position in the family (e.g. first daughter, third son), the father's name and profession, place of residence and – of great use to future genealogists – details such as names, occupation and residences of the father's and mother's parents. Burial records may have the age of the deceased, occupation, cause of death, names of parents and the name of a married woman's husband. Anyone who finds a Dade register will wonder why they aren't all like that.

The bad news is that the majority of Dade registers are for Yorkshire, and there are none for Welsh parishes, but they do exist for some places in Lancashire and Cheshire, where many Welsh turned up, as well as Nottinghamshire and (very rarely) in Devon, Essex and Surrey (see www.pontefractfhs.org.uk/Dade_registers.htm for a list).

The term 'Dade Register' has come to be used for any record that has more detail than might be expected, although, to be frank, the Dade system was not uniformly applied even in the York Archdiocese. As usual, a number of vicars, especially in larger towns, found it too much like hard work, so it didn't last long – the system was as good gone by 1812 (see the Rose Act, below). The vicars may have had a point, as they still had to produce bishops' transcripts, regarded by many as a duplication of effort. When the archbishop failed to impose any penalty on clergy who wouldn't comply, the death knell for Dade's scheme was sounded.

However, here is an example of the information to be found in a Dade register (a baptism in the Parish of Thorganby, Yorkshire).

Name:	Joseph Allison
Gender:	Male
Birth Date:	29 May 1796
Christening Date:	12 Jun 1796
Christening Place:	Thorganby, Yorkshire, England
Age at Christening:	0

Father's Name:	William Allison
Mother's Name:	Mary
Paternal Grandfather's Name:	John Allison
Paternal Grandmother's Name:	Mary
Maternal Grandfather's Name:	Robert Johnson
Maternal Grandmother's Name:	Frances

Barrington registers

Around the same time (actually, from 1783 or so) the Rev. Shute Barrington, then Bishop of Salisbury, put in place a similar, if less unwieldy, system to Dade's, and imposed it on Northumberland and Durham, when he became Bishop of Durham in 1797–98. Shute was a keen amateur genealogist, and it shows in the detail in the registers he inspired. Again, there are none in Wales.

The 1812 Rose Act

But it was, ultimately, all for naught. In 1812, an Act proposed by George Rose, a Scot by birth but Member of Parliament for Christchurch (and Richard Brinsley Sheridan's successor as Treasurer of the Navy) resulted in registers with printed forms and stipulated entry fields for baptisms, burials and marriages ('An Act for the better regulating and preserving Parish and other Registers of Births, Baptisms, Marriages, and Burials, in England', Cap.146, 28th July 1812). The Rose Act meant that from 1813 there were pre-printed forms for:

baptisms – mother's name, father's occupation and place of abode;
marriages – names of the couple and date (from 1754), condition (bachelor, spinster, widow or widower), parish of residence, occupation, whether the marriage was by banns or licence, names of witnesses, which often included relatives;
burials – name of the deceased, date of burial, sometimes age (more likely if a young child, and then often with the name of the father), age and abode.

The marriages are the most complete records, followed by burials and then baptisms.

Marriage banns, allegations, licences and bonds

The two main methods by which a couple could marry were by publication of banns and by licence, both of which are merely documentary proof that a wedding was intended, not that it actually took place.

Banns of marriage – Scotland, England and Wales

Banns are a declaration of intended marriage read in the relevant parish church or churches of the bride and groom. They are read aloud before the congregation, in both parishes if appropriate, on three successive Sundays, so that anyone with an objection could speak up ('or forever hold their peace', as the ceremony still says). By their very nature banns are public but they were not always written down until the Hardwicke Marriage Act (see above) made this compulsory in England (except for Quakers and Jews) from 1754 to 1812. Banns dating from before and after this time are often found in parish registers. During the Commonwealth (Cromwellian times) banns were read or published in the market square.

Marriage allegations

This worked as follows: the groom (usually) visited the diocesan registry or some other approved issuing body (such as a sheriff court in Scotland) and made an 'allegation' (a sworn statement) that church law had been complied with, that there was no known impediment to the marriage taking place and so on. If one of the parties was not 'of full age' (21 or over), the written consent of parents or legal guardians was required. Allegations usually give the names, ages and home parishes of the intended couple, and the church where the wedding was licensed to be solemnised.

Marriage bonds (cautions, pronounced 'kay-shuns', in Scotland)

A marriage bond was a contract by the groom or someone acting on his behalf (called a 'cautioner' in Scotland), with payment of the surety or bond against non-completion. It also absolved the church if an impediment was found later to have existed (a previous marriage, say, or consanguinity).

Then, if any statement sworn in the marriage allegation proved to be untrue and/or there was some impediment to the marriage, the bonded party would forfeit the sum stipulated. They were not required in England and Wales after 1823, and the application was by allegation only.

The bond documents themselves are interesting. They were in two parts – an obligation (written in Latin until 1733 in England) giving the names and parishes of those bound, which may or may not include the groom) and the bond or penalty; and a second part, always in English, laying out the terms under which the penalty would have to be paid, and naming the bride-to-be. Occasionally such documents still turn up – the Surrey Commissary Court licences were discovered archived with wills in about 1900.

Once the allegation and bond had been completed, the couple received a licence to marry to give to the celebrant (the minister). It contains nothing beyond what was in the original allegation and bond.

Marriage licences

Anyone wishing to avoid the reading of banns for whatever reason (privacy, keeping it quiet from the families, one or both of the couple away from his or her own parish, not prepared to wait three weeks) could apply for a licence to marry. Licences were the preferred route of the gentry and nobility, who felt the whole public banns exercise a touch too 'common'. But they cost money.

Typically, the parties applied to their diocese or to accredited deans and chapters, or archdeacons within their area, or if both lived in a 'peculiar' (a parish administered by an archdiocese), to the Ordinary of the Peculiar.

If the wedding were to be held in a diocese other than that of either of the intending couple, they would get a special licence from either the Faculty Office of Canterbury or the Registry of York, or from the Vicar-General of Canterbury. If they lived in different dioceses, they would apply to the vicar-general. If they were in different provinces (which were and are York and Canterbury) they would applied to the Master of the Faculties of the Archbishop of Canterbury. The Archbishop of Canterbury could issue a licence to any couple in England.

Not many marriage licences have survived, as they had no purpose after they were presented to the conducting vicar. However, it is worth looking in the records of the issuing body, usually the diocese in which the groom, bride, or both, lived. Marriage licences were dependent on two other documents, which were usually retained for record – allegations and bonds – and these are more likely to have survived.

The National Library of Wales has a searchable index of 'Marriage Bonds and Allegations' (http://isys.llgc.org.uk/) with details of some 90,000 marriages by licence in Wales between 1616 and 1837. A search produces a record that contains entries like this:

GRIFFITH, Thomas, bach., Welsh St. Donats, GLA. 1803, October 16. At W. St. D. Cecil Thomas. A,B. 97/43.

Gretna Green marriage registers

Between the 1754 Hardwicke Act in England, Wales and Ireland (which tightened up marriage, see p. 116) and Brougham's 1856 Act in Scotland (which attempted to much the same north of the border) there was no three-week residency requirement, no need in Scotland for parental consent for a groom over 14 and a bride over 12 and no real need for a church. Irregular marriage in Scotland was valid, even if at times illegal. It therefore became popular for English couples to head for one of the border towns, such Gretna Green or Lamberton Toll, to tie the knot. Among those willing to oblige were father-and-son team David and Simon Lang, who performed over 10,000 such marriages in Gretna between 1794 and 1828, possibly half of all the nuptials in the town during this period. This was known, somewhat scathingly, in England and Wales as the 'Scotch form of marriage', but it was perfectly valid.

This page from 1820 (above) happens to show a number of couples from the north of England, but although Gretna was handy for them, they weren't the only customers – these came from other parts of Scotland too, and in a few cases from Wales. The example shown starts with a record of an unpaid debt, then records the marriage on 29 February 1820 of John Hamilton from Arthuret and Elizabeth Cuthbertson of Camerton, both in Cumberland, and about 5 miles apart and some 35 miles from Gretna. These records can be found at www.scotlandspeople.gov.uk under 'Old Parish Registers'.

Finding and Using Parish Registers

Actual images of register pages are otherwise hard to come by, although they may be available alongside the widely available transcripts and indexes. Many are published by Phillimore and by local family history societies, and large libraries, as well as the Society of Genealogists in London, will have collections.

Unlike the situation in Scotland, parish registers for England and Wales are mainly held in the county record offices or archives (which have generally subsumed the old diocesan archives).

National Library of Wales

Almost all the parishes in Wales – over 500 – have deposited their registers at the National Library of Wales (NLW) or at the appropriate county record office (see Chapter 4 for contact details). At NLW, these are in the South Reading Room.

Society of Genealogists (London)

The SOG Library has copies of the Welsh parish registers (www.sog.org.uk/prc/wal.shtml) in their library at Goswell Road, London.

Family history societies

A number of FHSs are busy transcribing and indexing parish registers in collaboration with FindMyPast – see p. 111 for details.

LDS and other libraries

The family history centres of the Mormon Church and some libraries have the indexes on microfiche, and may have the record book images on microfilm (contact details on p. 53).

Online

FreeREG (www.freereg.org.uk).

Ancestry (www.ancestry.co.uk).

Borthwick Institute for Archives, previously the Borthwick Institute for Historical Research in York (www.york.ac.uk/library/borthwick/).

IGI (International Genealogical Index). IGI has the twin disadvantages of an unforgiving search facility and many flawed entries. It is not comprehensive, generally does not include burials, and in many cases has entries submitted by members of the LDS church, which may or may not be accurate and are uncheckable because there is no source information. However, it is a rapid and free way to do an initial quick search. There is a new search engine, but the 'old' interface is still available (www.familysearch.org/eng/) and many users prefer it for its flexibility. But do check both versions (see pp. 83–84). Collections include:

Wales Births and Baptisms, 1541–1907
Wales Marriages, 1541–1900
Wales Deaths and Burials, 1586–1885

National Burial Index for England and Wales, now searchable by county on the family history online web of the Federation of Family History Societies (www.ffhs.org.uk), which has now joined up with FindMyPast (www.findmypast.com).

Other indexes

These may be a good way of tracking down 'stray' Welsh, especially if they ended up in London. Boyd's marriage index, covering English parishes from 1538 to 1840, was compiled originally from parish registers, bishops' transcripts and marriage licences, and covers perhaps 12–15 per cent of the marriages in England but 95 per cent of parishes in East Anglia (see next entry).

Boyd's London burials index 1538–1872, which, with 243,000 records, indexes a few of the London burials (see next entry),

City of London burials 1742–1904 (but mostly 1788–1855) (www.findmypast.co.uk/content/sog/misc-series.html).

Pallot's marriage index, over 1.5 million entries from 1780–1837, which, although smaller than Boyd's index, is good for London and the Home Counties, as it covers all but two of the 103 parishes in the City of London and has some information from other counties (www.ancestry.co.uk).

In all of these, the information is sparse.

Common Latin terms found in early BMD records

General

aged – *aetatis*

and others – *et aliis* (*et. al*)

in the year of our Lord – *Anno Domini* (*AD*)

archive – *archivia*

born – *nata ex* (from), *de* (of)

Catholic Church – *ecclesia catholica*

cemetery – *cimiterium, coemeterium*

foresaid – *praedicto*

his/her – *ejus*

household – *familia*

first, in the first place – *imprimis*

name (given or Christian) – *nomen, dictus* (named), *vulgo vocatus* (alias)

died – *obit*

died without offspring – *obit sine prole* (o.s.p.)

parish – *parochia, pariochialis*

parish priest – *parochus*

surname (family name) – *cognomen, agnomen* (also nickname)

witness – *testis, testator*

town – *urbe*

namely – *videlicet*

village – *vico, pagus*

will/testament – *testamentum*

Records

baptismal register – *matricula baptizatorum, liber*

census – *census*

church – *ecclesia*

death register – *adnotet mortis, liber defunctorum*

index – *indice*

knight – *miles*

marriage register – *matrica* (marriage register), *liber bannorum* (register of marriage banns), *liber*

military – *militaris, bellicus*

of/in that place – *de eodem/eadem*

parish – *parochia, paroecia, vicarium*

registers – *matrica*

Events

banns (of marriage) – *banni, proclamationes, denuntiationes, notificationes matrimonii*

baptism/christening – *baptismi, baptizatus, renatus, plutus, lautus, purgatus, ablutus, lustratio*

birth, born – *natus, genitus, natales, ortus, oriundus*

buried – *sepulti, sepultus, humatus, humatio*

death – *mortuus, defunctus, obitus, denatus, decessus, peritus, mors, mortis, obiit, decessit*

divorce – *divortium*

marriage – *matrimonium, in matrimonium duxit, copulatio, copulati, conjuncti, nupti, sponsati, ligati, mariti*

solemnised – *solemnizat*

Relationships

ancestor – *antecessor, patres* (forefathers)

aunt – *amita* (paternal aunt), *matertera, matris soror* (maternal aunt)

brother – *frater, fratres gemelli* (twin brothers)

brother in law – *affinis, sororius*

child – *ifans, filius* (son of), *filia* (daughter of), *puer, puella*

children – *liberos, proles*

cousin – *sobrinus, gener*

daughter – *filia, puella, filia innupta* (unwed daughter), *unigena* (only daughter)

descendant – *proles, successio*

father – *pater, pater ignoratus* (unknown father), *novercus* (stepfather)

grandchild – *nepos* (grandson), *neptis* (granddaughter)

grandfather – *avus, pater patris* (paternal grandfather)

grandmother – *avia, socrus magna* (maternal grandmother)

great-grandchild – *pronepos* (great-grandson), *proneptis* (great-granddaughter)

great-grandfather – *proavus, abavus* (great-great-grandfather), *atavus* (great-great-great-grandfather)

great-grandmother – *proavia, proava, abavia* (great-great-great-grandmother)

All fields are optional EXCEPT Record Type, Surname and at least one County and Place. Tick the Soundex option to use a Soundex search on the Surname. Multiple Counties or Places may be searched by pressing and holding the CTRL key while making your selection. The list of Places includes an All places option. The list of Places is for **All Counties** not just the counties you have selected. If your County or Place of interest are not in the lists then the data has not yet been transcribed. Go to SEARCH HELP for advise on how to get the best results out of your search.

Record Type: ⦿ Baptisms ○ Marriages ○ Burials

Surname: Griffiths

Soundex: ☐ Check for Soundex

Forename: Ebenezer

Year: ⦿ Exact ○ +/- 2 years ○ +/- 5 years ○ +/- 10 years

County (Maximum of 10 can be selected)
Leicestershire
Lincolnshire
London (City)
Merionethshire
Middlesex
Midlothian
Monmouthshire
Montgomeryshire
Norfolk
North Riding YKS

Place
All
?
Abbas Combe
Abberton
Abbess Roding
Abbey Cwmhir
Abbey St. Bathans
Abbeycwmhir
Abbots Rippon
Abbots Ripton

Search | Reset

The FreeCEN search screen.

husband – *uxor, maritus, sponsus, conjus, coniux, ligatus, vir*

mother – *mater*

niece/nephew – *amitini, filius fratris/sororis* (nephew), *filia fratris/sororis* (niece)

orphan, foundling   *orbus, orba*

parents – *parentes, genitores*

relatives – *propinqui* (relatives), *agnati, agnatus* (paternal relatives), *cognati, cognatus* (maternal relatives), *affines, affinitas* (by marriage, in laws)

single – *innuptus, innupta* (usually of a female unmarried when she died), *coelebis/coeleba*

sister – *soror, germana, glos* (husband's sister)

sister-in-law – *gloris*

son – *filius, natus*

son-in-law – *gener*

uncle – *avunculus* (maternal uncle), *patruus* (paternal uncle)

widow – *vidua, relicta*

widower – *viduus, relictus*

wife – *vxor/uxor, marita, conjux, sponsa, mulier, femina, consors*

Case study – Ebenezer Griffiths b. c. 1828

We are still on the hunt for Ebenezer Griffiths, b. *c.* 1828 in Monmouthshire according to census and other records (Chapters 5 and 6).

Baptism search

Below are examples of searches for Ebenezer GRIFFITHS in all the historic counties of Wales. The search screen looked like this:

Notice that:

1. This is the search for baptisms.

2. It was a very wide search – no assumption about date range, no variants used (but there is a Soundex option).

3. You must select at least one county, but multiple counties can be searched at once – the limit is ten, which is a shame as Wales had 13 historic counties (see Chapter 4) – and the three shown were selected by using Ctrl+click.

4. No 'place' was selected.

#	Record Type	Baptism Date	Surname	Forename	County	Place	Name Found As
1	Baptisms	13 Jan 1851	GRIFFITHS	Catherine	Cardiganshire	Henllan	Father Surname
2	Baptisms	30 Jan 1816	GRIFFITHS	Ebenezer	Cardiganshire	Llanbadarn Fawr	Father Surname
3	Baptisms	19 Sep 1855	GRIFFITHS	William	Cardiganshire	Llanbadarn Fawr	Father Surname

4	Baptisms	19 Sep 1855	GRIFFITHS	Elizabeth	Cardiganshire	Llanbadarn Fawr	Father Surname
5	Baptisms	19 Sep 1855	GRIFFITHS	Ann	Cardiganshire	Llanbadarn Fawr	Father Surname
6	Baptisms	29 May 1795	GRIFFITHS	Ebenezer	Cardiganshire	Brongwyn Circuit	Father Surname
7	Baptisms	29 May 1795	GRIFFITHS	Ebenezer	Cardiganshire	Brongwyn Circuit	Father Surname
8	Baptisms	29 May 1795	GRIFFITHS	Ebenezer	Cardiganshire	Brongwyn Circuit	Father Surname
9	Baptisms	23 Aug 1829	JAMES	Ebenezer	Cardiganshire	Brongwyn Troedyaur Penbryn	Mother Surname
10	Baptisms	05 Aug 1849	JONES	David	Cardiganshire	Troedyraur	Mother Surname
1	Baptisms	17 Aug 1823	GRIFFITHS	Ebenezer	Monmouthshire	Blaenavon	

The only results were ten in Cardiganshire and one in Monmouthshire. The search found individuals who are not called Ebenezer Griffiths, but these two names crop up elsewhere in the particular record – for example, record # 1 in Cardiganshire is for a Mary, bapt. 13 Jan 1851, father Ebenezer, mother Mary. Notice also that this record is post-1837 – the churches did not stop parish registers suddenly in 1836 when statutory registration came in, and continue them right up to the present day, although it is rare to find one after this date.

Clicking on the numbers in the # column (#2 in Cardiganshire and #1 – the only one – in Monmouthshire) produces these search record details:

County	Cardiganshire	County	Monmouthshire
Place	Llanbadarn Fawr	Place	Blaenavon
Church	Parish Church	Church	Parish Church
RegisterNumber		RegisterNumber	304
DateOfBirth		DateOfBirth	
BaptismDate	30 Jan 1816	BaptismDate	17 Aug 1823
Forename	Ebenezer	Forename	Ebenezer
Sex	M	Sex	M
FatherForename	William	FatherForename	Edward
MotherForename	Margaret	MotherForename	Jane
FatherSurname	GRIFFITHS	FatherSurname	Griffiths
MotherSurname		MotherSurname	
Abode		Abode	Varteg
FatherOccupation		FatherOccupation	labr
Notes		Notes	(deceased)
FileNumber	23809	FileNumber	8829

The Cardiganshire record is very unlikely in terms of date and place (Llanbadarn Fawr is near Aberystwyth), but may indicate a nest of Griffiths relatives if 'our' Ebenezer or his forebears at some point travelled 85 miles south-east for work, which is possible. As for the Monmouthshire record, Blaenavon is about 10 miles east of Tredegar, and the date is out by five years, so this isn't a terribly convincing result either.

Marriage search

Just to make a point, in this case, the search was made for 'Griffiths', no forename, no date, only in Monmouthshire and with the place as Bedwellty. The results were:

#	Record Type	Marriage Date	Surname	Forename	County	Place	Name Found As
1	Marriages	11 Feb 1804	David	LEWIS	Monmouthshire	Bedwellty	Bride Surname
2	Marriages	01 Feb 1811	Daniel	JONES	Monmouthshire	Bedwellty	Bride Surname
3	Marriages	08 Jul 1805	Edward	BASKAWIS?	Monmouthshire	Bedwellty	Bride Surname
4	Marriages	20 Feb 1808	Henry	CENVIN	Monmouthshire	Bedwellty	Bride Surname
5	Marriages	07 Oct 1811	Jacob	PHILLIPS	Monmouthshire	Bedwellty	Bride Surname
6	Marriages	09 Jun 1808	John	THOMAS	Monmouthshire	Bedwellty	Bride Surname
7	Marriages	12 Mar 1804	John	WILLIAMS	Monmouthshire	Bedwellty	Bride Surname
8	Marriages	10 Feb 1754	James	HOWELLS	Monmouthshire	Bedwellty	Bride Surname
9	Marriages	11 Oct 1805	Thomas	EVANS	Monmouthshire	Bedwellty	Bride Surname
10	Marriages	07 Oct 1803	Thomas	GEORGE	Monmouthshire	Bedwellty	Bride Surname
11	Marriages	22 Jan 1812	Thomas	MORRIS	Monmouthshire	Bedwellty	Bride Surname
12	Marriages	05 Oct 1807	Thomas	REES	Monmouthshire	Bedwellty	Bride Surname

There are lots of females called Griffiths married in Bedwellty, mostly from the first decade of the 1800s. That suggests either:

1. one big Griffiths family with many daughters;
2. an extended Griffiths family.

Sadly, in no case are parents' names given, so we can't tell. Here are two examples of such records (#5 and #9). Note that 'Pheby' (the bride in the second record) might be a misheard 'Phoebe', but the first spelling was popular in Wales in the 1800s.

County	Monmouthshire	GroomParish	Bedwellty
Place	Bedwellty	GroomCondition	
Church	Parish Church	GroomOccupation	
RegisterNumber		GroomAbode	
MarriageDate	07 Oct 1811	BrideForename	Elizabeth
GroomForename	PHILLIPS	BrideSurname	GRIFFITHS
GroomSurname	Jacob	BrideAge	
GroomAge		BrideParish	Bedwellty

BrideCondition			GroomParish	Bedwellty
BrideOccupation			GroomCondition	
BrideAbode			GroomOccupation	
GroomFatherForename			GroomAbode	
GroomFatherSurname			BrideForename	Pheby
GroomFatherOccupation			BrideSurname	GRIFFITHS
BrideFatherForename			BrideAge	
BrideFatherSurname			BrideParish	Bedwellty
BrideFatherOccupation			BrideCondition	
WitnessOneForename			BrideOccupation	
WitnessOneSurname			BrideAbode	
WitnessTwoForename			GroomFatherForename	
WitnessTwoSurname			GroomFatherSurname	
Notes			GroomFatherOccupation	
FileNumber	8836		BrideFatherForename	
County	Monmouthshire		BrideFatherSurname	
Place	Bedwellty		BrideFatherOccupation	
Church	Parish Church		WitnessOneForename	
RegisterNumber			WitnessOneSurname	
MarriageDate	11 Oct 1805		WitnessTwoForename	
GroomForename	EVANS		WitnessTwoSurname	
GroomSurname	Thomas		Notes	
GroomAge			FileNumber	8836

Burials search

Post-1837 deaths – and more information on burials generally – can be found in Chapter 6. However, we can look here at the burial of Edward Griffiths, father of the Ebenezer b. *c.* 1823, above. The baptism record says 'deceased': this may refer to Edward (in which case he must have died some time in the previous nine months or so, between the conception and the baptism) or could be a later addition referring to Ebenezer (who may have died soon after baptism, as many infants did).

#	Record Type	Burial Date	Surname	Forename	County	Place	Name Found As
1	Burials	02 Apr 1863	GRIFFITHS	Thomas	Monmouthshire	Chepstow Municipal Cemetery	Surname, Relative One Surname
2	Burials	02 Jun 1886	GRIFFITHS	Edward	Monmouthshire	Bassaleg	Surname
3	Burials	08 Feb 1764	GRIFFITHS	Edward	Monmouthshire	Llandogo	Surname

4	Burials	20 Mar 1853	GRIFFITHS	Edward	Monmouthshire	Llanarth	
5	Burials	20 Mar 1853	GRIFFITHS	Edward	Monmouthshire	Llanarth	Surname
6	Burials	27 Jan 1842	GRIFFITHS	Edward	Monmouthshire	Llandenny	Surname
7	Burials	04 Jul 1878	GRIFFITHS	Edward	Monmouthshire	Llanmartin	Surname
8	Burials	11 Jan 1874	GRIFFITHS	Edward	Monmouthshire	Trevethin	Surname
9	Burials	03 Jan 1873	GRIFFITHS	Edward	Monmouthshire	Trevethin	Surname
10	Burials	05 Jan 1746/47	GRIFFITHS	Edward	Monmouthshire	Trevethin	Surname
11	Burials	31 Aug 1901	GRIFFITHS	Edward	Monmouthshire	Trevethin	Surname
12	Burials	28 Jul 1912	GRIFFITHS	Edward	Monmouthshire	Trevethin	Surname
13	Burials	18 Apr 1831	GRIFFITHS	Edward	Monmouthshire	Chepstow	Surname

None of these burial places is particularly close to Tredegar or Bedwellty, but that may not indicate much – it may depend where he was living at the time and/or where he died. Notice entry #10, though – the date is given as 05 Jan 1746/47 not because of uncertainty about the year, but because before 1852 New Year was 25 March, so the date is 1746 Old Style and 1747 New Style (see p. 211 for more details).

Searching on FamilySearch

For the sake of completeness, a search was also made for marriages at www.familysearch.org/eng/ (using the 'old' and far more functional original search engine).

Results for: Ebenezer Griffiths Marriage, Wales Exact Spelling: Off
Ancestral File
1. Ebenezer GRIFFITHS – Ancestral File Gender: M Marriage: Jan 1835 Carew, Pem, Wal
International Genealogical Index – British Isles
2. EBENEZER GRIFFITHS – International Genealogical Index / BI Gender: Male Marriage: 20 OCT 1823 Merthyr Tydfil, Glamorgan, Wales
3. Ebenezer GRIFFITHS – International Genealogical Index / BI Gender: Male Marriage: Before 1858, Wales
4. EBENEZER GRIFFITH – International Genealogical Index / BI Gender: Male Marriage: 14 FEB 1837 Llanelly, Brecon, Wales

Record #2 was expanded:

IGI Individual Record	FamilySearch™ International Genealogical Index v5.0
EBENEZER GRIFFITHS	Male
Marriages:	
Spouse:	SUSANAH DAVIS
Marriage:	20 OCT 1823 Merthyr Tydfil, Glamorgan, Wales

Messages: Form submitted by a member of the LDS Church. The form lists the submitter's name and address and may include source information. The address may be outdated. Details vary. To find the form, you must know the batch and sheet number.

Notice the disclaimer at the bottom – there is no way to check the source documentation unless it is listed on the original submission form, which is rare. The information should be treated with caution.

Summary

Obviously, all of this needs to be verified by reference to other records, that is, cross-checked with censuses, post-1837 statutory records and so on, but it shows the sort of approach that might be taken. It will also be necessary to check Nonconformist registers (Chapter 8) and bishops' transcripts (below). Incidentally, take care with cross-border dioceses – the indexes for the Palatinate of Cheshire contain almost all of the ecclesiastical records of Flintshire.

Bishops' Transcripts

From 1597, an annual copy was required of all entries from the parish register for the twelve months to about Easter or Lady Day (25 March), which was sent to the bishop. These are variable in quality – some are better than the originals and some not, but occasionally the churchwarden included more detail than is in the register, which is useful. In many cases, the original parish register no longer exists and the bishops' transcripts are all that survive. Even then, the coverage is patchy – the National Library of Wales has none before 1661, there are many missing before the eighteenth century, and most were no longer kept after civil registration began in 1837 (although there are a few from the early 1900s).

Those that remain are available to view in the South Reading Room of the National Library of Wales, Aberystwyth. A typical bishops' transcript entry looks like this:

Baptised 1672
December the 12th – William Burton the sonne of John Burton and Anne his wife
January the 16th – Elizabeth Grey the daughter of William Gray and Margaret his wife

The New Year started on 25 March until the change to the Gregorian calendar in 1752 (see p. 210–11); these entries are dated 1672 although today we would consider the first one to be December 1672 and the second 1673 (New Style). To avoid confusion, dates up to 24 March are usually given as, for instance, 1672/73.

A typical bishops' transcript entry.

Transcripts of bishops' transcripts

Some family history societies (FHSs) are collaborating with findmypast.co.uk to index and transcribe these, as well as parish registers. This is a work in progress, and the FHSs contributing at present include:

- Cardiganshire Family History Society
- Glamorgan Family History Society
- Gwent Family History Society
- Montgomeryshire Genealogical Society
- Powys Family History Society.

See p. 50–52 for contact details. It may also be worth checking those near the Welsh border, such as the North Cheshire FHS and also the Catholic Family History Society. There is more detail at www.findmypast.co.uk/content/ffhs/societies

Transcriptions at GENUKI

Katherine Hocking has transcribed many of the bishops' transcripts from the Parish of Trelêch-a'r-Bettws (Tref-Llêch-a'r-Bettws), a few miles north-west of Carmarthen; for the years 1727–97 (www.genuki.org.uk/big/wal/CMN/Tre-LecharBetws/BTs.html). The detail is sparse, but may be enough to pin an ancestor to a parish and time. Examples from 1797–98 look like this:

Baptism – Hester daughter of John Bowen	January 17th
Marriage – William Richard and Rachel David by Banns	Nov 2nd
Burial – David Lewis	Jan 18th

Non-established church and religious records
Nonconformist, Protestant and other religions are dealt with in Chapter 8.

Other Church Records

The church generated records beyond BMD. The ministers were assiduous compilers of lists for various purposes, not always to do with charging money for services rendered, or because a higher authority made them. Often they made lists to help them with their pastoral duties.

Marriage tax

In 1695 the Marriage Duties Act or 'Marriage Tax' was introduced on births, marriages, burials, bachelors over 25 and childless widows in England and Wales. It only lasted ten years but it meant that parishes or townships had to make lists of those inhabitants liable to pay tax. A small number of these lists have survived in county, borough, parish and some private archives.

See Chapter 10 for hearth tax and poll tax lists.

Ecclesiastical 'censuses'

Some of these so-called censuses were records used by the parish itself – such as visiting books, lists of communicants, Easter books and so on.

Visiting books, compiled by the incumbent of the established church parish may well include Nonconformist parishioners, with details of the households, and even small sketches or rough maps of the parish and places within it – including houses and the names of the residents, and occasionally other details like births, marriages, family relationships, employment and occupations, schooling and literacy (or otherwise), religious observance and character.

Lists of communicants and Easter books are more like censuses, recording the faithful (i.e. members of the Church of England). In Tudor times, these included those aged 12 or upwards, who would be considered fully grown and even able to marry – later, the age rose to 15 or 16. Part of the function of such records was to account for tithes chargeable to church members at Easter. The survival of these records is not uniform, so check at the National Library of Wales, county record offices and The National Archives (Kew, London). See also *Further reading*.

Poor Law records

Records of poor relief, settlement certificates, churchwardens' accounts, and other records generated by parochial boards are useful for genealogists (see Chapter 10). A settlement certificate showed that a person had a right to settle in a particular parish and could be in receipt of poor relief or be taken into the workhouse. The Overseers of the Poor were scrupulous about ensuring they were a charge on only the parish of legal settlement, and would send the poor 'back home' or charge the parish of settlement for them. In many areas the unit of local administration was the township or the Poor Law Union rather than the parish. Check with the county record office (p. 50–53).

Lists of clergymen

It may be useful to refer to the list of dioceses of the Church in Wales, p. 132–137.

There are many printed lists of clergymen, but they are harder to come by for Nonconformist and minority denominations. The best place to start is at the Clergy Database (www.theclergydatabase.org.uk), which contains details of the careers of all clergymen of the Church of England between 1540 and 1835, including the Church in Wales. It is searchable by name, diocese and parish, with date ranges.

As for printed information, among the easiest to find are those listed below.

Fasti ecclesiae Anglicanae

Fasti is Latin for 'calendar' or 'list' and that's exactly what this is. It is subtitled *A calendar of the principal ecclesiastical dignitaries in England and Wales, and of the chief officers in the Universities of Oxford and Cambridge, from the earliest time to year M.DCC.XV.* Complied by John Le Neve (1679–1741) and later edited and updated by Sir Thomas Duffus Hardy (1804–78) in 1854, this three-volume work initially went from the earliest times up to 1715. However, Hardy extended it to the early 1800s. The *Fasti* contains the names, dates of consecration, admission preferment, removal or death of almost every archbishop, bishop, dean, precentor, treasurer, chancellor, archdeacon and prebendary.

The books are organised by dioceses, so Wales is scattered through out all three volumes – so, for instance, St Asaph (then covering the counties of Flint and Montgomery, Denbigh, Merioneth, and also Salop or Shropshire) and Bangor (parts of Caernarfon, Merioneth, Montgomery, Denbigh and the whole of Anglesey) are both near the beginning of volume 1.

Each volume has an index. All three volumes are available at www.archive.org as downloadable or screen-readable PDFs.

ARCHDEACONS.

DANIEL AP-SULGION or SULGHEIN; he was elected bishop of St. David's in 1076, and being forced to fly
thence, took shelter at St. Asaph, and became archdeacon. Ob. 1127.

Example of detail in the Fasti Ecclesiae Anglicanae.

Crockford's Clerical Directories

These are a great source of information on the clergy. They were published annually from
1858, and contain biographical details of each incumbent, details of study and ordination, all of
their previous posts, and full address at the date of publication. Copies are usually only held in
larger reference libraries, but facsimilies on CD can be bought from Archive CD Books (www.
archivecdbooks.org/) and other providers, and through family history societies, the Parish Chest
(www.parishchest.com/) and so on.

Cox's Clergy List

Cox's Clergy List was published annually from the early 1800s as a catalogue of all clergy and their
place of appointment, until it was superseded by *Crockford's Clerical Directories*. The *List* has the
names and livings of clergy in England, Wales, Ireland and the Scottish Episcopal Church, those
working throughout the British Empire, and military, naval and prison chaplains. For benefices
in England and Wales it gives the value, population and patrons.

   These books are extremely rare, and likely to be found in major libraries only, but facsimiles
and CD versions are available as with *Crockford's* (see above).

Alumni and matriculation lists

Almost all clergymen attended the universities of Oxford or Cambridge, but may have been at a
Scottish university or Trinity College, Dublin. Check the records of these and later universities.

Catholics

For Catholic clergy, consult the Catholic Family History Society (www.catholic-history.org.
uk/cfhs) and the Catholic Record Society (www.catholicrecordsociety.co.uk); be aware that the
latter specifically states that it does not help with genealogical enquiries.

Dioceses in Wales

The Anglican Church in Wales has been a separate province since 1920. There are currently six
dioceses – deaneries and parishes are listed alphabetically under the appropriate diocese.

Diocese	Cathedral	Parishes/Deaneries
Bangor	St Deiniol Cathedral, Bangor	Aberdaron, St Hwyn
Aberdyfi/Aberdovey, St Peter		
Betws-y-Coed, St Michael (redundant since 2000)		
Botwnnog, St Beuno and Llaniestyn, St Iestyn		
Cricieth with Threflys and Llanystumdwy and Llanarmon with Llangybi		
Benefice of Dolgellau (St Mark, Brithdir; St Paul, Bryncoedifor; St Mary, Dolgellau; St Illtyd, Llanelltyd; St Machreth, Llanfachreth)		
Dwygyfylchi Parish		
Holyhead, St Cybi		
Llanallgo, St Gallgo 'Royal Charter Church'		
Llanbedr, St Peter		
Parish of Llandudno (Holy Trinity; St Tudno)		
Llandwrog and Llanwnda		
Llanfaelog, St Maelog		
Llanfairfechan, St Mary and Christ Church		
Llangeinwen a Llanfair-yn-y-Cwmwd, St Ceinwen		
Peris Valley Churches: Llanberis, Nant Peris, Llanrug, Cwm-y-Glo and Llandinorwig		
St Gallgo, Parish of Llanallgo		
Parishes of Valley, Bryngwran and Caergeiliog		
Llandaff	Llandaff Cathedral	Deanery of Rhondda
Parish of Aberaman and Abercwmboi with Cwmaman (St Margaret, Aberaman; St Joseph, Cwmaman)		
Parish of Aberavon (St Agnes; Holy Trinity; St Mary; St Paul)		
Parish of Baglan (St Catharine and St Baglan)		
Caerau, Parish of Caerau with Ely		
Caerau, St Cynfelyn		
Cadoxton, Parish of Cadoxton juxta-Barry: St Cadoc and St Mary the Blessed Virgin in Barry Dock		
Cardiff, Cathays Parish		
Cardiff (Roath Park), Christ Church		
Cardiff Centre, Dewi Sant		
Cardiff, Lisvane, St Denys		
Cardiff (Llanishen), St Isan and St Faith		

Cardiff Central, St John the Baptist		
Cardiff (Gabalfa), St Mark		
Cardiff, Parish of Roath Saint Martin		
Cardiff (Grangetown), St Paul		
Cardiff (Roath), St German		
Cardiff (Splott), St Saviour		
Parish of Cilybebyll (St John the Evangelist, Cilybebyll; St John the Baptist, Alltwen)		
Coity, Parish of Coity with Nolton: St Mary the Virgin, St Mary in Nolton and St Mary in Brackla		
Cowbridge, Parish of Cowbridge (Rectorial Benefice)		
Cwmafan, St Michael		
Cymmer, Parish of Cymmer and Porth		
Benefice of Dinas and Penygraig with Williamstown (St Barnabas, Penygraig; Dinas Mission; St Illtyd, Williamstown)		
Parish of Eglwysilan (St Ilan, Eglwysilan; St Peter and St Cenydd, Senghenydd)		
Ewenny, Ewenny Priory Church		
Glyncorrwyg, St John the Baptist		
Parish of Kenfig Hill (St Theodore, Kenfig Hill; St Colman, Cefn Cribwr)		
Laleston, Parish of Laleston		
Parish of Llandyfodwg and Cwm Ogwr (St David, Wyndham; St Twyfodwg, Glyn Ogwr)		
Llanharry, St Illtyd		
Parish of Llansantffraid, Bettws and Aberkenfig (St Bride, Llansantffraid; St David, Bettws; St John, Aberkenfig)		
Parish of Llantrisant (Ss Illtyd, Gwynno and Dyfodwg; St Michael, Beddau; St David, Miskin)		
Llantwit Major, Rectorial Benefice of Llantwit Major		
Margam, Margam Abbey (St Mary the Virgin)		
Parish of Merthyr Dyfan (St Dyfan and St Teilo, Merthyr Dyfan; St Paul, Barry)		
Merthyr Tydfil, Christ Church		
Merthyr Tydfil, St David		
Neath, Parish of Neath with Llantwit		
Nolton, St Mary		
Parish of Penarth and Llandough (St Augustine, Penarth; Holy Nativity, Penarth; Saint Dochdwy, Llandough)		
Parish of Penmark with Porthkerry (St Mark, Penmark; St Curig, Porthkerry; St Peter, Rhoose)		
Penrhiwceiber, St Winifred		

Pontypridd, St Catherine		
Port Talbot, Parish of St Theodore		
Porthcawl, Parish of Newton, Nottage, and Porthcawl		
Parish of Porth Newydd (St John the Evangelist, Cymmer; St Luke the Evangelist, Llwyncelyn; St Paul, Porth)		
Parish of Radyr (St John the Baptist, Danescourt; Christ Church, Radyr)		
Roath, Roath Parish: St Margaret, St Anne and St Edward		
St Brides-super-Ely, St Bridget		
St Brides Major, St Bridget		
Parish of Tonyrefail (St David, Tonyrefail; St Alban; St Barnabas, Gilfach Goch)		
Treharris, Trelewis and Bedlinog, St Matthias		
Parish of the Vale of Neath (St Mary, Blaengwrach; St Cadoc, Glynneath; St David, Resolven)		
Whitchurch, St Mary, St Thomas, and All Saints		

Monmouth	St Woolos Cathedral, Newport	Abergavenny, St Mary's Priory
Bassaleg Benefice (St Basil, Bassaleg; St Anne, High Cross; St John the Baptist, Rogerstone)		
Parish of Bedwas (St Barrwg, Bedwas; St Thomas, Trethomas)		
Blaenavon, St Peter (Parish of Blaenavon with Capel Newedd)		
Caerwent Parishes Group		
Caldicot, St Mary		
Chepstow and district churches together (St Mary, Chepstow; St Christopher, Chepstow; St Tewdric, Mathern; St Peter; St Pierre; St Andoenus, Mounton; St Luke, Titshill; St Mary, Tidenham; St Michael, Tidenham Chase)		
Cwmbran, Llantarnam, St Michael and All Angels		
Goetre, Parish of Goetre and Llanover		
Gwent, Risca, St Mary		
Llangybi/Tregrug, St Cybi		
Monmouth, Churches Together in Monmouth		
Monmouth, St Mary's Priory		
Newport, All Saints, St Julian, St Paul, St Stephen and Holy Trinity		
Overmonnow, with Mitchel Troy and Wonastow		
Pontnewydd, Holy Trinity		
Raglan Group (St Cadoc, Raglan; St John, Llandenny; St Peter, Bryngwyn)		
St Arvans, St Arvans		
Skenfrith, St Bridget		
Tillery Churches (St Michael, Abertillery; St Paul, Cwmtillery)		

St Asaph	St Asaph Cathedral	Rural deanery – Dyffryn Clwyd
Deanery – Llanfyllin		
Deanery – St Asaph		
Abergele, St Michael		
Bistre, Parish of Bistre		
Bodelwyddan, St Margaret		
Bryneglwys, St Tysilio		
Parish of Buckley (St Matthew, Buckley; Good Shepherd, Drury)		
Bwlch-y-Cibau, Christ Church		
Chirk, St Mary (with St David, Froncysyllte)		
Colwyn Bay, Parish of Colwyn Bay and Bryn-Y-Maen		
Connah's Quay Parish, consisting of St Mark and St David		
Dyserth, St Bridget and St Cwyfan		
Eglwysbach, St Martin		
Greenfield, Holy Trinity		
Gresford, All Saints		
Gwaenysgor, St Mary Magdalene		
Gwersyllt, Holy Trinity		
Hope Parish (St Cynfarch, Hope; Emmanuel Church, Penyffordd)		
Llanasa, St Asaph and St Cyndeyrn		
Llanbedr, Llanbedr group of parishes		
Llandyrnog, St Tyrnog		
Llanfair Caereinion, Llanllugan and Manafon (St Mary, Llanfair Caereinion; St Mary, Llanllugan; St Michael, Manafon)		
Llanfair Dyffryn Clwyd, St Cynfarch & St Mary		
Llanfwrog group of parishes		
Llanfyllin, St Myllin		
Llangollen, St Collen		
Llangynog, St Melangell		
Llanrhos Parish (St Hillary, Llanrhos; St Paul, Craig y Don; St David, Penrhyn Bay; All Saints, Deganwy)		
Llansantffraid Glyn Dyfrdwy, St Ffraid		
Llanynys, St Saeran		
Llay, St Martin of Tours		
Meliden, St Melyd		
Mold, St Mary the Virgin		

Montgomery Parish		
Newtown Parishes (All Saints, Newtown; Llanllwchaiarn Church; St Gwynog, Aberhafesp)		
Pontblyddyn, Christ Church		
Powys, St Melangell		
Prestatyn Parish		
Rhosnesni, St John		
Rhosymedre, St John		
Rhuddlan, St Mary		
Parish of Rhyl (St Thomas; St Ann; Holy Trinity with St John the Baptist)		
Rossett, Christ Church		
Ruabon, St Mary		
Ruthin, The Collegiate and Parochial Church of St Peter		
St Asaph, All Saints Sinan		
St Asaph, St Asaph and St Kentigern		
Sandycroft, St Francis		
Parish of Shotton (St Ethelwold; St Andrew)		

St Davids	**St Davids Cathedral**	**Deanery – Emlyn**
Aberaeron Parish (Holy Trinity, Aberaeron; St David, Hênfynyw; Llanddewi Aberarth Church; St Padarn, Llanbadarn Trefeglwys)		
Abergwili Group (St David, Abergwili; St Michael, Llanfihangel uwch Gwili; Capel y Groes)		
Aberystwyth (Trinity Place), Holy Trinity		
Aberystwyth, Eglwys y Santes Fair (St Mary)		
Aberystwyth (Parish of Aberystwyth), St Michael		
Carmarthen, St Peter		
Churches of Cothi Valley and Brechfa Forest (St Teilo, Brechfa; Dewi Sant, Abergorlech; Llanfihangel, Rhos Y Corn)		
Llanbadarn Fawr, St Padarn		
Llandeilo Fawr: Parish Church of St Teilo, Llandeilo		
Steynton, Parish Church		
Rectorial Benefice of Tenby (St Anne, New Hedges; St Julian, Tenby Harbour; St Mary, Tenby; St Laurence, Gumfreston; St Nicholas and St Teilo, Penally)		

Swansea and Brecon	**Brecon Cathedral**	**Rural deanery – Hay**
Parish of Bronllys with Llanfilo		

Caereithin, St Teilo		
Cockett, St Illtyd		
Crickhowell, St Edmund		
Parish of the Irfon Valley (St Cadmarch, Llangammarch Wells; St Cannen, Llangatten; St Afan, Llanfechan; Parish Church, Llanlleonfel) Killay, St Hilary and St Martin		
Llandrindod Wells, Holy Trinity		
Parish of Llwynderw (Holy Cross; Clyne Chapel)		
Llyswen Group (five parishes in rural mid-Powys)		
Parish of Manselton and Cwmbwrla (St Michael and All Angels, Manselton; St Luke the Evangelist, Cwmbwrla)		
Oystermouth, All Saints with Norton Mission		
Paincastle group of parishes: Bryngwyn, Newchurch, Llanbedr Painscastle and Llandewi Fach		
Sketty, Parish of Sketty		
Swansea, Collegiate and Parish Church of St Mary; St Gabriel; St James		
Parish of Talgarth and Llanelieu		
Waunarlwydd, St Barnabas		

Further reading

Books

Jeremy Gibson and Mervyn Medlycott, *Local Census Listings 1522–1930: Holdings in the British Isles* (Federation of Family History Societies, 1997). Available from the SoG bookshop (sales@sog.org.uk).

R.W. McDonald in The National Library of Wales Journal, vol. xix, pp. 113–31 'Cofrestri Plwyf Cymru' (in Welsh); 399–429 'The parish registers of Wales' (in English).

D.J. Steel, *National Index of Parish Registers, i: General Sources of Births, Marriages and Deaths before 1837* (Society of Genealogists, 1968). Both articles are available at http://welshjournals.llgc.org.uk/browse/listissues/llgc-id:1277425 under Cyf. 19, rh. 2 Gaeaf 1975 and Cyf. 19, rh. 4 Gaeaf 1976 respectively.

C.J. Williams and J. Watts-Williams, *Parish Registers of Wales/Cofrestri Plwyf Cymru*, 2nd edn (National Library of Wales, Welsh County Archivists' Group and the Society of Genealogists, 2000).

National Index of Parish Registers – published by the Society of Genealogists as a series, these include a separate volume on Nonconformist churches.

Protestation Returns – the lists of men of aged 18 and over who signed an oath in 1642 'to live and die for the true Protestant religion', distributed by the sheriff of the county to every parish. The printed text was read out in the church and lists were taken of those who signed – and those who didn't. These may be available in the county archives, or from the appropriate family history society.

Online resources

National Library of Wales – www.llgc.org.uk/index.php?id=485. Page on Church in Wales Records, including a link to the online index to pre-1838 bonds and allegations at http://isys.llgc.org.uk/

Parish locator programme, freeware download – www.dmbceb.me.uk

Yny lhyvyr hwnn (the first printed book in Welsh, by Sir John Price of Brecon, 1546) – www.llgc.org.uk/index.php?id=digitalmirror

Dade registers – www.pontefractfhs.org.uk/Dade_registers.htm

Welsh parish registers at the Society of Genealogists, London – www.sog.org.uk/prc/wal.shtml

8

Nonconformist and Other Church Records

The definition of Nonconformist is anyone who belongs to a Protestant church other than the Church of England, the Church in Wales (*Yr Eglwys yng Nghymru*) and the Church of Ireland. It does not cover Catholics, or those of other faiths (Judaism, Islam, Hinduism etc.). In contrast to the Church of England, the Church in Wales (not 'of' Wales, notice) is not the established church, as a consequence of the controversial Welsh Church Act of 1914, forced through by Nonconformists who objected to paying tithes to a church to which they did not belong. However, as a member of the Anglican Communion, the Church in Wales does recognise the primacy of the Archbishop of Canterbury as the overall leader of the Anglican Communion, despite the fact that he has no formal authority in Wales except in certain ecclesiastical court matters and in some border parishes that escaped disestablishment, and certain other remaining functions. The current archbishop (until January 2013), the Most Reverend Rowan Williams, is Welsh and came up through the Welsh church, as Bishop of Monmouth (1992) and Archbishop of Wales (1999). Thus, the Church in Wales is an independent Province of the Anglican Communion, composed of six dioceses (see p. 132–137 for a list) led by six diocesan bishops (one of whom is the Archbishop of Wales, currently the Most Reverend Barry Cennydd Morgan, Bishop of Llandaff) and two assistant bishops.

The equivalent Anglican Church north of the border is the Episcopal Church of Scotland, but the established church there is the (Presbyterian) Church of Scotland.

It is also necessary to clear up any confusion between 'Church' and 'Chapel'. It is widely held that 'Church' refers to the Church in Wales and 'Chapel' to any, often Nonconformist, denomination – in Wales, the chapel is the building used for worship and a church is the congregation or community that worships there and belongs to the parish.

Nonconformists

To the matter in hand: there was considerable dissent from the Act of Uniformity passed in 1662. The original 1558 Act of Uniformity was abolished by Cromwell's Rump Parliament in 1650. This embedded the freedom of worship ensured four years previously, when Cromwell finally defeated Charles I in the field, and the Long Parliament had abolished the episcopacy in the Church of England in favour of a state-run Presbyterian system. It had also replaced the Book of Common Prayer with the Directory of Public Worship.

Charles II, however, dearly loved the bishops, and in 1662 got the Cavalier Parliament to pass another Act of Uniformity, which put everything back more or less where it had been. The Book of Common Prayer was restored as the official liturgy, while any minister who refused to 'conform' would be removed from the Church of England.

To be frank, most ministers did 'conform' and had continued to use the Book of Common Prayer during the Cromwellian Interregnum, even though they didn't have to – but many of them (and their parishioners) resented being told they now *had* to. As a result, some

2,000 clergy resigned their livings in the Church of England clergy and became known initially as Puritans, later as Nonconformists or Dissenters. These ministers continued to preach to their flock in private houses and in other places, often outdoors and generally in secret, at meetings known as conventicles. Out of this grew the English Presbyterian, Congregationalist and Baptist denominations, differing by sometimes minuscule matters of doctrine or (more usually) church management and control. They were later joined by Methodists and other 'Independents', and the 'Quakers'. The Society of Friends, as the Quakers are properly called, got their name as a jibe when their founder George Fox told Justice Bennet to 'quake at the word of the Lord', and it stuck. They were persecuted more than most, so it's no surprise that a number of Welsh Quakers upped sticks in the 1680s and headed for the Quaker colony of Pennsylvania (p. 152).

The initially small number of these Independents and their lack, for a while, of organisation and buildings, meant that surviving records are sparse, but they were relatively few in number anyway for the next 200 years or so. William and Mary's Toleration Act of 1689 wasn't particularly tolerant; it wasn't until the late 1800s that non-Anglicans could attend Oxford or Cambridge, for example.

The individual churches themselves schismed and reformed at various times, and to this day there are Wesleyan Methodists, Primitive Methodists, Independent Methodists, the Wesleyan Reform Union and other factions, and an uncountable number of different form of Baptists (especially in America, where one commentator reeled off about twenty, finishing with 'Buzzard Baptists – them who only goes to Church when somebody dies!').

Nonconformist records

These are considered 'non-parochial', which means they do not appear in standard pre-1837 parish records. However, there is good news:

1. There weren't as many Nonconformists in existence as is generally thought until the period covered by civil registration and the censuses.

2. Many Nonconformists chose to be baptised, married and – especially – buried by the Anglican Church, which means they may well turn up in 'normal' registers.

3. After civil registration started in 1837, two parliamentary commissions were established to collect registers from Baptist, Presbyterian, Methodist and other non-Anglican denominations – these are mainly held by The National Archives, Kew, but microfilm copies of the Welsh records for Wales are at the National Library of Wales, many Nonconformist births or baptisms are indexed in IGI/FamilySearch, and several societies have an interest in Nonconformist ancestry.

The Welsh Church Commission of 1910 collected the names of all chapels in existence at the time, so that's the best place to start looking for the place of worship of an ancestor. One way is to check a census –1881, for example, for the term 'minister' or a building called 'manse'. Another good place to start, especially for photographs, is Jill Muir's Welsh Chapels & Churches website (www.welshchapelsandchurches.org) and the GENUKI church database (www.genuki.org.uk/big/churchdb/), although this mostly contains Anglican parish churches at the beginning of the 1800s. Better still is to find a *Gazetteer* entry (www.genuki.org.uk/big/Gazetteer/) or consult Jones and Williams, *Church and Chapel Data from the Religious Census of 1851* (see *Further reading*, below). The extract below shows just how many places of worship there were in Manmoel Hamlet, Tredegar, at that time (there were more in Ushlawrcoed Hamlet).

St Georges Church, Tredegar
Rhymney District Church
Ebbw Vale School Room (used by those living 3 or 4 miles from the district church)
Jerusalem Chapel, Rumney, Particular Baptist
Moriah Independent Chapel, Rumney
Mormonites, Uchlawreved, Rumney
English Wesleyan Methodist Chapel
Cwm Shon Mathew, branch of the Welsh Wesleyan Cause at Twyn Carno
Goshen Independent Chapel
Paran Calvinist Methodist Chapel, Manmoel
Wesleyan Methodist Tabernacle, Rumney
Sion Independent, Rumney
Penuel Particular Baptist
Ebenezer Calvinist Methodist
Bethel Independent Chapel
Primitive Methodist Chapel, Victoria
Caersalem Welsh Baptist Chapel
Sharon Independent/Congregational Chapel
Zion Independent Chapel
Zion Particular Baptist Chapel
Penuel Welsh Calvinist Methodist Chapel, Ebbw Vale
English Wesleyan Chapel
Nebo Particular Baptist Chapel
Bethcar Welsh Wesleyan Methodist Chapel
Primitive Methodist Chapel, Sirhowy
Penuel Calvinist Methodist Chapel, Tredegar
Siloh Particular Baptists (Welsh)
Welsh Wesleyan Chapel, Tredegar
Sharon Independent Chapel
Wesleyan Chapel (English), Tredegar
Ebenezer Primitive Methodist Chapel, Tredegar
Adulam Independent/Congregational Chapel, Tredegar
English Baptist Chapel, Tredegar
Salem Calvinist Methodist Chapel, Tredegar

Finding Nonconformist records

- Many of the Nonconformist records collected after civil registration began in 1837 are held at The National Archives (TNA) at Kew – see their research guide (www.nationalarchives.gov.uk/records/research-guides/nonconformists.htm) – and many of the registers catalogued under series codes RG 4, RG 5, RG 6 and RG 8 are available at BMD Registers (www.bmdregisters.co.uk). This includes records for Baptists, Methodists, Presbyterians, Protestant Dissenters (from Dr Williams's Library, below), Wesleyans and Independents.
- Dr Williams's Library in Gordon Square, London, established in 1729, is the main research library for English and Welsh Protestant nonconformity – www.dwlib.co.uk/dwlib/.
- The National Library of Wales has microfilm copies of the collected Nonconformist records for Wales, the originals of which are held at TNA, Kew (above).

- Local record offices (p. 50–52) may have details on particular chapels or denominations in their areas, as well as indexes to church records compiled by local family history societies in Wales (p. 52–54).
- Search for 'nonconformist' and 'non-conformist' at Archives Wales – www.archiveswales.org.uk.
- IGI/FamilySearch has many Nonconformist births/baptisms indexed.
- Baptist Historical Society – http://www.baptisthistory.org.uk/.
- Quaker Family History Society –www.rootsweb.ancestry.com/-enggfhs/.
- United Reformed Church History Society – www.westminster.cam.ac.uk/index.php/urc-history-society.
- Strict Baptists Historical Society – www.strictbaptisthistory.org.uk/.

Roman Catholic Records

- Many Roman Catholic mission registers are held at the Catholic National Library, which has a county list of mission registers – www.catholic-library.org.uk/.
- Catholic Archives Society – www.catholic-history.org.uk/catharch/index.htm.
- Catholic Family History Society – www.catholic-history.org.uk/cfhs/index.htm.

Recusants

This is not a denomination as such, but a general term for anyone who did not belong to the established church (realistically, mainly Catholics). Recusants were initially subject to criminal penalties and later to civil penalties, the inability to take certain offices or occupations, and general discrimination. There was a 'Test' of faith so written that almost anyone asked to take it would be bound to fail. Laws passed under James VI and I and Charles I mainly targeted Roman Catholic recusants; most such laws were not repealed until the time of George IV, although they had ceased to be enforced by then. Recusants initially also included Protestant dissenters, although after the restoration of Charles II these were what came to be known as Nonconformists, Dissenters, Independents and so on.

The genealogical importance of this was that various people drew up lists of recusants within the local parish, burgh or court area. The best source is court records, but local archives may have papers too.

Jewish Records

Many Jewish records are still held by Jewish burial societies or at synagogues, but the London Metropolitan Archive has some records from the Federation of Synagogues. However, the best places to start are:

- the Jewish Genealogy Society of Great Britain – www.jgsgb.org.uk;
- avotaynu, a good general site for researching Jewish genealogy, which includes the Jewish Consolidated Surname Index (CSI) containing some 2 million names from thirty datasources – www.avotaynu.com.

Case study

Below is the edited output from a simple search at www.bmdregisters.co.uk for everyone named Ebenezer Griffiths, which in some cases produces a relative rather that the subject, because the 'search all' box was ticked. The search was free, but to see more details and images, buy credits.

Surname(s)	Forename(s)	Year of Event	Event Type	Place	Recordset
Griffiths	Ebenezer	1779	Baptism	Hertfordshire	RG4_0743
Griffiths	Ebenezer	1784	Birth	Shropshire	RG4_2921
Griffiths	Ebenezer	1784	Baptism	Shropshire	RG4_2869
Griffiths	Ebenezer	1784	Baptism	Shropshire	RG4_2921
Griffiths	**Ebenezer**	**1795**	**Baptism**	**Cardiganshire**	**RG4_3803**
Griffiths	Ebenezer	1808	Baptism	Lancaster	RG4_0052
Griffiths	Ebenezer	1808	Baptism	Lancashire	RG4_2694
Griffiths	Ebenezer	1809	Baptism	Sussex	RG4_3313
Griffiths	Ebenezer	1809	Baptism	Lancashire	RG4_2694
Griffiths	Ebenezer	1813	Baptism	Anglesey	RG4_2902
Griffiths	Ebenezer	1815	Burial	London	RG4_3993
Griffiths	Ebenezer	1815	Baptism	Pembrokeshire	RG4_4039
Griffiths	Ebenezer	1818	Baptism	Carnavonshire	RG4_3871
Griffiths	Ebenezer	1821	Baptism	Breconshire	RG4_4006
Griffiths	Ebenezer	1822	Baptism	Northamptonshire	RG4_3190
Griffiths	Ebenezer Jones	1832	Birth	Lancashire	RG4_2557
Griffirhs	Ebenezer	1835	Baptism	Glamorganshire	RG4_4118
Griffiths	Ann★	1835	Baptism	Pembrokeshire	RG4_3913

★(Father: Ebenezer Griffiths)

The entry in bold expands to:

Register of Baptisms at Trewen Independent Chapel in the Parish of Bron-gwyn, Cardiganshire from 1785 to 1816

TNA Reference: RG4 / Piece 3803 / Folio 12
Full Name: Ebenezer Griffiths
Date of Baptism: 29 May 1795
Place of Abode: Llandinam
County of Abode: Cardiganshire
Registration Town/County: Bron-Gwyn, Cardiganshire
Father: John Griffiths
Mother: Ann Griffiths

Sometimes the records have extra detail such as: father's profession, mother's maiden name, mother's parish, date of marriage, place of marriage, maternal parents (name(s), profession, town and county), paternal parents (name(s), profession), plus a helpful pedigree chart.

The original page can be downloaded as a PDF image (see p. 277) – and note that this Ebenezer is a twin, a detail that might have been missed by looking at the index alone.

Crown Copyright (courtesy of The National Archives)

Further reading

Geoffrey R. Breed, *My Ancestors Were Baptists: How Can I Find Out More About Them?* (London: Society of Genealogists, 1988).

Dafydd Ifans (ed.), *Cofrestri Anghydffurfiol Cymru (Nonconformist Registers of Wales)* (National Library of Wales and Welsh County Archivists' Group, 1994).

Hugh Jones, *Hanes Wesleyaeth Gymreig (History of Welsh Wesleyans)*, 4 vols (Bangor, Wales: Llyfrfa Wesleyaidd, 1911–13).

I.G. Jones and D. Williams (eds), *The Religious Census of 1851: A Calendar of the Returns Relating to Wales*, i: *South Wales* (Cardiff: UWP, 1976).

William Leary, *My Ancestors Were Methodists: How Can I Find Out More About Them?* 2nd edn (London: Society of Genealogists, 1990).

Edward H. Milligan and Malcolm J. Thomas, *My Ancestors Were Quakers: How Can I Find Out More About Them?* (London: Society of Genealogists, 1983).

Rosemary Wenzerul, *Tracing Your Jewish Ancestors* (Pen & Sword, 2008).

9

Welsh Emigration and Immigration

It's fair to say that the Welsh are fairly disinclined to migration, rarely venturing further afield than a hop across Offa's Dyke into England for work, or moving within Wales as employment patterns shifted from agriculture to industry. Also, the Welsh are small by population terms – perhaps 500,000 in the late 1700s and barely three times that by 1881. Therefore, they have made a much smaller numerical impact on the colonies than, say, the Irish, Scots and Jews, who seem to have migrated – admittedly often due to adverse circumstances – at the drop of a hat. Even so, there are sizeable pockets of Welsh all over the globe, now finding a renewed sense of identity and cultural heritage.

Types of Migration

Welsh population trends are covered in the chapter on censuses (Chapter 5) and only touched on in the context of migration. However, it is important to consider both together, as the population of any area is obviously (births + migrations in) – (deaths + migrations out). Migration itself can be expressed as gross migration in and out, or as net migration (migrations in) – (migrations out).

Migration is the permanent or semi-permanent movement of a person, family or whole community to another place. One well-known non-Welsh example of whole-community migration is the *Mayflower* voyage to America in 1620 of 120 Nonconformists (wrongly called 'Puritans'), plus the ship's crew, drawn together by their religious affiliation. Another is the clearance of entire families off lands in the Highlands of Scotland (which happened less than is commonly told). But there are Welsh examples of such forms of migration, as we shall see.

Specialists consider several classes of migration events:

- In-migration – movement within a nation, such as Welsh migrating into England and vice versa, or the movement away from rural north Wales to work in the industries of the south.
- Out-migration – the same event seen from the other side of the coin, so a family may have out-migrated from Anglesey and in-migrated to the Rhondda.
- Emigration – movement to another nation, as when Welsh went to America or Australia, or the Irish or Polish went to Wales.
- Immigration – when the emigrants arrive at the destination.
- On-migration – subsequent movement after the first event, as happened when over 100 immigrant Welsh families left the so-called Welsh Barony in Pennsylvania and went to East Tennessee (now the area around Knoxville) after the American Civil War.

With luck, there will be records at both ends of these events – such as a passenger list of those leaving on emigration, and an arrivals list at the other end when immigrating. However, that is not always the case, and other classes of records have to be searched (see below).

Reasons for Emigration from Wales

There could be one of several rationales for migration, including the following.

Voluntary

- Free migration – trade. As early as the 1630s, the Welsh went overseas to set up or garrison military outposts, or in the interest of trade – setting up trading-posts and ports for merchant ships.
- Free migration – economic and social necessity. Many free emigrants simply sought better opportunities elsewhere, away from poverty or what they felt was political and religious oppression back home. The possibility of land ownership (as opposed to tenanting or subsistence agriculture for a large landowner) was an added draw, particularly after the poor harvests and famines in Wales around 1800. Many simply went for steady work and a better life, such as the many miners who settled around the areas with coal, mineral and slate that needed skilled mining. Are the motives of a tin worker who moved to America in the 1890s for economic advantage any different from those of actors Richard Burton and Anthony Hopkins when they moved to Hollywood?
- Free migration – religious. This is distinct from those who left from a feeling of religious persecution, as when thousands of Welsh members of the Church of Jesus Christ of Latter-Day Saints (Mormons) emigrated to the United States, mainly Utah, in the 1840s. The Welsh Quaker communities in Pennsylvania and the Baptists who founded Rehoboth and Swansea, Massachusetts, are other examples. There are other forms of persecution – Joseph Jenkins, a farmer from Cardiganshire, famously headed for Australia in 1868 at the fairly advanced age of 51 to get away from his nagging wife, as recorded in a series of not-quite-believable diaries recording his life as a 'swagman' in the bush country of Victoria!
- Assisted migration – typically from 1815 to about 1900. Migrants were paid, or had their passage paid, to move elsewhere; this could be at the instigation of the home country (as when it was used as an alternative to poor relief) or the target country (after 1840, the British colonies in South Africa, New Zealand and Australia provided passage money and/or land grants, especially to skilled workers, artisans and professionals, to encourage in-migration at a time when these countries were growing).
- Military service – another form of sponsored settlement (see Chapter 14). Often, soldiers serving overseas were offered, at discharge, parcels of land or other incitements to settle in the colony where they had last serving, as happened in Australia from 1791, Canada from 1815 and New Zealand from 1844.

Involuntary

- Transportation of prisoners. Up to 1870, over 200,000 'criminals' in Britain received a sentence that included a conditional pardon, subject to exile and transportation to a penal colony, typically for seven years, after which they were free to stay there, or come back. It is not always clear how many of these prisoners were from Wales. Until America declared independence in 1776, more than 50,000 prisoners were sent there, mainly to the Virginia and Maryland areas. After this, the newly independent America was not a possible destination, so from 1788 to 1869 over 160,000 people (including some 2,500 Welsh) were transported to Australia (see Text Box, Prison Hulks, p. 72).
- Children. To Britain's great shame, right up to the 1960s about 130,000 children or perhaps more were deported – there is no other word for it. Mainly, these were children

in orphanages or in the care of the authorities. Some were told their families had died, and the parents often got no information about where they had gone. Perhaps 10–12 per cent of all Canadians – maybe 4 million people – are descended from what were called 'British Home Children'. The Scottish website Golden Bridge (http://content. iriss.org.uk/goldenbridge/migration/journey.html) has shocking stories of the 100,000 or so abandoned and orphaned children sent to Canada alone between 1869 and 1930, and Library and Archives Canada has a site dedicated to immigration records and Boards of Guardians records (www.collectionscanada.gc.ca/databases/home-children/index-e. html). Canada has designated 28 September as British Home Child Day (www.children. gov.on.ca/htdocs/English/britishhomechildday/index.aspx).

Many children were sent off to virtual slavery in Canada, Australia and elsewhere by various charities and religious bodies, and more than a few were subject to ill-treatment, abuse and poor living conditions. There has been considerable publicity recently about the horrors many children suffered at the hands of church organisations in Australia. These children received an official apology from the British Government in 2011. It is interesting that this started exactly at the time transporting convicts to Australia was stopped.

Semi-permanent and 'boomerang' migration

- Not everyone who left stayed away for ever, and many never intended to. There are examples of Welsh people who left, made some money (or didn't!) and returned to Wales, often with families. Some left, came back, and left again. These can often be found in censuses when one or both parents were born in Wales but the children were born in Canada, for example.

Emigrants' letters
There is a partularly poignant series of nineteen letters plus a ballad available for view at the National Library of Wales website (http://digidol.llgc.org.uk/METS/HMJ00001/frames). Most are from Henry Jones (1824–52), who emigrated to Holland Patent, New York, in 1850, and his sister, Mary Jones (1831–61), who emigrated to Ballarat, New South Wales, in 1856, and are addressed to family in Llanfihangel-y-Pennant, Gwynedd.

General Sources for Migration Information
The thing to remember here is that movements within the UK (England and Wales, Scotland, Ireland), the Isle of Man and Channel Islands, and the colonies (Australia, Canada, India, South Africa, New Zealand etc.) required no documents, and such voyages may not have generated much by way of records. Free emigrants were, in the main, not recorded, except perhaps on a passenger list, if they went to the United States before 1776, Canada before 1865, or Australia, New Zealand and South Africa until well into the twentieth century.

Sometimes, the evidence of migration is 'negative' – a person is found in the censuses of 1881 and 1891, say, but disappears by 1901 and there is no record of a death. That suggests migration away from England and Wales, and is a clue that a search of censuses and other records in America, Australia and elsewhere might prove fruitful. There is an example of this on p. 165.

Of course, positive evidence is far better! As mentioned above, migrations should trigger records of some kind at one or both ends of the voyage. There are records of people emigrating and immigrating, including passenger lists, permissions to emigrate, naturalisation and passport records, lists of transported prisoners or registers of assistance to emigrate. These records may contain such details as: name, age, occupation, place of origin or birthplace, destination, ship, date of arrival and other information, but very often not all of these. Passengers may be grouped as

George Baxter (1804–67), an artist and printer from Sussex but based in London, invented commercially viable colour printing based on relief and intaglio methods, using coloured steel and copper-engraved plates. Despite having patents and producing an estimated 20 million prints, he never made any money. He was insolvent in 1860, bankrupt by 1865 and died two years later, run over by a horse omnibus. His son, also George Baxter, emigrated to Sydney, New South Wales, Australia, in the 1880s, where he opened a shop selling his father's prints and gave art lessons. These two famous prints were made in 1854 and 1853 respectively, and show the letter home (top) and the letter from home (below).

families and it may be possible to infer groups migrating together – a shared place of birth or destination, for example.

There may be later records at the destination, such as overseas censuses (which may give a place of birth and date of naturalisation) and death records. But it's not always as simple as looking up a passenger list (see below) or checking a census (Chapter 5).

Do not forget that people moved on – from one American state to another, and even between countries, such as the many who found New Zealand disappointing and headed for Australia or even California, or those who moved to America after disembarking in Canada and vice versa.

Migration records

To search migration records, you will need to know the name of the migrant(s) and the date of emigration (approximate). It helps if the name of the ship is also known, and the reason for migration (forced, voluntary, assisted etc.). Do not confuse point of departure with previous residence – someone from Wales could have left from Liverpool, Southampton, Glasgow, or even Queenstown or Moville in Ireland, and they might be listed on a passenger list as 'English' or 'From England' regardless of their origin in Wales. If the ship's name is known, it may be possible to find details of typical ports of embarkation and arrival in, for example, *Lloyd's Register of British and Foreign Shipping*, which is usually available at large municipal or specialist maritime libraries.

The Board of Trade in Britain started keeping passenger lists in and out in 1890. TNA has over 160,000 passenger lists (listing some 25 million passengers arriving at and leaving UK ports on long-haul voyages), and makes these available through commercial partner websites.

Outward-bound passenger lists of travellers from ports in the United Kingdom and Ireland to long-haul destinations (including Australia, Canada, India, New Zealand, South Africa and the USA) for the years 1890 to 1960 are at findmypast.co.uk (free to search but with a charge for downloading passenger list images). Find My Past also has over 350,000 UK passport applications made between 1851 and 1903.

Inward-bound passengers from foreign ports outside Europe and the Mediterranean are available on ancestry.co.uk, which also has certificates of alien arrivals and returns and papers (1836–69) plus aliens' entry books (1794–1921) and Hamburg passenger lists (1850–1934), useful for north European and Jewish passengers and those on their way through the UK to elsewhere.

TNA has a multi-partner site called Moving Here (www.movinghere.org.uk), which covers immigration into England and Wales over the last 200 years, in particular by Irish, Jewish, Caribbean and South Asian communities.

Other passenger lists

These are port of entry or embarkation records listing the names of arriving or departing passengers; although departure lists from Britain and Ireland are rare before 1890. After 1890 they are arranged chronologically by port of departure.

Possibly the best places for passenger lists are two wholly wonderful, free and volunteer-driven websites – The Ships List (www.theshipslist.com) and Immigrant Ships Transcribers Guild (www.immigrantships.net).

Assisted emigrants registers

Those applying for assistance to emigrate were recorded in special registers, which often have information beyond the usual name, age and residence – such as occupation, destination, name of sponsor, address of relative (if any) and size of family (see p. 165). Some parish and estate records list emigrants if they received help from the parish or landlord – common at a time when emigration was used as an alternative to poor relief (p. 153). These can usually be found in Welsh church records (Chapters 7 and 8) and land and property records at the National Library of Wales or local records centres (see Chapter 4 for lists).

Wills and probate records

It may not seem obvious at first, but a will or death duty register might make mention of an emigrant relative. The will of someone from Wales who died abroad but had property in Wales would have been proved in the Prerogative Court of Canterbury (1184–1858) or at the Principal Probate Registry (1858 and after). Start by searching:

- Prerogative Court of Canterbury (PCC) Wills at TNA, Kew (www.nationalarchives.gov. uk/documentsonline/wills.asp).
- National Library of Wales (www.llgc.org.uk/index.php?id=487).
- Archives Network Wales (www.archivesnetworkwales.info/cgi-bin/anw/fulldesc_nofr?inst_id=1&coll_id=77933).
- GENUKI (www.genuki.org.uk/big/eng/Probate.html).
- Peter Coldham's book *American Wills and Administrations in the Prerogative Court of Canterbury, 1610–1857* (Genealogical Publishing Company, 1989).

Other sources

- Emigration map from Wales to America at Data Wales (www.data-wales.co.uk/emmap. htm).
- David Peate, *Emigration in Welsh Family History: A Guide to Research*, 2nd edn (Federation of Family History Societies, 1998).

American Welsh

We have already seen (p. 145) that comparatively few Welsh emigrated to the USA (unlike Scots or Irish), and that those who did so predominantly went to certain places. However, the estimated 250,000 Welsh who migrated to America over the last 350 years have left a considerable number of descendants – as many as 1.75 million (or perhaps 2 million) Americans claim to have Welsh ancestry, and that's only the ones who are aware of it. Given that the present-day population of Wales is less than 3 million, that is a considerable diaspora in proportional terms. Presidents with Welsh ancestry include Thomas Jefferson, Abraham Lincoln, John Adams, John Quincy Adams, James Garfield, Calvin Coolidge, Richard Nixon and Barack Obama, not to mention Confederate President Jefferson Davis and Vice President Hubert Humphrey. And let's not forget the outlaw Jesse James, screen stars Richard Burton, Bette Davis, Ray Milland and (more recently) Anthony Hopkins, author Jack London and financier J.P. Morgan. However, the alert genealogist will notice that similar claims are made for almost all of these, especially the presidents, to Scots, Irish, Dutch, German, Swedish and other ethnic heritages – we should never forget that America is a real melting pot and almost everyone is an admixture of almost everything, including Native American and African.

Surnames (Chapter 3) like Davies, Hopkins, Humphrey(s) and Morgan are quintessentially Welsh (just as Nixon is Scottish and Lincoln is English), and when we track such names, the highest proportion are in the mid-Atlantic states, the Carolinas, Georgia, Alabama and the Appalachian parts of West Virginia and Tennessee. There are relatively few in New England, the northern Midwest, and the south-west. However, surnames are not always a reliable indicator – tracing Welsh migrations and census returns of people who claim Welsh background shows a radically different pattern. As more and more people have DNA analyses (Chapter 2), the overall picture will become clearer.

The first 'migration' to deal with is the mythical tale of Prince Madog, son of Prince Owain of Gwynedd, reaching North America in 1170, where he is said to have founded the Welsh-speaking Native American tribe known as the Mandan. There is absolutely no evidence for this, and a great deal to the contrary. In many ways, it mirrors the story of St Brendan and his voyage sometime between 512 and 530 AD, and was consciously fostered in the Elizabethan times to provide Britain with a prior claim to the Americas over Spain.

Madog was said to have taken 100 men to form a colony, setting off from Llandrillo, then returning to Wales to gather up settlers. Ten ships left, and landed somewhere in western Florida or perhaps on the Alabama coast, then moved up the great river systems until settling down somewhere in the Great Plains of the Midwest. As for Welsh-speaking Native Americans, this was a later graft onto earlier stories of tribes speaking Irish, Portuguese or even Hebrew. Various stories of Welsh-speaking Indians (near Louisville, Kentucky) and even a copy of the Bible in Welsh have been discounted and disproved over the years but the geographers Lewis and Clark were ordered to keep an eye (or ear) out for them, and in the eighteenth century explorer John Evans of Waunfawr embarked on his great Missouri River expedition partly because he hoped to find the Welsh-descent 'Madogwys' tribe. Even Brigham Young got in on the act, sending a Welshman with Jacob Hamblin in 1858 to the Hopi. They brought back three Hopi to Salt Lake City, where other Welshmen desperately tried to communicate with them, to no great end.

The Daughters of the American Revolution didn't help either, setting up a plaque in 1953 at Mobile Bay, Alabama, in memory of Prince Madoc – which was later removed by the Alabama Parks Department.

One of the first documented groups of Welsh migrants to North America was the congregation of Baptists who settled in Rehoboth, Massachusetts, under the leadership of John Miles (c. 1621–83). A quite remarkable man, Miles (or Myles) was born in Wales, educated at Brasenose College, Oxford, and became a member of the early Particular (Reformed) Baptist congregation at Glasshouse, London. Miles went to Ilston and founded the first Baptist Church in Wales, where he was minister from 1649 to 1662 and an adherent of Oliver Cromwell. At the restoration of King Charles II and the insistence on the Book of Common Prayer in the 1660s, Miles left England for the Plymouth Colony, along with others from Swansea and Ilston.

Originally attached to the Congregationalist church in Rehoboth, Massechussetts, Miles and his group found their Baptist persuasion unwelcome, so they went on to found their own church and a new settlement (which was later incorporated as an independent town), and, for obvious reasons, called it Swansea. Miles was pastor there for twenty years, but during King Philip's War in 1675–76, the Native Americans made life a little dangerous, so Miles pastored at the First Baptist Church in Boston while others of the 70-odd Welsh settlers moved to nearby Taunton. Swansea was burned, but was rebuilt after the hostilities died down, and became a place of ironworks, foundries and fishing, although it is now mainly agricultural.

This makes John Miles the founder of one of the first Baptist churches in America, as well as one of the earliest recorded Baptist churches in Wales. He had with him the 'Ilston Book', the record of the chapel at Ilston Beck in Gower. It contains the complete list of 261 members of that chapel up to 1660, and where they came from in South Wales. It is therefore of immense historical and genealogical significance, and is now held at Brown University in Providence, Rhode Island. It has been transcribed and republished (*The Ilston Book: Earliest Register of Welsh Baptists*, transcribed and edited by B.G. Owens (Aberystwyth: National Library of Wales, 1966)).

After this, any Welsh who came to America tended to congregate in and around certain states, until the steady push west and the increased immigration of the late 1800s. During the period of peak migration, 1850–70, an estimated 60,000 Welsh emigrated to the USA. This was largely a consequence of poverty among Welsh tenant farmers and labourers, and unreliable employment in the coal and steel industries. Radicals such as Samuel Roberts (1800–85) and Michael D. Jones (1822–98) stoked up interest in emigration, attracted by the possibility of owning arable land or working in more economically stable mining, quarrying and steel-making industries. Many of these naturally headed for pre-existing Welsh communities, especially in Pennsylvania, Ohio and upper New York State.

Pennsylvania and early settlement

It is not well known that the colony of Pennsylvania was originally called New Wales. The most significant early migration of Welsh to America was the settlement of Welsh Quakers in the 'Welsh Tract' or 'Welsh Barony' north-west of Philadelphia, at the invitation of William Penn. This started in the 1680s but continued for decades after as more Welsh – mainly Nonconformists – migrated to join them. By 1700, the Welsh constituted about 7,000, or a third, of the population at that time. Welsh place names abound from then, and increased after a second wave of Welsh migrants turned up in the late 1700s – the best known is Cambria (now Cambria County) established by Morgan John Rhys (1760–1804) in 1797. This wasn't so much a settlement as speculative investment, and the first community at Beulah near Ebensburg didn't last long. Rhys, from a farm called Graddfa near Llanbradach in *Caerffili* (Caephilly), was largely self-educated, and became a Baptist minister, which put him in a good position to start free day schools and Sunday schools in Beulah to teach children to read or write – including in Welsh. Morgan agitated for the rights of the 'Indians', was active in helping the poor, and even went over to France to hand out Bibles.

A further migration in the 1800s was to provide workers for the anthracite and bituminous mineral mines, but not always as mere mine workers. The Welsh had other skills and experience, including the qualities needed to manage and run the businesses. This was a double-edged sword (from some perspectives) as these organisational talents and a certain typically Welsh independence of mind manifested themselves in the establishment of labour unions, notably the United Mine Workers, led by John Lewis, born of a Welsh family in Iowa. The Welsh also exercised their talents in other aspects of politics in colonial Pennsylvania, notably the Legislature. Philadelphia City Hall bears a plaque, which says:

> Perpetuating the Welsh heritage, and commemorating the vision and virtue of the following Welsh patriots in the founding of the City, Commonwealth, and Nation: William Penn, 1644–1718, proclaimed freedom of religion and planned New Wales later named Pennsylvania. Thomas Jefferson, 1743–1826, third President of the United States, composed the Declaration of Independence. Robert Morris, 1734–1806, foremost financier of the American Revolution and signer of the Declaration of Independence. Governor Morris, 1752–1816, wrote the final draft of the Constitution of the United States. John Marshall, 1755–1835, Chief Justice of the United States and father of American constitutional law.

Later that century there was a large immigration of tin workers to the Pittsburgh area. This came about because until 1890 the tin mines of Wales (so prized by the Romans) were the world's biggest producer of tinplate, which was used primarily for food cans, and America was the largest customer. Protectionist as ever, the US Government passed the McKinley Tariff in 1890, which raised the duty on imported tinplate. The natural result? Many Welsh entrepreneurs and skilled tin workers followed the economic tide and headed across the Atlantic to take advantage of an opportunity that had supplanted the one at home.

Afficionados of the daytime soap opera may know of *One Life to Live*, which is set in a (fictional) Pennsylvania town in the Welsh Tract called *Llanview*, supposedly Welsh for 'Church View' (although, while *llan* does mean 'church', the Welsh for 'view' would be *golygfa*).

More realistically, the famous Bryn Mawr (Welsh for 'big hill' but also the name of a market town in Blaenau Gwent, South Wales) was founded by Welsh Quakers and is now a highly respected private and selective female-only liberal arts college.

The nineteenth century

Emigration to America dropped off in the 1700s but in the first half of the 1800s it increased again – particularly after 1815, when it was used as a cheap (and politically expedient) alternative to having the local parish look after and pay to support the poor back in Wales. At this time, the Welsh established further communities in Pennsylvania as well as in Vermont, Ohio, and upstate New York. Many of these (especially after the 1840s) were made up of skilled coal miners and ironworkers.

These early settlements became the nucleus for later migration into the neighbouring states of Wisconsin, Minnesota, Illinois, Missouri, Iowa, Ohio, Idaho and elsewhere, mirroring the general trend of 'Go West, young man!' prevalent at the time, as America's frontier was opening up. In fact, there was so much Welsh migration to Wisconsin that the state constitution was translated into their native language.

Tennessee

In the 1860s, after the Civil War was over, as many as 100 families of immigrant Welsh left Pennsylvania to settle in East Tennessee, to the place later called Mechanicsville, which is now part of Knoxville. This was at the instigation of two brothers, Joseph and David Richards, and their partner John H. Jones, who needed workers for the Knoxville Iron Works (the site of which was later used for the 1982 World's Fair). The Welsh built a Congregational church, and Reverend Thomas Thomas was the first pastor in 1870. Something approaching 250 families in the greater Knoxville area can trace their ancestry back to these 'founding families', and St David's Day (1 March) is celebrated each year with great gusto.

New York

A major centre of Welsh community in the nineteenth century was Oneida County. The Welsh arrived there after poor harvests in 1789 and 1802, attracted by the prospect of owning land, especially good-quality agricultural land. An initial five families were soon joined by other agricultural migrants, who moved mainly to the townships of Utica, Steuben and Remsen, and by 1855 Oneida had a Welsh-origin population of over 4,000. They were not all farmers, however – those from North Wales were skilled as slate quarriers, and found ready employment in the 'Slate Valley' area of upper New York state and Vermont.

Maryland

Slate-working also accounts for the Welsh population in five townships especially built for them on the border of northern Maryland and southern Pennsylvania (around the area of Peach Bottom and Delta, PA) between 1850 and the 1940s. This was the source of the famous 'Peach Bottom' slate, considered exceptionally hard-wearing and therefore the best for roofing. Traditional Welsh cottage architecture can still be seen in the Whiteford-Cardiff Historic District of Harford County.

The push West

After the Civil War, many of the Welsh moved west (as did many other Americans), particularly to Michigan and Wisconsin, where they engaged in the small-farm activities they knew well. It is typical in America that a defined cultural group, with its own religious and cultural traditions and its own language, forms a strong community. The church was the centre of every community, and a Welsh-language press maintained historical, cultural and linguistic identity – but not to the exclusion of more general assimilation, as seen with the Amish, for example.

Ohio

The mass emigration from Wales to America in the 1800s featured Welsh incomers to Ohio: Canal Dover, Niles and Gloucester being particularly popular destinations. Mainly, especially in the early 1800s, they were farmers, but later there was considerable migration to the coal-mining areas. Jackson County and neighbouring Gallia County, both in the Appalachians of south-east Ohio, have come to be called 'Little Wales', or, even more specifically, 'Little Cardiganshire', and the Welsh language was still commonly heard there well into the 1950s. The University of Rio Grande established a Madog Center for Welsh Studies in the 1990s.

Illinois

There is a long history of Welsh engagement in Illinois, especially with Chicago. Thomas Jefferson Vance Owen, first president of the town in 1833, is said to be the 'Founder Father of Chicago'; his grandparents were immigrants from Wales. All over Chicago there is evidence of Welsh influence – avenues called Berwyn and Bryn Mawr as well as nearby towns like Cambria, Cardiff, St David, Edwardsville, Evanston and Swansea. Chicagoans of Welsh descent include architect Frank Lloyd Wright, actor Robin Williams, Hillary Rodham Clinton and (best of all) Murray 'the Hump' Humphreys (1899–1965), labour racketeer, and mobster Al Capone's Number Two, whose parents were from Llanidloes, Powis (once Montgomeryshire).

Indiana

By the early 1900s, many Welsh had immigrated or on-migrated to the north-eastern part of the state, particularly Grant County and Madison County, and the cities of Anderson, Gas City and Elwood. These were mainly industrial workers.

Minnesota

Blue Earth and Le Sueur counties are famously fertile farmlands, and so attracted many Welsh farmers in the 1850s and later. The 1880 census shows as many as 3,000 Welsh and about forty churches and chapels. There is a particularly good review of this in Phillips G. Davies's article, 'The Welsh Settlements in Minnesota: The Evidence of the Churches in Blue Earth and Le Sueur Counties', *Welsh History Review*, vol. 13, pp. 139–154.

Kansas

This is similar to Minnesota – 2,000 Welsh immigrants and some 6,000 on-migrants of Welsh ancestry went there for the rich farmland, mainly around Arvonia, Bala and Emporia, and many churches and chapels held services in Welsh. Again, Phillips G. Davies has provided a masterful analysis of this in 'The Welsh in Kansas: Settlement, Contributions and Assimilation', *Welsh History Review*, vol. 14, pp. 380–98 (available at http://welshjournals.llgc.org.uk/browse/viewpage/llgc-id:1073091/llgc-id:1080171/llgc-id:1080573/get650). The period covered is 1868 to 1918.

The West

Idaho

Malad City is the centre for the Welsh population in Idaho, but for slightly different reasons. This was originally a Welsh Mormon settlement, and proudly claims to have more people per head of Welsh ancestry than anywhere outside Wales itself (about 20 per cent). The Welsh dragon is seen on flags everywhere.

Utah

As expected, most Welsh Mormons settled in Utah, and most Welsh who settled in Utah were Mormons. This is a special study in its own right, and the website www.welshmormonhistory.org has a great deal of information, journals, images and stories, as do various websites of the Mormon Church and the Genealogical Society of Utah (GUS), especially www.familysearch.org.

California and the West Coast

With their strong tradition of mining, it is not surprising that the Welsh headed for California during the gold rush of 1849–51 (as they also did to the gold fields of Australia, New Zealand and South Africa). But the Welsh who moved west were not all miners – the California Gold Rush also saw an influx of sheep farmers, shopkeepers, traders and merchants. Welsh settlements were established in northern California, particularly the Sacramento Valley and Sierra Nevada regions – a good example is Cherokee, near Oroville, California, about 80 miles north of Sacramento (see www.rockincherokee.com/CHEROKEE/CHEROK~1.htm); a quarter of Amador County's population has Welsh ancestry. To celebrate Welsh heritage, there was a West Coast *Eisteddfod* (a Welsh arts festival and outdoor market) held in Los Angeles in 2011. There are Welsh Society meetings and annual gatherings held regularly in many states, plus the National Welsh Gymanfa Ganu Association (*cymanfa ganu* is a traditional Welsh hymn-singing gathering) organises an annual National Festival of Wales around the country, with workshops and seminars on culture, history, music etc., a Welsh market and even more hymns – although it should be said these have yet to reach the extremes of the Irish-focused St Patrick's Day parades or the kilts-whisky-and-haggis Tartan Weeks and Highland Games beloved of ex-pat Scots.

The Pacific Northwest and Rocky Mountain states also saw the spread of the Welsh diaspora after the 1850s.

United States records

- The US National Archives and Records Administration (NARA) has guides to migrant archives – www.archives.gov/genealogy/immigration.
- From 1892 to 1924 over 22 million migrants passed through Ellis Island (www.ellisisland.org) and FamilySearch (see below) has transcribed the lists.

FamilySearch (www.familysearch.org) allows free access to a comprehensive set of migration records and guides. Subscription or pay-as-you-go sites with good record sets include ancestry (www.ancestry.co.uk and www.ancestry.com) and Find My Past (www.findmypast.co.uk), which also has a database of 24 million passengers leaving UK ports on long-haul voyages between 1890 and 1960, in partnership with TNA, Kew.

A few books about Welsh arrivals are also available, such as: Charles H. Browning, *Welsh Settlement of Pennsylvania* (Philadelphia: Wm. J. Campbell, 1912).

Canadian Welsh (*Cymry Canada*)

Canada was the one of the primary destinations of Welsh emigrants from 1815 to 1850. Most immigrants before 1900 arrived in Quebec City or Halifax but passenger lists are rare before 1865.

- Transatlantic passenger lists to Canada for the period 1865 to about 1908 have been microfilmed by the National Archives of Canada – there is a catalogue (www.collectionscanada.gc.ca/genealogy/022-908.002-e.html) with links to online search resources including 'Passenger Lists 1865–1922'.
- The National Archives of Canada has an online database of immigration records for the period 1925 to 1935 (www.collectionscanada.gc.ca/databases/immigration-1925/index-e.html).

Patagonian Welsh (*Y Wladfa Gymreig ym Mhatagonia*)

The Welsh have a reputation as reluctant emigrants, and much nineteenth-century Welsh migration was internal, or was directed across Offa's Dyke into England by the prospect of employment. The total Welsh population has always been small, with no more than 0.5 million before the late eighteenth century and a little over 1.5 million by 1881.

Even so, there was an attempt at colonising a part of South America, which was ultimately not a great success. The rather remarkable and enterprising Rev. Michael D. Jones had taken the view that the second-generation Welsh in the USA had more or less forgotten their Welsh heritage, so he arranged for 153 emigrants to go to Argentina aboard the clipper *Mimosa* in 1865, embarking at Liverpool to pick up up passengers who had assembled at Aberdare, Birkenhead, Mountain Ash and Rhosllannerchrugog. The idea was to form a Welsh community eventually named *Y Wladfa Gymreig* (The Welsh Colony) in the Chubut Valley. On landing at Porth Madryn (*Puerto Madryn* in Spanish) they were met by two Welshmen, Lewis Jones and Edwyn Cynrig Roberts, who had already arrived in Patagonia to prepare for the arrival. The Argentine Government granted the Welsh settlers ownership of the land in 1875, which encouraged hundreds of other Welsh to join them.

The small Welsh-speaking population still survives, in a way. Many of the Welsh and their descendants later left, often for Australia, as they were not keen on being conscripted into the Argentine army, resisted pressure to become fully Argentinean (all teaching was in Spanish, for instance), and were frustrated by the scarcity of suitable land for farming. Sadly, although one of the first settlers, Richard Jones (known as *Berwyn*), kept a BMD register for years, most of the records were lost in a flood in 1899.

- *Y Wladfa* – The Welsh in Patagonia – www.h2g2.com/approved_entry/A1163503.
- History of Welsh Patagonia (bilingual site, English/Welsh) – www.teithiautango.co.uk.
- BBC: The Welsh in Patagonia – www.bbc.co.uk/cymru/patagonia/.
- Glaniad: stories and images of the Welsh settlement in Patagonia – www.glaniad.com/.

Australian Welsh (*Awstraliad-Cymreig*)

About one in three people living in Britain have an Australian in their family tree – that's 18 million Brits, with an Aussie in the background (the vast majority are unaware of this). The implication is that roughly the same will be true for ⅓ of the 3 million people currently living in Wales – 1 million Welsh residents should consider looking for an Australian connection (see p. 159).

Other than mining, the Welsh are possibly most famous for their sheep. That would seem to be the perfect combination for a life in early colonial Australia.

Captain Cook had Welshmen among his crew. Francis Wilkinson of Bangor, Caernarfon, was master's mate on the *Endeavour*, although it is not clear if he travelled with Cook to Australia.

The *Discovery*'s surgeon and medical officer, who was present at Cook's death in 1779 in the Sandwich Islands (now Hawaii) was David Samwell; Samwell was also a noted poet and known in that context by his bardic name *Dafydd Ddu Feddyg* (Black David the Doctor).

However, the first Welsh immigrants to Australia were hardly voluntary – they were four male and two female convicts who arrived with the First Fleet at Botany Bay, Australia, in 1788 to establish the first European colony in Australia.

By the time of the 1851 census, about 1,800 of the convicts transported to Australia (283 of them female) were Welsh, or at least had been tried and sentenced in Wales. That is only just over 1 per cent of all convicts sent to Australia by that time. Many were Welsh-speaking only, so they were not only strangers in a strange land, they were condemned to communicate with the English-speaking majority.

The four convicts who had been tried and sentenced in Wales to be transported on the First Fleet in 1788 were (ships' names in brackets):

Man Watkins, aged 19, given seven years for burglary at Glamorgan Quarter Sessions (*Friendship*);

Frances Williams, no age, given seven years for burglary at the Great Sessions of Flint (*Prince of Wales*);

William Davis, no age, given transportation for life at the Brecon Quarter Sessions (*Alexander*);

William Edmunds, no age, sentenced to death but later reprieved and transported for seven years at Monmouth Lent Assizes for stealing a heifer (*Alexander*).

It is noticeable in the records that most transported Welsh were from the industrialised south – chiefly Glamorgan and Monmouthshire – which had all the social problems attendant on industrialisation and urbanisation.

It is a feature of transportation – or rather, the crimes considered punishable by transportation – that aside from petty criminals and other felons sent overseas, a considerable number of well-educated, able and radical-thinking people ended up in the colonies. Welsh transportees in the first half of the 1800s include figures from the early trade union movement in Wales, such as Lewis Lewis (*Lewsyn yr Heliwr*, Lewsyn the Haulier), who was condemned to death but transported as a commutation for his part in the Merthyr Riots of 1831, and Chartist leaders John Frost, William Jones and Zephaniah Williams, convicted for causing the siege of the Westgate Hotel in Newport in 1839 and sent to Van Diemen's Land. (Frost was pardoned in his old age and went back to Newport, where he was greeted as a returning hero – which, to many, he was. Williams had a later and extremely successful carreer as an industrialist in Launceston.) It should be no surprise, then, that the Eureka Stockade rebellion of 1854 – the first outbreak of Australian nationalist, democratic and anti-colonial feeling – had among its organisers the Welsh-born Chartist John Basson Humffray.

That is not to say there weren't also 'free' emigrants, but they are harder to track down due to the sparse records of the time, and they were often lumped together in the category of 'England and Wales' We do know, for example, that fourteen of the congregation of Bethlehem Chapel in Blaenavon, Monmouthshire, left for Australia between 1828 and 1836, as recorded by the minister, Morgan Morgans. As far as we can tell from the earliest proper census, dated 1851, a small proportion of the Welsh in Australia were free settlers, attracted by the advertisements placed in the Welsh press by the migration agencies who organised the packet voyages.

The gold rush period of the 1850s changed the picture considerably, but that wasn't the only draw. Copper had been discovered at Kapunda in South Australia in 1843 and at Burra in 1845, and there were later finds at Wallaroo and Moonta, all of which attracted Welsh mineral miners and smeltermen. As a consequence, the Welsh-born population of South Australia tripled from 300 to 900 between 1846 and 1851, and Burra had a Welsh quarter called Llwchwr. One of the copper mineworkers was William Meirion Evans (1826–83) from Llanfrothen, Merionethshire, who has the distinction of being the first person in Australia to hold religious services in Welsh, at Burra in 1849. He later became ordained and was the founding editor *Yr Australydd* (the *Australian*) and its successor *Yr Ymwelydd* (the *Visitor*).

When gold was found in the Ballarat-Sebastapol area in 1951, the Welsh influx to the Province of Victoria increased markedly. Between 1851 and 1871 – the 'boomtown years' – the number Welsh-born settlers in Victoria increased from about 400 to nearly 7,000, although it later fell back. The Welsh still outnumbered other British groups in Victoria in 1881. Not all were miners – apart from shopkeepers, traders and artisans, professionals were also attracted to the area and its main port, Melbourne. For example, David John Thomas (1813–71) arrived in Melbourne in 1839 from his native Carmarthen, became the best-known surgeon in the area, and established the Melbourne Hospital.

The Welsh population also grew in the other Australian provinces, swelled by on-migration from New Zealand, so that by 1901 there were 12,000 people of Welsh descent all across the country.

Of all the provinces, New South Wales is the one with the most obvious connection. Not only was it the pre-eminent coal-mining region, it is said that Captain James Cook thought the eastern coast reminded him of the Vale of Glamorgan in South Wales, which he knew well; he thus named the area accordingly. Later settlements were given names like Aberdare, Cardiff, Neath and Swansea. As with Welsh immigration everywhere, the cohesion provided by the chapel and the Welsh language maintained and enhanced a sense of identity and social cohesion.

Sydney's most famous department store chain is David Jones – no surprise, then, that it was started by a young man of that name from Llandeilo, Carmarthenshire.

Sydney, like Melbourne, was a major port and often had merchant ships visiting whose captain or crew were Welsh-speaking, and who had sailed from Swansea and Cardiff or the North Wales harbours of Caernarfon or Porthmadog. They would naturally seek out Welsh churches and society.

From Sydney, many new arrivals would travel north to Queensland, heading for the gold mines at Charters Towers where they established the first Welsh church in Queensland in 1868. However, most Welsh were in the Ipswich coalfield, south of Brisbane, around Blackstone. The so-called 'coal king of the Queensland' was Lewis Thomas from Talybont, Cardiganshire, who built a frankly extravagant mansion, Brynhyfryd, but was happy to let it serve as a central point for the Welsh community locally.

The chapels and Welsh culture

Cymanfa Ganu (Welsh hymn-singing mass gatherings) were organised in Australia – largely by the Nonconformist churches – attracted hundreds and could last for days. Initially – just for reasons of economy and congregation size – most of the chapels were interdenominational and ecumenical, but eventually and predictably they split into Baptist, Methodist and 'other' Independent, just as had happened in Wales.

The churches and chapels were also the focal points for Band of Hope gatherings and tea meetings (both an expression of the strong temperance tradition), literary societies, fellowships and preaching assemblies, all more often than not conducted solely in Welsh, as well as the usual Sunday worship. Early on there was more than one Welsh–Australian periodical, the best known of which was *Yr Australydd* (the *Australian*) mentioned above.

The chapels found by the early 1900s that their services had to include English. A move to establish an all-Welsh community similar to the one in Patagonia, Argentina (p. 156) was proposed, but by 1910 the Patagonia experiment had failed and the Welsh colony there was mainly heading for Australia in any case.

However, there was an opposing trend. In the late eighteenth century the Welsh back at home had revived (some say 'reinvented') the literary, bardic and antiquarian tradition of the *Eisteddfod*, and by 1863 Australia had followed suit with what was to become the National *Eisteddfod*, then held annually around Victoria. Other provinces had *Eisteddfodau* at this time, but with a small Welsh population diluting itself and dispersing throughout the 'Lucky Country', anglicisation and assimilation took their toll. However, to this day the Ballarat South Street Festival, the Sydney *Eisteddfod* and many other events do a great job of keeping alive the flame of Welsh music, literature, language, the arts, traditions and cultural heritage. St David's societies, many founded in the 1800s, have also survived, and still prosper.

The twentieth century

By 1914, Cardiff was the world's largest port for coal export, but people were also exported in droves. The mass emigration from Wales to Australia in the early twentieth century, particularly to New South Wales and Victoria, was mostly comprised of farmers, and later miners going to work in the Australian coalfields. This was in contrast to the Welsh population movement of the nineteenth century, which was (unlike the Irish equivalent) mostly internal, with the rural population leaving their pastoral livelihoods to feed the growth of the iron industry in South Wales in the late 1700s, and the necessary coal mining in the valleys of the Rhondda and south-east that followed soon afterwards. The earlier Welsh migrations to Australia had taken place before the split between the Welsh-speaking, agricultural north and the industrial, English-speaking south was completely embedded, but the later migrations were after this. It would be expected, then, that the Welsh-only element in Australia would become diluted by Anglophone southern Welsh migrants.

How many Welsh, and where?

The population of Australia swelled from 53,000 in 1826 to 5.6 million by 1922; and around half of there were of UK origin. It is also said that some 20 per cent of the population of New South Wales is least partly Welsh, although the figure for Australia as a whole may be as low as 1 per cent. In 2006, Australia overall had 25,317 citizens of Welsh birth and 113,242 of claimed Welsh ancestry. However, a study in 1996 identified the 'ethnic strength' of Welsh Australians at almost 250,000, an interesting formula that took into account about 45,000 of Welsh-only origin and nearly 700,000 of mixed origin. The Welsh are therefore fifth in the Australian Anglo-Celtic league table, behind English, Irish, Scots and – amazingly – Cornish.

Other well-known Australian Welsh:
- Sir Samuel Walker Griffith (1845–1920), Chief Justice and Premier, proponent of Aborigine rights, free compulsory education and trade union legislation, and responsible for drafting the Constitution for the Commonwealth of Australia in 1891, was born at Merthyr Tydfil, Glamorganshire.
- Alf Morgans (1850–1933), Premier of Western Australia, was born in Wales but migrated to Australia in 1896.
- William Morris ('Billy') Hughes (1862–1952) migrated from Llandudno, Conwy, to Australia in 1884 with his Welsh parents, was the founding father of the Australian Labour Party, and became prime minister in 1915. During the Second World War he returned to Britain as part of David Lloyd George's war cabinet, and they would speak together in Welsh.
- The most famous – to Brits, at least – must be entertainer and artist Rolf Harris, born in Australia in 1930 of Welsh parents, Cromwell Harris and Agnes Robbins, who married in Redfern, New South Wales, in 1922.
- The singing-dancing-acting Minogue sisters, Kylie (b. 1968) and Dannii (b. 1971) have an Irish father and surname, but a mother born in Wales.

'Ancestry' figures should always be taken with a pinch of salt – if someone's four grandparents were born in, say, Scotland, Wales, Spain and Greece, why would the Scots or Welsh lineage predominate? It comes down to perceived identity, and may have as much to do with the overall make-up of the local area – there isn't much point choosing a Welsh identity in a town of predominantly Irish or Swedish descendants. Or perhaps there is!

Another way to estimate Welsh ancestry would be by surname, but this isn't always reliable. 'Jones' is one of the commonest surnames in the English-speaking world (apologies to the Welsh for that statement!) but *isn't* the commonest in Wales by a long chalk. However, it is among the most frequent in Australia – over 1 per cent. But any ancestors of an Australian Jones could be English, Scottish or Irish, who may or may not have had an earlier Welsh heritage.

Australia and the 'Ten Pound Poms'

Take another look at the numbers above. About 22 per cent – between a fifth and a quarter – of all Australians who claim in some way to be Welsh, were born in Wales. That suggests a continuing and recent pattern of immigration, most likely swelled by the 'Ten Pound Pom' assisted migration scheme run by the Government of Australia, when many British subjects were enticed to escape the greyness and austerity of postwar Britain for the sunnier climes and more relaxed lifestyle in the southern hemisphere – not to mention an ocean cruise with a stop-off at exotic ports. It sounds like a dream come true!

The reality wasn't always quite so rosy, though. The scheme had been set up in 1945 by the first Minister for Immigration, Arthur Calwell, as part of a policy called 'Populate or Perish' and a wider 'White Australia' strategy. Part of the idea was to support the rapidly growing industries with skilled workers and managers, but there was also a not-too-deeply buried feeling that Australia might soon be dominated by Asians (from the Far East as well as the dwindling British Empire) and Afro-Caribbeans. It wouldn't do – Australia was a white British colony and should remain so! We see this today as overtly racist, but times were different then.

The scheme worked this way – each adult migrant paid a fare of £10 sterling (equivalent to about £400 or US$620 in 2012, but less than a week's average wage), with children travelling free. Employment, housing, a great lifestyle and excellent prospects were promised. On arrival, though, unless they had relatives to stay with and a job organised, the migrants often found themselves in dormitory hostels of a rather basic kind, and the 'guaranteed' work opportunities turned out to be less than readily available. Those assisted migrants who read the small print would have noticed that they were required to stay in Australia for two years, or refund the cost of passage, and the return to Britain would cost at least £120 (almost £5,000 in today's terms). Nevertheless, the scheme accounted for over a million migrants from the British Isles alone between 1945 and 1972. There was a particular 'Bring out a Brit' campaign from 1957 to 1982, peaking in 1969 when more than 80,000 migrants went in that year alone. The cost of the assisted passage went up to £75 in 1973 until the programme closed.

This was not restricted to the United Kingdom of Great Britain and Northern Ireland – anyone born in the Irish Free State or the southern counties of Ireland prior to the 1949 establishment of the Republic of Ireland could apply, and the category 'British Subject' included residents of British colonies such as Cyprus, Gibraltar, Malta, some Caribbean states, Hong Kong and elsewhere. Until 1947, India was still 'British'. There were parallel assistance schemes, though more selective in terms of occupations and skills, for the Netherlands and Italy (1951), Greece and West Germany (1952) and Turkey (1967), among others.

Citizenship was another carrot dangled in front of the migrants – until the end of 1973, Commonwealth migrants could apply for Australian citizenship after only one year's residence (this was then extended to three years but reduced again to two years in 1984). Interestingly, few British migrants took up the offer, possibly feeling they didn't need to – unlike the millions of postwar European migrants from Greece, Italy, Turkey and elsewhere.

Those who left lost their Australian residency status, and, in the event, about a quarter of British migrants returned home, although half of these – known as 'Boomerang Poms' – went back to Australia. Therefore, if you lose genealogical track of someone from Wales in the 1950s, '60s and '70s, but suddenly find them again, only to lose them once more a few years later – think 'Australia'!

Add to this the renowned tendency for young Australians to travel the world, and it would not be surprising to find an Ozzie from Adelaide called Owain Morgan working in a restaurant in Cardiff or Llandudno.

Probably the best-known Welsh Ten Pound Pom (although she went free, being only 5 years old at the time) is the first female prime minister of Australia, the Honourable Julia Gillard. The family migrated from Barry, Glamorgan, to Adelaide in 1966 when she was five and her sister eight, hoping the better climate would help combat Julia's bronchopneumonial infection. It clearly worked.

Finding Australian relatives

It was said on p. 157 that around one in three people living in Britain have an Australian ancestral migrant and that the vast majority will be unaware of this. Where does that figure come from? We know the number of British-origin travellers to Australia, and can estimate that about 16 million people living in Britain will have free settler ancestors, and a further 2 million or so will have convict ancestors – meaning they will have Australian cousins today.

Australian resources

- 'Ten Pound Poms' at the State of Victoria Immigration Museum – http://museumvictoria.com.au/immigrationmuseum/discoverycentre/your-questions/ten-pound-poms/
- 'Ten Pound Poms', University of Sussex, Brighton – www.sussex.ac.uk/press_office/bulletin/05may00/article5.html
- Immigration to Australia During the 20th Century – Historical Impacts on Immigration Intake, Population Size and Population Composition – A Timeline (Australian Department of Immigration), www.immi.gov.au/media/publications/statistics/federation/timeline1.pdf
- Population Size and Population Composition Timeline, Australian Department of Immigration – www.immi.gov.au/media/publications/statistics/federation/timeline1.pdf
- Australian BMD indexes covering almost 15 million Australians back to 1788 and up to 1980 in some cases (mainly New South Wales, Northern Territory, Queensland, South Australia, Tasmania and Victoria, but not the Australian Capital Territory)
- Welsh Australian, cultural and other links – www.welshaustralian.com/
- Useful portal to the genealogical sites in Australia by category (BMD, census, convict records, wills and probate, etc.) – www.coraweb.com.au
- New South Wales State Records with databases and guides to immigration – www.records.nsw.gov.au/
- The Australian National Archives is useful for tracing migrants after 1920, and those who served in the First World War (as many were born in Britain) – www.naa.gov.au/
- Australian family history societies are listed here – www.coraweb.com.au/society.htm
- The Welsh in Australia: a bibliography – www.llgc.org.uk/index.php?id=1095
- Cardiff Centre for Welsh American Studies – www.cardiff.ac.uk/welsh/subsites/welshamericanstudies/index.html

New Zealand Welsh (*Cymry Seland Newydd*)

If any two nations are famous for their sheep, it's Wales and New Zealand. It is therefore not a surprise that when the British began colonising New Zealand in 1840, the Welsh were right there. Immigration records usually give settlement details plus the names and ages of wife and children (if any). Most immigrants received assistance from either the New Zealand Company or from a government or church association formed to encourage immigration.

- Check the Find My Past database of passengers leaving UK ports (1890 to 1960).
- Look at passenger list sites (listed above), but more specifically lists of migrants to New Zealand (http://freepages.genealogy.rootsweb.ancestry.com/~ourstuff/OurPassengerLists.htm).
- Denise & Peter's 'Auckland' Stuff (http://ouraucklandstuff.freeservers.com) has pioneer rolls, shipping arrivals and more besides.
- New Zealand Bound (http://freepages.genealogy.rootsweb.ancestry.com/~nzbound/index.htm) has NZ passenger lists and useful tips on finding NZ immigrant and ship arrival information, plus links to other sites.

South African Welsh (*Cymry De Affrica*)

After Britain took South Africa from the Dutch in 1795 there were various waves of settlement, mostly promoted by the British Government, in order to stamp their mark on the southern part of the continent. Not many Welsh went to South Africa until a well-documented group of almost 4,000 British settlers went to the Eastern Cape Province in 1820, Welsh among them. (Before 1836, only Cape Province had any white settlements.)

- 1820 Settlers to South Africa (www.1820settlers.com) has a great deal of information on these settlers and their descendants.
- The Albany Museum in Grahamstown has genealogies and other records of the descendants of Cape Province settlers (www.ru.ac.za/albanymuseum/).
- Arriving passengers were usually listed in the *Government Gazette* for the province at which they arrived.
- The South African Genealogy site (www.sagenealogy.co.za) has a data archive with lists of passengers arriving at Cape Town in the period 1849–1951.
- The South African Passenger Lists site (http://sa-passenger-list.za.net/index.php) has some lists of passengers – ships to Durban, Port of Natal (1845–58) and Cape Town (September–December 1852 only).
- Rootsweb has a lively mailing list for British migrants to South Africa before 1900, which can be searched by keyword as well as surname (http://lists.rootsweb.ancestry.com/ index/intl/ZAF/SOUTH-AFRICA-IMMIGRANTS-BRITISH.html).

Welsh in British India (*Cymry yn yr India Brydeinig*)

The links between Wales and India are stronger than ever, now that Indian steel giant Tata has invested almost £1 billion in Welsh steel including in plants in Port Talbot and Shotton. The way English is spoken in Mumbai has such a lilt to it that it is known as 'Bombay Welsh'. This may be the influence of Welsh missionaries (see below).

Many British subjects went to East India for trade or to settle. Until 1834, no British subject could go to India without permission from the Honourable East India Company, who ran the whole subcontinent until the Mutiny of 1857, after which India was under the direct rule of Britain – the period known as British Raj – until independence in 1947.

- Most of the Honourable East India Company (HEIC) records are at the British Library, London, Oriental and India Office (www.bl.uk/reshelp/findhelpregion/asia/india/ indiaofficerecords/indiaofficehub.html).

The wonderful people at the Families in British India Society are extremely helpful in tracing ancestors (www.new.fibis.org).

- Check military resources for ancestors who were in the armed service in India (Chapter 14).
- Many Welsh missionaries went to India (and elsewhere). In particular, in 1833 scores of missionaries from Welsh chapels headed for the Khasi hills in Assam by sea, a long trek across India, then ascent by the rather fragile *Khoh Kit Briew* rope baskets 4,500 ft up to the Khasia and Jaintia hills. This was officially the wettest inhabited place on earth, so it suited the Welsh Calvinist Methodists perfectly. Dr Griffith Griffith from Montgomeryshire preached the Word of God and made the locals give up alcohol in favour of tea, of which Assam had plenty. It must have worked, because by 1901 nearly a fifth of the 100,000 Khasi were worshipping in Welsh chapels. In particular, Rev. Thomas Jones (1810–49) is famous as 'The founding father of the Khasi alphabets and literature', as his gravestone says; it is in the Scottish Cemetery at Calcutta for some reason. The last Welsh missionary was still in Assam in 1966. Each of the various Christian denominations may have records of their missionary work abroad.

Emigration to Australia

By the time Mary Jones (p. 147) emigrated to Ballarat in 1856 and started writing her letters home, many other Welsh migrants had already established themselves in the area. Large numbers had arrived during the gold rush of the 1850s. Most of the main towns and cities in Australia had Welsh chapels and some areas held an annual *Eisteddfod*. However, Welsh culture here was not as long-lived as in Patagonia and parts of America, and the Welsh migrants were soon assimilated into mainstream Australian society and culture.

Contents of the letters

Henry Jones settled in an area that already had many Welsh inhabitants. In Holland Patent, New York State, today over 16 per cent of the population has Welsh ancestry. His long and detailed letters describe his new home and life with references to other Welsh settlers. Unfortunately, he lived for only two years after arriving in his new home. When Mary's letters begin she lived in Welshpool but then emigrated from Liverpool to Australia on the White Star line. In one letter she describes the voyage, life on-board ship, and some of her fellow passengers. While she was living in Australia she composed a ballad entitled 'Hiraeth am fy ngwlad' ('Longing for my country'), which was published after her death in 1861.

Immigration into and Within Wales

Immigration into British Isles was mainly from Europe and tended to involve refugees from wars (the French Revolution, for one), from religious persecution (Jews and Huguenots) or what we call today 'economic migrants' (looking for work when there is none at home). Alien arrivals' certificates from 1836 are arranged by port, giving name, nationality, profession, date arrived, country last visited and a signature. Incoming passenger lists start in 1878, giving name, birthplace, last residence, and often the address of a relative in the home country. Remember that passengers from Europe or the Mediterranean did not have to be listed.

The best way to find these individuals is in the censuses, where the place of birth will be given. At the bottom of the page is an example.

Coal miner Domico Baseiglas, b. abt 1843 from Italy (no place given, although it sometimes is) and his wife Mary Baseiglas, a local girl, plus their Italian–Welsh children John (13), Mary (10), Llewellyn (8), William (5) and Evan (2), living at 13 Coed Lane, Merthyr Tydfil, Glamorgan. Notice that John (13) is also working down the coal mine. However, this is a good example of a

1881 Census. Crown Copyright (courtesy of The National Archives)

census enumerator being unfamiliar with foreign names – from his death in 1905, it seems the father's name was actually Dominic M. Basagelao.

There is a specific website dealing with in-migration to the South Wales coalfield – www. agor.org.uk/cwm/themes/Life/society/migration.asp

Case study – Frederick Ebenezer Griffiths

We wondered back in Chapter 5 why Frederick disappeared after the 1901 census, and didn't appear to have married or died in the UK. Now we can find the answer, using a variety of overseas sources, all found via www.ancestry.co.uk, although other sites could have been used for certain searches.

1. New York Passenger Lists, 1820–1957

Name: Frederick E Griffiths
Arrival Date: 5 Sep 1906
Birth Year: abt 1879, Age: 27
Gender: Male; Ethnicity/Race/Nationality: Welsh
Port of Departure: Liverpool, England; Port of Arrival: New York, New York
Ship Name: Caronia

Notice that Frederick is a blacksmith, is heading for Pittsburgh (although he doesn't have a ticket), and will be joining his uncle A.F. Griffiths (presumably Alphonso) who lives there, and that while Frederick can read and write, he is neither insane, a polygamist, an anarchist or crippled. So that's all right then. The *SS Cariona*, sailing from Liverpool on 28 August, was a brand-new Cunard two-funnel, two-masted, twin-screw, quadruple expansion-engined beauty of some 19,782 tons, capable of 18 knots, and built in 1905 by John Brown of Glasgow.

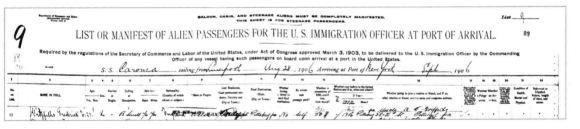

A New York Passenger List, 1906.

2. First World War Draft Registration Card, September 1918

Name: Frederick Ebenezer Griffiths
City: Pittsburgh; County: Allegheny; State: Pennsylvania
Birth Date: 18 Jul 1879; Race: White
FHL Roll Number: 1909241; Draft Board: 13

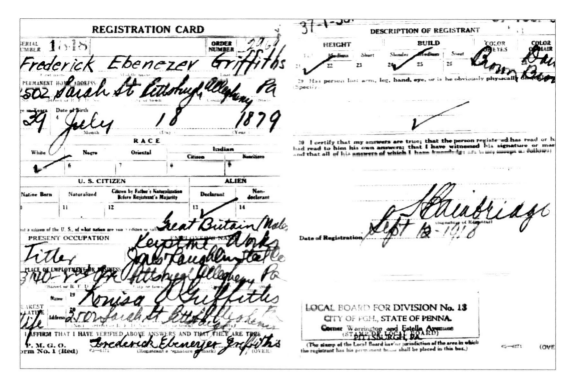

First World War Draft Registration Card, September 1918.

Frederick registers as an alien. He has brown eyes and dark brown hair. Also, he is married, to Louisa. Does he have any children?

3. US naturalisation, 16 July 1920

Name: Frederick Ebenezer Griffiths
Age: 40; Birth: 18 Jul 1879, Tredegar, Wales
Arrival Year: 1904; Naturalization Date: 16 Jul 1920
Spouse Name: Louisa; Children: Remelia, Irma, Iona

So, now Frederick is a citizen of the USA. Notice that he claims here to have first arrived in the USA by ferry from Port William, Canada, to Duluth, Minnesota, in 1904 – which is at odds with his passenger list entry of 1906 (above). Was that his second trip, perhaps? We also have the birth dates of his wife and three children, his occupation, and his renunciation of 'all allegiance and fidelity' to King George V.

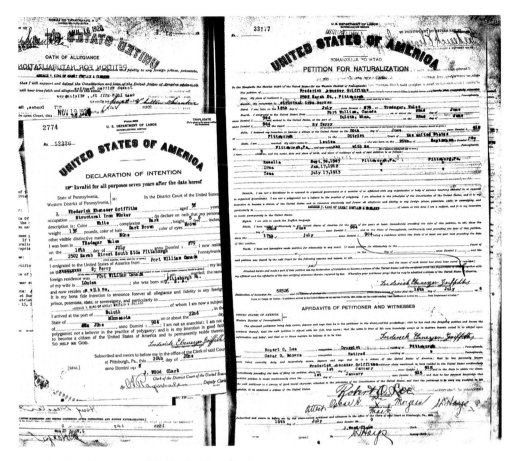

A Declaration of Intention and Petition for Naturalization, 1920.

4. 1930 United States federal census

We can pick them up in a census – this one happens to be 1930 – and notice that they have been recorded as 'Griffith' and his wife as 'Leonia'. This is an error in the transcription, not the original record.

Frederick did indeed arrive for the first time in the USA in 1904, his wife was born in Pennsylvania but had a Welsh father (although the 1920 census says he was Scottish), they married when he was 27 and she 20 (so about 1906, which suggests b. *c.* 1879), her mother is widowed and lived with them, Frederick spoke Welsh, and he is not a veteran.

1930 US federal census.

Second World War Draft Registration Card, April 1942.

5. Second World War Draft Registration Card, 27 April 1942

Frederick Evenezer Griffiths (Notice: wrong middle name in the index but correct on the card)
Birth Date: 18 Jul 1879; Birthplace: Tredegar, Wales
Residence: 58 S 25th St Pittsburgh Allegheny Pa; Telephone HE 2370
Age 62; Mrs Louisa Griffiths (same address)
Employer: Jones & Loughlin Steel Corp, Keystone Dept Pittsburgh Allegheny Pa
White, 5 ft 6 in, 150 Lb, Eyes Blue, Hair Grey, Complexion Light, Obvious physical characteristics None

Frederick obviously thought enough of his adopted homeland to sign up for two world wars, the second when he was aged 62!

6. Social Security death index
We can now pick up his death, from the Social Security Death Index (there is no image for this).

Name:	**Frederick Griffiths**
SSN:	168-01-3439
Last Residence:	15236 Pittsburgh, Allegheny, Pennsylvania, United States of America
Born:	18 Jul 1879
Last Benefit:	15227 Pittsburgh, Allegheny, Pennsylvania, United States of America
Died:	Jan 1979
State (Year) SSN issued:	Pennsylvania (before 1951)

We have a birth date for the first time (18 Jul 1879) and, from his death date, we can see that he almost reached 100, and that he was still living in Pittsburgh.

Further reading

Books
Charles H. Browning, *Welsh Settlement of Pennsylvania* (Philadelphia: Wm. J. Campbell, 1912).
Peter Coldham, *American Wills and Administrations in the Prerogative Court of Canterbury, 1610–1857* (Genealogical Publishing Company, 1989).
David Peate, *Emigration in Welsh Family History: A Guide to Research*, 2nd edn (Federation of Family History Societies, 1998).

Online resources
Library and Archives Canada – www.collectionscanada.gc.ca/
Moving Here – www.movinghere.org.uk
The Ships List – www.theshipslist.com
Immigrant Ships Transcribers Guild – www.immigrantships.net/
Prerogative Court of Canterbury (PCC) Wills at TNA, Kew – www.nationalarchives.gov.uk/documentsonline/wills.asp
National Library of Wales – www.llgc.org.uk
Archives Network Wales – www.archivesnetworkwales.info
GENUKI – www.genuki.org.uk
Welsh Mormon History – www.welshmormonhistory.org
FamilySearch – www.familysearch.org
US National Archives and Records Administration (NARA) – www.archives.gov/research/immigration/index.html
Ellis Island – www.ellisisland.org
Ancestry – www.ancestry.co.uk and www.ancestry.com
Find My Past – www.findmypast.co.uk
Y Wladfa The Welsh in Patagonia – www.h2g2.com/approved_entry/A1163503
History of Welsh Patagonia – www.teithiautango.co.uk

BBC: The Welsh in Patagonia – www.bbc.co.uk/cymru/patagonia/
Glaniad: The Welsh Settlement in Patagonia – www.glaniad.com/
Ten Pound Poms – www.sussex.ac.uk/press_office/bulletin/05may00/article5.html
Immigration to Australia – www.immi.gov.au
Welsh Australian – www.welshaustralian.com/
Genealogical sites in Australia – www.coraweb.com.au
New South Wales State Records – www.records.nsw.gov.au/
Australian National Archives – www.naa.gov.au
Australian family history societies list – www.coraweb.com.au/society.htm
Cardiff Centre for Welsh American Studies – www.cardiff.ac.uk/welsh/subsites/welshamericanstudies/index.html
1820 Settlers to South Africa – www.1820settlers.com
Albany Museum, South Africa – www.ru.ac.za/albanymuseum/
South African Genealogy site – www.sagenealogy.co.za
South African Passenger Lists site – http://sa-passenger-list.za.net/index.php
Rootsweb mailing list for British migrants to South Africa – http://lists.rootsweb.ancestry.com/index/intl/ZAF/SOUTH-AFRICA-IMMIGRANTS-BRITISH.html
British Library Oriental and India Office – www.bl.uk/reshelp/findhelpregion/asia/india/indiaofficerecords/indiaofficehub.html
Families in British India Society – www.new.fibis.org
Golden Bridge – http://content.iriss.org.uk/goldenbridge/migration/journey.html
South Wales coalfield – www.agor.org.uk/cwm/themes/Life/society/migration.asp
National Library of Wales Digital – http://digidol.llgc.org.uk/METS/HMJ00001/frames
Passenger lists to New Zealand – http://freepages.genealogy.rootsweb.ancestry.com/~ourstuff/OurPassengerLists.htm
Denise & Peter's 'Auckland' Stuff – http://ouraucklandstuff.freeservers.com
New Zealand Bound – http://freepages.genealogy.rootsweb.ancestry.com/~nzbound/index.htm
Emigration map at Data Wales – www.data-wales.co.uk/emmap.htm

10

Taxation and Representation

Benjamin Franklin said '… nothing can be said to be certain, except death and taxes' (1789) and he may have been describing a genealogist's concerns. Individuals often get 'captured' by more than BMD records and censuses – they also have to pay tax and, in many cases, register to vote. The earliest taxes were mainly carucages (taxes on land) and tallages (taxes on individuals), plus feudal levies such as aids and scutages, all of which generate records. Many of the earliest ones do not relate to Wales, as there was no unified tax system until the Act of Union of 1536, and until the mid-1600s the clergy was taxed by Canterbury and York rather than Parliament, so there are separate documents for lay and clerical taxes (hence 'lay' subsidies). It is worth looking at these, in near-chronological order.

Lay Subsidy Records (1290–1332)
Lay subsidies were a tax levied on personal wealth (but not land) from 1290 to 1332. They often say not much more than:

> And 40s, from Lawrence de Hastings, Earl of Pembroke, for one knight's fee in Inkberrow, which the Bishop of Hereford formerly held, etc.
> From Lady Bergavenny, holding one fee in Inkberrow, which Henry Hastings, Earl of Pembroke, formerly held. 6s, 8d. (*6 Henry VI. I 427–8*)

But occasionally there is glorious extra detail: 'From the same Thomas for the escape of a certain Welchman indicted for the death of another Welchman, whom he slew at Wyke … 100s' (*32 Edward III. 1358*). The number before the king's name is the regnal year (see p. 215).

A number of local record societies have published printed versions of these, with translations for the Latin; the originals are mainly held at TNA, Kew. Most of the records of assessment and collection of taxes in England and Wales from the thirteenth to the seventeenth centuries are in series E 179. There is a good online guide to taxation records: www.nationalarchives.gov.uk/records/research-guides/taxation-before-1689.htm

Poll Tax and Hearth Tax
These were two rather clever ideas, dreamed up – or rather reinvented – to pay for the ruinous wars that underpinned the 'glorious revolution' of William III (r. 1689–1702) and his Stuart wife and co-ruler, Mary (d. 1694). The difference is that a poll tax is a capitation, based and levied on an individual. A hearth tax, by contrast, is levied on the 'hearth', essentially per house, regardless of who lived there.

Poll tax, 1694–99
The poll tax was a 'good' idea that did not quite work. An earlier incarnation of this had led directly to the Peasants' Revolt of 1381. The poll tax was first imposed in England during the financial crisis at the end of the reign of Edward III (1377), when everyone in the kingdom, except mendicants and minors under 14, had to pay one groat (fourpence) per head. This 'tallage

of groats' was regressive – it hit the poor more than the rich – and failed to rise as much as expected. So, there were graduated poll taxes in 1379 and 1380 in which the common herd (older than 16) paid a groat as before, and the scale rose up to barons (who paid 3 marks = £2), earls, bishops and abbots (6 marks = £4) and viscounts and royal dukes (10 marks). This was effectively an income tax, and again failed to solve the fiscal issues. The poll tax of 1380 had a narrower banding – 4d to 20s (£1) – and had a built-in safety net by which the better-off should help the less fortunate. Whatever its intentions, it was seen as the poor bailing out the rich, which finished it off as a taxation method for almost three centuries, and ultimately brought down Margaret Thatcher in the 1990s for many of the same reasons.

The poll taxes of 1694, 1695 and 1698 (twice) were meant to settle the arrears and debts of the army and navy. This was means- and rank-tested, with the poor and minors under 16 exempt. Again, collection proved complicated and the records are incomplete. Those that exist are arranged by county and parish, but the information is variable – some give names of the 'Head of Household' as well as children and servants. There are local extracts available from some family history societies. Also, like hearth tax, the surviving records are not country-wide and, although they cover just about everyone, the information given is limited.

Hearth tax (1662–89)

Hearth tax has an equally chequered career. It was an idea of Charles V of France, and just as the poll tax led to dissent in England, the taxes Charles levied to support the wars against the English caused the French peasantry to become disaffected. On his deathbed (fearing God's view of the iniquitous hearth tax, perhaps) he announced its abolition. The government, realising the disastrous effects on the country's finances, refused to lower any other taxes, so leading to the Maillotin revolt in 1382.

William and Mary faced a similar situation to the English and French monarchs of the fourteenth century. Also, they knew that one of the most valuable lessons learned by both sides in the English Civil Wars of 1642–46 and 1648–49, was the unreliability of voluntary contributions. The days of melting down plate and ornaments to pay for armies were over. Parliament had also abolished feudal tenures and dues in England, so hearth tax (and poll tax) were back on the fiscal scene.

The hearth tax was on each hearth in every home during this period, 1662 to 1689, and was levied twice a year at the two terms of Lady Day (New Year, 25 March) and Michaelmas (29 September), at 1s per term per hearth of every householder whose property was worth more than 20s annually, and who paid rates and poor rates to the local church – the only exemptions were the poor living on parish charity and in hospitals. At times, collection was licensed out to private collectors who paid a fixed sum for the privilege and kept the rest. Just as unpopular with the lower classes as it had been 300 years before, this tax was thought rather simple to collect, as hearths do not move about the way people do, and houses cannot hide from the tax collector. William abolished English and Welsh hearth tax, so increasing his popularity at the beginning of his reign, but he had no such scruples in Scotland. Each hearth in a house attracted its own levy, which would seem to be progressive – richer families had more fireplaces – but required an internal inspection. Counting chimneys from the outside would have been easier. The tax proved difficult to collect in practice, especially in remote communities.

At first sight, these lists would seem to be excellent sources for genealogists – almost everyone had at least one hearth, tenant as well as landowner – so they should be almost a census of heads of households, but there are problems. They are arranged by county and parish, and some give names of the owners or occupiers, and the number and names of those exempt by reason of poverty. However, some lists only provide the total number of hearths under the name of the landholder, but do list the individual poor, while others list only the total number of hearths and the monies collected. The accuracy of many of the lists has also been called into question, and by no means all have survived. The only hearth tax records surviving are for 1662–66 and 1669–74, most of which are at TNA, Kew.

Land Tax Records (1692-1963)

Land tax was introduced in 1692 and lasted right up to 1963 (in the guise of valuation rolls). This tax has the inbuilt advantages of being administered at a local level and based on a certain amount to be paid by each parish. The surviving land tax records are mainly from the period 1780 to 1832, but as they list annually both owners and tenants (plus occupiers, if different in some cases), they are good pre-census substitutes.

The assessment records from 1798 for England and Wales (except Flintshire) are available at TNA, Kew, but some county record offices may have the originals or copies.

Death Duty Records (from 1796)

These are records of the tax liability on wills and bequests. They have details of the estate and approximate value, the name, address and date of death of the deceased and an outline of the will (beneficiaries etc.).

The indexes and registers for the period 1796 to 1857 have been microfilmed and can be seen at TNA, Kew, or at an LDS family history centre (see p. 53 for addresses). The indexes for 1858–1903 can be viewed at TNA, but book in advance. No registers exist after 1903 but there are some records held in separate files.

Other Tax Records

The 1700s saw a veritable ferment of taxation, which means fertile ground for genealogists. There is a list below, but bear in mind the fact that even though certain taxes would appear to apply to all households or householders (such as commutation tax, inhabited house tax, window tax and consolidated assessed tax), in reality they were only paid by the well-off and thus do not provide complete lists of residents in any given area. Some were levied for specific purposes, such as the additional property taxes to pay for the war with France from 1793. Some were frankly ridiculous – dog tax and clock tax shine out. Notice how almost all of these taxes were replaced by income tax in 1799. They are organised by county and parish. It is by no means guaranteed that any of these exist – but just in case, search at www.nationalarchives.gov.uk/ e179/ and individual county record offices.

Tax	Dates	Description
Window Tax	1747/8–98	Gives names of householders in houses with seven or more windows or a rent of over £5 a year.
Male Servants' Tax	1777–98	Certain categories of manservants, with the names of servants, their masters or mistresses given and sometimes the servants' duties. Bachelor householders paid double.
Inhabited House Tax	1778–98	Names of householders and annual value of houses.
Commutation Tax	1784–98	Similar conditions to window tax, in commutation for excise duties on tea.
Cart Tax	1785–98	Names of owners of carts with two to four wheels.
Carriage Tax	1785–98	Names of owners of carriages with two or four wheels.
Horse Tax	1785–98	Names of owners of carriage and saddle horses.

Female Servants' Tax	1785–92	Names of masters or mistresses, names of servants and, in some records, their duties.
Shop Tax	1785–89	Names of retail shopkeepers (but not usually the nature of the business) where the annual rent exceeds £5. Not comprehensive.
Income Tax	1799–1802	Names of individuals with annual incomes of £60 or more from property, profession, trade or office. This was replaced in 1803 by an income-based property tax (below).
Farm Horse Tax	1797–98	This is the most useful of the 'minor' taxes as it gives the names of owners of (and numbers of) horses and mules, and is therefore a list of tenant farmers and tradesmen. It carried on as Consolidated Schedules of Assessed Taxes (below).
Dog Tax	1797–98	Gives names of owners and the number of dogs owned.
Clock and Watch Tax	1797–98	Gives names of owners of clocks and gold, silver or metal watches, and the number owned. One for the horologists.
Aid and Contribution Tax	1797–98	The only lists that survive are for Peebles-shire. This was an 'additional' tax for one year only on those already assessed to pay duties on houses, and was replaced by income tax in 1799.
Consolidated Schedules of Assessed Taxes	1798–99	Names of householders, value of houses, number of windows, male servants, carriages, horses and dogs.

Electoral Registers

Nowadays, we rather take voting for granted. To an extent, it's hard to avoid. But for a considerable period of Britain's history, and until quite recently, the franchise was restricted to certain classes of people (see below) and the political obscenity of the 'rotten boroughs'.

When the vote did become more widespread, it was necessary to have lists of those who could vote. That meant names, usually addresses, and sometimes even ages and occupations, all of which are beloved of genealogists. The reason was that the eligibility criteria had to be recorded. Some records even give the name of the representative voted for by each individual – so much for the secret ballot, which didn't happen until 1872.

The study of who could vote and when that happened justifies a book all to itself (and the book by Gibson and Rogers in *Further reading* is just that), but in simple terms it happened this way:

Before 1832 – hardly anyone could vote. Representatives of the counties were elected by freeholders (owners of land or other heritable property in the county above a certain value).
1832 (Reform Act passed) to 1867 – owners, tenants and occupiers (male) of land and houses – fewer than 14,000 in the whole of Wales (one in every seven men).
1868 – male 'prosperous lodgers' – those paying rent of over £10 annually (one in three men).
1882 – unmarried females and married women not living in family with their husbands, if proprietors and tenants, could vote in burgh council elections (two in every three men by 1884).
1889 – females as above could vote in county council elections.
1918 – males over 21, females over 30.
1929 – almost everyone over 21, except lords and lunatics.
1969 – all adults over 18.

The effect of the 1832 Acts (not a single Reform Act, but a series of related statutes, passed by Westminster in 1832: Representation of the People Act; Parliamentary Boundaries Act; Corporate Property (Elections) Act and the Scottish and Irish versions of these) was that most of the counties continued to be represented by one member. There were some boundary changes, so a burgh for parliamentary election purposes might not be coterminous with boundaries for other purposes. The main change in Wales was that the proportion of electors in the population changed from one in 125 to about one in eight. However, that didn't feed through into the numbers who actually voted in the earlier elections – this went down in most parts of Britain, except Wales, between the 1832 election and 1868, after the 1867 Reform Act had its effect.

The registers
Different forms of electoral registers (also called voters' rolls) were kept during these various periods. Local election records were separate from parliamentary elections, and burgh registers may not be held with counties. Burghs were separate parliamentary constituencies from the counties, and some burghs were grouped together as one constituency. Large towns and cities were organised by electoral ward, county registers were arranged by civil parish. Information provided (from 1832 to 1918) included (by address) name; street number; occupation; whether owner, tenant or boarder; property entitling the individual to vote (because someone may not be living at the address by which he is made eligible). Female voters were kept in supplementary registers. Voters' rolls are also useful in that they give the descriptions of wards and districts, with street names. In 1832 it was possible, and indeed common, for those with qualifications in different constituencies to register and vote in all of them, so an individual might appear on more than one roll, not all of which reflected an actual address.

Sadly, not all registers have survived. There are no historic electoral registers available online and no complete collections of electoral registers at TNA, Kew, but there is a collection of electoral registers from 1947 at the British Library. However, the National Library of Wales holds many of the electoral registers and most local record offices and local studies centres have a good collection of electoral registers from the earlier years for their own areas – see pp. 46–54 for details.

Poor Law
In England and Wales poor relief was originally the province of the local parish, with Acts of 1597 and 1601 codifying the Tudor laws, and ordering the election of an Overseer of the Poor, responsible to the parish vestry and the local Justices of the Peace, and with tax-raising powers. There were also charities for relief, often administered on the behalf of these and the parish by *feoffees* (trustees). The Act of Settlement (1662) formalised this and defined the responsibilities of the parishes. The resulting system was not, however, satisfactory and demands on local funds increased as the population grew. Various reports and commissions led to the Poor Law Amendment Act (1834), which established Poor Law Unions (of parishes) each run by a board of elected 'guardians'. This system, with its Dickensian workhouses made purposely unattractive to live in, and other familiar props, carried on right up to the reforms of the Liberal Government from 1906 to 1914, championed by, among others, David Lloyd George. These provided what we would recognise today as social services (including old age pensions and national insurance) without the stigma that the Poor Law brought about.

The poor relief system from 1845
Under the Poor Law Amendment Act 1834, parishes formed Poor Law Unions, each with a Union workhouse. Unions were administered by Boards of Guardians, elected by local landowners and ratepayers who were, after all, paying for the system by a 'poor rate'. For example, Carmarthenshire had the Poor Law Unions of Carmarthen, Llandeilo Fawr, Llandovery and

Llanelli. Not only did the amount of relief vary from one area to another, the responsible parish was in theory the parish of birth, or where the individual concerned had been 'settled' for the past seven years, and often paupers were transported back to their home town, or one parish asked another to contribute to the upkeep of a 'stray', sometimes looking to the law to resolve where the responsibility lay.

Poor Law records

In the main, records after 1845 contain far more individual information, such as names and ages. The information can be extremely rich and can include: date and hour of application; name, residence and country of birth; date of inspector's visit to applicant; condition (married/single etc.); age; occupation; religion; weekly earnings; disabilities; names and ages of dependants; names of children not dependant; previous applications and their results; disposal (i.e. how settled); grounds of refusal (if refused). The records of most unions are with local record offices, and details can be found at Archives Wales (www.archiveswales.org.uk).

Other sources

A number of crafts, trades guilds (see Chapter 13), friendly societies and similar bodies had a fund to help poor members, or established schools, hospitals and other institutions. Their minute books may include donations to the poor by named individuals.

Further reading

Books

Paul Felix Aschrott, *The English Poor Law System, Past and Present* (Knight, 1902) (available online at www.archive.org).

John J. Bagley and Alexander J. Bagley, *The English Poor Law* (Macmillan, 1968).

Richard H.A. Cheffins, *Parliamentary Constituencies and their Registers since 1832* (British Library Publishing Division, 2000).

Simon Fowler, *Poor Law Records for Family Historians* (Family History Partnership, 2011).

Jeremy Gibson, *The Hearth Tax, Other Later Stuart Tax Lists, and the Association Oath Rolls* (Federation of Family History Societies, 1985; reprint Gemealogical Publishing Co., 1990).

Jeremy Gibson and Colin Rogers, *Electoral Registers since 1832* (Federation of Family History Societies, 1989).

David Hawkings, *Pauper Ancestors: A Guide to the Records Created by the Poor Laws in England and Wales* (The History Press, 2011).

Online resources

Guide to taxation records – www.nationalarchives.gov.uk/records/research-guides/taxation-before-1689.htm

11

Welsh Heraldry

Heraldry looks at first sight to be impenetrable. It uses obscure jargon, appears to involve only the landed and titled, and has a medieval feel about it. For these reasons and others – not least a form of inverted snobbery – the whole issue of coats of arms is often dismissed as irrelevant to modern life in general and genealogy in particular. However, nothing could be further from the case, and Voltaire's slight that heraldry is 'the science of fools with long memories' is wide of the mark.

Heraldic Origins in Wales

There is a sense in which Welsh heraldry is indistinguishable from English – both are controlled from the College of Arms in London as the heraldic authority, and the use of armorial bearings as we now know them was imported into Wales by the English conquerors. However, there are some particularly Welsh aspects, notably to do with the concepts of 'nobility' and 'gentility'.

The concepts of nobility and gentility

Nobility, as an idea, existed in Wales long before the twelfth century when coats of arms came to be used in their present form. A Welshman considered his status to be derived from 'gentility of blood', in other words, by virtue of his genealogy, especially if descended from one of the ancient princes or chiefs. This is distinct from the English concept of an 'armigerous gentleman' (someone who has 'gentility' because he bears arms) and the Scots idea of 'nobility' (where everyone is considered to be of 'noble and ancient heritage'). In Tudor times (possibly bearing in mind that the Tudors arose from Wales) the English heralds recognised this 'biological aristocracy' when evaluating Welsh claims to armorial bearings. (Henry VII was grandson of a Welsh knight, Sir Owen Tudor, Tewdor or Tudur – Owain ap Maredudd ap Tudur – a descendant of Ednyfed Fychan, steward of Llewellyn, the last Welsh king, c. 1220. Owen married Henry V's widow Catherine of Valois in secret, or perhaps not at all, and got beheaded for it in 1461, but not before fathering the half-brothers of the infant king, Henry VI, including Edmund Tudor. Edmund's son was Henry Tudor, born at Pembroke Castle in 1457; he killed Richard III in 1483 and thereby became King Henry VII.)

We could consider armigers in Wales as being of three categories – the existing Welsh aristocracy, the non-tribal Welsh and the Anglo-Norman *advenae* (new arrivals) who became the feudal overlords. Twenty-odd princely dynasties and the hierarchy below them spawned more than 150 heraldic ancestors.

The concept of gentility is inextricably interwoven with both heraldry and pedigree. The word usually translated as 'Gentleman' was *Gwr bonheddig*, which really meant 'man with a pedigree'. Gentility of descent (as evidenced by pedigree) implied education, at a time when this was restricted to the higher echelons of society and therefore attracted esteem. At a time before surnames (Chapter 3) were widely used (which was the situation in Wales right up to Elizabethan times, except for Norman families), having a correct pedigree was crucial, especially when it came to property inheritance, so the prevention of forgery was vitally important. This in turn required someone of unimpeachable probity who could investigate – and who would record or remember – genealogies, and so a second bardic order was instituted:

the *Arwyddvardd* (plural *Arwyddveirdd*) or herald-bard, who registered arms and pedigrees, and, just as with heralds in England, Scotland and elsewhere, had a quasi-ambassadorial function within the state.

The *Arwddvardd* was originally a nationally appointed officer, whose duties were later devolved upon the *Prydydd* (poet), including attendance at the birth, marriage and death of any *Gwr bonheddig* and entering the vital data in his genealogy – much as the registrar does today, and equivalent to the *Sheanachie* (variously spelt) in the Irish–Scots Gaelic tradition. When someone died, a *marwnad* (elegy) was composed, which had to expound their genealogy accurately (preferably at some length) from their eight immediate ancestors, but bringing in the various branches of their family, and those of the surviving wife or husband, plus all the in-laws and children. The *marwnadau* that existed formed the basis for the later work of heralds and genealogists.

The details of the *marwnad* were copied in the books of the *Arwyddvardd*, and a further copy was given to the heir, to be preserved in the family muniments, and produced one month from the day of the funeral, when the important family members got together to hear a recitation – a form of attestation as to the reliability of the evidence of descent, the public nature of such was another bulwark against forgery. The bard made a circuit every three years (a forerunner of heraldic visitations) at which pedigrees and genealogies could be collected and corrected. These are named either for herald/bard/poet responsible for the composition (e.g. *Llyvyr Llewelyn Ofeiriad*, the Book of Llewelyn the Priest) or the place of deposit, usually the chief mansion house in the relevant province (the Cotterell Book in Glamorganshire, for instance) and were handed on by one *Arwyddvardd* to his bardic heir or successor. Some go back 600 years.

Such Welsh heraldic registers do not seem to have survived beyond the mid-1400s, leaving an uncomfortable 100-year gap before the College of Arms took up the task with visitations (p. 198 and 204). The pedigree books themselves are held at various places. The National Library of Wales has a summary of this at www.llgc.org.uk/index.php?id=492 and Francis Jones (see p. 82) published the best account of them in his 'An Approach to Welsh Genealogy' (in *Transactions of the Honourable Society of Cymmrodorion* (1948), pp. 303–466). Possibly the best collection of written pedigrees is the Protheroe manuscripts, held by the College of Arms. One of the best, though, is the *Golden Grove Book of Pedigrees*, compiled around 1765 and continuing pedigrees originally composed 200 years before. A copy is at the Carmarthenshire Record Office but can be seen online at www.gtj.org.uk/en/small/item/GTJ08664 – click through the 600-odd pages of volume 2.

Early Welsh heraldry

There is a distinction made between *tynnu Arvau* (blazoning of arms, see below), and *casglu Achau* (compilation of pedigrees) although the two are inextricably related. Robert Vaughan of Hengwrt, Merionethshire (*c.* 1592–1667), the renowned antiquary and collector of old manuscripts, wrote in his *British Antiquities Revived* (1662) that in the eleventh century,

> Prince Grufydd ab Cynan, Prince Rhys ab Tewdwr, and Prince Bleddyn ab Cmvyn, made diligent search after the arms, ensigns, and Pedigrees of their ancestors, the nobility, and kings of Britain. What they discovered by their pains in any papers and records, were afterwards by the Bards digested, and put into books. And they ordained five royal tribes, there being only three before, to whom their posterity to this day can derive themselves; and also fifteen special tribes, of whom the gentry, especially of North Wales, are for the most part descended. And in our books we have mention of the tribe of the Marches, &c., besides other tribes called Gwehelyth and Gwehelaetliau.

Although it arrived with the incomers, the Welsh took to heraldry. There are equestrian seals of Morgan ap Caradog of Afan (1183), Prince Gwenwynwyn of Powys (c. 1200), Llewelyn the Great (c. 1222) and others. By 1246 Llewelyn's son, Prince David, had what we could consider an armorial seal, with a lion rampant, as did John ap John of Grosmont about the same time (a lion rampant within a border charged with six escallops). Arms became properly hereditary from 1300 (as in England), and from that date there is evidence of heraldic crests, such as the maiden's head with a coronet that Ithel ap Bleddyn bore with his shield (two lions rampant addorsed, tails intertwined).

Why heraldry is useful

Heraldry is a vital tool for genealogists and a valid subject for study, here are a few reasons why:

- heraldry can be a visual 'family tree', recording details in all ancestral branches;
- heraldic documents (grants of arms, registers, visitations) may be the only records extant of a pedigree;
- a knowledge of heraldry can help surmount 'brick walls' and puzzles;
- it is helpful in determining places as well as people;
- armoury (which encompasses heraldry) is a fascinating subject of study in its own right.

Far from being a dead subject buried in the past, heraldry is a living, breathing science. There is increasing interest in it, as witness the many websites that offer to sell you 'Your Coat of Arms' or, even worse, 'Your Family Crest'. As shown below, neither of these claims is valid. Alongside this, more than ever, individual people and bodies corporate of various sorts are applying for properly granted arms. In 2009, the College of Arms made over 230 grants and transfers of armorial bearings of various kinds, including to Glyndwr University, Wrexham.

At the very least, it is guaranteed that after reading this chapter you will suddenly see heraldry everywhere (although it was there all the time). There are coats of arms and other armorial insignia on buildings, bookplates, school and club badges, regimental banners and the like, as stained glass windows and signs at the boundaries of towns, carved on chairs, engraved on family silver, depicted on pub signs ('The Such-and-Such Arms') and, at various times during the year, displayed on standards up and down many streets (there are some examples in the extracted colour plate section). In fact, heraldry is hard to avoid once you start to notice it, and you will never again look at an armorial gravestone or a statue in the same way. So let's start at the beginning.

The two most contentious issues in the whole subject can be dealt with very simply:

1. A coat of arms is often referred to as a 'crest', when they are quite different – the crest is one component of arms, as discussed later.

2. There is NO SUCH THING as a 'family coat of arms' in the sense that anyone of a certain surname can simply find arms of that name and start using them – arms are individually granted and are the legal and heritable property of one person at a time, anyone who pretends otherwise in order to sell you something is knowingly misleading you.

This is all much more straightforward in Scotland, where such things are a matter of statute law. Arms must be granted by the Lord Lyon King of Arms (www.lyon-court.com) and anyone simply adopting arms relating to a certain surname will find that it is illegal, and runs the risk of having confiscated their stained glass windows, dinner services, silver cutlery or anything else made carrying arms they do not legally possess, and a fine imposed. In England and Wales, matters heraldic are controlled by the College of Arms in London (http://college-of-arms.gov.uk)

but it is a issue for civil law – in other words, if you have arms properly granted, and find someone else using them, it is up to you to sue them. The college and its activities are dealt with in more detail later.

The other distinction is that in Scotland the 'undifferenced' arms can only be borne by the person entitled and, after death, by his or her direct heir, and so on down one line; in England and Wales, any child of an armiger (person bearing arms) can use the undifferenced coat. This makes it a lot harder to trace lines of descent, but there are niceties to this that can help in that regard.

The components of an achievement of arms

It is best to start with an understanding of what a coat of arms consists of. On p. 181 there is an 'achievement' of arms with its various components:

- Shield – also known as the escutcheon, this is the main and most recognisable component of the arms.
- Helmet – the actual configuration of this denotes the rank of the armiger (p. 194).
- Wreath – also called a torse, this has the same colours as the mantling (below).
- Mantling– this takes the main colours of the 'livery' (the overall coat of arms, banners etc.).
- Crest – this arises from the wreath (below) and is the element used in a crest badge in Scotland; it was physically worn atop the helmet and served as a further identifier of the armiger etc.). It probably started as protection from the sun in the Holy Land, where the crusaders realised that wearing a metal pot on the head in the blazing sun was not a great idea. They noticed that the locals wore a cloth, held down by a burnous (the origin of the wreath or torse, above), to keep the sun off. The mantling is usually depicted cut and tattered (in a very florid and stylised way) to indicate the swordplay of battle.
- Coronet of rank – if the armiger is noble, the coronet will indicate baron, viscount, earl, marquess, duke, prince or sovereign (p. 196) – not shown in the illustration below.
- Motto – the motto is usually at the bottom, except in Scottish arms, where it should be at the top (but this is often ignored in, for example, civic arms on buildings).
- Supporters – not everyone merits supporters, but where granted they are usually animals, humans or mythical beasts of some sort (p. 196).
- Compartment – in Scotland, the supporters always stand on a compartment or ground, which is sometimes adorned with the family's plant or flower, while in English and Welsh arms the supporters often float in mid-air.
- Slughorn – as well as the motto at the top there may be a subsidiary slogan under the compartment, often the war cry of a clan or family, for example, or a subsidiary motto acquired when arms are merged as a result of marriage or assumption.

The details below were copied verbatim from p. 86 of the fifth edition of *Armorial Families: A Directory of Gentlemen of Coat-Armour* by Arthur Charles Fox-Davies (1905). This is available for download at http://ia700407.us.archive.org/0/items/armorialfamilies00foxd/armorialfamilies00foxd.pdf.

Fox-Davies is a comprehensive and reliable source of arms in England and Wales, and his work is probably the best place to start when researching arms. Other places include the various compilations by Burke, Debrett, Cracroft and so on (see *Further reading*, p. 208). Notice that a fairly full biography is given, with some genealogical information, military service, and address and the blazon (the description in heraldic terms) of the arms themselves. We will deal with the vocabulary and structure of the blazon later, but for now, see if you can follow it from the armorial bearings (below):

THOMAS BATE. Esquire. Deputy-Lieutenant and Justice of the Peace for the county of Flint, for which he served the office of High Sheriff in the year 1887, late Captain in the Denbighshire Hussars. Born 1849, being the only son of the late Edward Bate. Esquire, of Kelsterton. Justice of the Peace by Martha his wife, only daughter of the Reverend Edward Whitley of Berse Drelincourt. Clubs – Junior Carlton. Livery – Dark blue coat, red waistcoat, drab boxcloth overcoat, with blue cuffs and collar. Armorial bearings – He bears for Arms: Sable, on a fesse cotised Argent between four dexter hands couped at the wrist three in chief and one in base bendways Or, an arrow fesseways proper; and for the Crest, upon a wreath of the colours, in front of a stag's head couped Argent, attired Or, pierced in the neck by an arrow in bend proper, a hand couped at the wrist fesseways also Or; with the Motto, 'Live to live'.

Married July 11, 1878, Perenna, daughter of William Owen, Esquire, of Shanvaghey, Queen's County, and of Blessington, Ireland, Justice of the Peace; and has Issue – (1) Roger Whitley Bate, Gentleman, born October 12, 1882, killed at Rostpan, Dec. 7, 1901; (2) Thomas Bate, Gentleman, born July 1, 1889; Gwendoline Mary Owen; Dorothy; Gladys Annie; Marjorie Perenna; and Pauline Janet Whitley. Estates and postal addresses – Kelsterton, and Plas Bellin, Flint, North Wales.

Arms

1. Sable (the background of the shield is black);
2. on a fesse (a bar across the middle);
3. cotised (with two smaller bars above and below);
4. Argent (silver, but usually depicted as white, or the background colour of the page);
5. between four dexter (right) hands couped at the wrist three in chief (in the top third, above the fess) and one in base (below the fess) bendways (at an angle, pointing upwards and to the dexter side);
6. Or (gold);

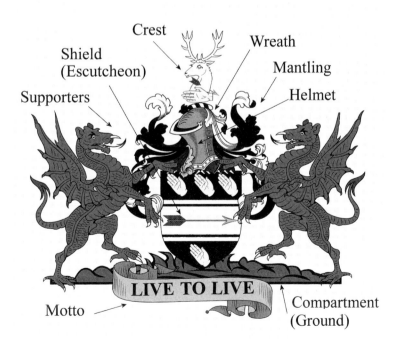

A full 'achievement'
of arms.

7. an arrow fesseways (straight across, same as the fess);
8. proper (the 'real' colours of an arrow).

Crest
1. Upon a wreath of the colours (that is, Sable – black – and Argent – silver/white);
2. in front of a stag's head couped (cut straight across) Argent (silver/white);
3. attired Or (the antlers are gold);
4. pierced in the neck by an arrow in bend (at an angle, same as the hands) proper;
5. a hand couped at the wrist fesseways also Or (gold).

Motto
'Live to live'

Supporters: the arms shown below are real, but this armiger does not have supporters. They were added, just for the sake of illustration, and Welsh dragons Gules (red) seemed appropriate!

How did arms originate?
Arms started from the need to identify knights and nobles on the battlefield and at jousting tournaments after the invention of the barrel helmet, which completely covered the face. There are no examples of arms as we know them (designs on shields etc.) among the Normans, as a look at the Bayeux Tapestry will confirm (see www.tapestry-bayeux.com). For the record, it wasn't made in Bayeux, and isn't a tapestry – it was embroidered in wool, possibly in either Winchester or Canterbury, England, and probably by nuns of noble Saxon background. There was no need for the Normans to be identified by arms, because the fighting men wore an open helmet with a nose-guard and everyone could recognise friends and enemies.

When the need to identify warriors became an issue, the practice arose of painting a high-contrast design on, possibly first, a banner, standard or other flag, and then on the linen surcoat worn over armour and mail to keep it clean, hence the term 'coat of arms'. This naturally spread to the whole livery – the shield and even the horse's caparison.

Although the Normans had no heraldry in the sense that we understand it – the use of individual and inheritable emblems borne on armour – and therefore did not introduce it to the British Isles, the practice had already started in Europe, probably around Flanders. By the time of Henry I of England it had started to take root in Britain – there is an account in 1127 of Henry knighting his son-in-law Geoffrey V, Count of Anjou, and placing around his neck a shield painted with golden lions. When Geoffrey died (1151) the funerary enamel on his tomb at Le Mans Cathedral depicted him bearing a blue shield emblazoned with golden lions. This may be the first recorded portrayal of a British coat of arms.

By this time coats of arms were considered heritable by the children of armigers throughout Europe. There are seals dating from the 1130s and 1150s showing a figure of the owner bearing a design on his shield, and by the end of that century the heraldic design appears as the single device on armorial seals.

Heralds and armorials
The functions and powers of the heralds and the College of Arms are explored on p. 198. For now it is enough to recognise that heralds had ambassadorial status from the earliest times, and were trusted emissaries of the king, with the equivalent of diplomatic immunity. As arms proliferated, someone had to keep a record of what these were, and ensure that there were no duplications. From this came a system of armorials (pictorial and textual descriptions of coats of arms).

The first roll of arms we know of was the mid-thirteenth-century *Chronica Majora* by Matthew Paris. Another early armorial was the *Dering Roll* (*c.* 1270–80). A particularly famous example is *Roll of Carlaverock*, essentially an epic poem describing the arms of all the nobles and knights who accompanied Edward I in his fight against southern Scotland in 1300, and including the arms of the Prince of Wales (later Edward II). It soon became the practice for heralds to swap these rolls at battles, and they were copied for the benefit of other knights and nobles. Similarly, at jousting tournaments in later centuries, heralds controlled the fixture lists. These even crossed to the continent – the Flemish Armorial de Gelré, for example, collated between 1370 and 1414, has arms of armigers from the British Isles.

How does heraldry work?

Heraldry has its own language. This is based on the Norman French of the Angevin kings of the time, and stems from the need to describe arms in an unambiguous way when it wasn't possible to draw or paint them. This is known as the 'blazon'. As arms became more elaborate, the language of their blazons acquired its own rules, vocabulary and syntax. It is necessary to get used to the terminology – and that comes with practice.

Rules of heraldry

- Each coat of arms should be unique (within each heraldic jurisdiction – there are examples of English or Welsh arms being the same as Scottish, German etc.).
- The arms should be distinguishable at a distance, so the majority of components should be large, simple and composed of a very few tinctures (colours).
- The main charge (design on the shield) should cover its field (the whole of the space available on the shield).
- There are two metals, four main tinctures (colours) and six furs (p. 184). The metals are Or (gold) and Argent (silver but usually depicted as white or the background colour of the paper, parchment, ornament etc.); the four tinctures are Gules (red), Azure (blue), Vert (green) and Sable (black), plus the rare Purpure (purple) and even more uncommon Tenne (tawny) and Murrey (sanguine); the main furs are Ermine, Pean, Vair and Potent, with variants.
- Metals may not be displayed on top of metals. For example, do not display an Or charge on an Argent field unless the charge is outlined in a tincture.
- Do not display a tincture on top of another tincture; an Azure charge may not be displayed upon a Gules field unless the charge is outlined in a metal.

Of course, there are exceptions: a charge may overlay a partition of the field and contrast cannot be avoided. When Godfrey of Bouillon was made King of Jerusalem he chose arms with five crosses Or potent on a field of Argent.

Incidentally, there is no standard for colours, like a pantone reference. As long as green is obviously green (as opposed to, say turquoise), it's fine, and some heraldic artists actually like to depict Or with gold paint rather than as yellow.

The colours of heraldry and the Petra Sancta system

Because black-and-white printing, engraving, stone carving and the like cannot use colours, a system of hatchings was developed to indicate what the colours would have been. This was popularised in the 1630s by either Silvester Petra Sancta (a Jesuit printer in Rome) or Marcus Vulson de la Colombière (a French heraldist and poet), but was based on an earlier method developed by the Flemish engraver, publisher and typographer, Johannes Baptista Zangrius.

'Attributed' arms of King Arthur (Arthur II, ab Uthr Pendragon), the first in Petra Sancta, the second in 'trick'.

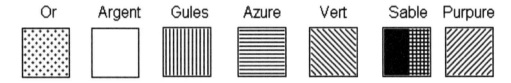

The Petra Sancta system of hatching.

Furs: Ermine (Sable on Argent), Ermines (Argent on Sable), Erminois (Sable on Or), Pean (Or on Sable), Vair and Counter-vair (Azure and Argent). Although furs operate as colours, there is no need to worry so much about the colour-on-metal rule so much – you could, for instance have a chevron Gules over an Ermine background, or vice versa.

Another way to indicate colours is 'in trick' – using standardised abbreviations. Early examples of this (such as the system of Don Alphonsus Ciacconius (1540–99), a Spanish Dominican scholar, based in Rome, naturally used the Latin initials for the tinctures – A (*Aurum*) for gold, a (*argentum*) for argent or white, c (*cearuleus*) for azure (blue), r (*rubeus*) for gules (red), v (*viridis*) for vert (green), and sable (black) was indicated by solid black itself. However, this is confusing to modern English speakers, so one system in use is as follows: Or (gold), Ar (Argent, silver or white), S or solid black

(Sable), G (Gules, red), Az (Azure, blue), V (Vert, green) and P (Purpure, the rare purple). Opposite are two versions of the same arms, showing how the Petra Sancta and tricking systems work.

The arms depicted are the completely spurious arms back-attributed to King Arthur Pendragon – a mythical person given arms relating to a time when no heraldry existed, and including the ostrich feathers not adopted by a Prince of Wales until Edward, the Black Prince, eldest son of Edward III, about 1346 (p. 207).

Blazon: Azure, three crowns in pale Or lined Gules, and on a wreath of the livery a king's helmet barred Or with a crest of three ostrich feathers Argent. (See pp. 195 and 207.)

So, the shield is Azure (blue), the three crowns are in a vertical line (in pale) and Or (gold) lined with Gules (red). The wreath and mantling reflect the two main colours of the livery (Azure and Or, so there is really no need to trick them), the helmet, as befits a king, has Or (gold) grilled bars and the feathers are Argent (white).

Points on the escutcheon (shield) and the blazon

The details below were copied verbatim from *Armorial Families* by Arthur Charles Fox-Davies, p. 85 (see p. 180 and p. 186, below).

WILLIAM RICHARD BASSET BASSET, Gentleman. Born November 23, 1863, being the eldest son of the late Major William West Bruce, Esq., J. P. co. Glamorgan, 74th Highlanders and 94th Regt. He assumed by Royal Licence, 1865, the surname and arms of Bassett, by his wife Eliza, daughter of Richard Weeks, Barrister-at-Law. **Armorial bearings** – Argent, a chevron between three buglehorns stringed Sable. **Mantling** – Sable and Argent. **Crest** – On a wreath of the colours, a stag's head caboshed, between the attires a cross fitchée at the foot Argent. Motto – '*Gwell angau na chywilydd*'. Seat – Beaupré, near Cowbridge. co. Glamorgan.

Read the blazon in this order:

1. The field of the escutcheon (shield) – gives the colour, here Argent.
2. The main charge or partition on the field – in this case, a chevron, and its tincture, Sable.
3. Charges not central – here, three buglehorns with strings, tincture Sable.
4. The crest – the stag's head and the cross are all Argent, 'caboshed' (or 'cabossed') is the head alone looking forward, and the cross is 'fitchée at the foot', meaning pointed.

The motto, by the way, translates as 'Better death than shame'.

Notice a few things here:

1. The two sides of the shield are referred to as sinister and dexter, yet the dexter side seems to be on the left – but if you were holding the shield, the dexter side would be on your right, which is why heraldists ONLY use the terms 'dexter' and 'sinister' and NEVER 'right' or 'left'.

2. The shape of the shield is not specified – the one shown is the most common shape, known as a 'heater' (like an old flat iron), but it is left up to the artist's discretion; however, because women traditionally did not go into battle, a shield is considered inappropriate so females' coats of arms are displayed on a lozenge or an elliptical shape (cartouche), except for the arms of a queen, as the sovereign is the commander-in-chief of the nation's armies (and in Canada, where there is no restriction against women bearing arms on a shield).

3. Colours and metals are given an initial capital (Gules, Or), largely to remove any confusion over the word 'or' as a conjunction.

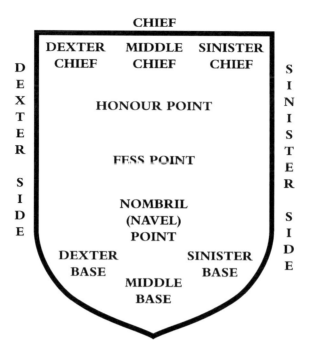

Positions on the field.

Arms of Basset (Glamorgan).

4. If the stag's head in the crest had had the colours as in nature, not heraldic colours (red, for instance), it would have been referred to as 'Proper', meaning the real colours, as in nature.

5. The mantling takes the main colours of the shield (here, Argent and Sable), with the first on the outside and the second as the 'lining' – however, a peer's mantling is always Gules doubled Ermine regardless of the colours of the 'livery'.

The ordinaries, diminutives and partitions

So far we have seen two examples of the charges called 'ordinaries' – the fess and the chevron. These are simple geometric shapes, and called 'ordinary' because they are the most common, and are often called the 'honourable ordinaries' (everything to do with arms is by definition honourable!) to distinguish them from their derivatives and diminutives. They also represent, in their simplest forms, the oldest arms on record, because in the early days there were fewer arms and therefore more choice. Unless specified, they extend to the edges of the field. The main ones, with examples of their use in arms, are shown on pp. 187–188, along with their diminutives, partitions of the field and charges arranged on the field. However, here are some Argent and Sable examples.

Argent, a pale Sable; Paly of seven, Sable and Argent; Palewise (or per pale) Sable and Argent; Argent, three fleurs-de-lys Sable in pale.

Some ordinaries.

Chief; Fess; Cross; Pale; Saltire; Chevron; Pile; Bend; Bend sinister; Bordure.
(Note that in Wales the chevron may be called a cwpl, from 'couple', the word used by carpenters to denote two timbers joined at the top and resting on opposite walls to hold up a roof.)

Some diminutives.

Bars (barry of four); Fess cotised; Pallets (paly of five); Pale endorsed; Chevronels; Piles (passion nails); Bendlet.

Partitions of the field.

Fesswise, per fess; Palewise, per pale; Per saltire; Per chevron; Per bend; Tierced in fess; Tierce; Tierced in pairle.

Positions on the shield (use more or less the same logic and terms).

In base; In pale; In chief; In fess; In bend; In bend sinister; In orle; Canton in dexter chief; Canton in Sinister chief; a martlet at fess point.

Sub-ordinaries (less common).

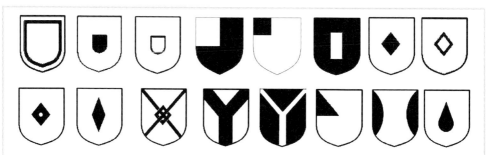

Orle or tressure; Inescutcheon; Inescutcheon voided; Quarter; Canton; Billet; Lozenge; Mascle; Rustre; Fusil; Frette; Pall or Pairle; Shakefork; Gyron; Flaunche; Goutte.

Patterning the field (the shapes of sub-ordinaries can be used to provide pattern).

Lozengy; Bendy of eight; Semy de gouttes; Gyronny of eight; Gyronny of six; Barry of ten; Chevronny of ten; Per chevron, checky and Sable; Fusilly; Quarterly. Note the double terminology – a pattern of gouttes may be goutty/goutée, which most heraldists find a bit ugly, or semy (semé) de gouttes. The gouttes tend to be of water or blood (gouttes-de sang, as on p. 193).

Lines of division

Lines do not have to be straight, but can take a variety of shapes such as: embattled (in the form of battlements), indented, dancetty, undy (wavy), nebuly (like clouds, supposedly), raguly, potente (like crutches), dovetailed, flory-counter-flory, engrailed (scalloped with points outward), invected (opposite of engrailed) and so on.

The lines of division and their blazoning as above: a chevron indented; a fess dancetty; a bordure invected.

Charges

Just about any object found in nature (or technology) may be a charge in heraldry, subject to the agreement of the granting authority. Sometimes these are highly stylised versions of animals, plants or objects, such as a quill pen, a book or a wheel. The most frequent charges are varieties of cross and the lion (an interesting choice for medieval Britain). Other common animals are stags and boars, fish, eagles, doves and martlets (a bird with no feet, as it is supposed never to land), and the mythical griffin, dragon, wyvern, mermaid and the like. The armiger is not limited, except by imagination and good taste. Note the difference in the examples shown between couped (cut straight across), as with the boar's head, and erased (as if torn off), like the bear's head.

Attitudes of animals

Quadrupeds are often rampant (standing on the left hind foot or both hind feet), arranged to show features such as claws and tail, passant (walking), salient (jumping), couchant (sitting) and their heads gardant (looking towards the observer), regardant (looking backwards) and other variants.

Different terms are used for beasts of prey (such as lions) and animals preyed upon (such as stags). Stags have their own attitude nomenclatures such as trippant (walking), statant (standing),

Common charges seen in heraldry.

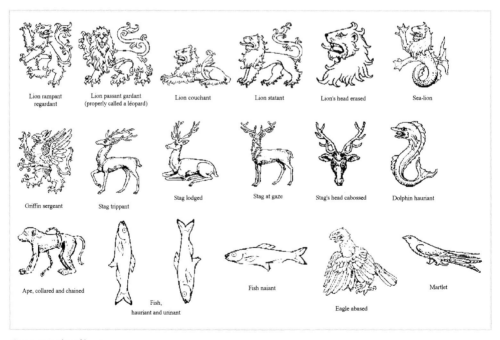

Some attitudes of beasts.

at gaze (head turned towards the observer), lodged (sitting) and cabossed (the head alone, facing forwards). Heraldic beasts often bear no resemblance to their natural counterparts, as with the heraldic dolphin and the sea lion, clearly conceived by someone who had never seen the real thing.

Eagles are usually shown with their wings displayed (spread). Fish have three attitudes: naiant (swimming), hauriant (head upwards) and urinant (downwards). Human figures are rare as charges, but often appear as supporters. The arms of John ap Gwilym ap Rhys and Owen of Caernarfonshire have examples of human heads used as charges.

Supporters

Dragons, unicorns and other exotics are more common as supporters. (For some reason, the iguanodon is a supporter in the arms of the borough of Maidstone in Kent, and Inverness has a camel.) There is more on this, with examples, on p. 196.

Marshalling arms

This is the term for merging two or more coats of arms in one shield, often to show the marriage of two armigers, the holding of office by an armiger (such as a bishopric), a claim to lands or some other circumstance. Marshalling is usually indicated by:

- impalement (where the shield is divided per pale into dexter and sinister halves, each with the full arms) or dimidation (half of the arms on each side);
- quartering (the shield is divided into four);
- adding an inescutcheon (a smaller shield in front of the main shield).

Quartering of arms: Impalement; Quartered; Inescutcheon of pretence; Sub-quartering of a grand quarter.

If more than four coats of arms are to be marshalled, there may be two rows of three (so-called 'quarterly of six') or more, but it is more usual to subquarter. An example of quartering is Rhys ab Einion Sais, and a particularly florid example of multiple quartering is in the arms of Hughes of Gwerclas (p. 192).

Shields impaled or quartered are read by rows from the dexter chief, with the first or main coat representing the highest or oldest title, or the paternal line. It works like this:

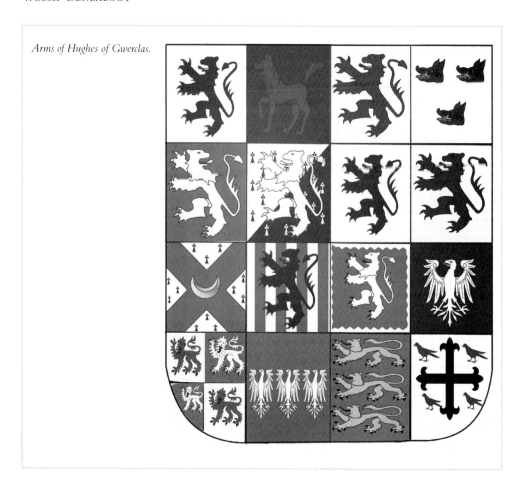

Arms of Hughes of Gwerclas.

Mr M., an armiger, meets Miss W. (who is not an armiger in her own right or an heraldic heiress, but her father has arms), and they marry, becoming Mr and Mrs W.-M. (Note that the man's name comes last, as it is the actual surname, and his arms go on the dexter side.) Their arms are impaled, with M on the dexter. The arms of their children are quartered, with M (paternal) in the first and fourth quarters, W (maternal) in the second and third.

Their eldest son marries a Miss P., they impale their arms, and the little P.-W.-M.s have subquarters in the first grand quarter. There is an example of such a thing on p. 193–4, concerning Brigstocke.

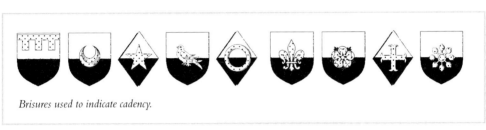

Brisures used to indicate cadency.

Cadency and difference – distinguishing children and branches

In England and Wales (and some other heraldic jurisdictions) all heirs of an armiger can bear the undifferenced arms. However, there are accepted systems of indicating younger children and derived branches of a family, called differencing or cadency (from the same root as 'cadet'). The following brisures (small charges) are typically added to a shield to distinguish younger children and cadet branches of a family, in order of birth: label of three (borne by the heir during the father's lifetime); crescent; mullet; martlet; annulet; fleur-de-lis; rose; cross moline; double quatrefoil.

Arms of Brigstocke.

Do not assume, however, that a shield bearing such brisures necessarily belongs to a cadet branch – they are also used as general charges. There is a similar system of brisures for females in Canadian heraldry – necessary because equal rights legislation over there means that women also get shields, not lozenges. Differencing can also be by changes in tincture or by the use of bordures. Finally, there can be differencing by quartering – but because this by itself does not always indicate cadency, an additional charge may be added, usually at the fess point, as in the first grand quarter of Brigstocke.

The original arms of Brigstockes from Blaenpant, Co. Cardigan, Pembroke and Carmarthen, first adopted in 1687, were Quarterly, Or and Sable, three escallop-shells counterchanged (as in the first and fourth grand quarters above). By a later marriage, the arms of subsequent generations incorporated the arms of Player of Ashey and Ryde (Azure, a pale Or, gutté-de-sang).

The helmet

All coats of arms may be displayed with an appropriate helm or helmet, which sits above the shield and carries the crest. The form of the helmet depends on the rank of the armiger and has a complex set of associated rules derived from conventions laid down in the 1600s. These are shown below, in this order; Sovereigns have a closed golden (Or) helm, affronty (facing forward); Nobles (peers of the rank of baron and above) have a closed helm with gold bars, facing to the side, usually dexter; Knights and baronets (entitled 'Sir') have an open-visored helm, affronty; Other armigers ('Gentlemen') have a closed tilting-helm, facing to the side; Corporations use another form of helmet called a sallet; But not everyone bears a helmet – churchmen, not being warriors, display above the shield a mitre (bishops and abbots) or a clerical tasselled hat called a galero (the number of tassels and the colour denotes the clerical rank).

Helmets as used in heraldry.

The crest

The crest sits atop the helm, arising from a torse (wreath) of twisted cloth in the two main colours of the coat of arms, sometimes within a coronet (simpler than coronets of rank). Crests identified a knight at a joust, and had the added advantage of deflecting blows. They were often (but not always) an animal. Since Tudor/Stuart times, crests have been granted with all coats of arms, except to women, who would not have fought in a medieval tournament. The crest must be capable of being fabricated in three dimensions. The crest usually rests on the helmet or is sometimes shown directly above the shield without a helmet, much to the annoyance of heraldic purists (how can you have a crest without a helmet to mount it on?).

The crest in heraldry can be almost any object, real or imaginary. The example in Brigstocke, above, is: a raven Sable holding in its dexter claw an escallop-shell Or.

Crests are also used on their own, with the torse, when there is insufficient space to display the entire arms, such as on stationery and the like – this practice may have led to the inaccurate use of the word to refer to a coat of arms. In Scottish heraldry in particular, the crest may be incorporated into a clan or family badge, which can be worn by any kinsman or kinswoman of the chief.

The motto

This is a word or phrase meant to describe the character or intention of the armigerous holder or corporation. Sometimes it is a pun on the name, as with Neville (*Ne vile velis* – 'Wish nothing vile'). It is usually on an escrol (a scroll) under the shield, or in Scots heraldry above the crest. A motto may be in any language, but English and Latin are the most frequent, despite Brigstocke showing off his familiarity with Matthew x.16 in Greek. In Wales, of course, mottos are often in Welsh – Basset Basset of Co. Glamorgan (p. 185) chose *Gwell angau na chywilydd* ('Better death than shame').

It is worth noting that, whereas in Scotland the motto can be registered at the same time as the arms, in England and Wales mottoes are not protected (see *Further reading*).

The arms of the City and County of Cardiff.

Supporters and other additions

An armiger may be entitled, depending on rank and other conditions, to certain additional items in the achievement. Peers of the realm, Scottish chiefs of clans and families, holders of the older Scottish baronies (chartered before 1587) and those who have continuously had supporters, inherit them with the title. Life peers (including law lords), Knights of the Thistle and of St Patrick, Knights Grand Cross or Knights Grand Commander of British orders of knighthood, Bailiffs and Dames Grand Cross of the Order of St John, corporate bodies established by royal charter or an Act of Parliament (including some local authorities), and certain other classes of individuals and institutions are entitled to supporters on either side of the shield, but only for life. Lords spiritual (the bishops who sit in the House of Lords) do not have supporters. Otherwise, the queen may grant supporters as an acknowledgement of some special merit.

The arms of the City and County of Cardiff (p. 195) are a good example of having two different supporters (granted in 1907 and augmented in 1956), and two mottos. The shield bears a Red dragon, the emblem of Wales, holding a standard on which is the Gules, three chevrons Argent attributed to Iestyn ap Gwrgant, last Prince of Glamorgan c. 1030–80, which became the arms of the Lords of Glamorgan and Cardiff. Where the dragon plants the standard, the leek, floral emblem of Wales, emerges. The motto below the shield (*Y ddraig goch ddyry cychwyn*) means 'the Red Dragon will lead the way' and the motto above the crest is *Deffro mae'n ddydd* (Awake, it is the day).

The crest incorporates a Tudor rose (the Tudors were Welsh) and the three ostrich feathers Argent from the badge of the Princes of Wales, issuing out of a mural coronet (indicative of a town or city with a royal charter of some kind).

The supporters are a Welsh goat on the dexter (emblematic of the Welsh mountains) and on the sinister, a hippocamp or sea horse (for the Severn and the transport trade of Cardiff port), both wearing the Royal Badge for Wales by a golden chain from the neck – these augmentations were granted when Her Majesty Queen Elizabeth II gave a royal warrant to Cardiff as the capital of Wales.

Coronets of rank

If the armiger has the title of peerage baron or higher (or hereditary knight in some countries), he or she may display a coronet of rank above the shield, usually below the helm in British heraldry, often above the crest (if any) in continental heraldry. For example, an earl has an eight-pearl coronet (but only five pearls are visible from the front). These derive from the actual coronets designed for the coronation of Charles II, which are still worn today.

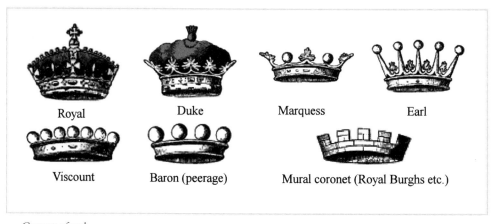

| Royal | Duke | Marquess | Earl |

| Viscount | Baron (peerage) | Mural coronet (Royal Burghs etc.) |

Coronets of rank.

Civic heraldry

There is a complicated set of coronets for the different forms of local authority – city, island, unitary authority, community council and so on – but the historic mural coronet (for royal burghs) has not been used in Scotland since burghs were abolished in 1975. For more on this, consult www. heraldry-scotland.co.uk/civic.html.

Corporate arms

Institutions and companies can have a grant of officially recognised coats of arms from government heraldic authorities. This is effectively a registered trademark.

The first recorded corporate coat of arms was granted to the Drapers' Company of London in 1438. However, many users of modern so-called 'heraldic' designs do not register with the authorities, and some designers do not follow the heraldic design rules.

Heraldic law

The first work on heraldic law, *De Insigniis et Armiis* (On Insignia and Arms) was written by Bartolo de Sassoferrato, professor of law at the University of Padua, in the 1350s.

From the earliest times of European heraldry, arms have passed by inheritance from father to sons (and daughters), and are strictly speaking the heritable property of the holder. A coat of arms may be borne by the original bearer's legitimate lineal descendants, with the eldest heir using undifferentiated arms and the others with modifications (cadency) to express the difference and maintain uniqueness, as we have seen. In some countries, such differences are not necessary in heraldic law and the arms of the original armiger pass equally to all male descendants. In other countries it is only the senior heir who can bear the original arms. In Scotland, all arms must be granted or matriculated (registered) and differentiated from those of the original armiger, except where they pass to the eldest heir.

The practice of all descendants bearing undifferentiated inheritance in some countries has led to the unfortunate misconception – first encouraged by unprincipled printers and stationers in the nineteenth century and perpetuated by 'Your Family Crest' merchants today – that a coat of arms somehow belongs to everyone with the same surname, whether or not there is any real family relationship. 'Family crests' (which is wrong anyway, since the crest is only one part of a full armorial achievement) are sold to a gullible public. What they will probably get is a version of the arms of the chief representer of that name (which is, of course, the legal property of the current armiger), or of the first person of that surname on their database, and with an inaccurate narrative. An armiger has paid an exchequer tax on the arms and any impostor displaying falsely acquired arms risks legal prosecution – by civil law pursuit in England and Wales, but by statute law in Scotland. In England and Wales, the only legal recourse for someone who feels his or her arms have been usurped is to mount a civil action in the Court of Chivalry, which has not met in such a matter since the 1950s and is not an integrated part of the English judicial system.

In any case, if your name is Jones, which of the examples of Jones arms would you choose? You can't be descended from all of them. There is a convenient fiction in heraldry that everyone of the same surname is related – it is recognised that this is not so in reality, but it does mean that new arms will reflect those of a previous armiger of that name. However, you are not justified in simply picking one of these arms and printing it on your stationery or having it embroidered on a tea-cosy.

Legally, it is the blazon (the word description) that is important, and which is inherited, rather than the design as such, so coats of arms can be thought of more as a patent than a logo. Hence, there may be differences in detail between depictions of arms – the exact size or placement of charges on the field, the number of claws of a dragon, the look of a fish or a castle.

Wales and the College of Arms

Wales comes under the jurisdiction of the College of Arms in London, and always did. English heralds accumulated evidence of arms and pedigrees by travelling around the country making 'visitations' (exactly what it sounds like), and it was common, and sensible, to take on a Welsh deputy when visiting Wales. The best known of these was Lewis Dwnn (died *c.* 1616), and his visitations records concerning the three counties of South Wales (Carmarthen, Pembroke and Cardigan) and part of the Marches (the border with England), compiled between 1586 and 1597, are highly regarded (see *Further reading* on how to obtain these and p. 206 for a sample page).

The chief herald is Garter King of Arms, operating under the authority of the Earl Marshal of England, and aided by two other Kings of Arms and a court of six heralds and four pursuivants (see below for a list). The two subsidiary Kings have theoretical territorial jusrisdiction – Ulster and Norroy for north of the Trent and Clarenceux for the south (and therefore Wales). There had been a March King of Arms in the time of Edward IV, called '*Rex armorum partium occidentalium*' (King of Arms of the West Parts), whose responsibility was the West of England, including Cornwall and the whole of Wales, but Richard III changed this by creating the Gloucester King of Arms for Wales. This office did not, however, survive beyond the first incumbent, until it was revived along with the Order of the Bath in 1725, but with no Welsh remit. There is now no specifically Welsh King of Arms or Herald, except that Michael Powell Siddons was created Wales Herald of Arms Extraordinary – the term 'Extraordinary' indicating that it was an additional appointment, for taking part in ceremonial occasions, in light of his exceptional scholarship in the field of Welsh heraldry, and in distinction to the 'Ordinary' or official officers of arms at the college.

There have been officers and other members of the College of Arms who were Welsh – Thomas Chaloner of Chester; Griffith Hughes, deputy to the office of arms for North Wales (an interesting appeleation) in 1639; George Owen, Norroy King of Arms in 1658; Captain Robert Chaloner, Lancaster herald from 1665; David Edwardes, appointed in 1684 by Sir Henry St George, then Clarenceux, as his deputy herald over the then six Welsh counties (Brecon, Cardigan, Carmarthen, Glamorgan, Pembroke and Radnor); and others since.

For the record, the names of the other officers of arms are given below, with dates of creation, but the titles imply no particular territorial responsibility, although they once did:

Kings of Arms
Garter Principal King of Arms (1415, pre-dating the foundation of the college by royal charter in 1484)
Clarenceux King of Arms (1334)
Norroy and Ulster King of Arms (Norroy 1276, Ulster 1552)
Heralds
Chester Herald of Arms in Ordinary (1396)
Lancaster Herald of Arms in Ordinary (1347)
Windsor Herald of Arms in Ordinary (1338 or 1348)
Somerset Herald of Arms in Ordinary (*c.* 1448)
Richmond Herald of Arms in Ordinary (1421)
York Herald of Arms in Ordinary (1385, royal in 1484)
Pursuivants
Bluemantle Pursuivant of Arms in Ordinary (1448)
Portcullis Pursuivant of Arms in Ordinary (1490)
Rouge Croix Pursuivant of Arms in Ordinary (1418)
Rouge Dragon Pursuivant of Arms in Ordinary (1485, named after the red dragon of Wales)
Extraordinary Officers (ceremonial duties only)

Arundel Herald of Arms Extraordinary (1413, revived in 1727)
Beaumont Herald of Arms Extraordinary (1982)
Maltravers Herald of Arms Extraordinary (1540, revived in 1887)
Norfolk Herald of Arms Extraordinary (1539)
Surrey Herald of Arms Extraordinary (1856)
Wales Herald of Arms Extraordinary (c 1393 but short-lived and revived in 1963, see p. 198)
Fitzalan Pursuivant of Arms Extraordinary (1837)
Howard Pursuivant of Arms Extraordinary (1992)
New Zealand Herald of Arms Extraordinary (1978, with a special remit – see p. 200)

Can I have arms?

If you are Welsh, or of Welsh descent, and not currently domiciled in a country where there is a heraldic authority (such as Scotland, Ireland, South Africa or Canada), and if you are a 'worthy and virtuous person', arms are possible. There are three routes:

1. If you can prove that you are heir to someone who at some time properly registered or was granted a coat of arms, then you can petition the College of Arms to re-grant these in your name.

2. If you have no armigerous direct forebears, you can petition for a new Grant of Arms.

3. If you live in, say, America and have no property in Wales or residence there, it may be possible to petition for arms in the name and memory of a Welsh ancestor, then establish an honorary grant in the ancestor's name. This is useful – and cheaper – when a number of members of a family want to achieve arms.

Arms and crests are granted by letters patent, with the authority of the Crown delegated to the Kings of Arms, acting under the Earl Marshal, who first has to issue a warrant agreeing to this.

- First, contact the college and start a dialogue with whichever officer of arms is on duty that day. If it is considered likely that the petition will be acceptable, the herald or pusuivant (see below) will drawn up a petition (called a 'memorial') for signature by the petitioner. There are no fixed criteria as such, but awards or honours from the Crown, university degrees, professional qualifications, military commissions, service in the public or charity arena, and some reputation in national or local life will be taken into account. Submit a pedigree (or ask the officer to research this, at extra cost) and curriculum vitae.
- Next, the petition or memorial is submitted to the Earl Marshal. At this point, fees are payable – as of 2012 the fees payable are £4,725 (approximately $7,500 or €6,000) for a personal grant of arms and crest, £5,825 for parish councils (for arms alone without crest), and much more for a non-profit body (£10,075) or a commercial organisation (£15,000). A badge or supporters (if eligible), or the design ('exemplification') of a standard is extra. Also, factor in the cost of having a genealogist or one of the officers of arms prepare an acceptable pedigree, if necessary – one advantage of having the College of Arms heralds do this is that they have best access to the records.
- If the Earl Marshal approves the petition, a warrant is sent to the Kings of Arms, and the design process begins. The actual design is absolutely at the discretion of the Kings of Arms, but there is usually a discussion so that the wishes of the petitioner can be incorporated,

subject to matters of precedence, distinctiveness, simplicity, good taste and so on. You will not get away with something ugly or barbarous. References to profession, place of origin or residence, associated institutions and so on are suitable. For example, someone with maritime heritage or a career in the navy will likely be allowed an anchor if wished, but it is unlikely that a pole dancer would be able to depict a dancing pole. Puns ('canting' arms) have a long history in heraldry, and are usually appreciated if not too excruciating – for instance, someone called Harrison might choose a hedgehog (French, *herisson*).

- You will be sent an outline sketch for checking and, once agreed, the blazon (what really matters) will be finalised.
- There will be a final check against all previous arms on record at the College of Arms (to make sure it is absolutely distinctive), a piece of vellum will be chosen, a College of Arms heraldic artist commissioned to paint the arms and a scrivener engaged to engross the text. Then it is signed and sealed by the Kings of Arms, and a copy painted and scrivened, as they say, into the official registers for all time. The letters patent become the property of the armiger.

Can American citizens get arms?

Well, sort of. Americans may get honorary arms, provided they meet the criteria above, and if they first record a pedigree showing descent from a subject of the British Crown. This could be a recent migrant, or someone living in the North American colonies before the British accepted, in 1783, that independence had actually happened. A good example is Colin Powell, ex-Secretary of State of the USA, who established a link back to a British-subject ancestor – his father, Luther Powell, born in Jamaica and thus a subject of the Crown. However, despite the Welsh-sounding surname, Powell chose to emphasise the Scottish roots of his mother's family (McKoy) and was therefore granted arms by the Lord Lyon in Scotland. It also didn't hurt Colin Powell's case that he was an honorary Knight Commander of the Order of the Bath.

Doesn't the United States have a regulated heraldic authority?

Strangely, yes it does – but only within the Pentagon (United States Army Institute of Heraldry) where the arms and seals of all military units have been carefully and closely controlled since 1920. Department of Defense and Military Seals are protected from unauthorised use by law. There was an attempt in America to regulate personal arms as a tax-raising opportunity in 1868, but it dwindled away. Other than that, no – but the American Heraldry Society (www.americanheraldry.org) or the American College of Heraldry (www.americancollegeofheraldry.org) will happily register arms for you, but not in any official way. They will possibly ask you hard questions about the provenance of arms and your right to bear them.

How about Australians, Canadians and so on?

Much the same applies to people of demonstrable Welsh descent living in Commonwealth countries and elsewhere – establish a link to a British subject and take it from there. However, Ireland, Scotland and Commonwealth countries with their own heraldic authority – Canada, South Africa – will expect residents to register arms there, and the College of Arms will direct petitioners in that direction. But you can always ask. (South Africa, incidentally, has the reputation of granting arms to absolutely anyone who asks, regardless of where they live and almost regardless of whom they are – so that's a possible route if all else fails.)

New Zealand is a special case, having its own New Zealand Herald of Arms Extraordinary, a sort of 'Honorary Consul' post created in 1978, not as a member of the college but working with the college to grant new arms to individuals and bodies in that country.

There are other unofficial but recognised authorities such as in Spain (see below).

Heraldic authorities

Those who may legally grant arms to individuals, corporations or other bodies are:

- Scotland: The Court of the Lord Lyon — www.lyon-court.com/
- England, Wales and Northern Ireland: The College of Arms — www.college-of-arms.gov.uk/
- Ireland: The Office of the Chief Herald — www.nli.ie/en/heraldry-introduction.aspx
- Canada: The Canadian Heraldic Authority — http://www.gg.ca/document.aspx?id=81
- New Zealand: Herald of Arms Extraordinary — www.dpmc.govt.nz/honours/overview/herald-of-arms/
- South Africa: The National Herald at the Bureau of Heraldry www.national.archives.gov.za/aboutnasa_content.html#heraldry
- Flanders, Belgium: Flemish Heraldic Council — www.monument.vlaanderen.be/aml/en/heraldische_raad.html
- United States Army: The United States Army Institute of Heraldry — www.tioh.hqda.pentagon.mil/
- Spain: Cronista Rey de Armas — www.iagi.info/Cronista/. (Heraldry is not regulated in that there are no laws or rules and no official enforcement. The heralds — Cronistas Reyes de Armas — have judicial powers in matters of noble titles and are a registration office for pedigrees and arms.)

Other heraldry

Many more people see heraldry as a part of their national, and even personal, heritage, as well as a manifestation of civic and national pride. Those who have an interest in heraldry as a hobby participate in the Society for Creative Anachronism (www.sca.org) and other such medieval, living history and re-enactment groups.

The Royal Arms

Why does Wales not appear in the Royal Arms? Quite simply, it isn't a nation. As a principality, Wales has no independent legal status distinct from England. There is, of course, devolution of some powers to the Welsh Assembly, but not to the same extent as the Scottish Government. Her Majesty is separately Queen of England (and Wales) and Queen of Scots — in the same way as she is Queen of Canada, Bermuda and other Commonwealth countries. However, the Principality of Wales does have its own Royal Badge (seen on the necks of the supporters of the arms of Cardiff, p. 195), first granted over 200 years ago and added to in 1959 (see below). The Prince of Wales has his own allusions in his arms to Wales.

Princess of Wales?

The wife of the Prince of Wales at any given time is, obviously, the Princess of Wales. But the title can go to a daughter in the male line of the sovereign. The best example is Victoria of Wales — Princess Victoria Alexandra Olga Mary (1868–1935), daughter of Albert Edward, Prince of Wales (later King Edward VII) — eldest son of Queen Victoria and Prince Albert — and Alexandra, Princess of Wales (née Princess Alexandra of Denmark). Victoria never married (despite the attentions of King Carlos I of Portugal) and seems to have spent most of her energies in running the Iver Horticultural Society in Buckinghamshire. Her personal arms, interestingly, bore an inescutcheon of the shield of Saxony, but that was quietly dropped in 1917 as a result of the First World War. So, nothing to do with Wales at all, really.

Symbolism and vexillology (the study of flags)

Of course, the national symbol of Wales is the red dragon (*Y Ddraig Goch*).

The flag of Wales has the red dragon on the Tudor colours of white and green. Henry VII (a Tudor, and therefore of Welsh ancestry) flew it at the Battle of Bosworth Field in 1485, and the dragon was then included in the Tudor royal arms. It was not officially recognised as the Welsh national flag until 1959. The earliest recorded use is in the *Historia Brittonum* (The History of the Britons), written about 828 AD during Anglo-Saxon rule, possibly by the Welsh monk, Nennius, not to be confused with the British prince of the same name in the works of Geoffrey of Monmouth. The flag is said to have been the battle standard of King Arthur Pendragon and perhaps other Celtic warlords. After Wales was annexed by England, the dragon was a supporter in the English royal coat of arms, until supplanted by the Scottish lion at the time of the Union. The city of Puerto Madryn (Welsh, Porth Madryn) in the Province of Chubut, Patagonia, Argentina, has a flag inspired by the Welsh dragon, thanks to the migration of Welsh there (p. 156).

The Royal Badge of Wales is the red dragon, and in 1953, by decree of Her Majesty the Queen in the Privy Council, this badge was enclosed in a scroll carrying the motto *Y ddraig goch ddyry cychwyn* ('the Welsh dragon gives the lead') in green on a white background and surmounted by a royal crown, used on all government publications and by government departments in Wales.

The flag of Saint David (*Baner Dewi Sant*) is normally Sable, a cross Or (a yellow cross on a black field) and very similar to the arms of the diocese of St David's (based in the cathedral church in the City of St David's, Pembrokeshire, and also covering Ceredigion, Carmarthenshire and a part of western Glamorgan). The flag is used as an alternative to the national flag, as well as being flown on Saint David's Day (*Dydd Gŵyl Dewi*, 1 March), and is the flag of Cardiff.

The plant symbols of Wales are the leek (dating back to the sixteenth century) and the daffodil (first popular in the late nineteenth and early twentieth centuries, encouraged by prime minister and passionate Welshman, David Lloyd George). There may be a couple of linguistic confusions (or intentional puns) here – the Welsh for leek (*cenhinen*) is very similar to the word for daffodil (*cenhinen Bedr* or St Peter's leek) and 'daffodil' is similar to David (*Dafydd*).

The Welsh flag.

Flag of the diocese of St David.

Flag of St David.

The Royal Badge of Wales.

The feathers from the crest of the Prince of Wales.

LLAN RYSTYD[1] Y PLAS I MABWS FAWR.

Rys du ap Llewelyn ap Kydwgan o Garog([1]) Esg══Gwyrul ♀ Ienan ap Einion ap Gruffydd.

Rys Vychan Gentn:══...... merch Ffylip ap Mredydd o Gilsant.

Ieuan══...... merch a choeyr Mredydd ap Llewelyn.

Rys══Marged ♀ David ap Howel ap Ieuan ap Einion o Drelech ar Betws([2])

Rydderch══Elen ♀ Lewys ap Ieuan ap Lewys o Abermaed.([1])

Richart ap Rydderch gent: 1613══Lleuku ♀ Wiliam ap Llewelyn Esg[e].

David ap Richart gent: 1613══Elsbeth ♀ Hari Vychan ap Richart ap Sion ap Rydderch   Ieuan   Tomas   Marged

Ano R. R. Jams 1613.   RICHAHERD AP REDD[rh].

HARFFORT WEST[3] AND TRERFRAN K. Y GARN.

Syr Huw Haris k[t]. ap Syr John Haris k[t] off Essex══Ann ♀ Tomas Deier Esgwier.   John Syton Esg[r]══Annes ♀ Syr Rys ap Tomas k[t] off the Garter.

Huw Haris of Harffort west([3]) Esg══Marged   Gruffydd Chweit Esg([4])══Mari ♀ Syr Owen Perot k[t].

Sioned gwraig ...... Marichyrch Esg   Mawd gwraig Tomas Bwtler off Janston([3]) Esg   Lewis Haris Esg══Mari

Richiart Ffletcher Esg[r]══...... do to ...... Sbenser

Richart Ffetchier Esgob Leundon([5])══Elsbeth Holant.

John Haris══Elsbeth   Sara   Prysyh gwraig John Batmann   Nathaniel══...... do to Doctor   Theoffklws([6])   John
Esg[t] 1613 | Ffletchier   off Harffort West([3])   Fletchier   Weikam   sans   sans

Lewys koeyr   Elsbeth koeyr

Hi bereth .... Ail bais John Harbert o Lacharn

Ano R. R. Jams 1613.   JO HARRIES.

---

[1] These places are in Cardiganshire.
[2] In Carmarthenshire.   [3] In Pembrokeshire.
[4] The Whites were a family of opulence as merchants at Tenby in the 15th century. That church contains their monuments, one of which is dated 1482.

[5] Richard Fletcher, D.D., who had been elected Bishop of Bristol in 1589, was, three years after, translated to the see of Worcester, and was elected Bishop of London in 1594. He died on the 15th of June, 1596, and was buried in the Cathedral of St. Paul's.
[6] Theophilus.

SIR BENFRO PLWYF NEVERN YN GHEMES. TREF Y DRESSI[1]

PLANT Howel Iong ap Howel ap Siankin Iong ap Ieuan ap Gwilim ap Iankin Iong o Drefor yw:

1. Howel Iong o Dre Jwrdan.(1)
2. Gruffyth Iong o'r Kruge.(1)
3. Lewys Iong or Klastor
4. David Iong o Llandndock.(1)
5. Domas Iong o Dressy.

Mam yr hain Marged ♀ Mathe o Sir Fon.(2)

Plant Howel Iong o Dro Jwrdan,(2) Siankyn, Mathias, Sian, Elu, Mari.

O Rys, Wiliam ; o Wiliam David, sydd yn heddyw 1591.

Plant Gruffydd Iong—Ilys, Siams, Owen, Alson. Rydderch ap Rys, ai

Plant Lewys Iong, Tomas ; ai vab yntau yw Arthur, Tomas.

Plant David Iong, Richiart Iong sy vyw heddiw 1591, Elen Iong, mam David Domas o Bark y Pratt.(1)

Plant Tomas Iong; Ffylip Iong o Dre'r Dryssy a briododd

Not. o weithred i'r Rydd⁴ ap David ap Ieuan ap David dew ap Howel ap Howel Iong Y ssel yw Llew rampant or.

Not. o weithred eto y Ieuan ap Gwilim Iong Hari. I sel ef oedd karw passant gardant rwng 3 flowr de lis or.

Anes Meurig val o'r blaen :(2) Ai blant yw [1]Rolant Iong a briododd Sian ♀ Mathias Bowen ap Syr Jams Bowen marchog ; mam hono Mari Ffylibs.

Ai blant (1591) [1]Tomas Iong, [2]Einion Iong, [3]Ffylib Iong. [4]Giorg Iong, [5]Elsbeth gwraig John ap Rys ap John ap Gruffydd o Bhenporth,(4) Marged.

Gwedi hyny priododd ef Sioned ♀ Gruffydd Lloyd ap Rydderch o Benywern, Sir Aberteifi.(4) Mam hono Gwenllian ♀ Lewys ap Ieuan vachan o'r Bontvaen yn Ghemes.(4)

Ai blant yw Sioned.

Plant [2]John Iong ap Ffylib Iong yw Tomas Iong, Ffylib Iong.

Mam ydain yw Marged koeres Morgan ap Owen o Dre Rickert.(5)

3. Tomas Iong ap Ffylib a briododd Saeg koeres Tomas ap Piter val o'r blaen.

4. Owain Iong ap Ffylib a briododd Marged ♀ Tomas.

Dated the 23 dai off September Ano R. R. Elsbeth 33 Ano 1591

Reseved off ROLAND YOUNGE 2s

PLWYF NAMERNAFON.[5] TRE LLEWELYN.[1]

OWEN PHILLIPS.

AM Y BOWENS O GEMES.[1]

a, Page 163.

[1] In Pembrokeshire.

[2] Anglesey.

[3] Of Bodorgan, Anglesey. She was sister to the Right Rev. Dr. Rolant Meurig, Bishop of Bangor.

[4] In Cardiganshire.

[5] Manerawen, or Maenor Ieuan Parish, in Pembrokeshire.

[6] Cynghordy, an old Mansion House above Glanbrân Park, in Carmarthenshire.

[7] Bentibarch, or Pentiparh, near Haverfordwest, the property of J. Philipps A. Lloyd Philipps, Esquire, of Dale Castle.

[8] This is, no doubt, Newcastle Emlyn, on the Teivy.

Previous page and above: *'A page from the Book of Lewis Doon (LLyfr Lewis Dwnn), Poet, of Montgomeryshire, of Bettws in Cydhewain on Berriew, who is Deputy Herald at Armsover the three Provinces of Wales, and in the Marches of Wales, under the Patentand Seals of Clarencieux and Norroy, two King of Arms, under the Great Seal, for the Southward and the Northward, for North and South Wales.'*

The Prince of Wales's feathers, the heraldic badge of the heir to the throne, is often used by Welsh bodies, when granted by a warrant to use it in Wales – the Welsh Rugby Union, for instance. However, these have no connection with the native Princes of Wales, but are an English invention. Edward, the Black Prince (1330–76), eldest son and heir apparent of King Edward III, was the first Prince of Wales to use it as an emblem. Actually, Edward was never called 'The Black Prince' until a couple of centuries after his death, and as he died the year before his father, he was the first English Prince of Wales not to become king – the crown went instead to his son Richard II, with all the trouble that caused! The 'Black' soubriquet may stem from his personal arms, which were Sable, three ostrich feathers Argent (his younger brother, John of Gaunt, had similar arms but with the ostrich feathers in Ermine). There is a persistent myth that the Black Prince took the feathers from the helmet crest of blind John I of Bohemia, after the Battle of Crécy in 1346 – the prince is supposed to have incorporated the feathers and King John's motto *Ich Diene* or *Ich Dien* (I serve) for his own. However, there are a few things wrong with that, such as:

1) the story doesn't appear until 1376, when Edward died;
2) King John's crest was actually vultures' wings;
3) *Ich Diene* was never John of Bohemia's motto;
4) the first Prince of Wales to use three white feathers (encircled by a coronet and with the motto) was Arthur, eldest son of Henry VII, 150 years later. Edward probably inherited the feathers from his mother, Philippa of Hainault, herself descended from the Counts of Hainault, whose eldest son had the title Count of Ostrevent, similar to *autriche*, French for ostrich, and therefore another heraldic pun.

Titles

Barons and baronies

This is an area of great potential confusion. In England a baron is a peer of the realm, the lowest rank of the lords. Until recently, a peerage entitled the holder to sit in the House of Lords. The title has no implication of landownership, although the peer may (separately) be a landowner with land in or near the place from which he takes his title – Lord Tredegar, for example, did indeed have a lot of land around Tredegar (see Index for more references) and chose the name for that reason rather than being given the title land from which landholding followed. In Scotland, it was (and still is) different – a baron was a 'Great Man' who held lands directly of the king by a grant *in liberam baroniam* ('in free barony'), so barons were therefore large landowners. They could levy taxes and tolls for goods taken through their lands or sold on them; in exchange for which rights the baronies helped manage the kingdom through the barony courts. A Scottish baron is not a noble, in the sense of having a peerage, although individual barons may also have other noble titles.

A peerage baron may be referred to as a *baro major* and a Scottish feudal baron as a *baro minor*. For that reason, in Scotland they are 'Baron *of* Such-and-such', as opposed to a noble, 'Baron So-and-so'. One person could hold several, or many, baronies, and occasionally you will see these for sale on Internet sites. The barony does not necessarily carry with it any lands, houses or money, and has no real duties or rights any more.

By contrast, a peerage title is 'by writ', rather than 'prescriptive' (tied to land – when ex-Prime Minister James Callaghan was elevated to the peerage as Baron Callaghan of Cardiff in 1987, he did not suddenly own Cardiff or necessarily have any more rights there than any other citizen – although they did make him a non-executive director of the Bank of Wales (a private bank, not any kind of state body)).

Baronetcies

A baronetcy is different again – it's a kind of hereditary knighthood (but not exactly) dreamed up by King James VI and I in 1611, partly to raise money for wars (it was an early 'cash for honours' system) and partly to encourage settlement and development in the Province of Ulster in Northern Ireland. It was rather clever in that it did not depend on giving a seat in the House of Lords. Somewhat different were the Scottish baronetcies of Nova Scotia instituted in 1625 by King Charles I in an attempt to encourage settlement in the colony – but few even went to see their lands and by then Nova Scotia was in French hands anyway, although disputed for centuries. Nevertheless, the Mi'kmaq were there first!

Since the Union of 1707, all baronetcies are of the United Kingdom. Queen Victoria used baronetcies to honour the deserving middle classes without giving them grand peerages. Baronets are styled, for example, Sir Hufton Tufton Bart. or Bt. and his wife would have the courtesy title Lady Tufton. A female baronet ('baronetess') would be Dame Hilda Bracket Bt. Such people are not in any sense nobles, nor necessarily landholding; baronetcies are just an honour. Prime Minister Margaret Thatcher became a baroness (gained a peerage) in her own right when she retired from the Commons, but her husband Dennis was granted a baronetcy, now inherited by his son, which explains why he is Sir Mark Thatcher Bt. although he did nothing to earn it except belong to the right family. Baroness Thatcher's title is a life peerage and will die with her, so Sir Mark will not become a baron (Lord Thatcher). While prime minister, Mrs Thatcher rewarded her retiring deputy, William Whitelaw, with a viscountcy, which is hereditary. Rather cleverly, the succession was limited to his heirs male, and as he had only daughters, the title died with him.

Further reading

Books

The two best publications are both Scottish, but so much of heraldry is general that they serve as useful introductions:

Mark Dennis' beautifully illustrated and remarkably cheap *Scottish Heraldry* (available from the Heraldry Society of Scotland) and Sir Ian Moncreiffe and Don Pottinger's, *Simple Heraldry Cheerfully Illustrated* (1952), which is out of print but can often be found on eBay or other auction and bookselling websites.

More formal works include the staggering multi-volume opus by Michael Powell Siddons, Wales Herald of Arms Extraordinary at the College of Arms, *The Development of Welsh Heraldry*, 4 vols (National Library of Wales, 1991–2007) and his *Heraldic Badges in England and Wales*, 4 vols. Some of these may be available on Google Books.

Others worth checking are:

Stephen Friar, *Heraldry for the Local Historian and Genealogist* (Stroud: Sutton, 1992).

Ottfried Neubecker, J.P. Brooke-Little and Robert Tobler, *Heraldry: Sources, Symbols, and Meaning* (London: Tiger Books International, 1989).

Also consult the various publications of Burke (Peerage, Landed Gentry etc.), many available for download as PDFs from www.archive.org.

Likewise, the Society for the Publication of Ancient Welsh Manuscripts, Abergavenny, published a number of excellent early Welsh sources (such as that by Lewys Dwnn, *c.* 1600: *The Heraldic visitations of Wales and part of the Marches; between the years 1586 and 1613, under the authority of Clarencieux and Norroy, two kings at arms*, 2 vols, ed. Sir Samuel Rush Meyrick (1846) – which is available at www.archive.org).

Online sources

See p. 201 for heraldic authorities worldwide

Heraldic dictionaries etc. – Notre Dame: www.rarebooks.nd.edu/digital/heraldry/index.html

Heraldry Society of Scotland: www.heraldry-scotland.co.uk

François Velde's Heraldry Site: www.heraldica.org/

Canadian heraldry: www.heraldry.ca/

Coats of Arms from Ireland and around the World (Eddie Geoghegan): www.heraldry.ws/

Cambridge University Heraldic & Genealogical Society: www.cam.ac.uk/societies/cuhags/links/her_info.htm

Arthur Charles Fox-Davies, *Complete Guide to Heraldry* (first published in 1909): www7b.biglobe.ne.jp/~bprince/hr/foxdavies/index.htm

Collection of Welsh mottos (in Welsh, Latin, English etc.) taken from Michael Powell Siddons' *The Development of Welsh Heraldry* (vol. 3, pp. 171–81.) at www.doomchicken.net/~ursula/sca/motto/welshmottoes.html#languages

Civic Heraldry of England and Wales: www.civicheraldry.co.uk/contents.html

Civic Heraldry of United Kingdom: www.civicheraldry.com/region/uk

Cracroft's Peerage – *The Complete Guide to the British Peerage & Baronetage*: www.cracroftspeerage.co.uk/

12

Dates, Money and Measure

Dates and Calendars

This would seem to be a straightforward issue – today is today, the day before was yesterday and next comes tomorrow. But it isn't that simple. Dates are complicated by a number of things:

- calendar reforms between the 1580s and 1750s;
- the date of New Year;
- differences in ways of recording dates 'at the terms of Whitsun and Martinmas', for instance;
- regnal years.

Julian and Gregorian calendars

In Julius Caesar's time, the first century BC, it became clear to Roman astronomers that the solar and calendar years were out of synch. Midsummer's Day, for instance, on the calendar was clearly not the day the sun was highest in the sky. This mattered because of the importance to agriculture and various religious observances that had to take place on certain days.

The astronomers of Rome knew that the error had been introduced because of a 365-day year, whereas the sun takes 365¼ days (they reckoned) to go round the earth, as they saw it. Hence, they introduced the leap day every four years and set things back to rights.

Originally, the Romans had ten named months – *Martius, Aprilis, Maius, Junius, Quintilis* (July), *Sextilis* (August), *September, October, November, December* – plus two unnamed months corresponding to our January and February. *Martius* (March, the arrival of spring) was the beginning of the year, a point we'll return to. *Januarius* and *Februarius* were added around 700 BC (when Rome was just beginning to establish itself as a power) and the New Year was moved to *Januarius*. Occasionally they added an 'intercalendar' month to cope with leap years, thereby turning *September* (literally 'seventh month') into the ninth month, and the same for *October, November* and *December*, which had been eight, nine and ten in the calendar (although, from the point of view of a March year-start, they were still in the right place). Later, in the time of Julius Caesar, they made the number of days in some months an odd 'lucky' number and gave February an extra day every fourth or 'leap' year. This produces the so-called 'Julian' calendar and the year structure we now have – *Thirty days hath September* and so on – and the names of the months *Quintilis* and *Sextilis* eventually got named after Julius and Augustus respectively.

That didn't fix everything, though – the earth's rotation round the sun (as we now think of it) is actually a bit slower than 365¼ days, so there was still an accumulated error of some eleven minutes and fourteen seconds each year. In 1582, Vatican astronomers faced up to this just as the Romans had some 1,600 years before, because the calendar was again some days ahead of the sun. Under Pope Gregory XIII they reformed the Julian calendar to correspond to the solar year, took out ten days (5 to 14 October) and changed the rule for leap days so that centenary years would not be leap years, except when divisible by 400, which is why 1900 wasn't a leap year but

1600 and 2000 were. Naturally, all the Catholic countries did what they were told, but Protestant northern Europe – including Scotland and England – were certainly not going to obey anything that came from Rome.

This led to 170 years of confusion, which affected, for example, foreign trade and travel:

1.   It is often said that William Shakespeare and Miguel Cervantes died on the same day (23 April 1616), but Cervantes, living in Catholic Spain, went to his reward ten days earlier than the Swan of Avon, who was in Protestant England and so seemingly on the same date.

2.   Likewise, when William of Orange came to accept the English and Scottish crowns jointly with his wife Mary Stuart (the 'Glorious Revolution' of 1698), they appear to have arrived in London a week before they left the Netherlands.

So how could a merchant trading to, say, Catholic France or Spain rely on a contract with dates that could be interpreted two ways?

Other countries adopted the Gregorian calendar piecemeal – Sweden, for instance, started in 1700 by removing leap days over forty years, but missed the boat twice and reverted to the Julian calendar. Then, in 1753, they adopted the Gregorian fully. Denmark, Norway and the German Protestant states adopted the solar portion of the calendar in 1700 but took another seventy-six years to adopt the lunar adjustments that determined, for example, Easter.

In Britain, calendrical reform became obviously necessary by 1750, when 'Ruling the Waves' meant listening to the astronomers who were producing navigation tables and the like. The Calendar Act of that year, introduced by Lord Chesterfield, accounted for the (by then) eleven extra days by having Wednesday 2 September followed by Thursday 14 September – the 'Calendar (New Style) Act 1750' c. 23 Regnal. 24 Geo II.

Therefore, the year 1751 in Britain was 282 days long, running from 25 March to 31 December, and 1752 began on 1 January. Parliament also adopted the better (Gregorian) rules for leap years and for reckoning the date of Easter.

Contrary to popular myth there were no 'riots in the streets' by calendrical fundamentalists demanding back the days lost from their lives, although imagine how you would you feel if your birthday had been on 3 September. On the other hand, there was widespread disquiet about the fiscal implications, stirred up by Tories to embarrass the Whig Government in the lead-up to the 1754 elections. The change was portrayed as 'Popish' because of its Gregorian origin, and for some strange reason advantageous to 'foreign Jews', presumably because of their international trade and finance links – although it was mostly home-grown landlords, financiers etc. who thought to pull a fast one by insisting on earlier payments. There is a well-known 1755 Hogarth painting and engraved print in which the Tory campaign slogan 'Give Us Our Eleven Days' appears written on a newspaper on the floor, which later led to apocryphal stories of widespread insurrection. If you were paying an annual rent, think how you would react if you were told to pay for a full year, but eleven days earlier. And why should you pay a whole year's taxes on 354 days of economic activity? A fudge was introduced that moved the start of the financial year from 25 March (see Quarter Days and Term Days, below) to 5 and later 6 April (because of the non-leap year of 1800), which is what we still have today.

Old Style and New Style years

The year 1752 also began reckoning the first day of the year as 1 January rather 25 March (Lady Day, see below). Scotland had made that change in 1600, largely to give the Scots a Yule celebration that the church couldn't disagree with (because being joyful at Christmas, for some reason was seen as both pagan and inappropriate on the day of the birth of our Lord). That entirely accounts for the reputation the Scots have for Hogmanay, whereas in England and Wales, 31 December/1 January didn't matter particularly.

So, for dates up to 1752 in England and up to 1600 in Scotland, 31 December 1565 (for example) was followed by 1 January 1565 and 24 March 1565 by 25 March 1566. Dates between 1 January and 24 March are usually given as 1565/66 to make that clear. However, 1 January 1601 in Scotland would have been called 1 January 1600 in England and Wales, as the New Year wouldn't start south of the border until 25 March.

This is referred to as OS (Old Style)/NS (New Style). A well-known example is the execution of King Charles I, which took place on 30 January 1648 as recorded in English documents of the time, but which we would now consider to be 30 January 1649 NS, as the Scots did at the time. The confusion finally disappeared in 1752, but please do not confuse the New Year issue with the change to the Gregorian calendar. You may occasionally see explicit mention of 'New Style' in parish registers during and after 1752.

The 'American confusion'

Also, be careful with dates on American documents prior to 1752. British dates before them are usually given in the original OS, but dates of events in (then British) America prior to 1752 have usually been converted to NS. George Washington was born on 11 February OS, but his birthday is celebrated on 22 February NS, because as a 21-year-old surveyor he understood the point and changed it himself. Many American genealogists (and genealogical software programmes) ignore this, and the OS/NS designation, so be careful.

Then there's Alaska. The Alaska Purchase from Russia in 1867 meant that Friday 6 October was followed by Friday 18 October, due to the USA being on Gregorian time while Russia was still on the Julian calendar, and because the International Date Line was moved west of Alaska at the same time.

Nova Scotia, flipping from French to British control at various times, was Gregorian from 1605 to 1710, Julian from 2 October 1710 to 2 September 1752, and then Gregorian again from 14 September 1752.

The date of Easter

Easter is a *moveable feast* – the date changes every year. Easter Sunday can fall on any date from 21 March to 25 April. The reason is the origins of Easter in pagan festivals dedicated to the fertility goddess, Eoster, which the Christian church incorporated with the passion and resurrection of Christ. The date is based on the lunar calendar and takes place (by the official Western definition) on the first Sunday after the first full moon or after the vernal equinox (usually 20 or 21 March).

The Western churches use the Gregorian calendar to calculate the date of Easter while Eastern (Orthodox) churches use the Julian calendar. So, for example:

2011	2012	2013	
Shrove Tuesday (Mardi Gras)	8 March	21 February	12 February
Ash Wednesday (beginning of Lent)	9 March	22 February	13 February
Vernal equinox	21 March	20 March	20 March
Palm Sunday (beginning of Holy Week)	17 April	1 April	24 March
Good Friday	22 April	6 April	29 March
(Western) Easter Sunday	24 April	8 April	31 March
(Orthodox) Easter Sunday	24 April	15 April	5 May

Quarter Days and Term Days

Why was New Year on 25 March in England and Wales (and elsewhere, but not Scotland) until this was changed in 1752? It's because of the importance of quarter days. There were four specific days in the year when rents and so on were due, when church ministers' stipends were paid, when leases and other contracts would begin or end, and when workers and servants were hired. Some leasehold payments, business rents and bills are still payable by quarters.

The quarter days (England) fell on four important religious holidays about three months apart. The English cross-quarter days were holidays based on the old Celtic calendar, about halfway between quarter days. Of course, all of these dates started out as important pagan festivals. The church, wisely, decided not to interfere with them, except to give them a new Christian spin (see the table on p. 214).

Lady Day (25 March) was also New Year's Day in Britain and the British Empire until 1752 (except in Scotland, where this has been 1 January since 1600).

The UK financial year and tax year starts on 'Old' Lady Day (25 March OS = 6 April NS/ Gregorian).

English and Welsh terms (the dates on which courts sat) were complicated because they depended on the dates of Easter, and also because the ancient universities used these for academic terms, but they had differing dates.

Oxford had:

- Hilary or Lent term (14 January to the Saturday before Palm Sunday);
- Easter term (ten days after Easter to the Thursday before Whit Sunday);
- Trinity term (Wednesday after Trinity Sunday to whenever the university decided to rise);
- Michaelmas term (10 October to 7 December).

Cambridge had:

- Lent term (13 January to the Friday before Palm Sunday);
- Easter term (Wednesday after Easter week to the week before Whit Sunday);
- Trinity term (Wednesday after Trinity Sunday to the Friday after Commencement);
- Michaelmas term (10 October to 16 December).

Other important dates in early manorial documents, especially for the payment of rents and so on, or as an excuse for a party, were:

- Hockday or Hocktide, the second Monday and Tuesday after Easter, and therefore likely to be about the end of April or early May, originally a Saxon festival held to celebrate either the massacre of the Danes on St Brice's Day (13 November 1002), or the death of Harthacanute (8 June 1042) and the subsequent expulsion of the Danes from England;
- Epiphany, the feast and holiday held on 6 January to commemorate the presentation of the divine nature of Christ to the magi and also the day after Twelfth Night;
- *Natale* (Christmas);
- *Pascha* (Easter);
- St John's Day (24 June and also Midsummer Day).

	England & Wales quarter days, also observed in Ireland	English cross-quarter days	English term days	Corresponding Celtic festival
February		Candlemas (2 Feb)	Hilary term (23 Jan–12 Feb)	Imbolc
March	Lady Day (25 Mar)		Easter term (Wednesday, two weeks after Easter Day – Monday after Ascension Day)	Ostara
May		May Day (1 May)		Beltane
June	Midsummer Day (24 June)		Trinity term (Friday after Trinity Sunday – Wednesday, two weeks later)	Midsummer
August		Lammas Day (1 Aug)		Lughnasadh
September	Michaelmas (29 Sept)			Mabon
November		All Hallows (1 Nov)	Michaelmas (6–28 November) (Ireland – starts 13 Oct)	Samhain
December	Christmas (25 Dec)			Yule (midwinter)

Trinity Sunday falls one week after Pentecost Sunday (Whit Sunday) and in 2012 was 3 June. Ascension Day is the fortieth day of Easter – for example 17 May 2012.

Saints' Days

There are often references to holy days, not least when law terms start and contracts and so on were issued. Saints' days may also be responsible for the Christian name of a child baptised that day, and in many old documents (including manor and court rolls) the day and even the month may not mentioned, but given as 'the day after the feast of St Cecilia' for example; remember Good King Wenceslas looking out 'on the feast of Stephen'? We may have forgotten most of these 'red-letter days' but here they are for reference.

January
1 Circumcisio Domini
13 St Veronica
13 St Hilary
25 Conversion of St Paul

18 St Edward
19 St Joseph
20 St Cuthbert
25 Annunciation, Lady Day

February
1 St Bride (Bridget)
2 Purification of the Virgin, Candlemas Day
24 St Matthias the Apostle

April
23 St George
25 St Mark the Evangelist

March
1 St David
2 St Chad
4 St Lucius
14 St Benet (Benedict)

May
1 St Philip and St James the Less
2 St Athanasius
3 Invention (or discovery) of the Holy Cross
5 St Hilary, Bishop of Aries
26 St Augustine

June

11 St Barnabas
13 St Anthony of Padua
22 St Alban
24 St John the Baptist, Midsummer
29 Sts Peter and Paul
30 St Paul

July

2 Visitation of the Blessed Virgin
15 St Swithin
22 St Mary Magdalen
25 St James the Great
25 St Christopher, Lammastide

August

1 St Peter ad Vincula
5 St Oswald
6 Transfiguration of our Lord
15 The Assumption of the Virgin
21 St Bernard
24 St Bartholomew
28 St Austin (Augustine)
29 Beheading of St John the Baptist

September

1 St Egidius (Giles)
8 Nativity of the Blessed Virgin
14 Exaltation of the Holy Cross
21 St Matthew
29 St Michael and All Angels, Michaelmas

October

4 St Francis of Assisi
9 St Denis (Dionysius) of Paris
17 St Audry (Etheldreda)
18 St Luke the Evangelist
21 St Ursula and 11,000 virgins
25 St Crispin
28 St Simon the Canaanite

November

1 All Saints' Day
2 All Souls' Day
11 St Martin, Martinmas
16 St Edmund
21 Presentation of the Blessed Virgin
22 St Cecilia
25 St Catherine
30 St Andrew

December

6 St Nicholas
8 The Conception of the Blessed Virgin
13 St Lucy
21 St Thomas
25 The Nativity of our Blessed Lord, Christmas
26 St Stephen
27 St John, Evangelist and Apostle
28 The Holy Innocents
29 St Thomas à Becket

Regnal Years

These are the years in which a particular monarch reigned. They matter because many documents are dated by the year of reign, such as:

- Anno Domini 1490, Anno Regni 3 Jac. IV indicating the third year of the reign of James (Latin, *Jacobus*) IV, which is 1490, as he came to the throne in 1488.
- The Married Women's Property Act, 1882 (45 & 46 Vic. Cap. 75) passed in the session of parliament that spanned the forty-fifth and forty-sixth years of Queen Victoria's reign (1880, in this case).

There is a distinction between public acts, given Arabic numerals, 1, 2, 3 and so on (e.g. 50 + 51 Vic c.xx) and local acts, given Roman numerals, i, ii, iii and so on (50 + 51 Victoria c.20).

In 1963 this was simplified to using just the calendar year and not the reign of monarchs or the session of parliament (e.g. 1973 chapter 10 or just c.10), the tenth act passed in the year 1973.

There a number of traps for the unwary in there:

1. The regnal year starts when the monarch accedes to the throne, not the date of coronation. For example, Queen Elizabeth II (b. 1926) became queen on 6 February 1952, when her father, George VI, died, but she was not crowned until 2 June 1953, by which time it was 2 E. II.
2. The regnal year starts on the date of accession, so 1 January 1953 was still 1 E. II.
3. The count starts at 1, not 0; so 45 Vic. is 1837 + 44 = 1881, but will spill over into 1882 until 19 June that year.
4. The Stuart sovereigns, from James VI/I to Anne, were, separately, monarchs of Scotland and of England, and therefore James VI/I had two separate regnal years – counting from 24 July 1567 in Scotland (when Mary abdicated) but 24 March 1602/3 in England (when Elizabeth died). Therefore a date in 1615 after 24 March would be in 48 Jac. VI, but 13 Jac. I. After that, the accession dates were the same in both countries.

The tables below give the birth, accession and death (or deposition) of monarchs of England and Wales from about 1000 AD. There is a handy converter for English and Scottish regnal years to calendar years at www.bsswebsite.me.uk/Daysanddates/regnal_year_converter.htm.

	Born	Succeeded	Died
House of Wessex (Saxons)			
Edward the Confessor	1004	1042	1066
Harold II	1022	1066	1066
House of Normandy			
William I (the Conqueror)	1027	1066	1087
William II (Rufus)	1056	1087	1100
Henry I	1068	1100	1135
Stephen	1105	1135	1154
House of Plantagenet			
Henry II	1133	1154	1189
Richard I (Lionheart)	1157	1189	1199
John (Lackland)	1166	1199	1216
Henry III	1207	1216	1272
Edward I	1239	1272	1307
Edward II	1284	1307	1327
Edward III	1312	1327	1377
Richard II	1366	1377	dep. 1399 d. 1400
House of Lancaster			
Henry IV (Bolingbroke)	1367	1399	1413
Henry V	1387	1413	1422
Henry VI	1421	1422	dep. 1461

Abbreviations: exec., executed; dep., deposed; res., restored; d., died; abd., abdicated.

House of York			
Edward IV	1441	1461	1483
Edward V (one of the 'Princes in the Tower')	1470	1483?	1483
Richard III	1452	1483	1485
House of Tudor			
Henry VII	1457	1485	1509
Henry VIII	1491	1509	1547
Edward VI	1537	1547	1553
Jane (reigned 9 days) (Lady Jane Grey or Dudley)	1536/37	10–19 July 1553	12 February 1554
Mary I	1516	1553	1558
Elizabeth I	1533	1558	1603
House of Stuart			
James I (VI of Scotland)	1566	1603	1625
Charles I	1600	1625	exec. 1649
Commonwealth – declared 19 May 1649			
Oliver Cromwell, Lord Protector	1599	1653	1658
Richard Cromwell, Lord Protector	1626	1658	dep. 1659 d. 1712
Charles II	1630	1649 res. 1660	1685
James II (VII of Scotland)	1633	1685	dep. 1688 d. 1701
William III Mary II	1650 1662	1689	1702 1694
Anne	1665	1702	1714
House of Hanover			
George I	1660	1714	1727
George II	1683	1727	1760
George III	1738	1760	1820
George IV	1762	1820	1830
William IV	1765	1830?	1837
Victoria	1819	1837	1901
House of Saxe-Coburg (House of Windsor from 1917)			
Edward VII	1841	1901	1910
George V	1865	1910	1936
Edward VIII (reigned 11 months)	1894	1936	abd. 1936 d. 1972
George VI	1895	1936	1952
Elizabeth II	1926	1952	

Islamic dates

The Islamic Hijri date (*Anno Hejira*) is based on the lunar calendar starting from the 'Hijrah' – the year Mohammad moved from Mecca (Makkah or Yathrib) to Medina (Madinah) to avoid assassination. The year 1 AH corresponds to either 15 (astronomical) or 16 July (civil) 622 CE; because the moon rises progressively later than the sun as you move west, western Muslim countries will celebrate a holy day one (Gregorian) day earlier than in the east. For instance, *Isra* and *Mi'raj* were Wednesday, 29 June 2011.

Jewish dates

The Hebrew lunisolar calendar is based on the date of creation, worked out by Rabbi Yose Ben Halfta around year 160 CE, which equates to the Gregorian year of 3761 BCE. Each Jewish lunar month starts with the new moon. There is a fixed lunar year, with twelve lunar months of twenty-nine or thirty days, plus an intercalary lunar month added seven times every nineteen years to synchronise the twelve lunar cycles to the slightly longer solar year. This means that the Hebrew year can have from 353 to 385 days, and New Year (*Rosh Hashanah*, falling on 1 and 2 *Tishrei*, the seventh month of the ecclesiastical year) falls on a variable date no earlier than 5 September and no later than 6 October:

- Year 5772 was from sunset 28 September to nightfall 30 September 2011;
- Year 5773 is from sunset 16 September to nightfall 18 September 2012.

The major Jewish holidays (including New Year, *Sukkot*, Passover and *Shavuot*) correspond to important agricultural times of year such as the coming of rains, planting and harvest, but also have religious significance. *Shavuot*, for example, days 6–7 of the month of *Sivan*, falls on 26–28 May 2012 but in 2011 was 7–9 June.

Money and Coinage

Originally coins had an intrinsic value (they actually contained an amount of silver or gold equivalent to the value) but eventually became tokens of baser metal – valueless in themselves but signifying a value guaranteed by the Crown – and then paper notes.

Britain has had a decimal system since 1970. One pound sterling (£1) consists of 100 pennies (100p). There are notes in various denominations (£1, £5, £10, £20, £50 etc.) and coins (1p, 2p, 5p, 10p, 50p, £1, £2) plus rare 'crowns' (with a face value of £5), issued mainly to mark important occasions such as the Queen's Jubilee.

Before this, the monetary system was more complicated, with a confusing variety of coins of various values in circulation at various times. Add to this that, until 1707 (see examples, below), Scotland had an entirely separate monetary system based on the pound Scots and the merk (mark), and continued to use this in documents well into the nineteenth century, and the additional complication that three banks in Scotland and one in Northern Ireland continue to issue their own notes. These are all sterling, and are identical in value, despite the problems some Scottish and Northern Irish tourists have changing them abroad. The Republic of Ireland now uses the euro (€), in common with many other European Union countries, but not all (such as the UK). Sterling banknotes are also issued by British dependencies outside the UK: the Isle of Man; Jersey; Guernsey; Gibraltar; Saint Helena and the Falkland Islands. These are all for local use, but are exchangeable at par with the pound sterling, and they circulate freely alongside English, Scottish and Northern Irish notes.

Americans reading this and familiar with the standardised 'greenback' dollar bills might reflect that until almost the end of the Civil War (1863) notes were issued by over 1,600 state-chartered, private banks of variable liquidity, and until 1935 by a network of licensed national banks, and that not every dollar bill was considered to be worth the same – it depended on the bank.

British monetary system (pre-decimalisation in 1970)

Before 1970, money was calculated in pounds, shillings and pence (L.s.d.) with 1 pound = 20 shillings = 240 pence. The pound symbol in documents is either *l* (don't confuse it with a numeral), a stylised *L* (£) or *lb* or *lib*, all from the Latin *libra*, meaning a pound (originally, of silver).

1 shilling is represented by /- or *s* (for 'solidus', a Roman coin) plural *ss*, and often written as ß, which is really a long s (§) followed by a small s. This will be familiar to anyone who knows German as the *scharfe* or double-s.

1 shilling = 12 pennies and the penny is represented by *d*, short for '*denarius*', also a Roman coin.
1 halfpenny is written as ½*d* but also '*ob*', short for '*obolus*', yet another Roman coin.
1 farthing is written as ¼*d* and represented by '*qua*', short for '*quadrans*' = a quarter penny.
There was also a common coin called a groat, typically worth 4*d* in England, 6*d* or 1*s* in Scotland.

    4 farthings = 1 penny (1*d*)
    12 pence = 1 shilling (1*s* or 1/-)
    2 shillings = 1 florin (2*s* or 2/-)
    2 shillings and 6 pence = a half-crown (2/6*d*, 2*s* 6*d*)
    5 shillings = 1 crown (5*s*)
    20 shillings = 1 pound (a sovereign, £1 or 1L)
    21 shillings = 1 guinea (£1 1*s*)

There were 240 pennies (d) to the pound (£), thus one 'new penny' (p) = 2.4 'old pennies' (d) and 5p = 12d = one shilling.

The convention that £1 1*s* (21*s*, today £1.05p) is called a guinea, although there has been no coin of that value issued since 1813, derives from the high-quality Guinea gold used, which therefore made the coin worth more than the £1 value sovereign. Unlike the half-crown, the crown has not been a coin in general circulation since 1937. Americans who find this quaint or puzzling should remember that they call 25 cents 'two bits' although there is no coin equal to one 'bit' – a reference to the *peso* (meaning 'weight') or 'piece of eight' into which a dollar could be divided.

Scotland had a silver dollar (or ryal) in the time of Mary, Queen of Scots, and after, derived (as is the American version) from the *Thaler* or *Joachimsthaler* of central Europe, and popularised by Dutch traders. Charles II had a different value dollar worth 4 merks, or £2 16*s* Scots. Incidentally, the dollar sign is essentially that of the Spanish *Peso* (an S over a p) and two Scots immigrants – John Baine and Archibald Binney – can be thanked for first casting the dollar sign for use on coins in 1797; the dollar had been adopted as the standard currency by the United States in 1785.

Relative values

Once you have a value in sterling and a year, it is possible to calculate the equivalent value today – possible, but not straightforward. Economists use a variety of measures to calculate equivalences over the ages, and they give wildly differing results. One method is to compare the price of something still for sale, such as a pint of beer, a chicken or a loaf of bread. But what if the costs of producing these have changed? Another is a working man's wage, or a week's rental. But has labour got cheaper or more expensive compared to housing? A third is per-head of a nation's total gross domestic product (GDP), although this is perhaps the least relevant method as Britain has been both a far richer and a far poorer country in international terms than it is today. Yet another type of calculation is the price of gold or silver, but currencies are no longer tied to these precious metals.

There is far more detail on this, plus calculators, at the Economic History Services website (www.measuringworth.com/calculators/ppoweruk/), which also has converters from sterling to US$. If the value £100, the year 1830 and 'derive 2009 values' are entered, we get the following results:

£7,550.00 using the retail price index
£9,450.00 using the GDP deflator
£82,900.00 using the average earnings
£111,000.00 using the per capita GDP
£289,000.00 using the share of GDP.

That's a discrepancy of almost forty-fold across the five measures.

Here is a 'realistic' table worked out from prices and wages.

Year	value	Year	value	Year	value
1600	233	1750	205	1955	25
1620	221	1800	77	1965	19
1640	194	1850	126	1970	16
1660	156	1900	114	1980	3.5
1680	187	1914	107	1990	1.75
1700	158	1919	47	2011	1
1720	168	1939	60		
1740	166	1946	39		

To use the table, look up any year. £1 in that year would have the purchasing power equivalent to the value against that year. For instance, if something cost £2 in 1800, it should cost 2 x 77 = £154 in 2011. To reverse that, £1 in 1750 would be worth £205 now.

Even this apparently simple method yields surprises. For instance, in 1600 a bottle of French wine cost 2 shillings (about £38 now), a chicken cost 1 penny (£1), a tankard of ale a halfpenny (50p) and a pair of boots £4 (£931). Present-day tax on beer makes the current cost nearer £3 and the boots look expensive, but the wine (if it's really good) and chicken (if it's bargain-basement) are about right.

On the other hand, this is not a dependable index to wages. The weekly wage of a carpenter in the early 1600s was about 5 shillings (£100 per week or £5,000 per annum now) and a typical wage for a head footman in 1761 was £7 per year (£1,430 now). Try getting anyone to work for those salaries today!

In 1815 a newspaper cost 7d (mostly down to the taxes on the paper used to print it, and on advertisements), which should equate to about £2.25 today, but a craftsman's daily wage was 6s (£23) and therefore a daily paper cost about one-tenth of a day's pay – the average industrial wage now is about £100 per day, so a paper would cost, in relative terms, £10. Newsprint got a lot cheaper when the various taxes were dropped in the 1850s and the 'penny paper' was born, which is more akin to the prices we pay today, relatively speaking.

So, monetary conversion across the ages is not an exact science, but for a rule-of-thumb calculation, use 200x for 1600–1800 and 100x for 1800–1900.

Weight, Length, Distance, Area and Volume

In England and Wales, weights and measures were standardised by Henry VIII (hence 'imperial' measure). The historical units of measurement, a combination of Anglo-Saxon and Roman, were used in England and Wales up until the 1824 Weights and Measures Act redefined some of the old units, but with slightly different values. Be aware that they are not the same as the US Customary Systems of Unit (a UK pint is not the same as a US pint, for instance).

The commonest units encountered are the following.

Weight

The avoirdupois system was based on the legally defined weight of a grain seed from the middle of an ear of barley.

Grain – 1/7000 of a pound (about 65mg)
Dram/drachm (dr) – 1/16th of an ounce
Ounce (oz) – 16 dr = 437.5 grains (about 28g)
Pound (lb) – 16oz
Stone (st) – 14lb (an Anglo-Saxon unit changed to fit in)
Tod – 2st = 28lb ¼cwt
Quarter – ¼cwt = 28lb
Hundredweight (cwt) – 100lb (short) or, more commonly, 112lb (long)
Ton – 20cwt = 2240lb (just short of a metric tonne, 1,000kg)

Length and distance

Barleycorn – ⅓ of an inch
Hand (used to measure height of horses) – 4in
Inch (Anglo-Saxon *Ynch*) – three barleycorns, as defined in a number of medieval laws in England and Wales, including the Laws of Hywel Dda in the tenth century; bizarrely, this is still the basis for current British and American shoe sizes
Foot – the Roman foot was 11.65in but the Anglo-Saxons introduced the German foot of 13.2in, and in the late 1200s the modern foot was defined as exactly 10/11th of the Anglo-Saxon foot (12in)
Link – 100th of a chain (7.92in)
Yard – 3ft = 36in
Ell – fingertips of one hand to opposite shoulder, used mainly for cloth measure (45in)
Span – width of a stretched hand from thumb to little finger (9in)
Cubit – fingertips to elbow (18in)
Fathom – fingertips to fingertips of outstretched arms (6ft)
Rod, pole, perch or lug – still used in land and architectural measure and confusingly sometimes used as a unit of area or volume unit (5½ yards, 16½ feet)
Chain – 4 rods, named for the surveyor's chain used to measure distances (now 66ft)
Furlong – from 'furrow long', the distance a plough team could go without rest (but defined as 40 rods, 10 chains or 660 modern feet)
Mile – originally the Roman mile was 5,000ft but this was extended in 1592 to make it 8 furlongs (5,280ft)
League – an hour's walk (3 miles)

Area

Rood – area 1 furlong in length by 1 rod in width, or 40 square rods (¼ of an acre)

Acre – Saxon for 'field' and as much as could be ploughed in one day, nominally an area 1 chain (4 rods) wide by 1 furlong in length (4,840 square yards in England and Wales, but 6,150 square yards in Scotland and 7,840 square yards in Ireland)

Bovate, oxgate, oxgang – the amount of land one ox can plough in a year (roughly 4 rods & 1 furlong = 15 acres or ⅛ of a carucate.

Virgate, yard land – the land a pair of oxen could plough in a year (30 acres)

Carucate, plough or carve – the area that could be ploughed by a team of eight oxen in a year (8 bovates, 120 acres)

Perch – 1 square rod (30¼ square yards, 1/160th of an acre)

Hide – somewhere between 4 and 8 bovates, a measure of agricultural yield rather than area, that is, the amount of land nominally able to support a single family and therefore a unit of taxation

Knight's fee – the amount of land required to equip one soldier for a knight's retinue in war (5 hides)

Hundred (wapentake in the north of England) – 100 hides grouped together for local administrative and judicial purposes, enough to sustain 100 households, and headed by a hundred-man or hundred eolder (e.g. 'Bedwellty, a parish in the lower division of the hundred of Wentllooge, in the county of Monmouth')

Volume

Gill – 5fl. oz

Cup – 10fl. oz

Pint -20fl. oz

Quart – 2 pints

Gallon – 4 quarts = 8 pints

Peck – 2 gallons

Bushel – 8 gallons (the only unit introduced by the Normans)

Coomb – 32 gallons

Cask – 64 gallons

Barrel – a UK beer barrel is 36 imperial gallons (43 US gallons) but a US beer barrel is 31 US gallons (26 imperial gallons; 117 L) and a barrel of oil is 34.9723 imperial gallons (42 US gallons, 158.9873 L)

Hogshead – 2 barrels, but a hogshead of wine is 52.5 imperial gallons (63 US gallons, 238.5 L), while a hogshead of beer or ale is 54 gallons

Butt or Pipe – 2 hogsheads

Tun – 2 butts, 4 hogsheads and therefore weighing 2,560lb, slightly heavier than the English ton of 2,240lb

perch – volume measurement used for stone equal to 16.5ft × 1.5ft × 1ft = 24.75 cu. ft

cord – 128 cubic feet of firewood (a stack 4ft × 4ft × 8ft)

Money and coins in Wales

It is known that Hywel Dda had a coin struck in the tenth century and other Welsh princes may have issued coins, the best documented being Llywelyn the Great (Llywelyn ab Iorwerth, Prince of Gwynedd in about 1197, d. 1240). The Normans and English probably had coin mints in various parts of Wales, and English coins circulated there in Saxon times and, of course, after 1066. In 1637 the Tower Mint had a branch at Aberystwyth Castle to use local silver while the London Mint was using Spanish silver. However, the early Britons used sword blades as currency before they began minting coins (it is more or less the same technology). As late as the fourteenth century a common form of payment was in cattle – the English words 'capital' and 'chattels' share a linguistic root with 'cattle', the word 'pecuniary' derives from the Latin word for cattle (*pecus*) and the Welsh noun *da* means both 'cattle' and 'goods'.

Tokens during the Industrial Revolution

In the late 1700s there was a shortage of silver and copper coins in England so tokens (not the same as counterfeit coins, which were illegal and whose production was punishable by death) were often struck and used. An example in Tredegar is given on p. 73, while the Anglesey Copper Company, which had high-quality copper ore at its Parys mine, struck a Druid Penny in 1787, which could be exchanged at full value for coin of the realm at its offices and shops. Many other towns in Britain did this and by 1800 the circulation of these tokens, as well as foreign coins, exceeded that of the official currency.

Various banks also issued their own notes – the famous one is the Black Ox Bank, *Banc yr Eidion Du*, established by David Jones of Llandovery in 1799 (part of the Lloyds Group since 1909), whose notes bore the Welsh Black cattle and had a better reputation than English banks, so much so that Bank of England notes were simply not trusted in much of west Wales well into the nineteenth century (see www.lloydsbankinggroup.com/about_us/company_heritage/ Lloyds_heritage/davidjones.asp). There were a number of drovers' banks in mid-Wales, which were set up to serve the Welsh cattle trade with English markets. This was all stopped (in theory) by the Bank Charter Act of 1844, but it took a long time to be implemented – there were still some fifty banks issuing notes in 1900, and to this day, while only the Bank of England issues coins and banknotes in England and Wales, there are Scottish banks, plus the Bank of Northern Ireland, which issue notes at full sterling value.

In 1968 the Royal Mint moved to Llantrisant, Wales. It produces coins not only for the whole of the UK but for many overseas countries.

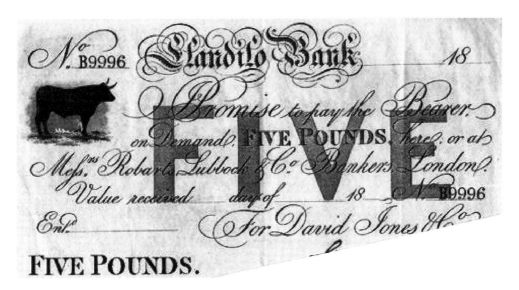

A note from the Llandilo branch of the Black Ox Bank. The original Sampson Lloyd (1699–1779) was a Quaker and iron founder of Welsh origin from Birmingham who, with button maker John Taylor (1711–75) created Birmingham's first bank. © Lloyds Banking Group

Further reading

Books

Glyn Davies, *A History of Money from Ancient Times to the Present Day*, 3rd edn (Cardiff: University of Wales Press, 2002).

R. Ian Jack, *Medieval Wales* (London: Hodder & Stoughton, 1972).

R.E. Zupko, *A Dictionary of Weights and Measures for the British Isles: The Middle Ages to the Twentieth Century* (Philadelphia: American Philosophical Society, 1985).

Online resources

Economic History Net – http://eh.net/hmit/

Current Value of Old Money – www.ex.ac.uk/~RDavies/arian/current/howmuch.html

Consumer Price Inflation Since 1750 – www.ons.gov.uk/ons/rel/cpi/consumer-price-indices/1750---2003/composite-consumer-price-index-with-description-and-assessment-of-source-data.pdf

13

Occupations and Professions

Examining censuses and BMD records, you may see abbreviations or occupations that at first glance make no sense. That is either because the trade has since disappeared, or the usage is local. There is a list of occupations and their typical abbreviations at the end of this chapter.

While censuses and other records give occupations, it is sometimes fruitful to look at lists of employees, tradesmen and so on to check if individuals appear. These may also be present in trade and street directories.

Local Trade Directories

Local trade, commercial and street directories – famous names like Kelly's, Pigot's and Slater's – have been published since the 1600s, but came into their own in the late 1800s (with the addition of lists of householders by street), until eventually superseded by the Post Office directories and

Directory. TREDEGAR, &c.

Butchers

Aubrey Morgan, 92 Queen st
Bowen William [& bacon curer], Rhymney   [Iron Works
Buchan Andrew & Co. Rhymney
Church Henry, 27 Park row
Collard Margaret, 43 Colliers' row
Edwards Thomas, Church st
Griffiths Caroline, Rhymney
Howells John, Rhymney
Hughes Jos. Carmeltown, Beaufort
Huish David, Beaufort
Husband Thomas, Rhymney
Jones Ann, 19 Church st
Jones Thomas, Charles st
Judd John, 95 Queen st
Lewis David, Rhymney
Llewellyn John [and farmer], Pontlotyn
Matthews Collins, Beaufort
Morgan Herbert, Morgan st
Morgan John, 42 Colliers' row

Havard Catherine, Rhymney
Hodges Richard, Market st
Jenkins John, Victoria rd Ebbw Vale
Morgan George, Rhymney
Morgan John, Pontlotyn
Morgan Lewis, Beaufort
Nicholas Rachel, Pontlotyn
Peters Margaret, Briery Hill
Price John, 35 Colliers' row
Price William, Church st
Rees John, Victoria rd. Ebbw Vale

Clothiers & Outfitters

Cox Thos. Briery Hill, Ebbw Vale
Evans William, Rhymney
Freedman & Barnett, Briery Hill, Ebbw Vale
Griffiths John, Rhymney
Harris Ephraim, 16 Church st
Horlick Egbert, Morgan st
Levy David, Briery Hill, Ebbw Vale
Lewis Evan, Morgan st
Morgan David, Rhymney

Shown here is detail of a page from Slater's Directory of Gloucestershire, Herefordshire, Monmouthshire, Shropshire & Wales, *1868 – the lady butcher called Caroline Griffiths and John Griffiths, clothier of Rhymney, might bear further investigation in the hunt for this family. It would also be worth searching later directories for the street and trade addresses of Griffiths individuals found in the censuses and elsewhere.*

Yellow Pages. Every local library or archive has a collection of these, but the best place to start is the University of Leicester's digitised versions of eighteenth- to early twentieth-century trade directories (www.historicaldirectories.org). The coverage of Wales is disappointing before about 1850, but that reflects the reality of the situation then. They do contain wonderful local detail – times of carriages, price of parcels, tide tables, local institutions and so on.

Professional directories
Specialist directories for different professions have been published since the nineteenth century for almost every occupation. Start at the professional body concerned, or in larger libraries.

Telephone directories
More than 1,700 British Telecom phone books published between 1880 and 1984 are searchable at ancestry.co.uk and ancestry.com. As these are annual, they are a good way to track someone down who moved (or disappeared) between decennial censuses, and also to take a family forward from the 1911 census.

Individual professions
Clergy are considered in Chapter 7. Schoolteachers, doctors and other medical professionals, lawyers and the rest of the regulated professions are usually found in trade and street directories (above), and in lists held and issued by the regulating bodies (the General Medical Council or the Law Society, for example).

Schoolteachers and education records
The Teacher's Registration Council registers those who taught in England and Wales between 1870 and 1948 (almost 100,000 names), which can be searched online at Find My Past (www.findmypast.co.uk/search/teachers-registrations/). This shows the teacher's name (also, often the maiden name of married women teachers), date of registration, address, qualifications and where trained, schools taught at and when. The database is only searchable by name, with a date filter.

School records
Many primary (elementary schools) and grammar (secondary) schools in the state system have registers and log books that go back to the 1850s, when the Victorians established school boards and built many new schools. Mostly these are in local record offices (see pp. 50–53), deposited by the old education authorities, although some are still with the schools themselves.

The Society of Genealogists (www.sog.org.uk) in London has an extensive collection of registers of pupils at public schools. Public schools (which are private) tend to hold their own records.

University records
Before the 1820s, the only universities in England and Wales were Oxford and Cambridge (there were five in Scotland at the time!). The University of London started about then, and after that, 'red-brick' universities were founded in larger cities, initially offering what were called 'External London Degrees'. Check with the university in question if you know it, or consult one of the many alumni and matriculation lists available in larger libraries or at the Internet Archive (www.archive.org).

Medical practitioners
The medical register, the official list of registered practitioners in Britain maintained by the General Medical Council, has been published annually since 1859. The British Medical

Association Library in London has most of these as well as membership lists of royal colleges and other professional associations, and will take biographical and genealogical enquiries. Contact the library staff if this would be useful (www.bma.org.uk). Another avenue is to contact the library of the Wellcome Institute for the History and Understanding of Medicine, also in London (www.wellcome.ac.uk/library). Doctors will also be listed (usually under 'Physicians and Surgeons' or 'Apothecaries') in local and trade directories.

The Guildhall Library has a large archive of records relating to apothecaries, surgeons, physicians and other medical practitioners (www.cityoflondon.gov.uk/Corporation/LGNL_Services/ Leisure_and_culture/Libraries/City_of_London_libraries/guildhall_lib.htm) and there is an online guide for records held at the library and elsewhere (www.history.ac.uk/gh/apoths.htm).

Lawyers

The National Archives, Kew, hold many documents relating to attorneys and solicitors as far back as 1656, and has an online guide for these records (www.nationalarchives.gov.uk/records/ research-guides/attorneys-solicitors.htm).

The Law Society holds the Registrar of Attorneys and Solicitors, established in 1843, with lists of admissions from 1845 plus lists of admissions for most courts from about 1790 and some registers of articles of clerkship from about 1860. Contact the Law Society of England and Wales (www.lawsociety.org.uk/) and the Solicitors Regulation Authority (www.sra.org.uk/ solicitors/solicitors.page) for solicitors, and the General Council of the Bar (www.barcouncil. org.uk/) for barristers – lawyers who appear in court in England and Wales (in Scotland they are called 'advocates').

Businesses

Many businesses have had their records deposited in local or other archives and some will have lists of employees, directors and shareholders, including wage books. Good places to start are Access to Archives, A2A (www.nationalarchives.gov.uk/a2a/) and Archives Wales (www. archiveswales.org.uk).

Coal and mineral mining

As mining was one of the major professions in the nineteenth and early twentieth centuries, there is a great deal of information in the records of mining companies. This will mainly be no more than a name, grade of work and pay, but in the absence of a census record, it may tie a person or a family (since women and children were employed too) to a particular locality. All mineworkers lived more or less on top of the pit, often in villages constructed specially to house them. This can be a help in tracing someone who disappeared from a locality, as they may have moved to find mine work elsewhere.

Coal export from South Wales peaked just before 1914 – in 1908 alone the Taff Vale Railway carried almost 19 million tons of coal and the port of Barry (near Cardiff, and later famous for its Butlin's holiday camp) exported a record 11 million tons in 1913.

Until postwar nationalisation, the mines were in private hands and the records may be in private archives (or perhaps donated to TNA or a county archive), or in a large archive such as a university. Those mines that became part of the National Coal Board (NCB) when nationalisation took place in 1947 may have their records collected, along with other NCB material, some of which dates back to the 1700s.

Some family history societies have collected names of local miners in their publications.

Specialist mining museums are worth contacting. The Coal Mining History Resource Centre (www.cmhrc.pwp.blueyonder.co.uk and www.cmhrc.co.uk/site/home/index.html) has a database of mining deaths and injuries in Great Britain.

Swansea's mining industry was based on mining and smelting copper, while North Wales specialised in slate (still to be seen around Blaenau Ffestiniog and on roofs and fences there, as are mounds of slate waste). All of this depended on the opening up of the railways.

Railways

Early railways – worldwide as well as in Britain – ran on rails of Welsh iron and had locomotives burning Welsh coal. Many of the world's steamships used Welsh coal, until this gave way to oil, just as sail had given way to coal-powered steam. The heavyweight industrial role of the valleys is now being consigned to history. Lighter, more environmentally friendly industries are appearing, and their arrival is helping eradicate the scars of the past.

Swansea's principal industry was copper, and, in its heyday, the entry from the east into the smoke-filled atmosphere of the town was between piles of copper waste.

In the north, it was slate that led to the opening of the area's railways, and in Blaenau Ffestiniog houses, fences and roofs are made of the material. High mounds of slate waste form a background to the town.

The many railway companies gradually merged, so the smaller ones were swallowed up or just disappeared. Tracking down their records can be a nightmare, but as ever TNA at Kew is a good place to start. These records may give a worker's date of birth, job and location (rather than an address as such, but it can help). Working out which railway companies existed at the time is a speciality all of itself, but Philip Conolly's *British Railways: Pre-grouping Atlas and Gazetteer* (1997) is great for lists and descriptions of the railway companies up to 1923 (very cheap used versions are available at Amazon and elsewhere).

The Great Eastern Railway Society has a specific page of genealogical hints, tips and sources for tracing railway staff at this and other rail companies (www.gersociety.org.uk/index. php?option=com_content&view=article&id=17&Itemid=23) – click 'Information', then 'Genealogy'. The Railway Ancestors Family History Society (www.railwayancestors.org.uk) and the Welsh Railways Research Circle (www.wrrc.org.uk) can also help.

Apprenticeship records

From 1583, the Statute of Apprentices made it illegal to work at a trade without first serving an apprenticeship, but there was no register of apprentices as such in England and Wales until the Statute of Anne (8 Anne c.5, 1710) made stamp duty (tax) payable on indentures – essentially the terms of their contract – except for those taken on by masters at the expense of the parish or a public charity (which were, in fact, quite a few). The Commissioners of Stamps kept registers of those who were not exempt, from 1710 to 1811, now known as the apprenticeship books, and held at TNA, Kew. They have the names, addresses and trades of the masters, the names of their apprentices and the dates of indenture (see www.nationalarchives.gov.uk/ records/research-guides/apprenticeship-records.htm).

There are summary abstracts of some 350,000 tax records relating to appenticeships, searchable by name only, between 1710 and 1774 at Find My Past (www.findmypast.co.uk/search/ apprentices-of-great-britain/) and they are starting to appear elsewhere, often on FHS websites or as local publications.

Before 1710, apprenticeships will be in local records of businesses, parishes and charities, and in private papers.

Police

The Police Index is (or was) an online database of almost 75,000 policemen, using details culled from local newspapers, police magazines and so on, for the period 1860 to 1920. It is part of a much larger – and extremely entertaining – website called the Black Sheep Index, which was at www.blacksheepindex.co.uk but has disappeared, to the disappointment of its many fans and followers. However, an archived copy is viewable via WayBackMachine at http://web. archive.org/web/20100722053825/http://www.blacksheepindex.co.uk.

Individual police forces often have an archive/museum, which will help trace an ancestor in the force. A good starting place is Stephen Ward's *Tracing Your Police Ancestors* (Pen & Sword, 2009).

Clubs, societies and subscriptions

If an occupation, profession or interest is known, it can be worth checking the records of relevant organisations. The society itself may have kept early records, often no more than a roll of members, but sometimes with an address or at least a town or village, and a date, and sometimes a father's name. If the minutes of clubs are available, they may have useful insights – if someone died, applied for relief or took office within the society, it may be noted.

Also, people subscribed to books which, essentially, they paid for up front, so that the author or publisher could afford to produce the volume. Local secondhand bookshops are a good source for these, but many libraries may also have them tucked away.

List of occupations and abbreviations

Adv.	Advocate
Advocate	Lawyer appearing in court, equivalent to English barrister
Ag Lab	Agricultural labourer
Alewife	Female owner or manager of an alchouse
Annealer	Finisher of metal or glass, by using furnace and chemicals
Annuitant	Person with an annual income or pension
Apoth.	Apothecary
Apprentice	Trainee learning a craft or trade, usually bound to a master
Argentier	Controller of finances, comptroller, treasurer
Army H P	Soldier on half pay
Assizor	Juror at a trial (assize)
B.	Burgess
Bailie	Magistrate in a Scottish burgh court
Banksman	Miner at the pithead unloading coal from cages
Baron (or barony) officer	Early policeman, who enforced the law within the barony
Baxter, bagster	Baker
Beadle	Parish or church official who assisted the minister with administrative work and acted as usher
Beadman, bedeman, bedesman, bedeswoman etc.	Licensed beggar
Beamer	Weaving mill worker who loaded yarn onto the beam of a loom
Beetler	Fabric embosser in a cloth mill
Black litster	Black dyer

Blacker, Berlin blacker	Varnisher of ironware products
Blaxter	Bleacher (of cloth)
Bleacher	Bleacher of textiles or paper
Blockcutter	Carver of wooden blocks used for printing
Blockmaker	Broker, trader
Blockprinter	Printer (on paper or cloth) using wooden blocks
Boatman	Boat operator at loch or river crossings
Bobbin turner	Maker of spools (bobbins) for textile mills
Bookmaker	Taker of bets for gambling on horse and dog races etc.
Boot clicker	Bootlace hole maker
Boot closer	Stitcher of boots and shoes
Boot laster	Shoemaker, using a metal 'last'
Boot sprigger	Shoemaker, using 'sprigs' (headless nails) to nail soles to uppers
Bottler	Bottle filler, usually in a distillery
Bower	Bowmaker
Bowman	Subtenant who looked after cows for a season
Boxmaster	Treasurer or deacon of a trade guild
Brasener	Brass worker
Brasiator	Brewer
Brazier	Brass metalworker
Brewster	Brewer (of beer)
Brodinster, broudster	Embroiderer
Brouster	Brewer
Brusher	Coal mine worker who kept mine roofs and sides in repair
Burgess	Enrolled as merchant or craftsman in a burgh
Byreman	Farm worker in the byre (cowshed)
Cabinetmaker	Wooden furniture maker
Cadger	Travelling pedlar
Cadie, caddie	Runner of errands or parcel carrier; later, golf club carrier
Caitchpeller	Keeper of a caitchpell or tennis court
Cal Prin	Calico printer (on cotton cloth from India)
Callenderer	Smoother of cloth or paper using rollers
Candler	Candle maker or retailer
Cap seller, cop seller	Seller of wooden bowls
Carbonarius	Charcoal maker
Carder	Brushed wool ready for spinning using wire 'cards'
Carter	Worked with horse and cart, carrying goods
Cartwright	Maker and repairer of horse carts
Catechist	Instructor in religion

Caulker	Repaired ships' hulls by sealing with 'caulk' (tar)
Causewaymaker	Road (causeway) builder using stone setts
Cellarman	Keeper of beer, wine and spirits
Chairman	Sedan chair carrier
Chair-master	Hiror out of sedan chairs
Chaisemaker	Carriage maker
Chandler	Dealer in supplies, usually for ships
Chapman	Stallholder or travelling salesman
Chapper, chapper-up	Knocked ('chapped') on doors to wake early shift workers
Charwoman	Female domestic cleaner
Check Weighman	Checked a miner's production so he could be paid
Chir apoth.	Chirurgeon-apothecary
Chowder	Fishmonger
Clagger	Removed clags (dirt and clumps) clots from wool
Clark	Clerk
Clicker	Lace hole maker (boots and shoes)
Clogged	Maker of wooden clogs
Cloth dresser	Cloth cutter in a textile mill
Cloth lapper	Cleaned cotton fibres before carding
Coachman	Coach and horse driver
Coal trimmer	Balanced coal barges or ships
Coalmaster	Owner and/or operator of a coal mine
Cobbler	Shoemaker or repairer
Cocquetour	Cook
Collier	Coal miner working at the coalface
Colourman	Mixer of dyes for textiles
Colporteur	Travelling bookseller
Combmaker	Maker of combs for textiles or hair
Compositor	Setter of type for printing
Conservator	Guardian or custodian
Cooper	Maker of wooden barrels and casks for beer etc.
Cordiner	Shoemaker
Cordiner, cordwainer	Leather boot and shoemaker
Cork Cutter	Cut and prepared imported cork bark
Costermonger	Street seller of fruit and vegetables
Cottar	Tenant with a cottage and minimal land
Cotton piecer	Leant over spinning-machines to repair broken threads (often small children)
Cotton warper	Cotton mill loom operator in weaving
Cotton winder	Wound threads onto a weaving looms

Cow-feeder	Tenant of small farm with dairy cattle
Cowper	Maker of cups
Creamer	Occupant of a cream or kraim (booth)
Creelman	Carried produce to market in a creel (basket)
Crofter	Tenant of farm and cottage (croft), usually in the Highlands
Curator	Person appointed by law as guardian, e.g. for a minor
Currier	Person curing or tanning leather hides
Customer	Receiver of customs or excise
Custumer	Collector of customs duties
Cutter	Cut cloth for a tailor
Dagmaker	Pistol maker
Dairymaid	Girl who milked cows and made butter in a dairy
Dapifer	Steward in a royal or noble household
Dempster, doomster	One who pronounces judgement, a sentencing judge
Dexter	Dyer of textiles
Diker	Builder of dry stone walls (dykes)
Docker	Docks worker, loading and unloading ships' cargo
Dom Serv	Domestic servant
Dominie	Schoolmaster
Draper	Retailer of cloth, fabrics, sewing threads etc.
Drawer	Mine worker who pushed or dragged coal carts
Drayman	Cart driver of a dray (long flatbed cart)
Dresser	1 Surgeon's assistant in hospital
	2 Stoneworker in a quarry, cutting rocks to shape
	3 Foundry worker cleaning metal after casting
Drover	Cattle dealer or mover of cattle to market
Drysalter	Dealer in salted and dried meats, pickles, sauces
Dustman	Street and domestic rubbish collector
Dyker	Builder of dry stone walls (dykes)
Engine Keeper	Operator of an industrial steam-driven engine
Exciseman	Collector of taxes, especially duties
F S	Female servant
Factor	Agent for land or property owner, rent collector
Farm servant	Farm worker under contract
Farrier	Blacksmith who shoes horses
Fencible	Militiaman, soldier recruited for war
Ferry-louper	Orkney name for arriving mainlander
Fethelar	A fiddler, musician

Fireman	1 Furnace stoker, e.g. on a train or ship
	2 Firefighter
Fishcurer	Drier and salter of fish for transport in barrels
Fishwife	Woman selling fresh fish door to door
Fitter	Assembled parts for machinery
Flax scutcher	Beat flax fibres before dressing
Flaxman	Flax dealer
Flesher	Butcher
Fletcher	Arrow maker
Flockmaster	Shepherd in charge of a flock of sheep
Forespeaker	Advocate, pleader in court
Founder	Maker of metal items in an iron or brass foundry
Freeman	Not feued to a feudal lord, and able to own property and trade in a burgh
French Polisher	Wood finisher, using sandpaper and oils
Fruictman	Fruit seller
Fuller	Cloth worker cleaning and thickening cloth by wetting and walking on it
Furnaceman	Looked after furnace in a metalworks
G.	Guild brother
Gaberlunzie	Travelling beggar
Gamekeeper	Kepper and breeder of game on an estate
Ganger	Leader of a gang of workmen
Gangrel	Vagrant, tramp
Gaoler	Jailer
Gasfitter	Fitted pipes for domestic gas supply
Gauger	Excise officer
Gen Lab	General labourer
Ghillie	Keper of wild game, especially deer on Highland estates
Gilder	Used gold leaf to adorn furniture, frames etc.
Girnalman	In charge of granary or grain store
Glover	Glove maker
Gowcher	Grandfather
Granger	Keeper of grain store (granary)
Grieve	Factor who collected farming rents
Groom	Looked after horses in a stable
Ground officer	Employee on a large estate who supervised tenants
Gudger	Grandfather (= gudsire)
H L W	Hand loom weaver, weaver of cloth at home
Haberdasher	Retailer of small clothing wares and sewing materials

Hackler	Lint dresser who separated coarse flax with a toothed hackle
Hammerman	Metalworker, smith
Hatter	Milliner, hat maker
Hawker	Pedlar, door-to-door seller of small items
Heatherer	Thatcher, roofer using heather divots or stems
Hecklemaker	Maker of flax combs for the hackler/heckler
Heckler	see Hackler
Heddler	Weaving loom operator in a textile mill
Hedger	Laid and repaired hedges around fields
Herd	Shepherd
Hetheleder	Person who cut and sold heather for fuel
Hewer	Miner cutting coal at the coalface
Hind	Farm servant
Holder-on	Rivetter's assistant in shipbuilding etc.
Hooper	Made hoops for barrels
Hortulanus	Gardener
Hosier	Seller of wool or silk stockings (hose)
Hostler	Looked after horses at an inn
Howdywife	Midwife
Husbandman	Farmer, farm animal keeper
Iron Dresser	Foundry worker who cleaned sand etc. from cast metal after moulding
Iron Miner	Miner of ironstone rock
Iron Moulder	Foundry worker who poured molten iron into moulds
Iron Planer	Planed flat surfaces onto cast iron
Iron Shingler	Operated a steam hammer on wrought iron
Iron Weigher	Weighed iron products in foundry for sale by the ton
J P	Justice of the Peace, magistrate
Jackman	Attendant or man-at-arms to a nobleman or landowner
Japanner	Applied black gloss lacquer to furniture
Jobbing man	Carried out a variety of small jobs e.g. minor carpentry
Joiner	Wood worker, carpenter
Journeyman	Qualified tradesman after serving apprenticeship
Kirk-master	Deacon in a church
Kish maker	willow basket weaver
Lamplighter	Lit the gas street lamps in towns
Lathsplitter	Made thin strips of wood (laths) for nailing to walls and ceilings as a base for plastering
Laundress	Washerwoman
Lawman	Officer with magisterial powers

Lawrightman	Controlled local weights and measures, and land tax
Leerie	Lamplighter (gas lamps)
Lengthsman	Rail worker who maintained a length of track
Letter Carrier	Delivered letters by hand (later, postman)
Liferenter	Had a tenancy for life
Limmer	Thief, scoundrel
Limner, limmer	Artist who decorates (limns) manuscripts
Lineator	Surveyor, measurer
Lithographer	Made printing plates from typeset paper or film
Litster	Cloth dyer
Litster, littister	Dyer
Lorimer	Maker of metal horse harnesses
Lotter	1 Batched up odd lots of wool for sale
	2 Croft or small farm divided into lots, usually worked by the crofter's sons
Loun	Young boy (north-east Scotland)
Lozenge Cutter	Cut and prepared sweets or preserves
M S	1. Male servant
	2. Merchant Service (seaman)
Maltster	Preparer of malt for brewing
Manf	Manufacturer
Mangler	Washerwoman who wrung out clothes through a mangle
Mantua Maker	Ladies dressmaker or bonnet maker
Marikin maker	Maker of dressed goat's skin or Spanish leather
Mariner	Seaman
Mason	Stone cutter and layer
Master	1. Head schoolteacher
	2. Qualified, self-employed craftsman or tradesman
Master Mariner	Ship's captain
Mendicant	Beggar living on alms e.g. mendicant monks
Miller	In charge of a meal or grain mill
Milliner	Maker of women's hats and headgear
Millwright	Mechanic in a mill
Min	Minister (or miner)
Miner	Worker at a mineral mine, usually coal, ironstone or shale
Minr.	Minister of the gospel
Moneyer	Mintmaster, maker of coins
Monger	Seller of goods, e.g. fishmonger, ironmonger
Moulder	Poured molten metal into moulds
Mouterer	Fee received by miller for grinding corn etc.

Mt.	Merchant
Nailer	Blacksmith who made nails
Navvie	'Navigator', canal and road digger
Night Soil Carrier	Removed toilet waste
Notary	Lawyer, solicitor able to notarise documents
Oakum Worker	Took old ropes apart for the hemp fibre (oakum) to be used for caulking (qv)
Orraman	Odd-job man
Orris weaver	Maker of gold or silver lace
Ostler	Hostler, looked after horses at an inn
Ourman	Overseer
Outworker	Employed at outdoor work
Overman	Colliery supervisor
P.	'Prentice (apprentice)
P.L.W.	Power-loom weaver in a textile mill
Pattern maker	Made metal patterns and moulds for iron casting
Pattesier	Pastry cook
Patton (or panton) heel maker	Maker of heels for slippers
Pauper	Without money or means of livelihood
Pavior	Layer of pavement slabs and flagstones
Pedlar	Door-to-door seller of small goods
Pendicler	Subtenant with some grass and arable land
Pensioner	Originally with an army pension after service
Periwig-maker	Maker of gentlemen's wigs
Peuterer	Worker in pewter
Philosophical Instrument Maker	Maker of scientific and astronomical instruments
Piecer	Mill worker who joined threads broken by spinning
Pikar	Petty thief
Pirn winder	Mill worker who threaded yarn on bobbins (pirns)
Pit brusher	Repaired coal mine roofs and sides
Pit roadman	Preparing and repaired coal mine passageways
Pitheadman	Coal mine (pit) worker above ground
Platelayer	Railway worker who laid and repaired rails
Plewman	Ploughman,
Plumber	Worked with lead on roofs, water pipes etc.
Pointsman	Railway worker who operated points
Polentarius	Malt maker
Pony Driver	Led ponies underground pulling coal hutches
Porter	Baggage carrier; gate keeper
Post Boy	Guard travelling on a mail coach

Postman	Delivers mail (letters and parcels)
Print compositor	Set up type for printing
Print cutter	Maker of printing blocks
Printfield worker	Mill worker who printed cloth with dyes and inks
Procurator	Lawyer or advocate
Procurator-Fiscal	Main public prosecutor in a burgh or district
Provost	Elected head of town or burgh council
Publican	Keeper of a public house (pub) selling ales, wines and spirits
Puddler	Iron worker operating a puddling or ball furnace to turn cast iron into wrought iron
Quarrier	Worker in stone quarry
Quine	A young woman (queen) – north-east Scotland
R C C	Roman Catholic clergyman
R.N.	Royal Navy
Ranselman	Empowered by a court to search houses for stolen property
Reader	Teacher of law, medicine, classics etc.
Red Leader	Painted red lead oxide paint onto metal surfaces
Reedmaker	Maker of reeds for weavers
Reeler	Mill worker who put yarns onto reels for weaving
Regent	Schoolmaster or professor
Reidare	Reader, lesser clergyman in early church
Relict	Widow
Resetter	Receiver, concealer or 'fence' of stolen goods
Riddler	Maker or user of coarse sieves (riddles) for grain, soil etc.
Riever	Robber, originally of cattle (esp. in the Borders)
Rivetter	Joining metal plates with hammered rivets
Roll turner	Winds knitted cloth onto machine rolls
Rope Spinner	Maker of rope by braiding yarns
Running stationer	Caddie (qv) stationed to run errands
Saddler	Maker and repairer of horse saddles and leathers
Salinator	Preserver who used salt, e.g. for fish
Sandpaperer	see French Polisher
Sawbones	Surgeon
Sawyer	Worker in sawmill or timber pit
Scallag	Poor farm servant of a tacksman
Scavenger ('Scaffie')	1 Dustman, street sweeper or refuse collector
	2 Worker in a jute mill who picked up loose material from the floor
Scholar	Child at school
Schoolmaster	Head schoolteacher
Sclater	Slater, roof tiler

Scourer	Washed raw wool with soap or in urine before processing
Scrivener	Scribe employed to draft contracts, accounts etc.
Scullery Maid	Kitchen servant (female)
Seafarer	Seaman, sailor, mariner
Seamstress	Woman who made, sewed and mended clothes
Seceder	Member of Secession Church (after 1733)
Sen. Coll. Just.	Senator of the College of Justice
Seriand	Constable or bailiff
Servitor	Clerk or secretary
Settmaker	Cutter of stones for cobbled streets
Sexton	Layman guarding a church and vestments
Sheriff	Chief officer of the Crown in a county
Shingler	Roof tiler using wooden shingles (cf. Slater; see also Iron Shingler)
Ship Master	Owner or captain of a ship
Ship stager	Put together the wooden scaffolding and platforms round a ship being built
Shipwright	Maker and repairer of ships
Sho.	Shopman, i.e. employed in retail
Skinner	Flayer of animal skins for leather, furs etc.
Sklaiter	Slater
Slater	Roof tiler using slates
Sledder	Driver of a sled, used over soft ground in preference to a wheeled cart
Smith	Metalworker, usually a blacksmith
Solicitor	Lawyer, usually not in court (cf. Advocate)
Souter	Shoemaker
Spargener	Plasterer
Spectioner	Third mate on a whaling ship, responsible for correct stowage in the hold
Spinster	Woman who spun textiles (also used for an unmarried woman)
Spirit Merchant	Dealer in spirits, but also vinegar
Sprigger	Embroiderer of lace and muslin (see also Boot sprigger)
Squarewright	Carpenter, but for fine furniture
Stampmaster	Official inspector with powers to fine for faulty or fraudulent maunufacture
Station Master	Railway employee in charge of a station
Steward	Chief servant of royal or noble household
Stoker	Stoked fuel into a furnace or boiler, e.g. on a ship
Stone Hewer	1 Sculptor or stonemason
	2 Miner who drilled holes in the coalface for dynamiting
Sugar Baker	Refiner in a sugar factory

Sumlier	Butler (sommelier)
Surfaceman	Laid and repaired surfaces of roads, railways or mine passages
Surg. apoth.	Surgeon-apothecary
Surveyor of taxes	Calculated and levied taxes on property
Sword slipper	Sword sharpener and sheath maker
Tacksman	Farm tenant who sublet rents (tacks)
Tacksman (taxman)	Tenant, holding the lease or 'tack'
Tailzeor	Tailor
Tambourer	Embroiderer, who used a hoop to hold the cloth
Tanner	Curer of leather hides
Tapsman	Head servant in charge
Tearer	Assistant to a cloth printer in a print mill
Tenementer	Tenant of a dwelling in town building (tenement)
Tenter	Mechanic for power looms
Thatcher	Roofer using natural cut reeds or heather thatch
Tick maker	Upholsterer
Tick manufacturer	A weaver of various fabrics (ticking)
Tidewaiter	Customshouse officer who received duty from merchant ships coming into harbour
Tinker	Travelling tinsmith, seller of pots and pans
Todman	Employed to kill foxes (tods) on an estate
Towsman	In charge of the halyards on a fishing boat
Trencherman	Cook
Tronman	Chimney sweep
Turkey Red Dyer	Turkey red (from madder root) was used to dye cotton
Turner	Lathe operator, wood or metal
Type-founder	Printer who set out individual letters on printing blocks
Vanman	Driver of a light commercial vehicle
Vermin Trapper	Employed to trap and kill rats and other pests
Vestiarus	Keeper of the wardrobe
Victualler	Supplier of food and provisions
Vintner	Wine merchant
Vulcanite Comb Maker	Made hard (vulcanite rubber) combs for the textile industry
W.S.	Writer (to the Signet) – Scottish equivalent of solicitor
Wainwright	Wagon maker
Walker	Cloth fuller
Weaver	Maker of cloth from yarns of wool, cotton, silk etc.
Webster	Weaver
Weigher	Weighed goods before sale (see Iron Weigher)
Weyverr	Weaver

Wheelwright	Wheel maker or repairer
White-iron smith, whitesmith	Worker in tin and light metals (cf. Smith)
Wincey Weaver	Weaver using string cotton thread
Winder	Textile worker who wound the thread on looms
Wobster	Weaver (see Webster)
Workman	Porter, chiefly at weighhouse
Wrecker	Plunderer of a shipwreck – some lured ships to destruction for the purpose
Wright	Maker, joiner or carpenter
Y.	Yeoman of the Guard
Yarn bleacher	Bleached textile fibres e.g. flax
Yarn dresser	Prepared flax fibres (see Hackler)
Yarn twister	Twisted silk into threads or yarn
Yauger	Pedlar of local fish and produce (Shetlands)
Ypor.	Apothecary

14

Military Records

Service Personnel

Almost all official records for the armed services before about 1920 are held at the National Archives (TNA) in Kew, London. There is really no option but to visit, request a search, or try to find digitised records via their website (www.nationalarchives.gov.uk) or a licensed partner, such as Ancestry, FindMyPast and others. On the positive side, they do have many resources online.

Medal Cards (First World War)

These are essentially an abbreviated record of service, searchable by name and downloadable as PDFs. These are six to a sheet, by surname, so it is possible to discover an unknown relative or ancestor by one of those happy accidents that pepper genealogical research.

Medal cards are also available on Ancestry's website, thanks to a deal with the Western Front Association. These have the advantage over TNA website records of having both sides of the card imaged – sometimes there is a correspondence address or other information on the back.

The medal cards records are remarkably complete – approximately 90 per cent of those who fought in the British Army in the First World War – and have the added benefit of including all ranks, whereas most services' sources list officers and warrant officers only. However, they are not of great quality and it takes some practice to interpret them. It is worth concentrating on one, as what seems like sparse information actually contains a wealth of detail. All six on the downloaded page (which cost £2) are shown on p. 242 and one is expanded below. It is possible to search by any combination of last name, first name or initial, regiment number, corps or rank. This search was for Godfrey Griffiths (for no particular reason) with no other information added, and indeed such an individual did appear, in the final two records on the right of the page of six that was downloaded, first as 'GRIFFITHS G. M.' but with 'Godfrey Morgan' added below, then (an added bonus) the record of a medal application from the same individual, this time listed as 'Griffiths Godfrey Morgan'.

Looking at the first entry:

Corps: Monmouthshire Regiment
Rank: 2/Lieut, Lieut – he was initially a second lieutenant, then was promoted to lieutenant. (The meaning of the star-shaped symbol is covered below.)
Regimental No.: (none given here).
Medals: He has been awarded the Victory Star, British Star and 15 Star (see p. 243) with roll and page given – the Army Medal Office references of the original medal rolls for each medal. The star-symbol like a dotted X is called a quadrant and is actually an asterisk, indicating that the medal marked was awarded at the rank or while in the regiment also marked – in this instance the Victory Star and British Star were awarded for service after the point when he was a lieutenant, which tells us this was after 1915.

The **Theatre of War first served in** is France (often it is just a number, such as 1, which would indicate Western Europe), and the date he went there, often left blank, usually indicating that the soldier was sent to France in 1916 or after, but here given as 7.15 (July 1915).

Remarks: here, they are simply annotations to the medals awarded – dates and authorisations. Other remarks might have included (but not in this case) a commission date, if commissioned from the ranks; date of death; whether taken prisoner of war; discharge date and other details.

His second card is unusual, and interesting for its extra detail. First, it tells us he was in the 1st Battalion of the Monmouthshire Regiment. Then it gives an address (Pencaemaur, Merthyr Tydfyl), which should enable the family historian to look backwards to birth and 1911 census records, and forward to marriage (if not already married), death and other details of this Godfrey's life. Finally, his application for a badge seems to have been refused, but the actual file (9/MonR/865) would have to be consulted at TNA, Kew.

Crown Copyright (courtesy of The National Archives)

Crown Copyright (courtesy of The National Archives)

For details of the medals, visit www.nationalarchives.gov.uk/documentsonline/medals.asp but here is the abbreviated version. These three are service or campaign medals, as distinct from gallantry medals. They were so ubiquitous – almost everybody got them – that they were known as 'Pip, Squeak and Wilfred'.

1914/15 Star (*left*)
Authorised in 1918, the 1914/15 Star was awarded to those individuals who saw service in France and Flanders from 23 November 1914 to 31 December 1915, and to those individuals who saw service in any other operational theatre from 5 August 1914 to 31 December 1915. This is not the same as the date of signing-up – it had to be a posting into an actual theatre of war.

British War Medal (*middle*)
The British War Medal 1914–20, authorised in 1919, was awarded to eligible service personnel and civilians alike. Qualification for the award varied slightly according to service. The basic requirement for army personnel and civilians was that they either entered a theatre of war, or rendered approved service overseas between 5 August 1914 and 11 November 1918. Service in Russia in 1919 and 1920 also qualified for the award.

Victory Medal (*right*)
The Victory Medal 1914–19 was also authorised in 1919, and was awarded to all eligible personnel who served on the establishment of a unit in an operational theatre.

The other medal cards

Some details on the other cards on the page are interesting.

1. What was someone so obviously Welsh (Gordon Llewellyn Griffiths) doing in the Lovat Scouts (a Yeomanry bicycle regiment) and attached to the KOSB (King's Own Scottish Borderers), both Scottish, and what did he do that merited promotion from private to second lieutenant? He must have done something terribly impressive in the Balkans. Amazingly, he has a web page all to himself – www.qohldrs.co.uk/html/lovat_scouts.htm.

2. Griffith I Griffiths served as a gunner (the equivalent of a private) in the Royal Garrison Artillery, probably on a gun emplacement somewhere on the British coast – he clearly never went into a theatre of war, at least not until after 1915–16.

3. Private George M. Griffiths of the Army Service Corps and later the West Riding Regiment (of Yorkshire) died of wounds on 13 October 1918 – less than a month before the Armistice.

The next step would be to fill in some details from other sources. Officers can be found the relevant army list (see below).

Other records for the Armed Forces

TNA website has excellent information guides (start with #359), which summarise the records held there and elsewhere, but a few others are worth mentioning.

Army

British Army WWI Service Records, 1914–1920 are available at Ancestry (licensed from TNA), although they are in no sense complete. Many of the 'burnt records' were lost or damaged during the London Blitz in the Second World War. The remaining records cover non-commissioned officers and other ranks, and include not only the expected name, age, birthplace, occupation, marital status and regiment number but other useful details such as height, hair colour and some detail of the service career, including misbehaviour.

Army service records from 1760 to 1915 can be searched and viewed online at Find My Past. Ancestry (via TNA) also has the British Army WWI Pension Records 1914–1920. These are essentially the service records of non-commissioned officers and other ranks who claimed disability pensions for service in the First World War after discharge, and payments to widows.

Information on an 'other ranks' (i.e. non-officers) may be found in the discharge papers at TNA. They run from 1760 to 1913, and are arranged by regiment until 1883, then alphabetically by surname for the whole army. TNA also has muster rolls 1730 to 1898, arranged by regiment.

The Army List (an official publication) was first published in 1740 and regularly from 1754, with officers indexed by name from 1766 and arranged by regiment. *Hart's Army List* is a multi-annual publication covering the period 1839–1915, and some volumes will be available in larger libraries. TNA, Kew, hold army lists from 1702 up to the present day while the Genealogist (www.thegenealogist.co.uk) has army lists for 1806, 1842, 1863, 1881, 1904, 1915 and 1920 to view online. Certain years are available on CD-ROM, and they are starting to become available as PDF downloads at Google Books (books.google.co.uk) and the Internet Archive (www.archive.org).

Remember also that the Honourable East India Company (HEIC) had its own armed forces up to 1857, and produced an *East India Register and Army List*. This also contains lists of civil servants, chaplains and judges and others, including a list of stockholders at the time. The 1819, 1845, 1857 and possibly other editions are available at Google Books, but also check the Internet Archive (www.archive.org).

Militia and yeomanry

As these are local forces, their records will be with sheriff court and county records, or in the private papers of local landowners, in some cases deposited at the NAS, which also has some Ministry of Defence records, including lists of Territorial and Auxiliary Forces Association members and volunteer forces. The largest collections are from the Napoleonic times when the whole country felt imminently threatened by invasion. Privy Council papers (NAS Ref. PC15/15) contain the registers of the East Lothian Militia 1680–83 and although there is little of immediate genealogical relevance (family connections can, however, be inferred from similar surnames), there are often ages and sometimes heights of the militiamen recruited. A nationality is often given in terms of Scottish, English, Irish or Foreign.

London Gazette

Service personnel commissioned, promoted, posted or awarded a medal or another honour are 'gazetted' – that is, listed in the *London Gazette*. Larger libraries may have printed copies of the *Gazette*, but the entire historical archive is being digitised, and the two world wars plus twentieth-century honours and awards are available online. Search the archive at www.gazettes-online.co.uk for a name. This will produce a PDF of the page in question – such as the one shown below, which would bear investigation:

Regimental museums

Not all Welsh soldiers served in Welsh regiments, of course, but many did. Such regiments have their museums, which are well worth a visit and can be a source of much fascinating detail and context.

1.   The Royal Regiment of Wales, the regular infantry regiment composed of the South Wales Borderers (24th Foot) and the Monmouthshire Regiment (41st/69th Foot), the amalgamation formerly known the Welch Regiment (1719–1969 and, yes, that does say 'Welch'), has two museums, one in Brecon (said to have the best gun collection of any regimental museum in the country) and one at Cardiff Castle – www.rrw.org.uk/museums/cardiff/about.htm

2.   The Royal Welch Fusiliers ('Welch' again) at Caernarfon Castle – www.rwfmuseum.org.uk

Monmouth Regt.
    Lt.-Col. C. H. Smith is restored to the estab.   17th June 1916.
    2nd Lt. (temp. Lt.) G. M. Griffiths relinquishes his comm. on account of ill-health. 1st May 1916.

London Gazette, issue 29625, 16 June 1916. Various legal notices, including insolvencies, were required by law to be published in the London Gazette (or its Edinburgh and Belfast counterparts), and so this can also be a useful source of information on companies, individual bankruptcies and property purchases.

3.   Monmouth Regimental Museum, Great Castle House, Monmouth, is the museum of the most senior regiment in the Territorial Army, the Royal Monmouthshire Royal Engineers (Militia) – www.monmouthcastlemuseum.org.uk/

Royal Air Force

Apart from records at TNA for officers serving in the RAF (formed in 1918 from the Royal Flying Corps and Royal Naval Air Service) there is the *Air Force List*, published from 1919. In many cases, the records of soldiers who transferred from the army to the RFC or RAF will be among army service records.

Navy

National Archives records include:

- Royal Naval seamen (www.nationalarchives.gov.uk/documentsonline/royal-navy-service. asp): covers non-officers in the Royal Navy 1873–1923. It is free to search the index, but there is a charge for image copies.
- Second World War merchant seamen's medals – over 100,000 (www.nationalarchives.gov. uk/documentsonline/seamens-medals.asp).
- *Steel's Navy List* (1782–1817), the official annual *Navy List* (from 1814) and the *New Navy List* (1839–55) cover officers; *The Naval Biographical Dictionary* by W.R. O'Byrne (1849, but covering lieutenants and ranks above active or retired in 1846) has more information, including details of the officers' fathers.
- Ships' muster lists 1667–1878 have the place of birth and often the age of ratings and officers, but only if the name of the ship is known. From 1853 it is possible to trace any seaman by name in the continuous service engagement books (1853–72) and the registers of seamen's services (1873–95), which also has date, place of birth and service details.

Ancestry has a database of Royal Naval Division Casualties of The Great War, 1914–1924, listing name, service branch and unit, date and cause of death, service history and burial information. Navy lists from 1756 to 1950 are available at the Society of Genealogists, London. Find My Past, by arrangement with TNA, has an online database of more than 40,000 Royal Navy sailors who died in the First World War.

Merchant seamen

- These records are rather different, as they are in effect commercial. From 1747 masters of merchant ships had to keep and file a muster roll, detailing the number of crew and the ship's voyages. Agreements between masters and crew were made compulsory in 1835 when the muster rolls were superseded by crew lists, which are at TNA (Kew) and the National Maritime Museum in London. These agreements give the name, age and place of birth of crew members, but usually the name of the ship or the home port is needed before any search is possible. Fortunately, they are being digitised and transcribed, albeit slowly. A worthy example is Bob Sanders and the Cardiff crew agreements at his maritime history website (www.angelfire.com/de/BobSanders/CREWIN.html).
- Find My Past has 30,000 records of crew lists 1861 to 1913 with details of over 400,000 crewmen, plus more than 900,000 Board of Trade records of merchant navy crew 1918–41, some with a photograph of the crewman.

War casualties

- The Commonwealth War Graves Commission has a wonderful, free online database with details of the 1.7 million Commonwealth forces who died in conflict, searchable by surname and initials (www.cwgc.org).
- The North East War Memorials Project has a helpful site for tracing world war casualties, see their Research War Memorials page (www.newmp.org.uk/category. php?categoryid=7).

Other sites

Welsh mariners – www.welshmariners.org.uk/. Index of 22,000 Welsh merchant masters, mates and engineers 1800–1945.

Crew List Index Project – www.crewlist.org.uk/index.html. Database of some crew lists from 1861–1913, with useful background information and links.

Service records and medals post-1920 – start at www.veterans-uk.info/recordsmedalsbadges. htm.

Military records and lists are available to purchase from the Parish Chest –www.parishchest. com/Army_Lists_Military_History_Books_CDs__LDD1786.

15

Welsh Language for Genealogy

Aside from a few vowels and double consonants, Welsh is more or less phonetic and pronounced pretty much as it reads. Welsh is really no more unpronounceable than English: to prove this, say these eleven English words out loud – borough (burra), clough (cluff), cough (koff), hiccough (hikkup), hough (hock), lough (loch), plough (plow), though (tho), thought (thawt), through (throo), tough (tuff). This chapter has a very simplified version of Welsh pronunciation, and takes no account of north/south differences, but it's as good as a non-native Welsh speaker can manage.

The Welsh Alphabet

C – **K**, as in English 'Car' – *Carmarthen* (**K**ar-mar-then)

CH – as in Scottish 'lo**ch**' and Johann Sebastian Ba**ch** – *Felinfach* (**V**elin-va**ch**)

DD – **TH**, as in 'brea**TH**e' – *Beddgelert* (be**TH**-gell-airt)

G – hard **G**, as in '**G**oat' – *Beddgelert* (beth-**G**ell-airt)

LL – roughly **THCHL**, **as in** 'lo**ch**', with a 'th' in front – *Llandudno* (**THCHL**an-dud-no)

F – **V**, as in 'of' – *Caernafon* (Kyre-nar-**V**on)

FF – pronounced as an **F**, as in English 'o**ff**' – *FFestiniog* (**F**est-in-i-og)

W – pronounced as an **OO**, as in 'm**oo**n' – *Bedwellty* (Bed-**OO**-ell-ti)

Y – in the last syllable of a word, as an **i** – as in 'it'; elsewhere, **U** – as in 'r**u**n' – 'mountain' is *mynydd* (m**U**n-**I**th) but 'mountains' are *mynyddoedd* (m**U**n-**U**th-oeth). In one-syllable words (such as *y* = 'the' or *ŵyr* = 'grandson'), the pronunciation **Y** is variable.

Mutations (*Treigladau*)

Watch out for these after and before vowels (as in the surnames ap Rhys but ab Owain) and in gender (*ei fab* = his son, *ei mab* = her son).

The basic rules are:

Soft Mutation	Nasal Mutation	Aspirate Mutation
c > g	c > ngh	c > ch
p > b	p > mh	p > ph
t > d	t > nh	t > th
g > – [missing]	g > ng	
b > f	b > m	
d > dd	d > n	
ll > l		
rh > r		
m > f		

Examples

Letter	Soft Mutation	Nasal Mutation	Aspirate Mutation	
b	*bara* (bread)	*ei fara* (his bread)	*fy mara* (my bread)	*ei bara* (her bread)
c	*cath* (cat)	*ei gath* (his cat)	*fy nghath* (my cat)	*ei chath* (her cat)
d	*dant* (tooth)	*ei ddant* (his tooth)	*fy nant* (my tooth)	*ei dant* (her tooth)
g	*gwal* (wall)	*ei wal* (his wall)	*fy ngwal* (my wall)	*ei gwal* (her wall)
ll	*llaeth* (milk)	*ei laeth* (his milk)	*fy llaeth* (my milk)	*ei llaeth* (her milk)
m	*mam* (mother)	*ei fam* (his mother)	*fy mam* (my mother)	*ei mam* (her mother)
p	*pren* (stick)	*ei bren* (his stick)	*fy mhren* (my stick)	*ei phren* (her stick)
rh	*rhaff* (rope)	*ei raff* (his rope)	*fy rhaff* (my rope)	*ei rhaff* (her rope
t	*tad* (father)	*ei dad* (his father)	*fy nhad* (my father)	*ei thad* (her father)

There is much, much more on this in the document from BBC Wales Education: www.bbc.co.uk/wales/learnwelsh/pdf/welshgrammar_mutations.pdf.

Emphasis
In Welsh, this is usually on the last-but-one syllable – Caernarfon (kyre-NAR-von), Bedwellty (bed-WELL-ti).

Welsh place names
Understanding how Welsh place names work can really bring geography to life, as most of them are descriptive – *Mynydd Bach* = 'small mountain'. The most famous is: Llanfairpwllgwyngyllgogerychwyrndrobwllllantysiliogogogoch (thchlann-vyre-pooth-gwinn-gith-gogg-erra-kweern-drobbooth-lann-tuss-ill-yo-goggo-goch).
Which is more or less: 'St Mary's Church by the pool with the white hazel near the rapid whirlpool by St Tysilio's church and the red cave'.

This was the result of a Victorian publicity stunt, in fact, and it worked, judging from the number of visitors ever since. The real name of the village is actually Llanfairpwllgwyngyll, usually abbreviated to Llanfair PG.

In addition to landscape features, some Welsh place names relate to animals, plants and structures. Often, a word can have two meanings, such as *ysgol* (school, Tai'r-ysgol) and *ysgol* (a 'ladder' formation on the side of a mountain, Craig-yr-ysgol). There is a much more comprehensive listing at www.ordnancesurvey.co.uk/oswebsite/freefun/didyouknow/placenames/welshglossary-a-b.html.

Welsh	Meaning	Example
abad	abbot	Tirabad
aber	river mouth, estuary, confluence, stream	Aberdaron
acer, aceri, acrau	acre	Ddwy-acer, Ty'n-yr-acrau
aderyn, adar	bird	Craig yr Aderyn, Brynyradar
adwy	gap, pass	Nant Adwy'r-llan
ael	brow, edge	Aelybryn

aelwyd	hearth	Aelwyd Brys
afallen	apple tree	Dolafallen
afon	river	Afon Dee
allt, gallt, elltydd, alltau	hillside, cliff, wood	Alltwalis
am	near, beside, around	Amlwch
amlwg	evident, visible, prominent	Grwnamlwg
angell	offshoot, tributary, leg, wing, limb	Afon Angell
anner, annair	heifer	Cwm Penanner
ar	on, upon, over	Pen-y-bont ar Ogwr
ardd, ard	hill, height	Pennard
argae, argaeau	dam, mill dam, embankment	Rhydargaeau
arglwydd -es	lord, lady	Waunarlwydd
argoed	wood, grove	Argoed
arian	silver	Carn yr arian
arth	bear	Afon Arth
asgwrn, esgyrn	bone	Mynydd yr Esgyrn
athro	teacher, father confessor	Pant Yr Athro
aur	gold	Llannerch–yr–aur
awel, awelon	breeze	Morawel
bach, bachau, bachell, bachell, bachellau	nook, corner, bend in a river	Eglwys-bach, Fachell
bach, fach	small, little	Felinfach
bala	narrow land between two lakes, outlet of a lake	Brynbala
ban, bannau	peak, beacon	Pen y Bannau
banc	bank, hill, slope	Pen-y-Banc
bangor	(ecclesiastical) settlement enclosed within a wattled fence	Bangor
banhadlen, banadl, banal	broom	Cefn-banadl
banhadlog	broom patch	Banhadlog
bannog	high, horned, turreted	Cefnbannog
banw	young pig	Blaen Cwm Banw
bar	top, summit	Crug-y-bar
barcud	kite, buzzard	Carreg y Barcud
bardd, beirdd	bard	Cwrtbrynbeirdd
bargod	boundary (eaves)	Bargoed
batin, bating (see betin)		

baw	dirt	Pig y Baw
bedd, beddau	grave	Beddgelert
bedwen	birch	
bedwen, bedw	birch	Craigyfedwe
bedwlwyn	birch grove	Bedwlwyn
beidr	lane, path	Penfeidr
beili, beiliau	bailey	Beili-glas
bela, bele	marten, wild beast	Trebela
bendigaid	blessed	Llanfendigaid
berw	rush of water	Berw-ddu
betin, beting, bietin, bieting	pared and burnt land	Batingau
betws	chapel	Betws-y-coed
beudy	cow-house	Beudiau
bid	quickset hedge	Twyn y Fidffawydd
blaen	promontory, projection	Blaengarw
blaen, blaenau	source of river, stream, highland	Blaenau Ffestiniog
blaidd	wolf	Castell-y-blaidd
bod, fod	abode, dwelling	Bodedern, Meifod
bol, bola	belly, swelling	Rhos-y-bol
bon	stock, stump, base	Bon-y-maen
boncen, boncyn (see poncyn, poncen)		
bont, pont	bridge	Pontnewydd
braenar, branar brynar	fallow land	Mynydd Branar
braich	ridge, arm	Pen-y-braich
brân, brain	crow	Cwm-brân
bras, breision	big, fat, rich	Bryn-bras
bre, bren	hill	Pen-bre
brenin	king	Rhodiad-y-brenin
brest	hill-breast	Brestbaily SN9838
brith, braith	speckled, coarse	Brithdir
briw	broken, shattered	Carn Briw SN0537
bro	region, vale, lowland	Llanbedr-y-fro
bron, bronnydd	hill-breast (breast)	Bronydd
brwynen, brwyn	rush	Cwmbrwyn SN2512
brwynog	place of rushes, marsh	Brwynog
brych, brech f	speckled	Brechfa, Llanfrechfa

bryn, bryniau	hill	Bryn-berian
bryncyn	hillock	Bryncyn-felen
buarth, buarthau	farmyard, pen	Buarth Berran
buches	milking fold	Buches y Foelortho
budr, fudr	dirty	Nant Budr, Rhyd-fudr
bugail, bugelydd, bugeiliaid	shepherd	Bugeildy
bustach, bustych	bullock	Nant y Bustach
buwch, buchod	cow, cattle	Cas-fuwch
bwbach	goblin	Bryn Bwbach SH6236
bwch	buck	Castell-y-bwch
bwla	bull	Nantybwla
bwlch	gap, pass	Bwlch
bwrdd	table	Bwrdd Arthur
bychan, bechan, bychain	little, tiny	Llanfairfechan
byr, ber	short	Byrgoed
cadair	seat, stronghold	Cadair Idris
cadno	fox	Pant y Cadno
cae	field	Cae Caled
caer	fort	Caermarthen
carreg	stone, rock	Carreg Samson
castell	castle	
cefn	ridge	Cefn-coed
cei	quay	Ceinewydd
celli	grove	Pencelli
cerdinen	mountain ash, rowan tree	Bryn-Cerdin
coch	red	Castell Coch
coed, coeden	tree, wood	Cefn-coed
croes, groes	cross	Croesgoch
cwm	valley	Cwmbran
cwrt	court	Cwrt Henry
dar, deri, derwen	oak	Abardar
dinas	fort, city	Dinas Emrys
dol	meadow	Dol-y-bont
du	black	Cwmdu
dyffryn	valley	Dyffryn Ceiriog
efail/gefail	smithy	Cefn-y-gefail

eglwys	church	Eglwyswrw
eryr	eagle	Tap Nyth-yr-Eryr
fawr, mawr	big	Fforest Fawr
felin, melin	mill	Felinfach
ffordd	road	Pen-y-fford
garth	promontory	Gartheryr
gwesty	hotel	
hendre	old house	Capel Hendre
llan	church, monastery, church lands	Llanfair
llyn	lake	Llyn Brianne
maes	field	Maesteg
melin	mill	Melin-coed
moel	bare hill	Moelfre
mynydd	mountain, moorland	Mynydd Bach
nant	brook, stream	Nant-glos
ogof	cave	Ogof Ddu
onn, onnen	ash tree	Trefonnen
pant	hollow, valley	Pant y Cadno
pen	top	Pen-y-bont
pistyll	waterfall	Pistyll Rhaeadr
ponc (pl ponciau)	hillock, tump	Pen-y-bonc, Ponciau
poncyn, poncen	small hillock	Clawdd Poncen
pwll	pool	Llanfair Pwllgwyngyll
rhos	moor	Rosnesi
rhyd	ford	Rhydfelen
tafarn	tavern, pub	Tafarnygelyn
tir	land, territory	Tirabad
traeth	beach	Malltraeth
twyn	hillock, knoll	Pen-twyn
tŷ, dref	house	Ty-croes
tyddyn	small farm	Tyn-y-groes
ynys	island	Ynys-las
ysbyty	hospital	Ysbyty Ifan
ysgol	ladder on mountainside	Craig-yr-ysgol
ysgol	school	Tai'r-ysgol
ystlys	side	Ystlys-y-coed-isaf
ystrad	valley, river meadow	Ystrad Rhondda
ywen	yew tree	Careg-ywen

Welsh vocabulary for genealogy

Days of the Week	
Dydd Sul (Sul)	Sunday
Dydd Llun (Llun)	Monday
Dydd Mawrth (Maw)	Tuesday
Dydd Mercher (Mer)	Wednesday
Dydd Iau (Iau)	Thursday
Dydd Gwener (Gwe)	Friday
Dydd Sadwrn (Sad)	Saturday

Months of the Year	
Ionawr, Ionor (Ion)	January
Chwefror, Chwefrol (Chw)	February
Mawrth (Maw)	March
Ebrill (Ebr)	April
Mai	May
Mehefin (Meh)	June
Gorffennaf, Gorphenaf (Gor)	July
Awst (Aws)	August
Medi (Med)	September
Hydref (Hyd)	October
Tachwedd (Tac)	November
Rhagfyr (Rha)	December

Cardinal Numbers	
un	I
dau	2
tri	3
pedwar	4
pump	5
chwech	6
saith	7
wyth	8
naw	9
deg	10
ugain	20
deg ar hugain	30

Ordinal Numbers	
cyntaf	first
ail	second
trydydd (3ydd)	third
pedwerydd (4ydd)	fourth
pumed	fifth
chweched	sixth
seithfed (7fed)	seventh
wythfed (8fed)	eighth
nawfed (9fed)	ninth
degfed (10fed)	tenth

Welsh Counties in Welsh

Historic County (Welsh name)	Historic County (English name)
Ceredigion	Cardiganshire
Meirionnydd	Merionethshire
Morgannwg	Glamorganshire
Sir Aberteifi	Cardiganshire
Sir Benfro	Pembrokeshire
Sir Ddinbych	Denbighshire
Sir Drefaldwyn	Montgomeryshire
Sir Faesyfed	Radnorshire
Sir Feirionnydd	Merionethshire
Sir Fôn	Anglesey
Sir Forgannwg	Glamorganshire
Sir Frycheiniog	Brecknockshire
Sir Fynwy	Monmouthshire
Sir Gaerfyrddin	Carmarthenshire
Sir Gaernarfon	Caernarfonshire
Sir Gâr	Carmarthenshire
Sir y Fflint	Flintshire

Welsh glossary

This includes relationships (father, daughter, first cousin twice removed) and the sort of terms seen on gravestones and in memorials ('in loving remembrance of', 'fell asleep in Jesus') and some useful phrases ('hello', 'goodnight'). It is no substitute for a decent Welsh–English dictionary and grammar, a good example being Gareth King's *Modern Welsh Dictionary: A Guide to the Living Language* (Oxford: OUP, 2007). See also www.1911census.co.uk/content/default.aspx?r=33&142 for terms found in Welsh censuses in particular.

a aned, a anwyd	who was born
a enwir/enwyd uchod	named above
a fu farw	who died
a gafodd ei ddiwedd	met his end
a gladdwyd	who was buried
ab, ap	son (of)
abades	abbess
abadesau	abbesses
aber	river mouth
addysgydd	tutor
adeiladau	buildings
adran	section, department
afon	river
afwyn	rein
amddifad	orphan
amgyffryd	width
amser	time
angeu, angau	death
anghysbell	remote
annwyl	loving
annwyl, hannwyl	beloved
ar hyd	along
ar hynny	then
ar led	abroad
ar un adeg	at one time
araf	slow
arall	other
archaf	I ask
archebu	to order
ardal	region
arfeu, arfan	weapons, arms
arfordir	coast

ariant, arian	silver, money
ar-lein	online
arweinydd y gân	precentor, leader of singing (church)
athrawes	teacher (f)
athro	teacher (m)
attaliaf	restrain
aur	gold
awr	hour
baban, faban	baby
bach, fach	small
bachgen	son or boy
bachgennyn	little boy
bardd	poet, bard
barf	beard
bedd	grave
bedydd	baptism
benyw	female
perthynas, berthynas	relative
blaen	promontory, projection
blaenor	elder, deacon
blaidd	wolf (masculine)
blant, plant	children
plentyn, blentyn, phlentyn	child
blwydd, mlwydd	year (after number)
blwyddyn	year
bodoli	to exist
pont, bont	bridge
bore da	good morning
braich	arm
brawd	brother
brawd, brodyr	brother
brawd yng nghyfraith	brother-in-law
brawdmaeth	foster-brother
brenin	king
briod	wife
briod	husband
brith	bread
bu farw	he (she) died
bugail	shepherd

bwlch	gap, pass
bwrdd	table
bwyd	food
byddwch yn ofalus	be careful
byrddiwr	boarder
cadarn	strong
caewch (y drws)	close (the door)
caf	get, obtain
caffaf	take
cam	step
cann, cant	hundred
car	relative (by kinship)
caraf	love
carchar	bonds, prison
cares	friend (female)
cariad	love
cariwr	carrier
carrai	lace
carreg	stone
carw	stag, deer
cawl	leek
cefnder	cousin (m)
cefn	ridge
cefnder (cefndryd) (m), cyfnither (-od) (f) eich tad/ mam	first cousin once removed (cousin of parent)
cefnder (m)/ cyfnither (f) eich taid /tad-cu (m)/ nain /mam-gu (f)	first cousin twice removed (cousin of grandparent)
ceisio	to seek, to ask
cennin	soup
cerddor	musician
cerennydd	friendship
chwaer, chwiorydd	sister
chwaer yng nghyfraith	sister-in-law
chware	sister
chwarelwr	quarryman
chwegr	mother-in-law
chwegrwn	father-in-law
ci	dog, hound
cilydd	companion
claddwyd	entombed, buried

claf	patient
cleddyf	sword
clod	fame, glory
clywaf	hear
coch	red
codwr canu	precentor, leader of singing (church)
coed	wood
coffadwriaeth	remember, remembrance
cog	cook
cogydd	cook (male)
cogyddes	cook (female)
colofn	column
corff	body
corn	horn
coron	crown
corph, corff	body
credyd	credit
criw	crew
croes, groes	cross
crydd	shoemaker, cobbler
cwm	valley
cwmni	company
cwn	dogs, hounds
cwsg	sleep
cyd	although, if
cyd	coupling, joining
cydymaith	fellow worker
cyfarchaf well	welcome
cyfeirio	to refer, direct
cyffes	confession
cyflogi	to employ, use
cyflwyno	to present
cyfnither	cousin (f)
cyfodaf	rise
cyfreithiwr	solicitor, lawyer
cyfreithlon	lawful
cyfrifiadur	computer
cyfrifol	responsible
cyfyngu	to limit

cyfyrder	second cousin (m)
cyfyrderes	second cousin (f)
cyhoedd	the public
cylchlythyr	newsletter
cymorth, cynhorthwy	help
Cymru	Wales
cymunedau	communities
cymydog	neighbour
cynhaliaf	support
cynorthwyol, cynorthwywr	assistant
cyrchaf	head for, approach
cysgaf	I sleep
cysylltiad	link, contact
tad, dad	father
dant	tooth
darganfod	to discover
darlledu	to broadcast
daw	son-in-law
deu	two
deunydd	material
dewch i mewn	come in
dewch yma	come here
dewch ymlaen	come on
dewredd	persistence, courage
diacon	deacon
digrif	pleasant
digrifa	entertain
dilledydd	draper
dim …	no …
dim mynediad	no entry
dinas	fort, city
dioddefwr, dioddefydd	patient
diogelu	to secure
diolch	thank you
diolch yn fawr	thank you very much
disgybl	pupil
diwrnod, dydd	day
dod o hyd i	to meet, come across
does dim clem 'da fi	I don't have a clue

does dim ots	it doesn't matter
dosbarth	administration, government
dros	across
drws	door
drych	look, appearance, mirror
du	black
duw	god
dwfr	water
dwg	take, lead
dwy	two
dyblyg	fold
dydd	day
dydd Gwener	Friday
dydd Iau	Thursday
dydd Llun	Monday
dydd Mawrth	Tuesday
dydd Mercher	Wednesday
dydd Sadwrn	Saturday
dydd Sul	Sunday
dynion	gentlemen
dyrnawd	blow
dysgu o bell	distance learning
dysgwr	apprentice
dywedaf	say
e-bost, e-byst	email
eglwys	church
ei (eu)	his/her★
ei annwyl wraig	his dear/beloved wife
ei fab	his son
ei ferch	his daughter
ei gŵr	her husband
ei mab	her son
ei merch	her daughter
eirch	she/he/it asks
eisieu	need
eisoes	already

★possessive, *ei fab/mhab* = his/her son (watch out for gender variants – *ei fab* = his son; *ei mhab* = her son; *eu mab/mhab* = their son

emynydd	hymn writer
enw	name
er cof am	in memory of
er cof tyner am	in tender memory of
er coffadwriaeth am	in remembrance of
er coffadwriaeth parchus am	in respectful remembrance of
er coffadwriaeth serchog am	in loving remembrance of
er serchog gof am	in loving memory of
erbyn	opposite
eu plentyn, plant	their child, children
eur, aur (primary)	gold
eurwisg	gold cloth
ewythr	uncle
ewythr mawr	great-uncle
fab, mab, mhab	son
faban, baban	baby
fal	like, as
fam, mam	mother
fawr, mawr	big
felin, melin	mill
ferch, merch, mherch	daughter
ffefryn	favourite
ffenestr	window
ffermwr	farmer
ffiniau	boundaries
ffordd	road
fforddio	to afford
ffrind	friend
ffurf	form, shape
flaen, blaen	before, in front
forwyn (morwyn)	maid, female servant
frenhines, brentines	queen
gallaf	can, be able
ganwyd, ganed	was born
garddwr	gardener
geir, gair	word
glöwr	collier
gogledd	north
gorchaifn	fourth cousin (m)

gorchaw	fifth cousin (m)
gorffwys, gorphwys	rest
gorhen dad-cu, gorhendaid	great-great-grandfather
gor-nai	great-nephew
gor-nith	great-niece
gor-or-nai	great-great-nephew
gor-or-nith	great-great-niece
gor-or-yr	great-great-grandson
gor-or-wyres	great-great-granddaughter
gorsaf	station
gorweddle	resting place of
gorŵyr, gor-yr	great-grandchild, great-grandson
gorwyres	great-granddaughter
gosodaf	strike
gwarandaf, gwrandawaf	listen
gwarchod	to look after
gwas	fellow, servant, lad, groom
gwas ffarm	farm lad
gwasanaethwr, gwasanaethydd	servant (male)
gwaudd	daughter-in-law
gwe, gweoedd	web
gweddw	widow
gwefan	had to
gweinidog	minister
gweinyddes	attendant, nurse
gweithredol	executive
gwelaf	see
gwenithfaen	granite
gwerin llong	crew
gwerth	worth, value
gwestai	guest
gwesty	hotel
gwisg f	clothes, garment
gwr, gŵr	husband
gwraig	wife
gwraig briod	matron
gwrda	'goodman', servant
gwreica	marries
gwreig	wife

gwrogaeth	homage
gwybodaeth	knowledge
gwyddoniaeth	science
gwyliau	holidays
gyd a	together with
gyda, gydag	with
gynt	formerly
gynt o	formally of
haearn	iron
hannwyl, annwyl	beloved
hawl	claim
hebawg, hebog	falcon
heddlu	police
hefyd	also
helo	hello
hen dad-cu	great-grandfather (south)
hen daid	great-grandfather (north)
hen fam-gu	great-grandmother (south)
hen hen rieni	great-grandparents
hen nain	great-grandmother (north)
hen rieni	grandparents
hirbell	distant
holaf	I claim
holl	whole, all
hon	this (f)
honno	that (f)
hun	sleep
hunodd	who died, he died
hunodd yn yr Iesu	fell asleep in Jesus
hwn	this (m)
hwnnw	that (m)
hwyl	goodbye
hyd	length
hyd	to, until, while
hyd at	as far as
hyd yn hyn	so far
hyd yn oed	even
hyn	this (n)
hynny	that (n)

hynt	path, way
i fynydd, i fyny	up
i gofio'n dyner am	in tender memory of
i maes	out
i ymdeith	away
iarll	steward, earl
iawn	OK
ieuanc	young
i'r llawr	down
llan	church lands
llannerch	clearing
llanw	tide
llawr	floor, ground
lle	place
lled	almost, partly
lled	breadth, width, broader, wider
lled	death
lledach	of ignoble birth or descent
llefarydd	spokesperson
lleol	local
lletywr	guest, lodger, boarder
lliw	colour
llong	ship
llu	host, throng
llwybr cyhoeddus	public footpath
llwytho i lawr	to download
llyn	lake
llys	court
llyschwaer	stepsister
llysdad-cu	step-grandfather
llysfab	stepson
llysfam	stepmother
llysfam-gu	step-grandmother
llysferch	stepdaughter
llysfrawd	stepbrother
llystad	stepfather
llyswyr	step-grandson
llyswyres	step-granddaughter
llythr	letter

lôn	lane
mab, mhab, fab	son
mabmaeth	foster-son
mabwysiadol	adopted
mab-yng-nghyfraith	son-in-law
maes	field
mam	mother
mamaeth	nurse
mam-gu	grandmother
mam-yng-nghyfraith	mother-in-law
march	horse, charger
marchawg	horseman
masnachydd	merchant
meddwl	think
medr	skill
meistr	master, boss
meistr tir	landlord (of property)
melinydd	miller
merch, mherch, ferch	daughter
merched	ladies
merch-yng-nghyfraith	daughter-in-law
mewn hiraethus gof	in grieving memory
milwr	soldier
milwraeth	valour, courage
mintai fawr	crowd, host, multitude
mis	month
misoedd	months
modd	means, mode
modryb	aunt
modryb fawr	great-aunt
moes	custom, usage
môr	sea
morwyn	maid, female servant
mwynwr	miner
mynegai	index
mynydd	mountain
nai	nephew
nain	grandmother (north)
namyn	except

neges	business, errand
neill, naill	the one (as opposed to *arall*, the other)
nerth	force, strength
ni, nid	not
nifer	retinue
nith	niece
nod	objective
nos	night
nos da	goodnight
noswaith dda	good evening
nyrs	nurse
o dan y garreg hon	underneath this stone
o flaen	in front
o hirbell	from afar
o hyd	always
o leiaf	the four corners of the earth
o ran	in part, as regards
oed, oedran	age
oedd	was
ôl	track, footsteps
o'r enw	in/by the name of
o'r gorau	very well (agreeing)
o'r plwyf hwn	of this parish
organydd	organist
os gwelwch yn dda	please
pali	brocade
parabl	speech
parchedig (parch.)	reverend (rev.)
parhau	to last, to continue, to persevere
parth	part, direction
pawb	every
pebyll	pavilion
pedestrig	walking pace
peidiwch	do not
peiriant chwilio	search engine
pell iawn	distant
pell, pellennig	far
pen	top
penderfynu	to decide

penllanw	high water, high tide
pen	head
pennau teuluoedd	head of family
penteulu	head of household
penyd	penance
perfedd	middle
perthynas, berthynas	relative
phlentyn, plentyn, blentyn	child
phriod, priod	husband
pistyll	waterfall
plant	children
plentyn	child
plentyn bach	infant or little child
plentyn (plant) eich cefnder (m), cyfnither (f)	first cousin once removed (child of one's cousin)
pluf	feathers
plwyf	parish
poen	punishment
pont	bridge
post	post
pregethwr	preacher
preswylydd	dweller, inhabitant, inmate
prif	chief
priod	spouse, wife, husband, married
profi	to test, prove
prynaf	buy
prynhawn da	good afternoon
rhan	host, company; part, share
rheolau	rules
rhieni	parents
rhoddaf	give
rhyd	ford
rhyfelu	make war
rhyngrwyd	Internet
saer coed	carpenter
saer maen	stonemason
safaf	stand
serchus, serchog	loving, affectionate
siaradwch yn arafach	speak more slowly
sicrhau	to secure

siop	shop
sobr	sober
swydd	office
swyddawg, swyddwr, swyddog	officer
swyddfa'r post	Post Office
syberw	proud
syberwyd	pride
syth	straight
tad, dad	father
tad-cu	grandfather (south)
tad-cu, taid	grandfather
tafarnwr	publican
tai	houses
taid	grandfather (north)
tarian	shield
tawelwch	silence
telynor	harpist
terfyn	end
teulu	household
teyrnas	kingdom
tigern	king
tir	land
tlotyn	pauper
toiledau	toilets
torf	crowd, host (many)
torraf	break
torri	to break, overcome
torri	to go bankrupt
torri ar	to interrupt
torri bedd	to dig a grave
torri cytundeb	to break an agreement
torri dadl	to settle a dispute
torri enw	to sign
torri geiriau	to say words
traeth	beach
trigiannydd	inmate, resident
trysorydd	treasurer
twg	success
twrf	noise

tyner, yn dyner	tender, tenderly
tyrfa	crowd
uchod	above
ufydd	humble
unben	lord ('own-head')
unrhyw	any
gŵr	husband
wraig	wife
ŵyr	grandson, grandchild
ŵyr (wyrion) (m) /ŵyres (wyresau) (f) eich cefnder (m)/ cyfnither (f)	first cousin twice removed (grandchildren of one's cousin)
wyres	granddaughter
wyrion	grandchildren
wythnos	week
y ddywededig uchod	the above mentioned (f)
y dywededig uchod	the above mentioned (m)
yma y claddwyd	here was buried
yma y gorwedd	here lieth, lies
ymadawedig	departed, deceased
ymddeol	to retire
ymdeith	journey
ymgeleddwr or ymgeleddwyr	guardian
ymwelwr or ymwelydd	visitor
yn (2) mlwydd oed	(two) years old
yn ogystal â	as well as
yn ôl	behind
ynglyn	concerning
yng-nghyfraith	in-law
ynifer	retinue, host
ynys	island
yr hon a fu farw	who died (f)
yr hwn a fu farw	who died (m)
ysbyty	hospital
ysgolfeistr	schoolmaster
ysgolhaig, ysgolor	scholar
ysgrifennydd	secretary
ystafell	room
ystlys	side

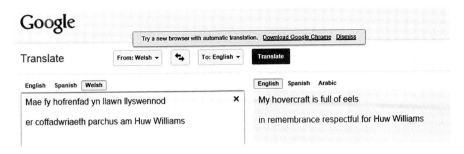

The Google Translate page.

Aids to translation

For single words, use the online dictionary at www.bbc.co.uk/wales/learning/learnwelsh/.

Best of all, probably, is Google Translate – http://translate.google.
co.uk/?hl=en&tab=wT#cy|en|.

Select the language pair and try a phrase. As can be seen below, it is not always perfect, but it gives a good approximation. The first phrase has translated perfectly ('My hovercraft is full of eels') but the second should say 'In respectful remembrance of Huw Williams'. There are similar translation facilities elsewhere, such as http://imtranslator.net/translation/welsh/to-english/translation/ but Microsoft's Bing (the replacement for Babelfish – www.microsofttranslator.com) hasn't yet learned Welsh.

Further reading

Books
Gareth King, *Modern Welsh Dictionary: A Guide to the Living Language* (Oxford: OUP, 2007).

Online resources
Terms found in Welsh censuses – www.1911census.co.uk/content/default.aspx?r=33&142
Welsh grammar from BBC Wales Education – www.bbc.co.uk/wales/learnwelsh

Online translators
Google Translate – http://translate.google.co.uk/?hl=en&tab=wT#cy|en|
IMTranslator – http://imtranslator.net/translation/welsh/to-english/translation/

16

Organising Your Research

It is very easy to collect lots of notes on loose bits of paper, documents, printouts, photographs and other information, and put it all in a drawer or a box file, promising yourself to 'sort it out later'. But there will come a time when it defies organising. So, start with a structure and stick to it. The method below is only one of many, but it works in practice.

1. Write everything down!
   DO NOT rely on your memory. Everything you see written, every book you consult, every website you look at, make a brief note of it. Even if you find nothing, it is useful to know that – it will save you repeating fruitless searches.

2. Use a hardback bound notebook.
   DO NOT use loose-leaf paper. Carry a bound notebook everywhere. Note everything. Later (but soon, preferably the same day), type this up into a document, spreadsheet, genealogy programme or whatever method you prefer for keeping your results.

3. Make full use of charts, research calendars and family group sheets.
   These are three of the most useful tools for genealogists. A pedigree chart is a visual aid of (usually) three or four generations of a family. A research calendar will remind you where you have been, what you found (or didn't find) and what you intend to do next. The family group sheet is all the information on one nuclear family (father, mother, children) with sources. There are examples of these available for download at www.brucedurie.co.uk/resources, which you are free to copy and use.

4. Keep the information on one (extended) family in a ring binder.
   Genealogists argue whether to file printouts, documents and notes by each person alphabetically. The problem is, any one document might refer to a number of people – a birth record will have information on at least three (child, father, mother) and a census could be as many as ten, or more. Alphabetical ordering takes no account of time and there may be multiple people with the same name, often in the same generation (cousins, for instance).

Therefore, set up a ring binder for each project and use tabbed dividers to separate the following categories (you can always add other later, e.g. military):

- Pedigree/ancestral charts (useful to have at the beginning as an aide-memoire)
- Family group sheets (all together, in chronological order of father's birth date)
- Births (every birth record, arranged chronologically)
- Marriages (as above)
- Deaths (as above)
- Censuses (by year)
- Wills and testaments abstracts (chronologically)

– Newspaper clippings etc.
– Plastic one-page wallets for documents (use archive-standard polyester, not PVC)
– Plastic wallets for photographs (polyester, not PVC).

5. Give each family a number (start with 001, so SMITH I001). Then number individuals from your index person (the person you start from). He/she will be 1, father 2, mother 3, paternal grandfather 4 and so on. See below for more information on numbering systems.

6. Photocopy, photograph, download or scan every actual document, print a copy, keep the print in your file and put the original document away in a safe place. Use plastic one-page wallets and a metal or acid-free cardboard file box. Your local stationery shop should be able to advise you about these, as will your local library or archive. Some A4 photocopy-paper boxes are acid-free, come with a lid, and are strong and stackable.

7. If you store images on your computer, put the images in meaningful folders, give them filenames that tie up with the document, and print out every image and store it in your file as paper. John-Smith1.jpg is meaningless as a file name; D-1905-SMITH-John-75-Scoonie-Fife456-0002.jpg will lead you straight to the paper file version (D = Death, B = Birth etc).

8. On each document copy or image printout, write the source and reference number, and the filename.

9. It's OK to have the same person in different family files. Copy all relevant papers.

10. At the beginning of the file, have two lists of everyone – alphabetically (with birth date), such as:

SMITH, Alfred b. 12 Jun 1887
SMITH, John b. 14 Apr 1890
JONES, Mary b. 10 Sept 1725

Charts and Numbering Systems

Genealogy uses charts and family group sheets to record data. Genealogy software programmes can help, and can print out information in a variety of formats, but there is still something to be said for the old paper and pencil.

The two basic forms for recording genealogical information are ascendant charts and descendant charts (see p. 277). An ascendant chart starts with you and moves back through the generations of your ancestors. A descendant chart starts with you or another individual in your family tree and lists all of the descendants coming down through the generations. On these forms you record the names of your ancestors or descendants, and the dates and places of the three major genealogical events (birth, marriage and death). They basically serve as a master outline for your genealogy information and make it easy to see at a glance where you have gaps in your knowledge of people or events.

Ascendant charts

The chart that most people begin with is the pedigree chart, a type of ascendant chart. The most common type of pedigree chart displays four or five generations of family data on a single page, but you can purchase paper charts that will accommodate as many as fifteen generations.

A four-generation chart is useful as it fits neatly on a standard size page and leaves enough room for data. The first individual named on the left of the chart is the one whose ancestry the tree documents. The chart then branches in two to show parents, then in four for grandparents, and so on. This chart only shows the index person's direct ancestors – there is no room on a pedigree chart for siblings, multiple marriages, and so on.

The pedigree chart is the more graphic representation of a person's ancestors, while an ahnentafel (German for 'ancestor table') presents the information in a neat, compact manner as a table or list. Ahnentafels are not used quite as often today as they were in the past. Ancestors are numbered on pedigree charts and ahnentafels using a system known as the ahnentafel numbering system. You (or the person whose ancestry is being traced) are number 1. A father is twice his child's number (1 x 2 = 2) and a mother is twice the child's number plus one (1 x 2 = 2 + 1 = 3). The numbers for men are always even and the numbers for women are always odd, with the exception of number 1, which can obviously be either. Notice that the first number for each generation is equal to the number of people in that generation (i.e. paternal great-grandfather is 8, and there are eight great-grandparents). Use the same numbering in your family group sheets.

Descendant charts

Descendant charts are most often used to chart all of the descendants (or at least as many as can be found) of a specific ancestor. You won't find these very useful as you start out, although you should prepare one to include your children and grandchildren if that applies. In general, however, descendant charts begin with a progenitor – the earliest proven ancestor in a line. This means doing some research before you can create this type of chart.

These use a different numbering system, with the progenitor as 1 and all children as 1a, 1b or 1i, 1ii and so on.

Family group sheets

This is the basic worksheet used for genealogical research. While a pedigree chart identifies your ancestry and serves primarily as a culmination of your work, the family group sheet is how you get there.

There are many different formats available, but each family group sheet is based on a single family unit – husband, wife and children. A family group sheet has space for the basic genealogical events for each family member, including dates and places of birth, marriage, death and burial. For each child on the list, a name of a spouse can be given, along with a date and place of the marriage. There is usually a place for notes, where you should record where you got your information (source) as well as make note of any discrepancies in your findings.

Family group sheets are essential because they:

1. serve as a simple means of recording data;

2. make it easy to see at a glance what information is known and what is missing; and

3. serve as a means of easily exchanging information with other researchers.

Recording names

There are some important conventions that should be followed with regard to names, dates and places. These help to ensure that genealogical data are as complete as possible and cannot be misinterpreted by others.

Genealogy software programmes will each have their own individual rules for entering names. Be sure to read the directions completely so that you get it right the first time!

1. Record names in their natural order – first, middle, last (surname). Use full names if known. If the middle name is unknown, use an initial.

2. Print SURNAMES in upper case letters. Example: Henry Michael DAVIES; Henry M. DAVIES.

3. Enter women with their maiden name (surname at birth) rather than their husband's surname. Example: Margaret JONES married Henry DAVIES, enter her as Margaret JONES.

4. If a female's maiden name is unknown, give her first (given) name followed by empty brackets (). Example: Margaret Ellen, maiden name is unknown, married to Henry EVANS = Margaret Ellen () or Margaret Ellen () EVANS.

5. If a woman has had more than one husband, enter her given name, followed by her maiden surname (m.s.) in brackets followed by the names of any previous husbands (in order of marriage). If the middle name is known then you may enter that as well. Example: a woman named Mary CLARKE at birth, was married to Jack SMITH prior to marrying Walter LEWIS = Mary (Clarke) SMITH or Mary LEWIS previously SMITH m.s CLARKE.

6. If there is a nickname that was commonly used, include it in quotes after the given name. Do not use it in place of a given name and do not enclose it in brackets. Example: Rev. Hector 'Heavens' Evans, Huw 'The Post' WILLIAMS

7. If a person is known by more than one name (due to adoption, name change etc.) then include the alternate name or names in brackets after the surname, preceded by a.k.a. Example: Bernard SCHWARZ (a.k.a. Tony CURTIS).

8. Include alternate spellings when you find them. Record the earlier usage first. Example: Daphne BROON/BROWN; Michael ROLLINS/RAWLINS.

9. Include titles, but feel free to abbreviate: Sir Hufton TUFTON; Lady Evadne BLIMP; Thomas, Lord GONSCATTY.

10. Use notes when you can. For example, if a female had a maiden name that was the same as her husband's surname, make a note of that, so you're clear in the future that this was not entered incorrectly.

Recording dates

It is especially important to follow genealogical standards when recording dates, as the usual way that you enter a date may be different from the standard date format in another country or a different time period.

Genealogy software programmes may have somewhat different standards for recording dates. Many will, however, allow you to record them in the format of your choice and still allow you to print out charts and forms with the standard genealogical format.

1. Use the accepted European standard of DAY, MONTH (spelled out) and four-digit YEAR. Example: 30 June 1993.

2. Americans often use dates with a number format as month/day (e.g. 9/11), which leads to confusion. Example: 02/01/01 – is it 1 February or 2 January?

3. Spell months out, although there are standard abbreviations you can use. (June and July are often not abbreviated.) Examples: Jan., Feb., Mar., Apr., May., Jun. (or June), Jul. (or July), Aug., Sept., Oct., Nov., Dec.

4. If you only have an approximate date, add 'about' (abt.) or 'circa' (ca. or *c.*). Examples: *c.* 1851; ca. 1873; abt. November 1881.

5. Use before (bef.) or after (aft.) a specific date, for instance, when you know someone was still living at some time, or was born after a certain date. Example: aft. 12 Jan. 1880; bef. 9 Apr. 1881.

6. If you can, narrow it down to a specific time span. For instance, if you know the date a will was signed and the date it was recorded or confirmed, it's reasonable to assume a death between those dates. Example: bet. 3 Apr. 1869 – 12 Jun. 1870.

7. If you find a date that could be interpreted more than one way, enter it exactly as it is written and give your interpretation in square brackets [ ] following the original. Example: 02/03/71 [2 Mar. 1871]. ALWAYS record EXACTLY what is given in a document, then add your interpretation after it.

8. If storing document references in a spreadsheet, it may be useful to have an extra column with the dates in a different format – yyyy-mm-dd, such as 1876-02-19 – so that these can be sorted automatically.

Recording places

The general rule of thumb when entering place names into genealogical records is to record place names from smallest to largest location (i.e. town/locality, county/parish/district, state/province, country). You may choose to leave off the country if it is the one in which you reside and the one where the majority of your research lies, but you may want to at least make a note of this in your files. The breakdown of these locations will vary by country. Here are two examples: Springburn, Glasgow, Lanarkshire, Scotland (village/hamlet/farm/area/district, town/city, county, country) and Calluragh, Inchicronan, Clare, Munster, Ireland (townland, parish, county, province, country).

If you have additional place name details, do include them, but be sure to make a note of what they are. For example, you could add the name of the barony (Upper Bunratty) to the above location details for Calluragh, Ireland.

Many paper pedigree charts and even some computer programmes do not include enough room to record full place names. Abbreviations may certainly be used as long as they are the ones in standard use. For example:

– Co. (county)
– Par. (parish)
– Twp. (township)

Check out this very useful list of genealogical abbreviations from Rootsweb for more commonly seen abbreviations (www.rootsweb.com/~rigenweb/abbrev.html).

Country and place names usually have accepted variations as well. See p. 40 for the three-letter Chapman codes for countries; for counties and other abbreviations for subdivisions of many countries check http://helpdesk.rootsweb.com/codes/.

If you only know the town or city in which an event occurred, then you should consult a *Gazetteer* to find the county, parish, province and so on. There are also many online sources from which you can obtain information on the county or province in which a town or city is now located.

Population changes, wars and other historic events have caused location boundaries to change over time. It may be something as simple as a town that no longer exists or has changed its name, or something a little more complex, such as a town which was originally part of one county and is now part of another. It is very important to know the history of the area in which you are researching so that you will be able to make educated guesses as to where to find the records for a given time period. When recording a place name for an event, you should always record the locality as it was situated at the time of the event. Then, if space permits, you may also include the information for the locality as it exists today.

Example: Beaufort Co. (now Pitt Co.), NC; Culross, Perth (now in Fife); Dyfyd (now in Powys).

If you aren't sure of a location, but you have records that suggest the most likely alternative (i.e. if you know where an ancestor is buried, you may make the assumption that he probably died in that locality), then you can record the place as a 'probable'.

Example: prob. St Michael, Bristol, Gloucestershire, England.

Pedigree charts
There are versions of these and other forms available at various places, often downloadable for free. Start at www.brucedurie.co.uk/resources

Blank census forms – England and Wales 1841–1911
There are versions of these and other forms available at various places, often downloadable for free. Start at www.brucedurie.co.uk/resources

17

Degrees of Kinship

How Related Are You?

Confused over whether two individuals are second cousins or first cousins once removed? Use the chart on p. 279 to determine the relationship between them.

1. Determine the ancestor which the two people share.

2. Starting with the shared ancestor, find the relationship of person 1 (P1) across the top row.

3. Again starting with the shared ancestor, find the relationship to person 2 (P2) down the left column.

4. Find the box where the P1 column and the P2 row coincide. This is their relationship.

Examples:

1. P1 and P2 share a great-grandfather. P1 is a great-grandchild; P2 is a great-grandchild; P1 and P2 are second cousins.

2. The grandfather of P1 is the uncle of P2; therefore the great-grandfather of P1 is the grandfather of P2; they are first cousins once removed.

3. P1 is the child of the shared ancestor; P2 is the great-grandchild; P1 is the great-aunt or uncle of P2, who is a great-niece or nephew.

Note: This excludes direct ancestry (for instance, if the grandfather of P1 is the great-grandfather of P2, they could be father (or mother) and child. It also only works for blood relations – not for uncles and aunts by marriage).

What is 'removed'?

This means one generation out of step. Your relationship to your first cousin's children is first cousin once removed. The relationship between your first cousin's children and your children is second cousin – they are in the same generation.

An easier way – count the Gs

Here is the simplest way to work out the relationships – work back to the common ancestor and count the Gs. Second cousins are connected at the great-grandparents (2Gs) and fourth cousins at the great-great-great-grandparents (4Gs).

   If Huw is Owain's great-great-grandfather, and also Megan's great-great-grandfather, that's 3Gs so Owain and Megan are third cousins.

If Huw is Owain's great-great-grandfather, but Jenny's great-grandfather, that's 2Gs plus a generation 'removed', so Owain and Jenny are second cousins once removed.

SHARED ANCESTOR	Child	Grandchild	Great-Grandchild	Gt-Gt-Grandchild	Gt-Gt-Gt-Grandchild	Gt-Gt-Gt-Gt-Grandchild
Child	Sibling	Niece/Nephew	Great-Niece/Nephew	Great-Great-Niece/Nephew	Gt-Gt-Gt-Niece/Nephew	Gt-Gt-Gt-Gt-Niece/Nephew
Grandchild	Aunt/Uncle	First Cousin	First Cousin 1 x Removed	First Cousin 2 x Removed	First Cousin 3 x Removed	First Cousin 4 x Removed
Great-Grandchild	Great-Aunt/Uncle	First Cousin 1 x Removed	Second Cousin	Second Cousin 1 x Removed	Second Cousin 2 x Removed	Second Cousin 3 x Removed
Gt-Gt-Grandchild	Great-Great-Aunt/Uncle	First Cousin 2 x Removed	Second Cousin 1 x Removed	Third Cousin 1 x Removed	Third Cousin 2 x Removed	Third Cousin
Gt-Gt-Gt-Grandchild	Gt-Gt-Gt-Aunt/Uncle	First Cousin 3 x Removed	Second Cousin 2 x Removed	Third Cousin 1 x Removed	Fourth Cousin	Fourth Cousin 1 x Removed
Gt-Gt-Gt-Gt-Grandchild	Gt-Gt-Gt-Gt-Aunt/Uncle	First Cousin 4 x Removed	Second Cousin 3 x Removed	Third Cousin 2 x Removed	Fourth Cousin 1 x Removed	Fifth Cousin

Envoi

This has been no more than a brief canter through some of the foothills of Welsh genealogy; there is always more to discover. We have not touched, except lightly, on newspapers, wills, DNA, maps, manorial records and much else besides. Another time, perhaps.

As you progress (or hurtle) along in your researches you will find other sources of information, and more and more documents will come to light all the time. Genealogists can help each other by publishing their findings in family history society booklets, genealogy journals, magazines and on the web. The document or archive you find that is of minimal value to your researches might just be the last piece in someone else's jigsaw puzzle.

Please just remember three things:

1. Never take anything at face value.

2. Do not trust anything that comes without a robust reference (preferably the original document, or where to find it).

3. Be prepared to justify every assertion you make – no leaps of faith, no wild guesses, no wishful thinking.

If you imagine yourself to be a forensic detective and think 'Could I swear to this in a court of law?' you won't go wrong.

As E.M. Forster said in *Howards End*: 'Only connect'.

But, above all, have fun.

Index

If you enjoyed this book, you may also be interested in...

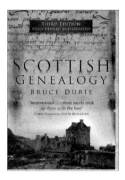

Scottish Genealogy: Third Edition
Bruce Durie
978 0 7524 6372 8

The Last King of Wales: Gruffudd ap Llywelyn
c. 1013-1063
Michael & Sean Davies
978 0 7524 6460 2

Bloody Scottish History: Glasgow
Bruce Durie
978 0 7524 8289 7

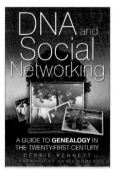

DNA and Social Networking: a Guide to Genealogy in
the Twenty-First Century
Debbie Kennett
978 0 7524 5862 5

Visit our website and discover thousands of other History Press books.

www.thehistorypress.co.uk